THE DEADLY RITE
OF HAZING

Hank Nuwer

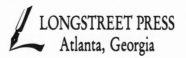

LONGSTREET PRESS
Atlanta, Georgia

Published by
LONGSTREET PRESS, INC.
2150 Newmarket Parkway
Suite 102
Marietta, Georgia 30067

Printed in the United States of America

1st printing, 1990

Library of Congress Catalog Number 89-063797

ISBN 0-929264-72-X

This book was printed by R. R. Donnelley & Sons, Harrisonburg, Virginia.
The text type was set in Bembo by Typo-Repro Service, Inc., Atlanta,
Georgia. Design by Laura Ellis.

For Jenine Nuwer and Fraser Drew with love,

but also for Louis Ingelhart,
to recognize his lifelong fight
for a free student press

ACKNOWLEDGMENTS

The idea of writing a book about hazing was supported by a grant from the Gannett Foundation which gave me the funds to research a portion of this book. Thank you.

I also thank my wife for incredible support during the more than two years it took me to complete *Broken Pledges,* particularly on those many eighteen-hour days when smiles, backrubs, and unlimited pots of coffee meant so much. I also wish to thank my sons for bearing with their dad during long hours spent on this book that might have been spent playing baseball.

At Longstreet Press, I wish to thank the entire staff, particularly Jane Hill, Allison Adams, and Trigg Robinson.

I also wish to thank certain people for their research expertise. Steve Jensen and Darryl Nitsch conducted important interviews at the 1989 Future Farmers of America convention and later interviewed FFA advisors at many schools. Don Slusher spent many hours imitating a mole in the Indiana University library. Hazing researcher Mike Moskos provided me with eleventh-hour information on some fraternity deaths for the appendix.

I also wish to thank the administration and faculty of Alfred University for giving me access to them and to the campus. While this book draws certain conclusions about the school's handling of some fraternity and sorority matters based on my observations and research, I wish to emphasize that I came away with many positive impressions about the school and its caring faculty. I also wish to emphasize that similar attention to problems within the Greek system could have been given to many other colleges and universities. This statement is not meant to excuse Alfred University. However, it is important to look at events that have occurred from the perspective that the involvement of the Alfred administration in Greek affairs exceeds the involvement of some other institutions. Among the Alfred individuals who cooperated were Donald King, Steven Peterson, Gary Horowitz, Robert Heineman, Stuart Campbell, and Edward Coll. Similarly, events depicted at Klan Alpine fraternity could and have occurred at many other local and national Greek organizations. I wish to thank the brothers of Klan Alpine for their cooperation under trying circumstances, particularly Kevin LaForge, Carl Pelcher, Ron Sember, Richard Sigal, Richard Klein, David Hoff, and Scott Sullivan.

I benefited from information and documents provided by sources who have insisted upon remaining anonymous. I also wish to acknowledge certain kindnesses given me by journalists Susan Ager, Read Kingsbury, and the library staff at the Buffalo *News*.

I wish to thank former colleagues at Ball State University, particularly Louis Ingelhart, Jim Willis, Warren Vander Hill, Earl Conn, Marilyn Weaver, Bev Pitts, Mark Popovich, and Fred Woodress. I especially want to thank my former students at Ball State, Greeks and non-Greeks alike, for cheery encouragement.

I wish to thank Fred Kershner, Maria Minardi, Lionel Tiger, Charles B. Wright, Ron Taylor, Mark Taff, Scott Doty, John Longo, Paul Engleman, Jeff Harmon, Ron Rash, Kevin O'Rourke, Greg Belanger, Jimmy and Nanci Arnoux, Doreen Stenzel, Mr. and Mrs. Joseph Nikiel, Tiny Jamison, Richard Harris, Gale Beyers, William Cunningham, Kate Hobble, Randy Belmont, Tish Zapata, Tom and Cher Mueller, and others who have assisted this project.

Finally, Eileen Stevens provided valuable press clippings from Committee to Halt Useless College Killings (CHUCK) files. She also permitted me unlimited access to her journals and diaries and then allowed me to read her all passages from *Broken Pledges* in which I have referred to her thoughts. Thanks are owed to members of the Stevens family, particularly Roy, Suzanne, and Scott, for allowing me to disrupt the household while researching this book. I also wish to thank Ray and Maisie Ballou, Mary Lenaghan, Joan Cerra, Dorothy Flowers, and Adrienne Harris. It is my prayer that this book can help prevent others' undergoing the strife that they continue to endure.

PREFACE

After the death of Charles (Chuck) Stenzel in a fraternity initiation ceremony, the then-president of Alfred University, M. Richard Rose, spoke at a memorial service. He said that no individual student could be blamed for the death in what Chuck's mother has called a senseless hazing incident. Rose ended his remarks with a quote from John 8:7 — "Let him who is without sin cast the first stone."

When I was twelve I accidentally brought home from the library a book by Upton Sinclair called *The Jungle*. I say "accidentally" because I had been reading about the adventures of Frank Buck, and the title misled me. I thought *The Jungle* might be about Africa and safaris.

Reading about the horrible goings-on of the meat-packing industry upset me, terribly. But, when I closed the book, I concluded that the author had done something important by exposing what he had found. Once those particular evils in the workplace had been dealt with, American students stopped reading *The Jungle*. Today they know only its title, if that, and Upton Sinclair's name is forgotten by most. That is as it should be. The author's name isn't important; solving a social predicament is.

Just before I abandoned graduate studies at the University of Nevada-Reno in 1976, a young man named John Davies died in a hazing incident. The death appalled me. As a freelance writer one of the first articles I wrote was for the now-defunct magazine *Human Behavior*. The article was on fraternity deaths. Eileen Stevens, the mother of Chuck Stenzel and founder of the Committee to Halt Useless College Killings, read the piece and contacted me. We met once in a New York restaurant in 1979, talked, and went about our separate lives except for occasional notes at Christmas.

I was too inexperienced then to write a book on hazing. I wanted to learn first-hand about the American experience. For more than three years I lived out of my pickup truck as a freelance journalist for six to eight months at a stretch, writing magazine articles in KOA campground offices, in shabby hotel rooms in remote outposts, and in the houses of friends I had just met. To make a living as a freelancer, I began writing "puff" pieces — the "ten best roadhouse bars" and other tripe — and, whenever I could, solid and solemn journalism that went into my portfolio. Following my marriage in 1982, my writing projects were more in line with what my vision of journalism had been as a twelve-year-old: books for boys on steroids and recruiting evils; magazine articles on alcoholism, a basketball scandal, and one aging professor's battle to keep the moribund American chestnut from extinction.

To support my writing addiction, I began to teach college classes in which students read the books I had come to cherish: the nonfiction novels of Norman Mailer and Truman Capote; the literary journalism of John

McPhee, Richard Rhodes, Joan Didion, Mark Singer, and Tom Wolfe; the nonfiction books and essays of Harry Crews, Edward Abbey, Ted Conover, Thomas McGuane, and George Plimpton. Since I had never taken a creative writing or journalism class, I began interviewing authors whose work I admired. Their genre didn't matter. Their excellence is what drew me to them. These interviews with the likes of Kurt Vonnegut, James Dickey, John Jakes, David Mamet, Mark Steadman, William Least Heat Moon, Maurice Sendak, Crews, and Plimpton appeared in popular and little magazines. But the publication credits were a secondary reason for doing the interviews. Quite simply, I wanted to ask the best writers in America questions about writing that I couldn't answer on my own. In turn, I fed their answers to my college students.

My work as teacher and advisor brought me many warm relationships with my students, a good many of them fraternity and sorority members. Hence, the idea of this book came into my head and wouldn't go away. I received a grant from the Gannett Foundation to do preliminary research on hazing.

Broken Pledges is the result of my investigation of that subject, particularly—although hardly exclusively—as it exists in college fraternities. Hazing, I've discovered, is a common, hidden cancer in the nation's high schools, armed forces, clubs, sororities, and adult fraternal groups. It is a problem that demands more scrutiny than a single book can give it.

Upton Sinclair alone didn't attack the problems of the meat-packing industry. As a result of *The Jungle* public policymakers and watchdog journalists did the real work to eliminate the horrid practices. My hope is that this book is so successful that it soon becomes as forgotten as *The Jungle* is today. One book alone cannot eliminate hazing, but an informed public, press, military, and government can.

No, President Rose, I'm not without sin. I pledged Sigma Tau Rho fraternity at the State University College of New York at Buffalo and was initiated in 1965. I was hazed as a pledge; I hazed as a member. But the problem of hazing is too demeaning, widespread, and dangerous for even sinners to ignore. It shatters the lives of perpetrators, as well as those of victims and their families. It destroys the reputations of otherwise admirable institutions and administrators. I concluded, finally, that a former sinner might be best qualified to expose hazing abuses. Since slavery, no institution has so deserved to be ended.

Having said that, I hereby cast the first stone. I hope that this book gives other hazers and victims the courage to fire away.

—Hank Nuwer
Fogelsville, Pennsylvania

The call came in the middle of the night. Eileen Stevens's son was dead.

She was alert and numb at once, her flesh no longer part of her. She wanted to hang up. She wanted the caller to stay on the line forever. She wanted to know what had happened and how. But most of all she wanted the call to be a dream, a very bad dream.

The pain in the caller's voice, the small break in his professional manner, revealed the truth, told her the worst had happened. She was ready to bargain with God. The devil. The caller himself: Take my life, my soul — take me. I've lived. But make it untrue. Take me, not Chuck.

But Chuck was dead.

She wandered through the house. A gong vibrated between her ears. She eyed the refrigerator. The freezer held the ingredients for chili. Chuck alone in her family loved it. Parents Weekend at Alfred University was approaching, and she had planned on taking him a special meal.

She went into his room. In the closet were the boots and skis she'd given him not two months earlier. He'd used them only once. She was glad she exceeded the budget to buy them. She could still hear his squeal of joy on Christmas morning. Twenty, he'd acted like a four-year-old. His joy was infectious; his hugs, genuine. If only she had kept hugging him forever, never let him go.

The caller's words roared like a waterfall in her mind. Chuck's "probable cause" of death was an overdose of alcohol, "at a party," the dean of students had said. He had also repeated that explanation to her husband, Roy, in a later call. But how was that possible? Sure, Chuck drank a few beers with his buddies, his fellow clammers on nearby Great South Bay, but he'd never had too many, to the best of her knowledge.

She wanted to leave immediately. But a winter storm had intensified, adding 3.4 inches of snow to the twenty-two already on the ground in Alfred. Flying into a commercial airport within a ninety-minute drive of New York's Southern Tier was going to be impossible until snowplows could do their work. She contemplated going by car, but Roy convinced her she would have to wait out the night.

A staunch Catholic, she spent the long night cradling her husband in her arms, taking comfort in her religion. Then the thought struck her. She'd have to ask if someone had summoned a priest to administer Extreme Unction, the sacrament her faith promised would permit her son straightways into heaven.

Little did she know that her boy's spiritual welfare was the last thing on the minds of those who shared his last hours. To the ghastly end, fraternity rites prevailed over last rites. And human rights.

PART ONE

1

Alfred University is the alma mater of Peter Jenkins, the young man who shouldered a backpack and left the upstate New York town to take, and write, *A Walk Across America.* The countryside near the university is rugged and particularly lovely in winter. The trees on the ridges poke through the snow like white knights on parade. In summers logging trails through the woods provide a serene landscape for joggers.

But danger can also lurk in the countryside. Death from hypothermia can waylay careless hunters or ice fishermen. Anyone who has read Jenkins's book recalls the chilling scene when Cooper, the author's half-malamute, snatches a northern copperhead from his master's path.

Jenkins's book also features an offbeat art teacher: John Wood came to class on a Bultaco bike in spring and on cross-country skis in winter. Apparently, such behavior was the norm, not the exception. The 1979 Alfred yearbook pictures an odd but intriguing faculty. An art teacher in a down vest plays darts, aiming at an unseen target. Four young women — one in a halter top — cling to another art professor, making him the stem of a human four-leaf clover. Conservatively dressed male teachers are the exception. Their duds look starchy and uncomfortable compared to the fatigue jackets, flannel shirts, and jeans favored by many male faculty members. There were too few women professors to generalize about their fashion taste. The 1979 faculty was overwhelmingly male: eighty-eight full-time men, only ten full-time women.

In 1979 the student paper, the *Fiat Lux,* asked Jenkins to reflect on his Alfred memories. He recalled turkey subs and all-night kiln firings, heated sidewalks in winter, snowball wars, beer chugging, and inspiring teachers. He confessed that Alfred's reputation made people "cringe," noting that it wasn't quite the same as saying you graduated from Yale. But he credited Alfred with making him do something with his life, inspiring him to want something better. Jenkins told the student paper that Alfred "is what you get from the place, what you take with you . . . when you leave the security of the valley."

But by 1979 the valley was insecure. Faculty attire may have been laidback, but the atmosphere in department meetings was anything but. Alfred released tenured professor Dmytro Sich — not because he was inept or immoral, but because the school had declared a financial emergency. History professor Stuart Campbell says that the concept of tenure at Alfred had "been seriously weakened." An untenured professor, timidly talking on condition of anonymity, questioned the strength of the tenure concept at the school as well: "Tenure is a legal guarantee of employment, but how secure is that guarantee now?" Tenure at Alfred had become as valuable as a first-class upgrade on the *Titanic*. A prof-eat-prof mentality surfaced. An associate professor of German says an unfortunate situation developed: "Negative feelings exist; people aren't pulling together. A kind of competitiveness has emerged among the faculty."

A scene ripe for a Shane in academic regalia. None emerged. The faculty stewed and grumbled, but did nothing. Academics "are not a very heroic breed," Campbell told the student newspaper.

From its inception Alfred University has been a backwater college. Many students, alumni, and faculty love it for precisely that reason. Before acquiring the sophistication and academic standing that inspired *U.S. News & World Report* in 1985 to rank it the second-best (although most expensive) small comprehensive institution in the nation, Alfred's appeal was its isolation. Conservative parents sent their children to this educational mecca set amidst woods and pastureland to shield them from corrupting influences. Eileen Stevens might flinch at *The Sesquicentennial History of Alfred University,* in which one faculty writer describes a time when "Parents could be assured their children were in safe hands." The school promoted its tranquility and virtue to impress New York state parents who shuddered at the thought of the Sodom that was Buffalo, the Gomorrah that was New York City. Founded by Seventh-Day Baptists who revered learning and despised weaknesses of the flesh, Alfred gained its university charter as one of the first U.S. coeducational institutions in 1857, having operated as a Select School since 1836.

But, truth to tell, what Alfred may have on Buffalo and the Big Apple in sanctity, it certainly lacks in variety. The deep snows of winter that make students wisecrack that Alfred has but two seasons—winter and bad sledding—often create depression in those unable to make friends quickly. The size of the village is revealed by the number of its white pages in the local phone directory, only ten-and-a-half in 1989. "What I remember about Alfred . . . is a feeling of loneliness," poet Marvin Bell, a 1958 graduate, once said. "I know such moments were few, but they were deep, and, therefore, they linger."

No city of any size is less than an hour away, and if you don't like a steady diet of outdoor sports or the culture and entertainment imported to campus, the chilling loneliness can freeze your marrow. Daily life in Alfred is slow and stagnant as pond water for students and faculty who lack the initiative to keep up socially and intellectually. For many youngsters, the choice is to drink; for others, to go Greek. Many say that at Alfred these are really the same.

The college's namesake is not an English butler nor a pet cat as some snide souls joke, but King Alfred, the ninth-century ruler and music-loving savant of the West Saxons. There is dismal irony in a youth's perishing at Alfred in a house of men he wanted for brothers. King Alfred translated the works of classic Roman writers, such as Boethius, into Old English. In one translation he rhapsodizes "how happy would this mankind be" if absolute friendships were possible. Alas, Alfred concluded, such bonds are impossible, except in the abstract. Men are too frail, too weak, too flawed to allow a perfect friendship to bloom for eternity. He who suffers most is the man whose belief in true friendship leads to his own destruction.

The village of Alfred and the school have supporters who won't allow themselves to be uprooted even after a scandal as nasty and as enervating as Chuck Stenzel's death. Donald H. King, the dean who called Chuck's family, is a career administrator with a yen for jogging and watching contact sports. He may not be a pillar of the community, but he is certainly part of its mortar. Its safe, caring environment keeps him there.

"You can't understand this place until you're immersed in it," says King, whose office has the wood paneling and subdued paint of an elegant restaurant. "What has drawn me to this place [is] what it stands for: the personalization, the individual attention that is given to people. . . . In this community, nobody locks doors. We had a rash of burglaries one year in the village, and people were really concerned. It wasn't serious, but people had to buy locks for their doors. We have trouble getting students to lock their doors in the residence halls. The tendency is that people are trusting. Those are the kinds of things that attracted me and keep attracting me to a place like Alfred—even though there've been difficult times."

But ask Sergeant Randy Belmont of the Village of Alfred police how nice, how safe Alfred is. He'll give you the same look he'd give if you asked if he's overpaid.

One of his worries is the tradition of the annual snowball fight between prestigious Alfred University students on one side of Main Street and those average Joes from the State University College of Technology on the other. In December of 1987 it took three officers to clear rioting students near the Delta Sigma Phi house. The fight resulted in twenty-three arrests. The 1986 fight brought only six arrests although snowball hurlers broke fifty-eight windows on campus and damaged four automobiles.

More serious were mysterious attacks upon students in 1985. After six were assaulted, the school and village police advised everyone to walk in pairs. Townsfolk still recall a brawl after two A.M. in September 1985, when Gamma Theta Gamma from State swapped knuckles with Alfred's Delta Sigma Phi, sending one youth to the hospital with head injuries. Then there was the incident in January 1986. A lone student said that a marauding gang of fifty youths pummeled him with their fists and snowballs.

Randy Belmont doesn't have King's idyllic view of Alfred.

"A lot of people don't want to admit that urban America has come to Alfred," explains Belmont. "We have all the problems that the big cities do—on a smaller scale, of course. Thefts and drugs—but no murders, thank God. People want us to solve problems the way they did fifty years ago, and that just doesn't work."

The village's longtime police chief Lldon "Tiny" Jamison has an opinion that lies somewhere between King's and Belmont's views. "It depends on one's terminology of the word *safe*," he says. "Compared to New York, Buffalo, and Rochester, it's a safe place. Now it's also true that we have isolated instances [of crime]. While there've been no real serious attacks, I'm not going to make this place sound like a monastery either."

Belmont is a muscular man with a tad of flesh over his gunbelt. Working in a town where policemen aren't favorites of drunken college kids, he's had to adjust his thinking from the noble goals he had in mind when he became an Alfred cop in the early seventies. "But I've gotten more used to it," he says. Tranquil nights can turn into riots if the right snowball hits the wrong fraternity man. Belmont has often had to leap into frays that look more like a *West Side Story* rumble than a good old American fistfight. "Other [policemen] break up fights of one or two," he claims, blowing cigarette smoke while he talks. "When we have a fight, it's fifty or seventy-five guys."

One of the more infamous street battles in Alfred history occurred in January 1977. The brothers of Klan Alpine engaged in a savage fistfight with another local fraternity. Don King blasted the Klan participants and put the group on social probation for nine months, but the dean made no public announcement of the disciplinary measure. Whose responsibility was it to tell Chuck Stenzel, other prospective Klan pledges, and concerned parents such as Roy and Eileen Stevens? "It was the responsibility of the [Klan] house to tell them," King told the student newspaper.

When the probation ended, King expected the fraternity's behavior to be angelic. Not quite two months later, Chuck Stenzel—Eileen Stevens's son—lay dead on Klan's beer-marinated floor while the brothers wailed and cursed their misfortune.

The night of February 24, 1978, was pandemonium in Alfred. In addition to the normal wanderings of drunks hopping from bar to bar on Main Street, it was Tapping Night, the term for the sodden spectacle that celebrates the entrance of initiates into the Alfred Greek system. "Throngs of people were on the street," recalls Randy Belmont. They were "drinking, drunk, or just or'nery."

No major brawls erupted, but Belmont and his partner Bruce Razey had to keep little fires from turning into conflagrations. Both anticipated a long night of minor arrests. "Monday morning is going to be like a zoo," they told each other, thinking about the scene when friends and lovers bailed out collegiate jailbirds.

In the midst of a minor confrontation around midnight, Belmont noticed flashing red lights about three blocks down on the south side of Main Street. "I wonder what's going on," he mentioned to his partner. But they couldn't leave. Another fracas had broken out near the town's traffic light.

The red lights were flashing in front of the Klan Alpine house at 61 South Main Street. The fraternity was often in conflict with the community. Neighbors frequently called the police to quiet Klan down. Labeled an animal house long before the movie was filmed, the Klan had no trouble living up to its reputation for wildness. Of course, Klansmen were often sharp in the classroom. Some studied harder than they partied. Several faculty rather liked having Klan members in their classes. According to Scott Sullivan, who was fraternity president in 1977-78, one member at the time of Chuck's death later became class valedictorian. But Sullivan admits too many others pledged Klan and flunked out a semester or two later.

"They weren't the same type of boy you saw in other fraternities," recalls Judith Archer, then a director of student plays, who rented the octagonal house bordering the Klan's backyard. "They were students by day and vikings by night."

In the months before the Stenzel incident rocked Alfred, Archer observed the hearts of both darkness and sunshine in her young neighbors. Without payment the Klan trimmed the Archers' hedges in summer and shoveled their walk in winter. "They were good neighbors," says Archer, although she also remembers mountains of open garbage outside Klan, a magnet that drew rats to the neighborhood.

During the day the Archer preschool children often cavorted on the basketball court with the hulking Klansmen. The Klan brothers stopped their games in mid-drive whenever the Archers' two-year-old wandered into the action.

"Give the baby the ball," one of them would say. The little boy looked like a dwarf carrying a medicine ball. When he tried to throw the ball back, the Klansmen would howl with laughter.

This sweet, private image faded on the nights the brothers had been drinking. "They had a rough-rider image," says Archer. "They were crude. You could walk by, and [a Klansman] would be urinating out the door or off the back porch."

Klan members snubbed their noses at authority figures they could not respect. The group's leaders were bright and independent, destined to become professionals or to form their own companies instead of working for someone else. Others, however, were jocks in the worst sense of the term, recruited because they looked good in Klan shirts and brought notoriety to the house. At their best, members were loyal to one another and their college, donating gobs of money as alumni. At their worst, they were student vikings, black hats. To those who failed to see their good side, they were arrogant, convinced of their own invincibility, braggarts, heavy partiers, coarse, sexist, and contemptuous of all not their own kind. Father Flanagan of Boy's Town said there were no bad boys. But he never observed a Tapping Night at Klan. Even in appearance Klansmen were different: long-haired, shirtless in summers, preferring macho-casual dress with just the right rips in their jeans and sweatshirts.

Judith Archer says, "They were big, they were handsome, they were intelligent." They were also sometimes exceedingly dangerous. A reckless initiation custom was to make their name synonymous with all that is bad about fraternities. What Klan regarded as an initiation, many called hazing—though not by law. That legislation was still two lost lives away in New York state.

Dave Schwert, a faculty member and volunteer with the local ambulance crew, was the first person to come to Chuck Stenzel's aid. When Schwert entered Klan Alpine that night, he blinked in disbelief.He felt as if he were seeing the lowest level of Dante's hell. The smell of stale beer overpowered him. A falling rope of urine issued from a young man on the nearby stairwell. Schwert reminded himself to stay composed. "Nothing made sense," he said later. "Nearly everyone had been drinking."

Schwert had taken one of six calls that went out to the emergency team. "One of the brothers at Klan had called—I'm not sure which," he says. "I went to Klan out of a sound sleep." Because his home was closest, he went on foot while others picked up the ambulance. Klan members later estimated that he arrived five or ten minutes after their initial call.

Schwert fought his emotions. He wanted to help, but he was in the middle of chaos. Some of the brothers and pledges were belligerent; more than a few were disoriented. The sober ones, who recognized the seriousness of the situation, were unnerved by the motionless body lying face up on a mat in a second-floor bedroom. It didn't take Schwert long to learn that someone was in serious trouble, but those he questioned either didn't know what had occurred or stonewalled him. Some brothers who didn't know Chuck well were afraid he had taken drugs. They couldn't comprehend that alcohol alone could kill. Schwert still didn't know what had happened when the rescue team arrived. "For three minutes the whole world was a blur," he says.

When the others arrived, Schwert warned them that he had found bottles of Sominex and Vivarin, both over-the-counter drugs. In the midst of drunks and panicked men, he told the crew that an overdose or tampering might have occurred. Without being completely certain what had transpired, the husband-wife rescue team of Dick and Margery Sands got to work. They hoped without hope that their CPR could revive the blue-purplish husk that was some mother's son.

Once Belmont and Razey solved their downtown fracas, they were dispatched to the Klan Alpine house. A citizen detained them with a minor complaint after they were already in their car. They spent several seconds extricating themselves. Then over the squawkbox came the clincher. "The coroner is on his way," the disembodied voice said. The squad car sped away.

The disorder they encountered astounded the police officers. "It was an atmosphere you could cut with a knife," says Belmont. "It was hostile."

Two young men danced around them like pit bulls. "Get the fuck out of here!" said one. "What the fuck do you want?" demanded another. A pledge clad only in a blanket joined the harangue, cursing and threatening the officers.

Belmont flexed his biceps and looked over at a group of gawking brothers. The profanity bothered him, but he was used to it. Whenever he passed a fraternity house with ten or more people on the porch, he expected to be cursed. He had long ago stopped vaulting out of his car to confront these animals. What was he going to do — arrest the whole crew? They simply stared at him, insolent as magpies, when he demanded, "Who said that?"

Belmont flagged down a couple of sober brothers. He wanted a muzzle on the bobbing, cursing, angry pledge. "Control him or I will," he promised.

They controlled him.

Two state troopers barged through the door. "The coroner is going to be mad as hell," they told Belmont. "We didn't wait for him."

Belmont grimaced at trooper J. J. Cosgrove and pointed to the floor. It was sloppy, stinking, sticking to his shoes. "Nice place, huh?"

Cosgrove nodded. "It was a shithouse," he recalls. Chief Jamison puts it more delicately. "A damn pigpen," he says.

Chuck Stenzel became friends with a few Klan Alpine members after transferring to Alfred from Doane College in Nebraska in the spring semester of 1977. He had several friends already at Alfred, and he and a buddy, Jimmy Arnoux, enrolled together even though they weren't able to be roommates. In May 1977 Arnoux gave up on his nursing studies and left Alfred. Chuck decided — against his family's urgings — to work that summer and through the fall to bank some money before returning to school.

In February 1978 Chuck re-enrolled at Alfred. This time he was able to choose his roommate — a straightforward, earnest kid who belonged to Klan Alpine, someone Chuck and Arnoux had hung out with the previous year. Although his parents didn't know it, Chuck had even had too much to drink at a couple of parties, including at least one Klan Alpine function. If Eileen and Roy had had even an inkling of the peer pressure to overindulge in alcohol at Alfred, they would have taken action. To them, both light drinkers, three drinks for students is tantamount to drunken revelry. At Alfred the party often starts Thursday night and ends Tuesday morning. But there are also students — including Klan brothers — who spend four years at Alfred stone-sober.

At the time of Chuck's death, Don King told the Rochester evening newspaper that five percent of the student body could be classified as alcoholics. The owner of Short's Liquor Store in Alfred told the paper that it wasn't unusual for fraternities to purchase sixty dollars' worth of liquor. "Yeah, they drink a lot," said Janet Short. "I personally think it's because they don't have enough to do in Alfred. . . . These kids aren't alcoholics.

. . . They just want to party for the . . . four years they're here. Most of them won't ever party again like this. Their stomachs wouldn't take it."

Eileen and Roy had no reason to suspect Chuck. After all, he had always been open with them. At Doane he had written his parents letters on three occasions when he had had too much to drink. One of those times he had been with a friend's parents at a football game. One Klan Alpine member who attended Alfred in 1978 says that Chuck was "not a virgin with alcohol," but not a drunk either. An Alfred administrator says there were two alcoholics in the spring 1978 pledge class. Chuck was not one of them.

Thus, when Eileen later began to tell packed audiences of Greek students that "It wasn't Chuck's experience with alcohol, but his inexperience, that killed him," she was partially correct. The relative inexperience of most Klan Alpine members with alcohol — although they beat their chests and claimed the opposite — was truly responsible for her boy's death. "At the time you think you're fairly indestructible," says Klan's Carl Pelcher. Pelcher speaks out so that others might be spared the hell he went through after Chuck's death. "Our problem was drinking. Drinking was fun and drinking was a manly thing to do. The more you could drink, the more in you were and the more one of the guys you were. But you're not indestructible — that's the main thing. Even though you're eighteen, nineteen, you're just not indestructible. You have to use some common sense."

Why did Chuck want to join this particular fraternity? Eileen Stevens has pondered that question a million times and likely will ponder it a million more. But the answers seem relatively simple. For one thing, he probably wanted to cement a bond with his new roommate, particularly since his relationship with his last roommate — Joe Bachman, a *Fiat Lux* writer — had been tortuous for both young men. Another possibility was that sports-loving Chuck saw Klan as an opportunity to try out for varsity lacrosse. Several members of the team — including one of the ten best goalies in America that year — belonged to the fraternity. In any case, it was the lacrosse players who vouched for Chuck a few days later when he put his signature on a Klan sign-up sheet. "He's a good guy," they said at a special meeting held in the Klan's Chapter Room. That testimonial was enough for the majority of brothers who didn't know Chuck by name or sight since he had not been on campus the previous semester. No one suggested he be blackballed — the fraternity method of rejecting a prospect — and he was assigned to be the little brother of one of the lacrosse players.

The decision to join a fraternity probably wasn't as momentous for Chuck as it is for many young men. He was anything but shy, and he had dozens of friends, both male and female, not only at Alfred but at nearby St. Bonaventure University. He wasn't joining out of loneliness. He wrote at least three letters in the ten days prior to his death, and in none of them did he mention Klan. He did, however, say in two letters that he had had enough of partying and was excited about the biggest decision he had made in his young life. Stu Campbell's classes had set him on fire intellectually, and he now knew what profession he wanted to pursue. "Chuck was just getting his feet wet, and he didn't know what direction he wanted to go in," says Roy Stevens. "He had decided that he wanted to become a history teacher."

In the days after Chuck's death the Alfred University administration would take the standard legal stance common to nearly all administrators and institutions in the wake of a fraternity death: although they deeply regretted the tragedy, etc., they could accept no responsibility for what had happened. Nonetheless, Klan Alpine and all other Greek organizations follow school guidelines for checking out prospective members at parties and social gatherings, known in their parlance as "rush." In 1978 those guidelines were determined by King, as dean of students, and the Pan-Hellenic Council, a representative body made up primarily of Greek presidents and designated advisors from each fraternity and sorority. Among other things, King and the Pan-Hellenic Council issued a memo that was photocopied and placed on bulletin boards all over campus. One purpose of King's involvement was to ensure that no fraternity or sorority gain unfair advantage by jumping the gun on rushing potential members.

Alfred rush parties were relatively mundane compared to the elaborate theme affairs some fraternities concoct. For example, the Tulane chapter of Delta Kappa Epsilon turned rush into a houseboat party in 1971. It resulted in the death of seventeen-year-old Wayne Kennedy. At Klan Alpine the basics were the order of the day: beer flowing from kegs and male chitchat about sports, school, and women, as members checked out prospects and vice versa.

Chuck telephoned his family around nine P.M. the night before his death. For several minutes he teased his little sister Suzanne—he alone was permitted to call her Sue—because she had gotten a cat for Valentine's Day despite Eileen's allergies. When Eileen got on the phone, Chuck's conversation focused on Roy and Eileen's upcoming vacation in the Bahamas. He said nothing about Klan Alpine, possibly to avoid his mother's questions—a tendency he kidded her about. His last words to his mother were "Have a great trip to the Bahamas, Mom."

After talking to his family, Chuck went to a local tavern and bought shots of liquor for some Klansmen. His last evening—Tapping Night—was the next day. Alfred yearbooks from the sixties and seventies provide a graphic idea of what Tapping Nights are like, says Gary Horowitz, who, in 1978, was not only a history professor at Alfred but also the village mayor. The 1971 book, for example, contains a close-up of a blonde youth vomiting over the Klan house's porch rail while another member holds onto his jacket to keep him from pitching over the side. The theme of Chuck's Tapping Night was "Don't Stop 'til You Drop."

Klan is an old, established fraternity at Alfred, having celebrated its fiftieth anniversary in 1968. From the beginning, the group preached the advantages of nonsectarianism, allowing blacks, Jews, and Catholics into its ranks when many fraternities practiced racial and religious discrimination. The early brothers of Klan Alpine knew that the actions of a few could destroy them. "Every man . . . should remember that his every act is one that will reflect credit or discredit upon his Fraternity," was a cherished credo in 1922.

According to a 1921 statement, the purpose of Klan is to "promote the ideal of the brotherhood of man, that each may be a broader and better man, better enabled to carry on his life work." The 1922 yearbook says that Klan "stands first, last, and always for scholarly ability, social equality, good fellowship, mutual helpfulness, and athletic progress." Another early motto was appropriated from the poet Kipling: "The Strength of the Pack is the Wolf and the Strength of the Wolf is the Pack." Initiated Klan members inherited such secret traditions, be they fact or fiction, that the fraternity is descended from Klan McAlpine, a staunch and ancient brotherhood from the days when bands of men called clans clove to one another for protection. A group of men who referred to themselves as Clan Alpine dined together at Burdick Hall in 1908 and possibly earlier.

The day of his death Chuck cashed a check for ten dollars and waited in his dormitory room at Openhym Hall after the dinner hour as a Klan member had instructed. Klan members who qualify their remarks as hearsay indicate that he had "maybe two or three beers" in his room, but no one recalls where that information originated. Sometime after seven P.M., Chuck greeted his big brother at the door. The lacrosse player appeared glum. He was sorry, he said, but the membership had voted, and a couple of guys thought Chuck wouldn't fit in. Sorry about that, guy, he said in effect, and departed.

The big brother allowed Chuck to fret over his supposed rejection for a few minutes. Then he knocked on the door again. Surprise, the joke's on you. We want you after all. He gave Chuck a gray tee-shirt with "Klan" in black letters and also handed him a bottle of congratulations, a pint of Jack Daniel's whiskey. After Chuck put on the shirt, the brother led him outside. The temperature that day varied between eight and twenty-seven degrees Fahrenheit. On the trip to Klan Alpine Chuck had to ride in the car's trunk.

Either before or after Chuck was picked up, the big brothers of two other pledges fetched their men from Kruson Hall. If Chuck was picked up last, the other two pledges waited in the cold trunk while Chuck's big brother pulled the ruse. If the other two were picked up afterwards, Chuck waited in the trunk. (A longer stay in the trunk could have affected Chuck's behavior. In October 1980 a University of Michigan student was placed in the trunk of a car and kept outside for ninety minutes, dramatically lowering his body temperature.) "The most dangerous thing you can do is stick a freezing creature—a lung breather—in a trunk like that because it's not sealed off from the exhaust," says the doctor who assisted at Chuck's post-mortem. "If it is well sealed, they may run into excess CO_2 as well as CO. If they're drunk and they're cold, it will kill them faster."

It is unclear whether the car, an old blue Chevrolet, was running with the heater on to keep the Klan brothers inside warm. The car eventually left for the fraternity house. According to confidential documents, the pledges in the trunk with Chuck later told authorities that he chugged not only his pint of whiskey but also most of another pledge's pint of Scotch, but a Buffalo *Courier Express* story printed the Monday after the incident cited an unidentified police source who said that Chuck was given "a quantity of whiskey, beer, and wine." To this day Eileen believes the *Courier* account, which says Chuck was given a pint of Jack Daniel's, a six-pack of beer, and a quart of wine. Klan's Rocky LaForge says that "the pint of Jack Daniel's is true; the six-pack of beer and quart of wine is inflated." A confidential document reveals that a lie detector test confirmed Chuck's roommate's statement that Chuck drank his pint and three-fourths of another.

The ride to the Klan house took fifteen minutes, according to one brother, although Eileen suspects it was longer. Once in the driveway, the driver opened the trunk and Chuck and the other pledges scrambled out. At that point, according to Klan accounts, the three toasted each other with what was left of their individual bottles. Chuck's precise condition at that point is unclear. According to a confidential document, the roommate's lie detector test is inconclusive because, while he answered all other questions truthfully, "he had trouble" with a question addressing Chuck's condition when he got out of the trunk. Scott Sullivan would insist in a deposition that Chuck didn't stagger when he left the trunk—in spite of his having allegedly downed nearly two pints of sipping whiskey. "There's no way he passed out in the car," said Joseph van Cura, an Alfred alumnus present at the house the night Chuck died.

Somehow Chuck walked or was helped into the fraternity house between eight-thirty and nine-thirty P.M. Inside were twenty-five to thirty members. No women were present until after the drinking games ended. Then a girlfriend or two showed up. In the entranceway stood a table loaded with full twelve-ounce glasses of wine—a variation on a one-time fraternity tradition in which members drank from a cup to celebrate their pledging. In 1978 van Cura said that Chuck chugged two glasses. Sullivan agrees, saying Chuck's "festive" mood matched that of the brotherhood.

Chuck either staggered or was assisted downstairs. In the barroom, for an undetermined time, he played a game, traditional to the Klan, called "races." The object was to grab a beer from your big brother or another member and gulp it down before the other pledges could down theirs. The pledges were also drinking in competition against the brothers, which would help account for the large number of drunken members that the police and rescue crew found on their arrival. However, some seniors pretended to drink and tossed their beers over their shoulders, making pledges think that they had drunk larger quantities than they actually had. The object was to fill a trash can, up to a line marked on the outside, with vomit.

That neither the school nor the fraternity chose to talk about this game is significant. Chuck's chugging alcohol by himself in the trunk is one thing. Visualizing Klan members handing beers to a fully intoxicated Chuck, then hanging all over him like ants on a picnic lunch some two hours before his death, is another. Horowitz, the 1990 Klan advisor, and Sullivan, the Klan president at the time of the death, were both surprised to hear that Chuck's blood alcohol content was .46 — more than four times the legal limit. "If it had gone to trial, it sounds like negligence," says Horowitz.

Eileen Stevens is repulsed by the vision of drunken pledges sliding in beer and vomit while brothers gleefully tossed more beer all around. One Klan member later insisted that Chuck went to the bar on his own and grabbed his own beers off the counter. If true, this is contrary to Klan's Tapping Night tradition. Rocky LaForge says that Chuck "certainly was not forced to drink," and Don King says his investigation supports that statement. But apparently no member felt either the legal or ethical responsibility to say stop, that's enough — an omission that haunts many Klansmen.

Sometime during the races, Chuck's speech became slurred. He began to make muttering sounds. Because he was soaked with beer, his big brother and Sullivan decided to give him a shower. Whether Chuck had soiled his clothing — a sign that the involuntary organs are in deep trouble — is not known. Since a member's girlfriend washed his clothes before returning them to Eileen, it may never be known. At one time Sullivan thought he put a clean pair of underwear on Chuck after toweling him off, but this is doubtful unless rescue workers removed them. He was naked when funeral director David Gardner dispatched his body to the morgue. Someone thought of forcing vinegar down Chuck's throat, presumably to make him vomit. No one did, however, because he was already unconscious, and they were afraid he might choke.

Instead of taking Chuck to a hospital, where he almost surely would have been saved, the big brother and Sullivan placed him on his stomach with his face to one side. Apparently they had seen enough pledges pass out that they thought he would sleep it off. The university said that he was put to bed but neglected to mention that the "bed" was an uncovered tick mattress.

Chuck started snoring immediately. His body's vital organs were in trouble, but no one recognized the snoring as a danger sign. Also in the room was another pledge, who had passed out and had been dumped on another mattress. Sullivan left to check on other pledges, including his real-life brother, and came back fifteen minutes later to check Chuck and the other unconscious pledge. He then departed with another brother for a sorority party, leaving LaForge to tend his little brother and a drooling Chuck.

LaForge slipped away to take a shower, returning about eleven-thirty P.M., the time of death listed on Chuck's death certificate. He observed that Chuck was barely breathing and that his fingernails had turned blue, but he believes that Chuck was still alive at that time.

LaForge called out. Carl Pelcher came into the room.

"I don't think he's breathing too well," said LaForge.

Pelcher turned Chuck over. He saw that the upper part of his body was blue-purplish. There was a strange red mark on Chuck's chest that mystifies Pelcher to this day. His body felt cold. Another brother entered the room at this point. None of the three men knew CPR or resuscitation techniques, another detail that haunts the Klansmen. Nor could these three sober brothers get much help from pledges and other members too drunk to do anything. "I have a mellow head in a crisis situation while other people panic," says LaForge. "If you don't help, get out of the way." But in a short while, after Chuck was pronounced dead, LaForge's emotions got the best of him.

Pelcher ran to the phone and dialed the operator. "This is an emergency," he said. "Give me an ambulance." The call went immediately to rescue crew members.

Dick Sands and his wife labored to save Chuck, one doing the compression, the other the breathing while performing CPR. They worked without much hope. They found no vital signs. His eyes were fixed and dilated. But ambulance personnel are not competent to judge whether a victim is deceased, so they worked as if he were still alive. They squeezed a goodly amount of liquid from his body while waiting for a physician to pronounce him dead.

By twelve-thirty A.M., or shortly thereafter, Don King and university president Richard Rose arrived separately at Klan Alpine. Dave Schwert had phoned King. Rose had been listening to the ambulance call on the CB radio in his Checker automobile while driving back from a meeting in nearby Hornell.

Rose asked if all pledges were accounted for. Finding that they weren't, he ordered the house searched. In the confusion, Klan Alpine members ran this way and that. The pledge class had eleven men, and only ten pledges—including Chuck, the other unconscious pledge who was receiving first aid in LaForge's room, and a basketball player who failed to show up for Tapping Night—could be accounted for.

The Alfred village police were angered when Rose, an ex-Marine, tried to take over and reminded him that he had no jurisdiction. "The university officials were out of bounds," says Randy Belmont. This tift gave rise to rumors rampant in Alfred that Rose had commanded students "to clean up this pigsty," inadvertently destroying evidence. Since both the state troopers and the Belmont-Razey team arrived right after the ambulance and before Rose, there was little time for anyone to destroy evidence. Four witnesses at the scene, including Tiny Jamison, say that rumor is untrue.

Finally, the unaccounted-for pledge was discovered curled up in a locked closet. Rose remembers that the door had to be forced open. The ambulance crew found a slight pulse on the youth and went to work. The pledge who had been in the room with Chuck also had a tremendous amount of alcohol in his bloodstream and added to the confusion by screaming when he came to his senses. Both of these men were taken to Bethesda Hospital in Hornell, halting what Rose and Eileen Stevens believe might easily have been a triple tragedy. Dave Schwert was distressed by what he saw but not surprised. Alcohol overdoses have happened too many times in Alfred to shock him. "This type of thing was very normal for Klan Alpine," he says. "In a college community with two campuses, it's several times a year we respond to calls like this. Of course it was extreme where you had a fatality and two near-fatalities."

The two state troopers still waited downstairs, observing a madhouse that grew worse when grief and rage overcame the Klansmen. The troopers kept picking their feet up and down to unstick their boots from the floor. One says he watched King and Jamison confer. He knew what was coming when they approached him. He and his partner were, in effect, told that the investigation was under control and not in their jurisdiction and that their presence was no longer necessary or desired. They left.

Jamison's investigation may have been more intensive than those conducted by the school and district attorney. "They had been doing a lot of drinking—that was evident," Jamison says. "There were kegs of draft beer. We confiscated several bottles. There was lots of Jack Daniel's. Stenzel drank a helluva lot." Through the night and early the next day, village police interviewed many Klan Alpine members present at the party, obtaining signed depositions. By the following week, they may have completed interviews with all witnesses.

But signed depositions were, unfortunately, not the only source of information at work in the community. Will Archer, Judith's husband, signed a statement saying he had no personal knowledge of alcohol's being poured down the throats of Klan Alpine pledges. Nonetheless, a rumor to the contrary found its way to Eileen and Roy Stevens in Sayville. That rumor, and others, such as one that said Klan members defecated into a hole in their party room, angered Klansmen such as Rocky LaForge. "It was total b.s.," he says. Despite his deposition, on the morning after Chuck's death, even Archer repeated false statements he heard from students. Without question, these rumors did additional, undeserved damage to the school's reputation.

As late as 1983 the wife (now widow) of dismissed Alfred faculty member David C. Jillson, a loser in an age discrimination suit, repeated an untrue statement about Klan Alpine.

"They got [Stenzel] drunk," Grace Jillson told the Boston *Globe*, which printed the remark unchallenged on August 24, 1983, "and when he was unconscious they poured the last drops of whiskey down his throat. . . . It got into his windpipe and killed him."

Randy Belmont says the rumors made his job harder because "the gruels and drools" —as he terms his critics from academia—got on his case, even though none of them had any facts. The police were unable to prove that Klan members tried to revive Chuck on their own before calling an ambulance, but in Belmont's opinion there could have been a delay before help was summoned. "It's not uncommon to cover up before [fraternities] call anybody in these instances," he says. Klan members deny that there was any such delay on the night of Chuck's death.

Tiny Jamison is a sturdy, smart old cuss whose uniform sleeves are too short. He gets to the point in few words, and although his speech is gruff, he's a kinder soul than he'd like to let on. His hair is thick; his eyes hold contact. His desk is covered with paperwork, but he puts his hands on anything he needs without much delay. A *Saturday Evening Post* poster of a benevolent cop hangs over his head. In Jamison's view Klansmen are "decent" and "different people when sober." On the street when he talks to them, they look the part of the all-American boy. "When they get in the booze, they're unresponsible asses if you want my opinion. But this is true not only of Klan, and not only fraternities, but society," he says. Jamison calls Chuck's death a waste.

Robert A. Heineman, a professor at Alfred since 1971 and the advisor to Klan until the previous September, hurried into the house about one-thirty A.M. A fraternity member had summoned him when he couldn't reach Steven Peterson, the current advisor and a one-time student of Heineman's at Bradley University. Heineman—an Alfred village official—was distressed by the scene he observed, never having attended a Tapping Night during four years as Klan advisor.

"Where is the boy having difficulty?" he asked a bystander.

"Upstairs."

Outside the room where Chuck lay, Heineman encountered Russ Johnson, an ambulance crew member. "Where is he?" he asked.

"In there."

The professor peered inside. The room was in disarray. Chuck's desert boots and a coverlet with a snowflake pattern lay on the floor. A partially filled case of pop and an empty beer case filled with schoolwork were conspicuous, as were a jacket, a pair of jeans, a heavy belt, a coffee cup, and a pitcher. A plaid couch, a chair made of phony, cracking leather, some files, and a six-drawer dresser with one glass replacement knob were the main pieces of furniture. A Buffalo Bills poster, a dartboard, and a poster depicting a semi-truck passing a church adorned the walls.

"Is he dead?" asked Heineman.

"Yes," said Johnson.

"Who's in there with him?"

"Dr. Eisenhardt."

Dr. Robert Eisenhardt, a physician who lived a mile out of town, was inspecting the body. It was he who first pronounced Chuck dead at 1:45 A.M. and released the rescue crew from their efforts.

Don King entered the room. The physician asked the dean if he could identify the body.

King looked. "No," he said.

Joseph van Cura, the Klan alumnus who came back to the house to be with the boys, was upset. He gave an interview to the Rochester *Democrat and Chronicle* and expressed his hope that people wouldn't get the wrong idea about what had happened at Klan that night. "The initiation ceremony has been pretty much the same since the fraternity started," he said. "I'm afraid people will look at this and think about closing down the fraternities, not only at Alfred but around the country, and at Alfred fraternities make up the social life for many students. These things make it look like fraternities are really bad, and that's not an accurate picture."

Twice more in the middle of the night, Roy Stevens and Don King talked by phone about the best way to get the couple from the Rochester airport to Alfred University. King came away with the impression that Eileen and Roy would be most at ease having two students from Sayville meet their plane and drive them to campus. Roy thought the students, two girls who knew Chuck, would be accompanied by a university representative — or at least be in a university car. Clearly, Roy and the dean had a misunderstanding — understandable given the late hour and the inherent stress. King insists that he was not insensitive to the couple's needs. The result was that two grieving, sleep-deprived girls met the Stevenses in the only transportation available to college kids on short notice: a clunker.

The conditions of their ride distressed Eileen. After the sad-eyed girls met them, Roy had to get both gas and oil before they could even reach their destination. Worse, the car's smoking condition caused a policeman to pull them over. The officer let them go undisturbed, but the incident only heightened the tension in Eileen.

Like every parent, Eileen had sent her son to college to help him prosper. Perhaps because she had been unable to attend college herself, she wanted to make certain that Chuck and her other children did. She respected people with an education. During her meeting with King, she would be intimidated by his title and stultified by the attractive campus. She had dreamed lofty dreams for her children. Why shouldn't her first-born succeed at college? Chuck had won science awards and belonged to the honor society in high school. His prospects were excellent. "Make that dean's list and get all you can out of college," she once wrote him. "It's an experience you'll never regret, and life holds good things for you."

Each stage of Chuck's growth, every achievement, had signified something larger in her mind. Chuck was independent. He had his own paper route and took on a second during a friend's vacation. He regularly woke up without prompting to ride his bicycle to six A.M. Mass. This kid of hers had ambition, she boasted to his doting grandparents.

Once he returned home from serving as an altar boy at a funeral Mass talking nonstop about the woman he had seen before the undertaker closed the lid. "Her name was Angelina," he said.

"How old was she?" asked Eileen.

"Not so old. Her children cried so hard."

Neither Roy nor Eileen knew the woman, but Chuck brought her to the dining table with him. He cared for people, and he wanted his parents to care too.

A tall, striking man whose hair turned prematurely white in his twenties, Roy Stevens was considered the ideal father by all Chuck's friends. He had worked his way through school, and he thought that having part-time jobs would strengthen his stepson's character. Eileen always referred to Roy as the love of her life. One of Chuck's friends who comes from a broken home says that Roy and Eileen have "the ideal marriage."

Nonetheless, immediately following Chuck's death, Roy went through a period of self-recrimination. He worked fewer Saturdays and became more demonstrative with his children. Having learned that opportunity can be snatched away in a heartbeat, he made saying "I love you" to Suzanne when he left for work a matter of routine. He remembered a time when Chuck had wanted to attend a basketball camp for high-school players. He was a good athlete, but not the natural his younger brother Scott was. Chuck was all hustle and push on the Catholic Youth Organization (CYO) teams he joined; Scott had finesse, grace, and a natural shooting touch. Chuck thought the camp might polish his skills and give him a chance to make a college team. To Roy's everlasting sorrow, he told the boy that he couldn't send him. It didn't help Roy's troubled mind that his family was living paycheck to paycheck back then; whenever the family got a few dollars ahead it was time to pay parochial school tuition.

One of the things he told himself on the long night before they left for Alfred was "I should have scraped that money together and done it somehow."

A sorority woman present at the party with Scott Sullivan coincidentally hailed from Sayville. She phoned her mother to tell her Chuck was dead. The mother called the Vollmers, neighbors of the Stevenses' who doted on Chuck. "You wished he was your boy," says Bob Vollmer. "That's what kind of boy he was." The Vollmers' son Billy, a gentle grizzly, was Chuck's lifelong friend.

As children, the two boys counted on Mr. Vollmer to be their playmate. In winter he hauled out a garden hose and made the boys a hockey rink. In summer he and his wife took them to camp at Moose River, a wild area in northwestern New York state. Chuck begged Roy and Eileen, unsuccessfully, to go there with him. Roy was too busy at the factory; Eileen was terrified of whatever unknown creepy crawlers skulked in the woods. Her idea of seeing wildlife in the flesh was a rugged trip to the Bronx Zoo.

Sometime in the middle of the night, after a police photographer took shots of Chuck's pale, naked body, the undertaker drove the corpse to Cuba Memorial Hospital for an autopsy. The next afternoon, Roy and Eileen Stevens sat grim-faced at the hospital.

The waiting room was tiny, equipped with only seven red chairs for visitors and illuminated by a gold lamp. A rendering of carousel horses by an artist named O'Grady hung on one wall. On another wall was an architect's idyllic vision of the hospital. Stacks of magazines and copies of the Cuba *Patriot* lay untouched on an endtable. Through the window the couple could see a stand of pine trees and a parking lot with a few snow-topped cars belonging to physicians. Down the hall a few paces were a water fountain, an old-fashioned wooden telephone booth, a meditation room, and, somewhere unseen, the morgue where Chuck now lay—minus vital tissues and fluids that Randy Belmont would soon drive to a Buffalo laboratory for analysis.

Eileen paced like a lioness deprived of her cub. Again and again she asked the head nurse if she could see Chuck. Again and again she was rebuffed. She listened idly to the voice of a switchboard operator. Once again she approached the nurse on duty, Debbie Hamilton, to insist—not to ask—that she be allowed to see her son. Hamilton left, and in a short time an odd little man with a grumpy manner ushered the Stevenses into the tiny but soothing meditation room. He introduced himself as Dr. Paul der Kolisch, a pathologist. He said that he had assisted the coroner, Dr. Irwin Felsen, on Chuck's autopsy. Kolisch, in his early sixties, had little hair on top. What remained grew long and wild. He had the sideburns of a Civil War general; wiry black hairs sprouted from his cheeks. With his thick glasses he could pass for the mad scientist in a Saturday morning cartoon.

He warned them that this was not a pleasant thing they were about to see and put his hand on Eileen's arm to steady her. He told them about the unbelievable amount of fluid in Chuck's body. The immediate cause of death was "diffuse pulmonary edema" as a consequence of "acute alcohol intoxication." In laymen's terms, Chuck's vital organs had drowned in all that liquor. The pathologist talked tough yet was anything but hardened. Eileen says, "He was gruff, but he was decent to me—the only one who was that whole trip to Alfred." The pathologist also explained the extent of the damage that had been done to the body in the morgue. He never does a partial "post" because he doesn't want to explain why he did only half the job to some prosecuting attorney in court. "When I get a drunk on the table, I don't fuck around," the pathologist snaps. "I take a piece of the brain." He adds, "I knew these people were devastated. . . . What this woman cannot face and what is probably churning around in her guts is the way she brought up this kid that he would accept this horseshit. . . . This is what bothers me. That people will ask to be let in to a fraternity, much less permit themselves to be abused. . . . You almost want them to climb back into the uterus and tie them to the placenta."

Eileen was unyielding. She wanted to see Chuck. Dr. Kolisch "filibustered" while some hospital aides tidied the body up. As they sat there, Eileen says, the physician told her that what had been done to her son was "manslaughter."

"Obviously a crime had been committed," the pathologist recalls. "A white-collar crime."

Dr. Kolisch and the head nurse escorted Eileen to the morgue. The nurse talked quickly, trying to dissuade her.

Eileen had a sudden fear. She grabbed Roy's arm. "Promise me something," she said.

"What?"

"Promise me on your life that if I faint we won't leave until I see Chuck."

"Eileen—"

"Promise me."

"Yes."

The doctor led the way. She took no notice of the half-dozen aides in green gowns, the tiled walls, the bottles on shelves, the hoses, and a sink—all in a room no bigger than sixteen-by-twenty feet. How she made it to the side of the metal gurney without collapsing she'll never know.

The aides had cleaned Chuck up as best they could. Nonetheless, despite the sheet that covered him, she knew that his whole body had been violated. The room was cold. She shivered. Eileen took her son's limp hand. She had to visualize his blue eyes. The lids were closed forever.

"I love you, Chuck," she said. She kissed him on the mouth and said a prayer. The nurse broke down and sobbed.

Roy stood by, ready to do whatever he had to do.

Receiving the news that your son is dead, over the phone in the middle of the night, is clearly one of life's worst blows. Almost as bad is having to make such a call to a parent. After phoning the university's public relations head to give him what scraps of information he knew, Don King left the Klan house sometime after twelve-thirty A.M. on February 25. From there, he took a short drive along Main Street to his office in the administration building to look up the home telephone numbers of the dead youth and the two stricken pledges.

King says that the whole affair was an ordeal for him. He feels he became a scapegoat. "I happen to be a very sensitive individual," he says. "For me to have to get on the phone and call a mother to tell her that she lost a son . . . is not anything that anybody wants to do or wants to be put in a position to do. Once [I did] that it was a natural progression that she blamed me for it happening."

King has severe critics at Alfred University, but no one charges that he is an unfeeling man. Gary Horowitz, now Alfred's director of alumni/parent relations and occasionally one of King's critics, tells a story about an injured football player. King not only called the boy daily but also helped him graduate on time by getting his assignments. The player, says Horowitz, thinks there isn't a nicer guy on this earth than King. "You hear time after time about the willingness of Don King to be there," concludes Horowitz. "He cares about the kids. He grieves when something happens, he really does. The guy is not a dispassionate person by any means."

Much of the criticism directed at King centered on his inability — and that of the Alfred administration, including President Rose — to deal with the Klan Alpine tragedy from a public relations standpoint. "Everybody on campus said that," says Horowitz. "The first rule of public relations is that you tell everything — everything." After phoning the Pennsylvania family of one stricken Klan pledge, King never followed-up, according to a letter the boy's father wrote Eileen. The Stevenses too charge King with being insensitive in their time of sorrow. If he had bent over backwards to help her in the days and months following Chuck's death, Eileen says, she would never have sued the university.

"I doubt that," retorts King. He says that from his very first conversation with Eileen Stevens, he had the perception that she planned to sue.

Don King is at his best with good students and loyal employees. With them he is good-humored, solicitous, and warm. He shows a different side under pressure — not a bad side, but irksome, perturbable. During an interview, he's his affable and charming self, but ask him the wrong question and his normally steady gaze starts to shift. His eyes dart, and he appears uncomfortable. When he considers a question too personal or impertinent, he can give "that look," as Ron Sember, a former Klan Alpine president, calls it.

King's eyes maintain contact when he discusses the Stenzel death. The pain and misery in his expressive face appear to be genuine. Accusatory letters, three hundred of them, that he received after Chuck's death had a devastating effect on his wife, children, and secretary, as well as on him.

King feels at ease with the Greeks because he is one of them. He talks with affection about his days as a fraternity president at Morris Harvey College (now the University of Charleston) in West Virginia and credits that office with helping him overcome shyness and self-doubt to get him where he is today.

King's fraternity was the Gamma Mu chapter of Alpha Sigma Phi — one of the most tradition-loving of traditional fraternities. The Morris Harvey group received its national charter on April 2, 1960. Founded at Yale University in 1845, Alpha Sigma Phi is one of the older fraternities. Its rolls number celebrity alumni such as television weatherman Willard Scott and actor Vincent Price.

A mystic ritual, in which all members — presumably including King — had to participate came to light in 1985. Fiery residue from a lit bowl placed on a coffin seeped onto a nineteen-year-old member. Martin Badrov, an Illinois Institute of Technology student, suffered severe burns to his arm, leg, chest, neck, and face during the ceremony, which members called the "flambeau."

Nothing quite that controversial occurred during King's days as a pledge and member. In the spring of 1963, Alpha Sigma Phi gave bids to forty-two of fifty-nine men seeking admission to the Gamma Mu chapter, including King. "So what if you have to get up at 6:30 for an early-morning coat-and-tie breakfast?" said a taunting blurb in the school newspaper.

"Well, just wait a week or so, pledge. You'll be lucky to get in bed that early. And smile when I say that."

During King's pledge period, Alpha Sigma Phi was involved in a flap. A sorority member blasted the group in the student paper for holding "an unchaperoned, banned playing-band dance" in violation of rules set by the Interfraternity Council (the fraternity governing body whose president at the time was an Alpha Sig). "It seems that the Alpha Sigma Phi fraternity is a little unethical, might we say?" wrote Sandra McKenzie. "Just as surely as birds of a feather flock together, so do unethical people."

One indication of the severity of King's pledge period is that only thirty-one of forty-two men made it to the traditional ceremony held at St. Matthew's Parish House on May 12, 1963, at two P.M. King and his fellow initiates were given an official Alpha Sig pen and the fraternity flower, a talisman rose.

Hazing was regarded as a problem at Morris Harvey College. Student antics caused locals to give the school the nickname of Harvey High. One administrator — Director of Freshman Admission W. J. Briggs, Jr. — wrote an editorial for the school paper (while Don King was a student) to attack the custom:

> The time is long overdue for the fraternities to discontinue the ancient role of serfdom for their little brothers. There is no doubt that the wide-eyed neophyte doesn't realize what an ogre the bright-eyed, hand-shaking, back-slapping, tooth-smiling brother can become after [the pledge] has signed his pledge card.
>
> The role of the fraternity member is to aid his little brother, not to break down his health (both mental and physical) and . . . lower his academic achievement no matter for how short a time. I realize fully that the fraternities have a difficult time policing their own brothers; there are sadists in all groups, but I also realize that if the tactics of the group were reported to the national officers, they would all be placed on suspension . . .
>
> If I were a college freshman, I would think more than once before signing a pledge to any social organization under the guise of a brotherhood organization founded for friendship that would force me to be subjected to public humiliating treatment and abuse, and subject to terms that would affect my academic average and in fact endanger the very reason for which I enrolled — a college education.
>
> So let's get with it, Morris Harvey College fraternities. Let's get on the band wagon and march toward our real goals — Brotherhood — Scholarship — Friendship.

* * *

On December 15, 1964, Don King was elected president of Alpha Sigma Phi. On a positive note, under his direction, his chapter announced in May that it had modified its pledge program to eliminate hazing and had substituted "Help Week" for Hell Week. A photograph accompanying the school paper's article, however, contradicted that announcement. It depicted Alpha Sigma Phi's pledges standing at attention in a lineup. The photograph buttresses Eileen Stevens's contention that King is against only hazing that meets his personal definition. What distresses her is that even today he quibbles that Chuck did not die by hazing because the death occurred at Tapping Night, which was only an entrance into pledging.

That argument might satisfy King's conscience, but it wouldn't satisfy the Fraternity Executives Association, an organization of national fraternity heads. That group defines hazing as "any action taken or situation created, intentionally, whether on or off fraternity premises, to produce mental or physical discomfort, embarrassment, harassment, or ridicule. Such activities and situations include paddling in any form; creation of excessive fatigue; physical and psychological shocks; quests, treasure hunts, scavenger hunts, road trips, or any other activities carried on outside the confines of the house; wearing, publicly, apparel which is conspicuous and not normally in good taste; engaging in public stunts and buffoonery; morally degrading or humiliating games and activities; late work sessions which interfere with scholastic activities; and any other activities which are not consistent with fraternal law, ritual, or policy or the regulations and policies of the educational institution." According to this definition, Chuck experienced hazing from Klan Alpine when his big brother played a mind game on him in the dorm room, when he was given a bottle of booze with the implied or stated expectation that he should drink it, when he was put in a trunk, and when he was expected to partake in drinking games.

Since Klan Alpine is a local fraternity—meaning that it is not one of the fifty-nine member fraternities in the National Interfraternity Conference (NIC)—unless King, or the university, accepts a broader definition of hazing, Eileen Stevens insists, there is nothing to prevent another death from occurring on some future first night of Alfred pledging. Ironically, according to Eileen, Alpha Sigma Phi is and has been tough on hazing perpetrators. Many national fraternity executives regularly and strictly enforce their organizations' policies against hazing. Local fraternities have no such executive intervention.

King, well-intentioned though he may be, perhaps still sympathizes with the traditions he took part in as a pledge and brother. He doesn't think paddles should be outlawed and disagrees with educators who have said paddles can't be sold in bookstores because they represent beatings. "Paddles can be explained because it's part of the tradition, part of the mystique of fraternity life," says King. "It's a symbol." He does not specify what meaning that symbol has for him.

King was a fraternity man at a time when doing awful things to pledges wasn't thought of as hazing. "We just thought it was part of tradition," he says. "I had never heard of anyone getting hurt. We used to get paddled and do stupid things—nothing of a malicious intent." His chapter "kidnapped" pledges and dropped them off in isolated areas of West Virginia. They poured unpleasant things all over initiates, sent them on scavenger hunts, deprived them of sleep, and, in general, treated them like plebes. "Some of it was degrading, but we didn't relate to it as degrading," says King.

The Stenzel death made headlines in New York state from Buffalo to Long Island. The initial headlines saddened Eileen and Roy because they felt Chuck was made to look entirely at fault for his own death. They blame King because he told the New York *Times* and other papers that the youth's death "was not a hazing" when he was interviewed less than twenty-four hours after the event. Roy and Eileen feel that King's comments put the burden of responsibility on their dead son. "Of course there is the question of peer pressure," King told the *Times*. "There was extensive drinking. . . . It is an unfortunate tragedy and one that is difficult to justify. . . . But certainly these things do occur when people get together drinking at these kinds of affairs."

It is not uncommon for administrators to downplay the incident after a hazing death. A spokesman for American International College in Springfield, Massachusetts, made the same claim after James E. (Jay) Lenaghan, Jr., died in February 1984. Dean of Students Blaine Stevens (no relation to Roy Stevens) said that early indications were that Jay had choked on his own vomit after drinking alcohol during a pledge dinner. "Whenever something like this happens, an antenna goes up and people suspect a hazing," Stevens said. "But we at the college don't condone or allow anything like that." The university was later embarrassed when the "pledge dinner" was revealed to be tiny amounts of spaghetti that all the pledges ate while chugging stupendous quantities of wine. Like Chuck Stenzel, these pledges were expected to fill designated trash cans with vomit.

The barbarity of these Greek-letter society customs is shocking. But even more disturbing is the institutional insensitivity alleged by survivors of victims. When six-foot, 220-pound Steven J. Call died from hyperthermia in 1980 after performing calisthenics required of him by Delta Kappa Phi members, a University of Lowell spokesman gave a statement to the Boston *Globe* that trivialized the 108.6 body temperature suffered by the pledge. "Apparently the boy had been doing thirty minutes of exercises, nothing extraordinary, as part of his initiation when he became disoriented and very hot," said University of Lowell spokesman Oliver Ford. Ford stressed that Call had been subjected to "ordinary harassment"—a revealing oxymoron. Ford also rejected any possibility that hazing had occurred. "The only thing we found that is even reminiscent of the old days of hazing is a bit of paddling that was done with a piece of carpet," said Ford. "The paddling is routinely applied. There is a certain amount of indignity involved but that's what being a pledge is all about. It's nothing compared to the horrible days of the past when fraternity pledges went through Hell Week."

When administrators have a limited definition of hazing, deaths and injuries that might be called hazing-related are labeled "unfortunate accidents." Unless university administrators are compelled by the public to call a hazing incident a hazing incident, many deaths and injuries will continue to go unrecorded, says Eileen Stevens.

It is impossible to make an accurate count of hazing deaths because universities tend to cover them up with euphemisms of every stripe. Newspapers reported forty-five to fifty deaths between 1978 and 1990, probably an inflated figure since it includes not only recorded hazing deaths but also deaths of Greeks from sundry causes, such as accidental deaths (including the increasing number of falls from fraternity house roofs) and suicides.

A young fraternity man named Mike Moskos keeps a partially verified list of deaths as a public service. Moskos's photocopied list has kept hazing in the consciousness of many national fraternities and sororities, but, as its disclaimer states, "Some of the information here may be wrong." Moreover, many alcohol overdose incidents involving hazing are never reported as hazing—particularly if the victim recovers. Nor are schools and fraternities required to report instances of hazing. Many Greek-letter societies are disciplined by their advisors or the nationals for hazing, and these incidents never make the papers—particularly in cases where there is "only" mental hazing and no bodily injury. Physician Mark Taff, the co-editor of a 1985 study of hazing deaths and injuries for the *American Journal of Forensic Medicine and Pathology,* says that reported hazings are only the "tip of the iceberg." Unless media and public pressure is brought to bear on colleges and other groups in which hazing is common, administrators will continue to call hazing by any other name.

3

The ride from the morgue to Happy Valley, as the Alfred area is sometimes called, seemed to last forever. As their smoking car passed through Friendship, questions about those who were supposed to be her son's friends plagued Eileen. Don King had said Chuck died at a drinking party. Didn't he have a single friend there to watch out for him? Couldn't someone have taken him to the health center?

Aware that she would need her strength for what lay ahead, Eileen managed to keep her composure during the drive. Chuck was dead, but at least, she consoled herself, she would soon know why. She wondered if Greg Belanger, Chuck's Sayville friend, would be at the dormitory. She hoped eyewitnesses would be able to tell her what her son might have been thinking at the end. Tears streaked her mascara, but she refused to crack.

Her mind was at war. Fixed in Eileen's memory was the sight of her strapping son in that cold, sterile room. She recalled the softness of the sheet covering the gouges an autopsy required. She could see only his hands and face; the rest was hidden under the white cloth. The aides had seen to it that he looked like he was sleeping. His color had not changed, but that would happen, she knew. The lips were not as cold as she had expected. But they were cold. The room had smelled faintly of disinfectant.

Questions assailed her. Can he see me now? Is he aware of my suffering? What does he think about what happened last night?

Her family had been her life. Now a void existed. How could she ever have imagined that she knew pain and sorrow? What petty problem had she been wringing her hands over only the day before? Bitterness welled inside her. In her mind she yet again questioned Chuck.

What happened last night?

Why did you drink so much?

What were you trying to prove?

The winter scenery in the foothills outside Alfred blurred past the window. Something in this sparsely populated country had stirred Chuck. He had spoken of the friendly, down-to-earth people he had met and the beauty of the outdoors, teeming with pheasant, black bear, whitetail deer, redtail hawks, and mallards. She glanced at the snow-laden hardwood ridges in the distance and at the occasional stands of pines lining the highway. Allegany County was beautiful, but she had no desire for pretty landscapes now. Chuck had looked forward to coming back here. Yet he had called to let them know that his arrival was tainted by sadness. He missed his family.

The family missed him.

Alfred was Chuck's second college. While he was in high school, a recruiter from Doane College in southeastern Nebraska sold him on that school. Doane was his first choice partly because he thought he might have a chance to make a smaller college's basketball team. But even there the talent proved too much for him. He worked out with the team when he arrived and learned that his hustle couldn't keep him from being over-matched by more skilled players.

Nothing worked for Chuck at Doane. His shirts were flannel, which, he joked in a letter, did him a lot of good. September temperatures were in the nineties, and it stayed sunny and warm into November. The boy from the Great South Bay of Long Island did not belong in the flat fields of Nebraska. Pizzas at El Toro in the college town of Crete couldn't satisfy a kid whose taste buds craved New York-style food. He referred to himself as "your stranded son" and felt pinned to the campus without a vehicle.

The subtle beauties of the Midwest simply didn't touch Chuck's soul. The hills, trees, and duck ponds on the Doane campus failed to excite him. His outdoor spirit craved an ocean or woods. He had brought only his clothing and a pillow. "The room seems so black with nothing in it," he said. He tacked up a photograph of his little sister to remind him of home.

Eileen badgered Chuck to write to all his relatives. She also spiced her letters with multiple questions. Chuck teased her for being nosey and called her a nag. She was undaunted in a return letter, baiting him by stringing a chain of questions together. "Have you heard from anyone yet?" she wrote. "Could you take more classes if you wanted? Have you thought about your major yet? Hey, what's this about a kid from Levittown? Maybe you can come home together? What do you do after classes? Do you have a lot of free time? Do you need money? How much did the books cost? (Only five more questions)."

In a letter he confessed that he really didn't mind his mother's Spanish Inquisition routine, adding an evaluation of her character that one day would haunt the Alfred University administration. "You wouldn't be the same if you didn't ask all those questions," he said.

Homesickness assaulted him, relieved only by a visit from Jimmy Arnoux and Mike Shivers in late September. He missed his friends. Worse, his classes were hard, and he struggled to keep a *C-* average.

While Chuck chafed in Nebraska, letters from Greg Belanger told him what terrific fun Alfred was. Belanger's classes were fantastic. The view from his dormitory room was idyllic. He had made the friends of a life-time. Oh, he had broken his leg in a touch football game, but, hey, three girls from his dormitory were fetching his food and washing his clothes. There was a beer party somewhere every night. Without trying, Belanger sold Chuck on Alfred.

Chuck asked his buddy to send him an application and catalog for Alfred. "[Greg] doesn't care if he goes home or not over the holidays," a shocked Chuck wrote his mother. He'd had enough of a state without an ocean. "I don't want to go here again. I like it, but I'd much rather be in New York somewhere. Greg's school sounds nice," he went on.

Chuck wrote another letter home in November. He planned to leave in nine days to enjoy Thanksgiving with his family. His heart was set on Alfred, but he knew it was too expensive. He was resigned to attending a state college.

Despite his loneliness, Chuck made close friends at Doane, a liberal arts school affiliated with the United Church of Christ, with a student body of only about seven hundred. He dated a pretty freshman named Sue Cantwell. She says that Chuck wanted to have a good time but drew the line at smoking marijuana. "I don't know if he even drank," she says. "He didn't participate much on that level at all. He was not a drinker, and he was not a smoker of pot."

Chuck would talk for hours about the Great South Bay and his boat back home. "He was homesick—he was real homesick," says Cantwell. "He really missed his family and friends a lot. Those people born on the East Coast have a real umbilical cord to the ocean."

Shortly before Thanksgiving Chuck and his parents had a heart-to-heart phone conversation. The upshot was that he would leave Doane at the end of the semester and enroll at Belanger's beloved Alfred in September—if he still liked the school after checking it out. Eileen and Roy agreed they would scrimp and help him all they could, and Chuck said that he would come home and work for a year to help defray costs.

Chuck visited Alfred and loved the campus. In the spring of 1977 he enrolled there, first majoring in economics. The letters from his family continued to flow, but Chuck began to phone more often than write. Peer pressure to drink occasionally caught up with him, according to Jimmy Arnoux and Joe Bachman, Chuck's roommate that spring. Chuck went with Arnoux to a Klan party, where the two of them "were blitzed on grain alcohol." Arnoux, who lived in Openhym Hall a few rooms from Chuck, says that they knew drinking and crazy antics went on at Klan, but not the severity of it. "I do not have the foggiest idea of what went on in his mind that night [of his death]," says Arnoux. "From the bottom of my heart I do not know. It had to be a spur-of-the-moment thing." Bachman says Chuck was trying to prove "he could drink with the big boys—the baddest dudes around—Klan Alpine."

Despite the nighttime antics, Chuck loved his classes at Alfred, and his grades were better. He raved about several, including his American literature class. In the months after his death, Eileen studied Chuck's class notes, trying to stay in touch with her son's mind. He took extensive notes on Thoreau's *Walden,* underlining references that struck a particular chord: "I went to the woods because I wished to live deliberately, to front only the essential facts of life, and see if I could not learn what it had to teach, and not, when I came to die, discover that I had not lived."

The references would haunt Eileen. The literature of nineteenth-century America is preoccupied with death, wickedness, and the moral failures of mankind. She couldn't help wondering if his reading had anything to do with his decision to join men who had declared themselves brothers. "The unpardonable sin," Chuck wrote, "was isolating yourself from man." She chastized herself for lionizing Chuck in her diary and journals, noting after his death that his real appeal was that he was "an ordinary kid."

His notebook also showed that, however content he was at Alfred, he still missed the beautiful bay. The pages were covered with doodles of his clamboat and the boatyard on the Great South Bay.

The smoking car entered the tiny village of Alfred. Eileen took no notice until her escorts pointed out the school. The drive to the dormitory from the campus entrance took less than a minute. The first thing Eileen saw was Chuck's pickup truck, the only one among the cars, a bold, blue reminder that he was gone. She sobbed. Roy's arm tightened around her. Chuck had loved that vehicle. It had been repainted only a few months earlier. He was always washing it, fixing it, driving it. It had been his recreation and his favorite status symbol. He had poured his money into it.

To Eileen, Openhym Hall didn't look special, but the hilly campus was pretty. Alfred University occupies 232 acres of land. Some of its older buildings are eye-catching. Alumni Hall, a white, churchlike structure with an ornate steeple topped by a twelve-foot quill pen, is lovely. The Steinheim Museum, an intriguing gothic building originally constructed as a house in 1875, looks as if the stone tower ought to harbor a madwoman or a hunchback.

Someone had gotten word to the men of Openhym that Chuck's parents would be coming by. Eileen walked into the building. What plans had Chuck had when he first passed through these doors? The boy with the laughing eyes and the mane of hair had a serious side, too. He was worried about the environment. He worshipped wildlife and worried about endangered species. Eileen believed Chuck would have been successful at whatever he tried. He would have been a superior history teacher. No one was better with kids.

Something was very wrong, Eileen thought as she walked to room 221, Chuck's room. Her son drinking himself to death? He couldn't have done that, could he? He was too conservative to be a risk-taker. He wasn't the type to accept dares. He was his own person, his own man, sure of himself. He had wanted to come to Alfred even when he didn't qualify for financial aid. He had earned a significant portion of his tuition, too, as he had promised. Her thoughts were driven from her head as young men walked toward her and Roy. They shook Roy's hand, comforted her. A couple offered hugs. Many were crying.

Inside room 221 there were two beds. Chuck's was made; the roommate's, rumpled. The room looked as if Chuck had merely stepped out for a moment. On the wall was a picture of Jonathan Livingston Seagull—a present from Suzanne — and a U-Haul poster that Mike Shivers had given him. On the desk were a letter to Eileen he had just begun and an unopened letter from her that must have come that day. A few weeks previously, she had sent him a schmaltzy Valentine's Day card, thinking at the time that it sounded too gushy, but he had displayed it. A snapshot of his boat on the Great South Bay was in view, along with a sketch of a house by his grandmother, Doreen Stenzel, and a picture of Suzanne. A wire spool from the Long Island Lighting Company that Roy had corked served as a table. A new history textbook was on his desk, and nearby was a pile of books by his three favorite writers: Jacques Cousteau, F. Scott Fitzgerald, and Kurt Vonnegut.

Eileen tried to touch all his things. Before leaving, she fingered Chuck's blue down jacket, the only coat other than his yellow slicker that he owned.

"Roy, why is his coat here?"

"I don't know."

"This doesn't make any sense. Why would he go to a party in the middle of winter without taking his coat?"

A few days later a recollection of this detail came back to Eileen, leading her to deduce, rightly or wrongly, that Chuck had been surprised and taken — coatless — from the room by Klan Alpine.

Greg Belanger sat in Alex's bar, a pitcher of beer in front of him, eyes fixed on the light in the Alfred administration building across the street. Ever since six A.M. when a friend told him ever so bluntly that Chuck was dead, Belanger had been rambling all over Alfred in a borrowed yellow Volkswagen. He had stopped by the quaint country house of Paul Kohler, a professor of languages who was battling the university for his academic life due to Rose's faculty cutbacks. Kohler had been in Europe during World War Two and had witnessed Nazi atrocities firsthand. "Young men do stupid things," was all he could say when Belanger asked him to make sense of his friend's death.

Chuck had been a part of Belanger's life from the time the Stevens family moved into his neighborhood just before both boys entered third grade. Belanger lived in a development on the backside of a tract of woodlands. He felt a strong bond with the new kid on the other side of the woods. Chuck lived on Marion Street, a dead end, which made it a fine place to throw a ball back and forth without traffic interruptions. Bronzed and golden in summer, the pair chased one another all over the woods, following the old wagon ruts that cut a swath through the trees.

When Belanger moved to an older section of Sayville, he and Chuck stayed tight. At St. Lawrence the Martyr Elementary School, Belanger and Chuck and Jimmy Arnoux made a single shadow. Strangers often assumed that Chuck and Belanger were twins. With platinum hair and a striking look, Belanger was a stockier version of Chuck.

When Belanger, Arnoux, and Chuck were hardly more than finger-lings, they gave their hearts to the bay on Long Island's south shore. They rolled in the warm sand like colts, and their spare time revolved around seawater adventures. By the ninth grade each owned a boat. Belanger's was a quixotic symbol for his romantic spirit. Chuck's and Arnoux's vessels satisfied more practical needs. Pragmatic Arnoux saw an opportunity to make a buck from his beloved sea. As a clammer, he became the captain of his life, rejoicing every day that he could make money without being entombed in a factory.

Chuck had a little of Belanger and a little of Arnoux in him. He had the imagination to get a near-mystic thrill from the sea, but he wanted to be paid for his hard work. His biological father, grandfather, and great-grandfather had been clammers and fishermen at one time or another. His father had courted Eileen by taking her for rides on the sound aboard his clamboat. Because Chuck hailed from a family of modest means — although hardly poor — he also saw clamming as a cash industry. If you pushed and had the will to learn that Arnoux and Chuck had, you could earn much more than you could flipping burgers. The three boys told one another that someday each would buy a monster pickup, the steed of choice among Sayville's working-class men. Boomer Esiason, the rugged quarterback for the Cincinnati Bengals, grew up on Long Island, and he, too, clammed for spending money. "That was my summer job," says Esiason. "You talk about hard work! Kids don't know what it means to spend six hours out in the boat digging for clams. That's unbelievable."

As Chuck, Belanger, and Arnoux aged, they graduated to bigger and bigger boats. The trio expanded into an unnamed fraternal society of clammers that at one time also included Billy Vollmer, Mike Shivers, Scott Doty, and Jim Schildt. The bond between these seven was strongest when they bought a ruined houseboat and worked as if they had hot coals in their pockets to restore it to its former grandeur. They furnished it with whatever used (and sometimes new) items they could borrow or steal from their various homes. Roy once pulled into the garage to find a rug missing that he had intended to put in the family's playroom. He rushed down to the boat to repossess it — a good thing too since the boat eventually sank, taking several mothers' silverware, dinner plates, easy chairs, and tables down with it.

Before it sank, however, the boys lived on that boat, and the regular crowd on Fire Island got to recognize it when the gang of seven docked to get Cokes and cheese sandwiches at a local cafe. Many local high-school girls pranced aboard its deck, prompting some jealous, luckless, boatless guys to dub the houseboat a "floating whorehouse."

No matter how much fun the gang of seven had, they respected the water as well as loved it. They knew enough to take care on days that were less than calm or shrouded in fog. Every so often on a howling day, a clammer gets lost on the bay. Usually, but not always, it's someone with an ill-equipped boat who has ignored small-craft warnings or overloaded the deck with men, clams, and equipment. Chuck and his friends never over-dramatized the danger, yet they knew it was there. Chuck's great-grandfather, after all, had perished in a storm at sea. Jimmy Arnoux's dad also died on a boat.

Year by year, the boys proved themselves seaworthy. Belanger held his own, but he was not the clammer that Chuck and Arnoux were. From Roy and Arnoux, Chuck learned a strong work ethic. From Billy Vollmer's father, he learned self-reliance: "You want water, you get water," Mr. Vollmer had taught him. "You want a fire, you build one." From Eileen he inherited a stubborn streak that wouldn't let him give up when his hands were raw and chapped in winter, or even when the clamboat sank, as it occasionally did, and required costly parts. Arnoux was equally self-reliant and stubborn, plus—as Belanger likes to say—"he had more integrity than anyone I knew." If Arnoux told Chuck and Belanger to meet him at the dock at six-thirty A.M., the two wouldn't have to wait one minute. The others always teased Belanger, who liked to sleep late.

At seventeen Chuck and Arnoux looked like weatherbeaten seamen in a Winslow Homer painting. They belonged to the sea. On the water they had the confidence of racecar drivers who have logged hundreds of wins. Belanger admired their efficiency and effectiveness. He himself never became an accomplished clammer. He was like the baseball player who thinks while swinging and thus watches every pitch whiz into the catcher's glove. Arnoux and Chuck were like batters who simply put good wood on the ball. Arnoux, silent by nature, and Chuck formed a lasting bond through clamming. They needed no secret handshake, no ritual to cement their brotherhood.

As they were preparing to leave Openhym Hall, Roy asked one of the women who had driven them to phone Don King. Eileen feels that their having to track King down is another sign of his insensitivity to their situation. King says he left his afternoon free to meet with Eileen whenever she finished at the morgue and dormitory. He too was exhausted after staying up all night, and Roy had spoken to him briefly from the hospital to let him know that they had arrived.

Before closing the door to Chuck's room, Eileen asked the students if anyone had seen his roommate. No one had. Nor had anyone seen Greg Belanger. She had no idea how she would get Chuck's truck and belongings back to Sayville. But one young man promised to see to it that the truck and everything else made it safely. Students wept in the hall as the Stevenses departed.

Eileen and Roy went from the dorm to King's office in Carnegie Hall, a boxy building with an attractive red roof. Only the dean's quarters were lighted; the rest of the building was dark. Only King was at work this cold Saturday afternoon, facing his grim duty.

King tried to be both cordial and professional, but Eileen sensed his trepidation and anxiety. A lean man, a daily jogger well before the national craze, King has the handsome features of a small canine. At this initial meeting, he kept directing himself to silent Roy even though Eileen posed nearly all the questions. Perhaps King knew instinctively that he had a better chance to understand this tall, uncomplicated man—obviously a jock like himself—than he did his wife. He chose his words carefully. At the time Eileen thought he did so because he feared she would break down. Later she decided that he spoke with caution to avoid having to eat his words in court someday.

King had to walk a tightrope that afternoon. He wanted to convey his personal feelings about the death. But as someone who not only loved but represented Alfred University, he had no divided loyalties. If Eileen's charge that King was evasive is valid, such conduct would not be atypical. The dean tends to "stonewall in crisis situations," according to a tenured faculty member.

Eileen could not have known at the time that Richard Rose, Alfred's president, had consulted with one or more school attorneys at some point on Saturday morning and was advised to clamp a lid on the Stenzel death. The lawyers instructed him to give minimal information to the family and the press, advice King had also given him at the Klan Alpine house in the middle of chaos. King says, "I conferred with him and told him what I thought we should do—he agreed." King denies that there was any stonewalling. "The institution wasn't trying to whitewash what had taken place," he says. Rose also insisted that all statements by university officials be "cleared" with him personally.

King is a few years younger than Eileen; he was two months shy of his thirty-fifth birthday at their first meeting. He came to Alfred in 1969 after working for two years at the State University College of New York at Brockport. His job at Alfred encompasses many responsibilities: he oversees residence halls, student activities, counseling services, financial aid, health services, intercollegiate athletics, and recreation. Although he met with fraternities and sororities to lay ground rules for rushing and other events, he did not require the Greeks to have faculty advisors. Alfred University had no formal policy to delineate the duties of advisors. "You have to realize that these [fraternity houses] are all off-campus places, and the advisors, in some ways, were in name only," King says.

The versions of what transpired during King's hour-long meeting with the Stevenses, as well as during a ninety-minute visit as he drove them to the airport in a university car, vary dramatically. Eileen learned that there was drinking, "lots of drinking." She learned that Chuck died at a Klan Alpine function and that two other pledges had been hospitalized. She says King reassured her that both the police and the university would investigate and keep her informed.

In February 1979 King gave this official version of what transpired in a media release:

> During the course of our discussion, we talked about
> everything I had learned up to that time concerning
> Charles's being invited to pledge Klan Alpine: the
> trip from his dorm to the fraternity house in the

> trunk and at a party in the fraternity house after he
> got out of the trunk, his passing out and being put to
> bed and checked on by others from time to time, and
> finally the discovery of his rapidly deteriorating
> condition.
>
> At this point, Mr. and Mrs. Stevens knew as
> much as I did about the incident.

In her journals Eileen criticized that release, and she still feels strongly about it. She says that King did not tell her and Roy about Chuck's being placed in the trunk of a car. She acknowledges that the passing of time and her distraught condition might have caused her to confuse minor details, but she believes she has complete recall of the gist of what King told her that afternoon. Roy Stevens concurs, saying he learned about the trunk of the car at Chuck's wake from his brother, a Long Island policeman who had been told the story by a colleague.

King admits that he isn't certain he told the Stevenses about the trunk. Asked if it might be possible that he discussed it on the drive to the airport, King says, "No, because I didn't even know [about the trunk] at that time — not when we were driving back to the airport. I went to meet the next day with students who were at the hospital to try to learn from them what had transpired."

Thus, part of the university's official statement, designed to destroy Eileen's credibility, is by King's own admission either inadvertently incorrect or an intentional falsehood. Eileen doesn't gloat over King's altered story. She believes it may show that the dean has changed, grown, in the time since Chuck's death.

At some point during the interview with King, Eileen asked to see Rose. She says that King told her that the president was unavailable — that he had planned to attend a basketball game that day.

King denies saying that Rose was at a basketball game. But a Rochester *Times-Union* story from 1978 sheds light on this point of contention. The paper's first story on the Stenzel incident included this fact: "Dr. M. Richard Rose, university president, was not available for comment and was reported at a basketball game."

Whether Rose was at that basketball game — a match pitting the Alfred Saxons against the Rochester Institute of Technology, whose presidency Rose would assume in a few months — is irrelevant except that Eileen was angered by what she perceived as his lack of sensitivity. The *Times-Union* article indicates a potentially greater relevance, however — that the basketball game may have been used as an excuse to keep the press and Eileen away from Rose. Was the basketball game a fabrication? If so, on whose part?

President Rose's first public response to Chuck's death was not printed until the Monday after he died. He said, "Drinking is a serious problem at college campuses in the United States, and Alfred University obviously is not immune," a position that deemphasizes the fraternity's role in the tragedy. His reasons for that approach puzzled Eileen for twelve years. Why would Alfred University try to make it look as though some dumb kid drank himself to death at a party—instead of as part of a fraternity initiation? Could the university's action have been designed to prevent the fraternity angle from instantly putting Chuck's death on the wires as a national news story?

The answers to these questions may lie in the fact that Alfred had a special visitor in its backyard all weekend. When Rose went to Klan Alpine on the night of Chuck's death, he was returning from a meeting in nearby Hornell. Rose says he cannot recollect precisely where he was that evening, but a newspaper account states that the annual dinner meeting of the Hornell Area Chamber of Commerce was held that night. The guest speaker that Friday evening—as part of "his weekend tour of the Southern Tier"—was New York Secretary of State Mario Cuomo.

Cuomo, an ally of Governor Hugh Carey, was one of the state's most powerful political figures, destined to become lieutenant governor in 1978, and eventually governor. The university was ultimately unsuccessful in downplaying the fraternity initiation angle in Chuck's death. Newspapers in Buffalo, Rochester, and Long Island, for example, put the story on page one Sunday morning. But one plausible reason for Rose's having ducked Eileen Stevens is that he wanted to avoid a possibly messy confrontation that might hit the papers. Similarly, he may have ducked newspaper reporters that Saturday so that Cuomo would be safely out of the Happy Valley area before his statement appeared in print on Monday.

Cuomo's presence at a function Rose attended on that February 24 made it an especially sensitive time for a messy frat death to hit Alfred. But if the institution thought it could clap a lid on this particular can of worms, it was mistaken. The can was filled with gunpowder. When it finally exploded, Alfred University suffered burns that still haven't healed.

4

The afternoon of the interview with King, Eileen phoned Long Island funeral director Gil D'Andrea, whom she knew from church. Calling someone she knew was easier than asking a stranger to embalm her son. D'Andrea handled all the arrangements for getting Chuck's body back to Sayville.

The Stevenses did not want to stay overnight in Alfred. King offered to drive them back to the Rochester airport, and they piled into the backseat of a university station wagon. As King pulled onto Main Street, a bearded man suddenly sprang in front of the car. King braked.

Seeing the university car from his perch in Alex's, Greg Belanger had run out the door. He pumped his legs like the fullback he once had been and headed straight for Eileen's side of the car. He put his face in the window. The door flew open, and Belanger was all over Eileen. They embraced. She thought her ribs would crack, but she didn't care.

King was confused. For a second he probably thought Eileen was being assaulted in a university car. He motioned Belanger to leave.

"No, it's OK," Eileen said a bit too loudly. She and Belanger babbled, neither quite hearing each other, leaving King to sort out the relationship between this bearded fellow and the Stevens family.

"God, I can't believe it's true," wailed Belanger.

"I guess I didn't hold back any longer," says Eileen. A logjam had been dynamited. The river sloshed over its banks. Belanger remembers mascara running down Eileen's face.

Quiet, practical Roy broke in. Belanger was more than Chuck's friend. He was family. Roy said quietly, "Do you think you could get Chuck's truck to Sayville, Greg?"

Belanger said he had intended to do just that. He could be in Sayville in ten hours and would get on the road just as soon as he packed Chuck's things. King had been looking in the mirror from time to time. Eileen hugged Belanger tightly once again, as if she were holding on to part of Chuck.

After he departed, Eileen and Roy were silent for a long time. King tried to make small talk. He brought up cross-country skiing, going on for several minutes. If he realized that Eileen wanted to reach over the seat and halt his chatter, he gave no sign.

Eileen ruined his monologue. She looked into those nervous, pretty eyes in the mirror. "Do you have sons?" she asked.

* * *

Greg Belanger's friends like him because he takes everything seriously, except himself. He was a member of the National Honor Society in high school. Alfred professors such as Stuart Campbell and Gary Horowitz remember him as a terrific student, although Horowitz is less enthusiastic about Belanger's idealism than is Campbell. Nanci Lunati, a pretty high-school cheerleader who once hung out with the gang of seven, used to tease Belanger for his use of ninety-nine-cent words where ten-centers would have done just as well. "We all know you memorized the dictionary, Belanger," she kidded him. "Say it so the rest of us can understand you."

During Chuck's first semester at Alfred, he and Jimmy Arnoux found Belanger preoccupied and his demeanor impenetrable. His passion was the People's Campaign, a hard-core group of perhaps six or seven activists. He was its president. Belanger's appearance suggested that he had been stranded too long on a deserted island. His hair grew in curls over his shoulders; his jeans were tattered. Professors who saw only superficialities lumped him with Alfred's flag-shirted space cadets of the waning seventies. "It's easy to write off people who have a politically inconvenient view by [calling them] a bunch of pot-smoking hippies on the hill," Belanger says with emotion. Still, the People's Campaign—earnest and well-meaning as it was—was ragtag, undisciplined, and in need of a member as orderly as Chuck Stenzel or Jimmy Arnoux.

Consequently, although the Campaign unsettled more than a few bureaucrats at Alfred, its members never became movers and shakers. Those bureaucrats tended to mispeg Belanger as a flaming radical with a penchant for spitting into a headwind. Little did they know that he saw himself as a moderate and that his girlfriend (and future wife) viewed him as an absolute conservative politically. His passion was saving the environment. His immediate target was a defunct nuclear reprocessing plant— "a sitting bomb" in his words—situated in the Southern Tier agricultural community of Westfield, New York. Belanger feared, correctly in retrospect, that this radioactive sludgepot was a hazard to human health.

The People's Campaign was atypical of the Alfred student population. So civilized was the campus that Richard Rose almost—but not quite—lamented the departure of campus left-wingers. "In a sense I miss the radicals," he told the student paper in the last issue before Chuck's death. "It was exciting, but when the demonstration ended, there was no follow-through."

Belanger was so involved with his cause that the semester came and went without his getting together much with Chuck and Jimmy Arnoux, an oversight he regrets because he believes his childhood friends felt slighted. But a chance for redemption came about three weeks before Chuck's death.

Belanger was walking past the Alfred administration building when a bold blue pickup caught his eye. He camped out on the bumper until Chuck emerged from a sporting goods store across the street, a package under his arm. The two embraced spontaneously. They were once again the golden twins who had discovered ancient wagon ruts in the woods off Marion Street. "So you're back!" Belanger said.

The two chanced to meet again in the school pub on February 21, three days before Tapping Night. Chuck left a table of Greeks to join Belanger, who asked him for a ten-dollar loan. Chuck happily complied. It was like old times. Chuck and the other clammers used to tease Belanger about miscalculating his checkbook balance, thereby necessitating occasional short-term loans. The conversation turned to school, and Chuck became animated. The two boys shared a passion for the teachings of Stuart Campbell. Chuck announced that he planned to switch his major from economics to history. When Belanger realized that Chuck had not discussed the move with Campbell, he suggested that they visit the professor at his office in Kanakadea Hall, a converted brick schoolhouse.

Campbell was glad about Chuck's decision. Belanger said something about all the smart ones ending up in history. He himself had been pre-med — until organic chemistry changed his mind. Campbell, who has a reputation for deflating overblown egos, fired a warning shot. "Watch out, Greg," he said. "He's smarter than you." The two friends went back to the pub to celebrate. Belanger never saw Chuck again.

After easing out of King's car, Belanger hopped into his borrowed VW and drove to Chuck's dorm. Perhaps as a release from Eileen's visit, a group of young men had gathered in front of Openhym. They pelleted the Bug with snowballs. Belanger parked and strode toward the building. He was disgusted. Not twenty-four hours earlier one of their own had died, and here they were acting like buffoons.

"Hold on," someone said. "That's Stenzel's friend."

Belanger went to the room, oblivious to bodies in doorways as he passed. He saw signs of his friend everywhere. On the desk was a partially eaten packet of cookies. A few of Chuck's friends in the dorm helped, but Belanger worked without talking. In his state of mind, a new friend of Chuck's was an enemy. In minutes possessions were boxed and piled inside the cab and atop the bed of the truck. A young man who helped told Belanger that he might have mechanical trouble. Chuck had been working on the electrical system and hadn't driven the blue Ford in days.

Belanger knelt on the floorboard. A spaghetti feed of wires greeted him from underneath the dash.

He grabbed a pair of pliers from some tools that Chuck had left in the truck. He was no electrician. Nonetheless, he started splicing left and right, memorizing which wires he connected so that he wouldn't repeat an unnecessary step if the truck failed to start. He slid behind the wheel. Not all his luck was bad that day. The truck fired up the first time. After a quick run home to fetch clean clothes, he headed toward Long Island.

Eileen placed a call home from the airport. Thank God for her family, she thought. Her sisters Mary and Teresa had come at daylight; her parents and two brothers were on their way when Eileen and Roy drove to the airport. She was glad they had each other. She hoped that the neighbors would wait a day to come by. Her kids needed reinforcement that only their grandparents, aunts, and uncles could give. The next three days would be hectic. She both dreaded and looked forward to seeing the mourners. She had no idea how many to expect. She had ordered three hundred thank-you cards from the funeral director. There would be overnight guests to feed and a constantly ringing telephone.

What she hadn't expected was the generosity of her neighbors. Even people she only nodded to on the street came, their arms laden with food. Someone prepared a ham. Others brought trays of cold cuts, rolls, donuts. The parents of her employer at the Town Squire clothing store brought a huge pot of spaghetti and meatballs. She was overwhelmed.

Chuck's father came from California. Roy insisted that he stay with them so he wouldn't have to face his ordeal alone.

Chuck was born nine months and eight days after her elopement. Her husband was bound for extended duty in Korea, but never once did she lament having Chuck. She couldn't say the same thing about her marriage. The soldier came home after twenty-one months to greet a son he had never seen and a girl-bride who had become a woman. Eileen's love had vanished like water from a long-dead lake. It wasn't her husband's fault, she later wrote in her diary. He had committed no sin greater than loving a girl who hadn't had time to discover herself.

Catholic sensibilities tortured Eileen. She prayed the love might be regenerated, but it wasn't. All of it had somehow been transferred to Chuck. He was her life, her center. His personality showed itself from infancy. His sense of humor captivated all who knew him. She stayed close to her husband's father even after his son became her ex; she loved to see him and her son walking to the fire station for a visit. Chuck's hand used to disappear in his grandfather's fist. Her own parents, too, doted on Chuck. He and her father had a daily ritual of going to the store. At least he'd had a lifetime of loving before he died.

So many things in life had seemed uncertain to Eileen. She had questioned her first marriage and annulled it, questioned her faith, and questioned her actions, too many times to count. She would, after February 24, 1978, question her past priorities and condemn herself for being complacent and too preoccupied with superficiality. But never had she questioned her love for Chuck.

Belanger hadn't been on Route 17 long when darkness began to seal the day. He jerked the headlight switch and nothing happened. Some wires remained unconnected. He drove through sparsely settled New York state until he came to a town. Under the light of a supermarket stanchion he again worked with Chuck's pliers. He connected two wires and pulled the switch. Headlights. He shook his head. Someone or something is watching over me, Belanger thought.

* * *

None of Eileen's children was quite like the others. Chuck had been the most well-rounded. Scott was the athlete. In between came quiet and serious Steven, her thinker; slowed by a heart murmur when small, he preferred to draw or read. Suzanne was the youngest, a lover of gymnastics and, like her mother, quick to develop. Eileen used to tell her she was eleven going on sixteen.

Chuck was close to each of his siblings in ways he knew they would appreciate. Scott was a superior athlete. Chuck was proud to have him join in basketball games. The two of them — joined by Roy many summer nights — shot at a hoop and backboard in front of the house. When neighbors complained about the constant bouncing, Eileen refused to heed their griping. She preferred knowing where her sons were and was pleased that they enjoyed each other's company. Chuck and Steven had a cerebral relationship; both loved books.

Chuck was Suzanne's hero. He was eight when she was born. She brought out the tease in him. "Suzanne is a brat," he'd write on her chalkboard. "Suzanne has a face like a monkey's." After he got his driver's license, at seventeen, he agreed to take Suzanne and a young cousin to see *Song of the South* in a neighboring town. He parked and grudgingly joined the girls, fearful of dropping them off to see the movie by themselves. "Don't tell anyone I saw that," he said gruffly when it ended. Nonetheless, for a year afterward, he whistled "Zip-a-dee-doo-dah" and winked at his sister. "It was our little secret," she told her mother long after Chuck's death.

Chuck loved the role of older brother. Late one night, when he was fourteen, Roy and Eileen drove to New York City and stayed out longer than they intended. When they came back to the garage where they'd left the car, they realized that they had not read the posted restrictions: the place was closed until morning. Feeling panic, Eileen phoned Chuck to explain the problem. Should they try to find a ride back to Sayville at this hour?

Chuck assured them that he could handle the situation. Before going to bed, he set the alarm for five A.M. When he awoke, he marched into the kitchen to make sandwiches and put them in sacks. That chore finished, he whipped up breakfast and rousted the troops. Unfortunately, by the time he pushed the last sibling out the door, he had missed his ride. Undaunted, he grabbed his bicycle and pedaled the seven-and-a-half miles to Seton Hall High School.

Part of his independence came from his insistence on earning his spending money. At nine he had his paper route and a job sorting clams for vendors after school. In addition to clamming all his adolescent years, he worked for a time at a department store in lawn supplies. Eileen kidded Chuck, calling him a little old man. She reared him according to Roy's instincts because her husband, the son of a neighborhood butcher, was so much his own man — having worked for everything he owned. From Roy, Chuck acquired a blue-collar industriousness and a hatred for labor fakers.

As small boys he and Steven loved to help Roy with home improvements. Chuck especially liked tinkering with his stepfather's progression of used cars. Gradually he shifted from merely holding the tools to using them. Eventually, he could fix a leak, replace a water pipe, panel a wall, and tune-up a vehicle. All through his teenage years, he learned the mysteries of his clamboat's choke cables, electrical wiring, and control box. More often than not his clothes stank of grease, WD40, and shellfish.

Chuck respected authority but refused to be buffaloed by it. He cherished his relationships with his teachers from elementary school on up. "Chuck was one of the nicest students I have ever known," his eighth-grade teacher, Helen Schwam, wrote Eileen after his death. "He was always respectful, kind, and so bright—a beautiful youngster through and through."

Because she had Chuck when she was so young, Eileen was as much his mini-skirted big sister as she was his mother when the boy was in grade school. Just as her three younger children defined—in many ways—who they were by how Chuck responded to them, so too did Eileen. She confided in him more than she did her other children. With them she was always the consummate, sometimes bossy mother; with him she was more the pretty, slow-to-age sister. Consequently, she disciplined him differently. Her word was less than law with Chuck. She both negotiated and squabbled with him—particularly when she played Mom instead of Big Sis. Chuck's first impressions of Eileen were of a twenty-year-old girl, playing house with a beautiful, blonde doll.

Klan Alpine's initiation ceremony killed Eileen Stevens's son and favorite confidante simultaneously. Chuck, she liked to say, had good instincts about people. Often she brought people into the house that he treated with all but rudeness. He'd complain to her that they were phony or worse. Months later, sometimes years later, something would happen between Eileen and these people. "Chuck was right about them," she would tell Roy. Perhaps because of her belief in his talent for judging character, after Chuck's death Eileen began to trust her own instincts about people more and more. Later, when she felt Don King had let her down, she would kick herself internally for listening to what his mouth said when he promised to share the results of his investigation. She had known during their initial meeting that his eyes told a different story. Foolishly, in retrospect, she had wanted to trust the dean whose favorite expression seemed to be "the institution this" or "the institution that."

Chuck also had good instincts for knowing when something was wrong with Eileen. He had a knack for penetrating the subtle side of her, ignoring her brassy, "what-the-hell" exterior. All those letters that had kept his mailbox free of cobwebs at Doane repeated one truth: his mother thought her life was dull, dull, dull. Her sole obsession was housecleaning. In January of 1978, one month before he died, he confronted her.

"Mom, why don't you get involved?"

"What do you mean 'involved?' I'm involved at the church, and I've got my little part-time job."

"Why don't you go to college too?"

The idea seemed ridiculous. He might as well have asked why she didn't consider becoming a priest or raising a musk ox. "I wouldn't know how," she confessed. "I wouldn't know how to go about it."

Chuck countered her arguments. She had helped both him and Steve with the paperwork involved with taking college boards and applying for financial aid. "Start with one course, Mom," he said. "Just one course."

"You think I can do it?"

"We've got a bet," he said. "If you get an *A*, I'll take you out to dinner."

Eileen signed up for a course in English composition at Suffolk County Community College. "It took all the courage I had to go to that first class, but I went because I wanted to keep the bet," she says. A few weeks into the course she lost her son. She considered dropping the class but didn't. "I did it for Chuck because he wanted me to do it. I strove to get that *A*." After burying Chuck, she continued to make the once-a-week drive to her class. It provided the only perspective she had after his death. It strengthened and fulfilled her, just as he had somehow known it would.

Something about driving Chuck's truck had Greg Belanger's emotions sanded down to the nerves. He had been in it dozens of times, but always in the passenger seat. Belanger thought nothing of borrowing ten bucks from his friend, but he had never considered asking Chuck to use the Ford. The vehicle was just too special. It symbolized more than Belanger could bear. The tears came. He drove down Route 17, his head thrown slightly back, shrieking as if his dead twin were in his hands instead of a steering wheel.

5

DEAR ANN [LANDERS]: My son, Chuck Stenzel, decided on Feb. 24, 1978, to pledge Klan Alpine. It is Alfred University's oldest fraternity.

Chuck was taken by surprise from his dorm, put into the trunk of a car with two other pledges. Each was given a pint of bourbon, a bottle of wine, and a 6-pack of beer. They were told they would not be released from the trunk until they had consumed all of it. It was February in upstate New York in freezing temperatures with snow and ice on the ground. The boys in the trunk had no jackets or coats.

Forty minutes later Chuck and the others were carried to their rooms in the fraternity house. When it became apparent that the boys were unconscious, they were rushed to the hospital. One had gone into cardiac arrest, another was in an alcoholic coma and Chuck was dead.

Sociology professor Richard Sigal of New Jersey's County College of Morris has a strong voice and a snappy delivery that keeps his students' attention most days. They're never quite certain what he's going to pull on them next. A holdover from the late sixties, he still gives a damn about his "kids," as he sometimes calls them. On the first day of each term he encourages students to visit his office. He tells them that their tuition has paid for his time, and he's there to talk about sociology, careers, personal problems. He has counseled students through the agonies of incest, abortion, suicidal inclinations. He's even lent his ear to a student who had committed two homicides. He speaks his mind on crucial issues and listens to what his students tell him. Sigal maintains the gaze of an eagle with both eyes on breakfast, but he is always sensitive to his listener's voice and facial mannerisms.

One of his specialties is deviant behavior. He holds nothing back, knowing too well that he has recovering substance abusers, alcoholics, and drug users in his classroom. He assigns his students questions to ask themselves each time they take a drink to make them more aware of their alcohol consumption: Am I drinking because I'm thirsty? Am I drinking because I'm in a social situation and want a beer or two? Am I drinking to celebrate an event? Am I drinking just to get drunk? What scenario am I playing here?

"Do any of [my students] go out and change their drinking styles?" he asks. "I don't know—I hope they do."

As Sigal reads the much-folded Ann Landers column, the class sees something in his face—pain, maybe—that has them hushed. Before he finishes, one young woman is pawing at her eyes, and several young men slide lower in their chairs. The students are certain that he's going to use this letter to generate discussion on recent hazing deaths. New Jersey has had its share of initiation catastrophes in the news: a Zeta Beta Tau pledge buried alive at Monmouth College; numerous alcohol overdoses at Princeton's eating clubs; the death of Richard C. Fuhs, Jr., of Rutgers in a car crash following a Delta Phi early-morning drinking session; and the death of Rider College's Sean Hickey in a vehicle driven by a fellow Theta Chi pledge whose blood-alcohol level was twice the legal limit.

The first couple of times Sigal read the next passage of the letter to his class, he had to make his body rigid as a mummy's to keep from weeping. Eileen Stevens's words made him think of his own son in such a fix:

> I buried my beautiful sophomore son three days later, with all his hopes and dreams for a promising future. The other two boys survived and joined Klan Alpine. Alfred University and the district attorney treated the tragedy as an "isolated accident." Everyone was sorry but no one was held responsible. There is a rigid code of secrecy surrounding hazing practices. Members take oaths of silence. Peer pressure is so great that seriously injured pledges remain loyal to their vows of secrecy. Meanwhile this life-threatening practice persists with all its talk of brotherhood and tradition.

Rich Sigal finishes three more paragraphs and faces his class. When he is composed, he says something that knocks the wind out of their collective sails. He tells them that before the discussion on group norms and socialization begins, there is one detail they should know.

"Klan Alpine," he says, "was my fraternity."

Sigal's class discussions on hazing always focus on the concept of rites of passage. He teaches his students that in fraternities pledging has traditionally been an important masculinity rite.

Tapping Night at Klan Alpine is a time when a pledge is expected to prove that he is a man. Since Klan values drinking, a kid such as Chuck Stenzel receives instant respect if he can drink a lot. He earns even more respect if he can hold his alcohol well. Klan is not atypical. Men seeking to join most fraternities are pressed to demonstrate their masculinity.

Sigal makes his classes a lesson in the Big Picture. Men may prove their masculinity in a variety of ways. Young adults, however, don't usually have the option of making tons of money in business and thereby confirming masculinity. They can build their bodies, achieve success in sports. They can score with young women, quantity being preferable to quality. But those are unreasonable options for some men, Sigal points out. It takes a certain amount of success, skill, savvy to be a good student-athlete, to attract women, and to build up your body.

Chuck Stenzel was a better-than-average athlete, a young man who never lacked for women, and a strapping six-footer. He also did a man's job as a clammer. He loved the status symbols his gang of seven valued—a sharp truck, a clamming boat, and outdoor clothing. Klan Alpine, unfortunately, offered this exceptional student, athlete, and rugged individualist only one viable option for proving his manhood on Tapping Night. He had to drink. "Any moron can drink," Sigal says. Unfortunately, that was the masculinity litmus test of choice for Klan Alpine.

Chuck Stenzel was trying to prove that he was a good fraternity man by the Klan's definition. Klan Alpine members put him and his fellow pledges through a drinking ritual on Tapping Night to validate their own sense of maleness. When an attractive young man such as Chuck showed submissive behavior, the men he submitted to naturally felt more manly.

"I think this masculinity thing is an important issue and needs to be addressed," insists Sigal. "People must see what it really means— especially with regard to drinking and drinking to excess. . . . Young men are being asked to prove they're men, and the way you prove yourself a man in this society is by blind compliance—by drinking to excess and doing things perceived as very masculine types of things." He blames the movie *Animal House* for projecting a mindless, pro-hazing, anti-feminist image that many fraternity men believe is a *sine qua non* for the Greek good life.

Students in Sigal's classes get accustomed to hearing him talk about the Big Picture. He tends to look at fraternity deaths, teenage suicide, and drug and alcohol addiction as problems symptomatic of society as a whole, all problems, but not *the* problem. *The* problem is the rapid rate of change in society. As that rate accelerates, people have trouble keeping up. What general practitioners understand the stress-related diseases they're asked to treat these days? Which professors manage to stay on top of their specialties and to give their advisees the time they need and deserve? How can executive directors of national fraternities know enough about the bombed-out party-people inhabiting their chapter houses from Alabama to Wyoming to do their jobs well?

Moreover, young undergraduates—less scholastically prepared, on the average, than their parents were as freshmen—are expected to assimilate information that gets more complex and detailed each year. If these students take classes from professors who have slipped through the tenure cracks to deliver tired lectures, boredom and resentment intensify the tensions. These students, claims Sigal, are more vulnerable than adults; thus, they look to suicide, drugs, and alcohol as releases. "Younger people have less insulation on their wires," he says.

Sigal believes that young people must be educated to be aware of why they do the things they do—particularly if harm can come to them or others. But he has discovered that such education is often startling to his students. "I talk in my classes, and I have kids with their eyes and mouths open," he says.

A student approached him after class. "How come they never told us this in high school?" he asked. "They gave us a substance abuse course, but they gave us factual data. If you drink this much, you become drunk. They brought in a cop, and he talked about Breathalyzers. But they never talked about the real meaning of drinking."

Sigal is not the only thinker to explore the issue of hazing, but he is one of a handful of academics who approach the emotional issue from an intellectual perspective.

Two important questions arise from Chuck Stenzel's death. Why did he choose to suffer the ordeal of an initiation requiring excessive drinking? Why did he do potentially dangerous things, such as getting into a car trunk and consuming enough alcohol to intoxicate a half-dozen men?

The answer to both questions, says Irving L. Janis, a Yale psychology professor emeritus and author of *Groupthink*, is "a basic aspect of group psychology." Quite possibly, according to Janis's theory, a pledge in Chuck's position has "the enormous fear . . . that to refuse puts one in danger of being a deviant by violating a group norm." Sigal recalls that in his day Klan Alpine pledges who refused to drink were booed and derided although, to his knowledge, they were not blackballed. Nonetheless, those pledges who did drink and asked for more earned praise: "Hey, we've got a good one here," Sigal says someone was sure to say. Even a youth as popular and as relatively successful as Chuck wanted the esteem, backslapping, and instant bonding with Klan members once he made his decision to pledge. "All of us are very hungry for that sort of thing," says Janis. "None of us can get enough of it."

Invariably, when discussion starts during Sigal's lecture on fraternity deaths, a student or two wants to know what was on Chuck Stenzel's mind when he put the bottle to his lips for the first time. Didn't he know that all that booze could kill him?

"When Chuck Stenzel got into the trunk, he wasn't thinking, 'If I drink all this stuff, I may die,'" says Sigal. "That wasn't in his head. He got into the trunk thinking, 'So this is what Klan people do?' He probably wasn't thinking even in that much depth."

Sigal tells the class what it's like. You're exhilarated because you've learned the blackball ruse was only that. You're not an outcast. This big brother of yours, the hotshot lacrosse player, has accepted you. You're relieved. You're emotional. "I'm in," he probably thought as he scooted into the trunk. "I'm anybody's equal," he might have thought as he raised the bottle to his lips for the first swallow of whiskey. Chuck Stenzel didn't think he was doing anything extraordinary. If this was tradition, as the brothers had said, then he was only doing what hundreds of men before him had done.

Sigal moves the discussion toward the issue of socialization, but now and then his students don't let him off the hook. The questions fly: What about you, Professor Sigal? Did you go through it? How could you?

"I'm shocked by what I did," he tells them frankly. "I can't believe I put up with what I put up with. If my head then had been where it is now, I wouldn't be in a fraternity. When I was there, I certainly drank to excess. When I was there, I certainly put people through that [custom] who drank to excess. I've dealt with people who had passed out."

He tries to take them back with him. He paints a picture of what his life was like in 1959. Picture kids wearing their hair in a flattop or slicking it back in a ducktail like Elvis's. You stood in front of a mirror for twenty minutes, the Wildroot Cream Oil thick as bacon grease on your scalp. You worked a comb like an artist into the front of your pompadour to fashion a spitcurl.

At that time in Alfred there were some special circumstances that made unlikely fellows like me choose fraternity life, Sigal explains. Alfred was a dry town. If you wanted to drink, you drove twenty minutes or so to a dive called the Beacon, where non-Greeks went to socialize. In the winter, the Southern Tier often had snow on the ground from Thanksgiving to Easter, which made it hard to get around on foot. Since freshmen were forbidden to own cars, you hitchhiked everywhere.

Like many freshman, Sigal threw out a thumb to snag a ride to the Beacon. At the end of the night, he trusted to luck that some passing upperclassman would feel sorry for him and give him a ride back to campus at two or three A.M. Alfred then had spartan facilities. The student center across from the library was hardly past the blueprint stage. There was no bowling alley, no pool hall, no movie house. On Fridays one movie played in Alumni Hall, and you went even if you'd seen it back in your hometown. "If you wanted any social interaction with women at all, you joined a fraternity," Sigal tells the class.

As a senior in high school, Sigal seemed an unlikely specimen to attend a school so close to the middle of nowhere that students joked that someone paid bribes to get the village's name printed on road maps. He grew up in Freeport, Long Island, another town on the Great South Bay, but instead of collecting clams he had a passion for rock-and-roll. He and a friend named Lou Reed participated in sports, double-dated, and played in a band called The Valets—"Here to serve you and yours," as the lead singer used to say.

Then Sigal visited Alfred as a senior in high school. He drove up with a Freeport girl who was dating a guy at Alfred. Her boyfriend happened to be a member of Klan Alpine. About fifteen seconds after the pair pulled into Klan's driveway, the grateful member turned Sigal over to his friends and disappeared with the girl.

"Did they give me a weekend!" recalls Sigal. They set him up with dates and practically ran IV tubes from his veins to a house keg. By Sunday when he and the girl departed, he interrupted her naps with unceasing chatter about what a great time he'd had that weekend.

So Sigal went to Alfred and joined Klan. He played in a group called the Klantones. Occasionally, the band warmed up audiences for Robert Klein, an Alfred student who thought he might have a future as a stand-up comedian. Sigal's friend Lou Reed went to Syracuse University, wrote poetry, became a leading figure in avant garde music, and ended up on the cover of *Rolling Stone* in 1989. While Reed took a walk on the wild side of the big cities in New York state, Sigal spent parts of six years in the hinterlands of Allegany County, finding out about his own wild side in the company of men known then and now as the "Klanimal House" fraternity.

He pledged Klan in 1960 and was responsible for his pledge class's being one of the fraternity's largest ever. He recruited in the dormitories, talking half the pledge class into rushing Klan with him. This immature, naive kid had the fire and drive of a missionary. Sigal's house was the last to bask in the rah-rah-sis-boom-bah fraternal good fellowship reminiscent of the twenties' fraternity boom. Members of Klan Alpine in the early 1960s had a loyalty to the house and one another and idealistic principles that fraternity members of the flower-child era would only mock. For the members of Sigal's generation, the fraternity was not unlike a traditional religion in its belief in rituals and worship of sacred items. Members felt a common bond, says Sigal, and the secret handshake and passwords, traditions, and shared initiation rites differentiated Klan from all other fraternities.

The one admirable characteristic of that era that has continued in the 1990s, according to current Klan advisor Gary Horowitz, is that "Klan kids" are the "tightest" fraternity at Alfred University. Sigal's Big Picture screen sees Klan's loss of commitment to cherished ideals, however, as one more indication of a valueless society. Klan Alpine members today seldom, if ever, invite the school's president or faculty over for spaghetti feeds, a tradition in former days that brought positive role models into the house.

Sigal's generation not only respected rules but wanted them. No-commitment sex that members in the late sixties and early seventies would expect as their due was not the norm in the Klan Alpine house Sigal remembers. "In the early sixties, you didn't join Klan to get laid," Sigal tells his class. "The truth is you never took a girl upstairs." A few Lotharios, it's true, snuck coeds into the house, but they snuck them back out the same way they'd come in. "You didn't want to jeopardize the house and put it on social probation, so you didn't do it," says Sigal. The sweet mysteries of love and flesh were unveiled in cars parked behind a high snowbank.

Sigal tells a story about the last time he saw Lou Reed, back around 1984. "When are you going to tour again?" he asked him.

"Never would be too soon," said Reed, who has been known to silence a heckler by giving him back a profane tirade.

"Why?"

"Because you take your life in your hands. You go onstage, and they go onstage and try to break your instruments. You need an army of armed guards. These people are animals. They throw stuff at you. I don't even want to be out there."

Sigal says that today's MTV videos flicker with images of musicians smashing thousand-dollar guitars and wrecking cars. For him, such waste reflects our valueless society. Everything is disposable," he complains. "You don't expect material things to last. You don't expect relationships to last." In this world, fraternity pledges are as disposable as throwaway cameras. The escalating rate of adolescent suicides suggests that, to young people, even one's own life isn't worth much.

How much less do some Greek brothers and sisters value the lives of the pledges they break?

Had Chuck Stenzel lived through Tapping Night, he would have had four to eight weeks of pledging still to survive. The members of Klan Alpine felt that their pledge period was less dangerous than that of other fraternities at Alfred. Paddling, for example, was nonexistent. Klan Alpine has traditionally disdained paddles as a pledge project, refusing to make the gigantic symbols that hang by the dozen in a restaurant across the street from Don King's office.

One initiation tradition in the seventies, says Carl Pelcher, was for a brother to brandish a paddle and eye the pledge class with fury in his eyes. "Who wants to be the first to get paddled?" the member would ask. "Who thinks he can take it?"

When several hands went up, the brother showed disgust. He poured lighter fluid on the paddle and flung it into the fireplace. "We don't do that in Klan Alpine," he would growl.

By the early sixties, during Rich Sigal's tenure in Klan, the Klanimal image began to intensify, as did the group's pride in how members were perceived by each other and outsiders. Members still dressed in suits for the group yearbook photograph, but they began to haul kegs of beer into the pictures. By 1965 the yearbook published a photograph of a Klan member, clad only in his underwear, stuck high in a tree outside the house. No one can say for sure when hazing became as fierce as it was for Chuck Stenzel, but certainly it was intense during the early sixties when Rich Sigal was a brother and member. Some nights he would be up past midnight to study trivia about Klan and its history. He set his alarm clock to wake up members with early classes, and he helped other pledges make breakfast. After attending his classes and possibly running an errand or two for a brother, he went to work on the current pledge project, usually something he enjoyed in retrospect, such as helping make the Klan Alpine entry for the annual St. Pat's Parade. He also enjoyed cleaning the house before parties on Saturday and after parties on Sunday because the members pitched in alongside the pledges to develop camaraderie. He says that the purpose of the scrubbing was to purge the odor of spilled beer from the house. Klan members then possessed pride in the ownership of the house.

But other pledging activities were dangerous. In addition to drinking bouts, Sigal's class endured traditions such as the notorious cigar gig. Every year pledges were expected to light big, foul-smelling cigars in a small broom closet. Exceptionally small classes experienced this ritual in a phone booth. Somehow the pledges learned about the tradition and worked in unison to circumvent it. Sigal, as a pledge, lived behind the house with nine other men in a small barn. He and a couple of other pledges snuck into the house, entered the closet, and punched holes in one wall, figuring that they could put out some of the cigars and hide them from the members.

The night of truth arrived, and all thirty-six pledges squeezed into the closet. The bigger football players stood on the bottom. Lighter pledges, such as Sigal, who was on the wrestling team, climbed atop their shoulders. "Light up," said the members. The door closed.

The pledges set to work. Many of them put out their cigars or broke them into two pieces, stuffing the larger ends into the holes. "The idea was great — except that it didn't work," Sigal says. The cigars were hard and about as easy to light as rain-soaked twigs. They had to be lit by matches, not by touching the end of a lit cigar to an unlit stub. The stogies began to fill the closet with smoke. Men started to panic as breathing air departed. A couple hyperventilated. Someone on top vomited, beginning a chain reaction. One football player on the bottom turned green. The pledges banged on the wall, yelling for someone to remove him before he died or became seriously ill from smoke inhalation.

The purpose of the exercise, says Sigal, was to teach blind obedience. The ideal pledge was a boot-camp recruit who followed orders without questioning them. On another occasion pledges had to take repeated mouthfuls of water from a sink filled with soggy cornflakes and other objectionable materials, then crawl down a flight of stairs to put out a fire in the fireplace by spitting on the flames. A favorite activity of Klan in the late sixties and early seventies, according to David F. Hoff, a 1971 Alfred graduate and fraternity member, was a dangerous practice in which members played Bombs Away, dropping empty beer kegs from windows as pledges scurried to get out of the way. "It was a wonder no one was killed then," says Hoff, now a St. Louis businessman, who doesn't donate to the fraternity since Chuck's death.

To satisfy the membership's warped sense of fun, Klan also had a demeaning annual practice called the Olive Race. Pledges picked an olive off a block of ice with their buttocks' cheeks and ran to the other side of the room. Supposedly, if you dropped the olive, you had to eat it. Sigal recalls a pledge who pretended to eat his soiled olive; a member vomited. During all these activities, notes Sigal, the housemother found an excuse to leave or retire to her room.

He has vivid recall of his Klan days. Although he cringes when he thinks of what he did as a pledge and required others to do when he was a member, the sociologist in him can explain, although not justify, his actions. "For one thing, what we did was based on tradition," he says. "[We believed] that this had been going on forever." In his mind—and in the minds of all pledges who have endured hazing—this was how it had always been. "You don't question it," he says, "because the thought never enters your mind. This is what they always did, and this is what we do, and they got through it."

Pledges do what they're told partly because members seem so unified when it comes to hazing. Pledges, in turn, must unify to survive the pledge period. Alumnus David Hoff acknowledges that pledging helped his class build solidarity but feels the same unity could have been achieved in a constructive manner. Even when members become brothers, few realize that these supposedly time-honored traditions are in many cases recent inventions.

The ride in the trunk that Chuck Stenzel took, for example, was not around in Sigal's Klan days. Since Hoff, who pledged in 1968, did ride in a trunk, the practice had to have begun in either 1966 or 1967. Hoff's big brother was hardly as cordial to him as Klan members in pretrial examinations after Chuck's death testified they had been to their pledges. Hoff was called a maggot when he was ordered into the trunk. When the trunk stuffing custom started isn't crucial although its relatively recent advent does puncture a hole in the popular myth that hazing customs go back to the fraternity's founders. What is important is that once a pledge has ridden in a trunk or chugged a pint of Jack Daniel's, he thinks nothing of requiring others to do the same or worse after he becomes a member. Just as abused children often become abusers, the hazed become the hazers.

Hoff hazed as a member. "You'd wish it would be different, but you did it because it was done to you," he says. Richard Klein—who was Sigal's pledgemaster and a member of the Klantones and remains one of the sociologist's best friends—says he may have felt pressured to continue Klan Alpine's tradition of foolish stunts. "I would like to think I was enlightened, but I'm not sure that was true," says Klein, a PhD in ceramic engineering who runs a corporate laboratory in a Boston suburb. "I'm sure there was pressure brought to bear that this is what pledging is all about. . . . With hindsight I would have liked to have taken a much more pro-active stance. But as a sophomore, I don't know if that's realistic."

Chuck Stenzel's death saddened Klein, and he questions whether the university's measures to ensure that the tragedy wouldn't recur were strong enough. "How can a college let that go on?" he asks. "I'm frankly surprised that fraternities still exist at Alfred."

These days, judging from his students, says Sigal, kids are unwilling to live by codes of conduct, don't know what the boundaries are. He no longer chaperones his college's field trips because he feels powerless to stop students from getting sloppy drunk, using drugs, and sleeping around.

Complicating the issue is the refusal of all but a few universities to enforce guidelines with respect to dormitory study hours and opposite-sex visitation rights, fraternity alcohol use, even "no talking" rules in many campus libraries, says Sigal. As a result of such permissiveness, an anything-goes atmosphere exists that he sees as the perfect breeding ground for hazing abuses. If you want to prevent hazing, he snaps, you have to get these kids on a regular basis and indoctrinate them from the first day of student orientation until they button up their robes on commencement day. And that goes for AIDS education and substance and alcohol abuse as well, he says. But that presumes that a school wants to get involved with Greeks, a scenario that is hardly the case at universities that keep a hands-off policy in order to plead ignorance in the event of a hazing incident. Sigal wants the schools to establish clear parameters, definite limits. And he wants them to involve parents by routinely sending them a list of school policies when their child is accepted for admission.

In Nobel laureate William Golding's *Lord of the Flies*, the scene in which the shipwrecked boys kill Simon is analogous to what happens in a hazing death, says Sigal. Young Simon runs down the mountain because he has discovered the beast. He rejoins the tribe to find the others involved in a ritual, chanting, "Kill the beast! Cut his throat! Spill his blood!" The crazed boys stab Simon, and his small corpse rolls out to sea. The next day two characters, Ralph and another doomed boy named Piggy, have a discussion. Piggy insists what had happened was an accident, "and that's that." Ralph justifies his own behavior, saying he was on the outside of the circle, and his companion agrees: "We was on the outside. We never done nothing, we never seen nothing."

Sigal has used this example in his classes to point out how fraternity members inevitably respond after a hazing death. "We didn't do it. Something happened. He died, but we didn't do it." So too with Chuck Stenzel. No one at Klan Alpine was responsible. "If you polled every one of the brothers and pledges, anyone would tell you it was pretty much a festive initiation," says former Klan president Scott Sullivan. "There was no maliciousness. . . . Deep down it's because he drank too much at an initiation party. . . . I saw him get out of the car. Who could tell if he was intoxicated?"

In any hazing death by drinking, responses can almost always be interchanged, according to Sigal's theory. The pledge died, but we didn't do it. He couldn't control his drinking that night, but how is that my fault? I gave him the pint of Jack Daniel's, or Jim Beam, or Cuervo Gold, but I didn't make him drink it. Oh, sure we played a drinking game, but he didn't have to join us. All the rest of us once did it. How did we know he couldn't take it?

According to Sigal, hazing is a rite that can only go wrong. Any fraternity member who has hazed cannot, in good conscience, feel superior to the devastated Klan Alpine members of 1978, or to any Greeks whose organization has suffered a tragedy. "We didn't haze to the point that we killed anybody, but we had some life-threatening things that went on," says Sigal. "Luck figures in there too."

Hazings by their nature take pledges to the edge of danger or tolerance. They leave no room for variables. No room for the pledge like Chuck, whose inexperience with hard liquor made him try to please the Klan brothers by chugging the stuff as if it were no more potent than equal ounces of beer.

No room for a pledge like Robert Bazille, whose University of Pennsylvania Omega Psi Phi brothers pushed him to exertion, not knowing his heart would blow all fuses if overloaded.

No room for the brothers of Tri Chi at California's Pierce College, who abandoned nearsighted pledge Fred Bronner in a remote area without his glasses, causing him to fall five hundred feet to his death as he took a shortcut.

No room, either, says Sigal for the sadists in nearly every large group who are in their element during hazings, by their nature often violent and degrading for pledges.

Klan Alpine had several members whose behavior Sigal questioned during his years as a member and pledge. There were always sadists or sociopaths who were entirely self-focused, who showed little or no concern for the feelings or welfare of others. Fraternities without an iron-willed president or advisor to run their affairs democratically always run the risk of hazing abuses because compromises regarding the welfare of initiates are sometimes made. Time and again, the person selected as fraternity president is not chosen for his power and sensitivity, but on the basis of seniority or popularity. Too often such presidents lack the diplomacy, intelligence, and grit needed to control, as well as lead, the membership — including the occasional sadists and sociopaths.

Not infrequently, says Sigal, the sadists in his day took their aggressions out on the fraternity house, like the time members ruined a cookout with a sorority by defecating on the grill. Everyone recognized "the mean, sadistic bastards," but no one did much about them, says Sigal. In a sense these men have a certain license to do what they want to do because part of the experience of being a fraternity house is that your norms differ from society's.

Fraternities allow brothers a great range of permissible behavior, according to Sigal. A sadist ordered one of Sigal's fellow pledges to strip, then sit naked in a sink with his legs in one basin and his buttocks in another. The initiator then filled the basins alternately with hot and icy water, while hand-feeding the victim a concoction of eggs, hot spices, thick sauces, and other garbage. He made Sigal and other pledges watch while the victim swallowed spoonful after spoonful. The sadist thought it was the funniest scene he had ever invented. "I never liked him from the word go, and I never had much of anything to do with him," says Sigal. "The pledges hated him. He was the drill instructor all the recruits despised. He was a vicious, hostile bastard, and nothing will change that."

Sigal says that the presence of a sadist can be dangerous during the height of hazing when all the norms have already broken down. "It may or it may not have happened during the Stenzel thing," he says, "I don't know. . . . You put a bunch of guys together, and the chances are pretty good that you're going to have a guy who has some problems." When a Greek president or other legitimate leaders defer power to the pledgemaster and the field-level members, they in effect allow tragedy to happen. The legitimate leaders are unwilling to stop a ceremony that's out of control because they fear defying tradition and because they've become a part of the collective behavior, says Sigal. "Once the ball is rolling, it's out of hand," he says. "People will do things in groups that they won't alone."

Fraternities who permit hazings in which booze, recklessness, and sadistic individuals are present and in which all rules and norms are suspended should not be surprised when members find themselves looking into the eyes of a dead pledge. But at Alfred University Rich Sigal had not yet formed these opinions. When a sadist threw pledges into an icy creek near the Klan house, so did he.

His students, however, are forewarned.

6

As he drove Chuck's truck back to Long Island, Greg Belanger agonized over his friend's decision to join Klan Alpine. Chuck hadn't thought
pledging worth mentioning when they went to see Stuart Campbell. Perhaps he hadn't been fully committed until the last minute. Still, Belanger
wished that Chuck had told him about Klan. Belanger had his own hazing
stories that his friend might have benefited from hearing.

If Chuck was hazed in high school, he never mentioned it to his
friends. Belanger, however, received his unfair share of abuse at fourteen.
Like many teenagers, he knew nothing about hazing until he learned from
sad experience. Soon after enrolling at Seton Hall High School with
Jimmy Arnoux and Chuck, Belanger stood in a line with other freshmen
to meet the seniors. It was an annual event until the Catholic high school
closed when Belanger, Arnoux, and Chuck were juniors. Supposedly, the
ritual gave the seniors an opportunity to share tidbits of wisdom with the
newcomers. Instead, the older boys dished out abuse.

One senior, in particular, decided to pick on Belanger, perhaps
because he was one of the tallest freshmen. The senior tried to ram a
wooden dildo up his intended victim. Belanger managed to get away.

On another occasion, Belanger was hazed by older boys on the varsity
football team after he was called up to replace an injured upperclassman.
The veteran players tormented the youngster, particularly after Belanger
held his own on the field, playing both offense and defense. In the locker
room, it was a different story. The seniors maligned him constantly.

One day the players caught Belanger alone while he was walking into
the shower. They introduced him to a Seton Hall custom. The bigger boys
formed a circle to prevent their intended victim from fleeing. They
chanted as they attacked him.

"Tape, Tape, Tape, TAY-YUP, TAY-YUP, TAY-YUP!"

Belanger was strong, but the seniors were a bulky bunch. They
wrapped him from ankle to neck in tape, leaving him helpless as a pinned
moth. Getting attacked while he was naked was bad enough, but when his
hands were freed, he had to endure pulling adhesive strips from his pubic
hair.

He has never fully understood why the older players chose him. They
called it tradition, a simple answer that seemed to satisfy them. In some
perverse way, they seemed to believe Belanger would be pleased to be
selected for the special treatment. A few days after the incident, after
some other "offense" of Belanger's, the upperclassmen again trapped him

outside the shower. This time they carried multi-colored electric tape. "TAY-YUP, TAY-YUP, TAY-YUP," they grunted.

Initiation had not been part of Belanger's Alfred experience. He knew Greek men and women, but fraternities never appealed to him. He talked to the football coach at Alfred but decided at the last minute not to try to make the team as a walk-on. Football was not the end-all for him that it is for some players. He had sung in the glee club his senior year at Sayville, a big fullback-linebacker performing a high-voiced "Maria" from *West Side Story* during his audition. All through high school and college he found himself "in this perplexed middle," as he called it. He had mainstream friends like Chuck and Jimmy, as well as counterculture friends. He bridged two worlds, feeling comfortable and uncomfortable by turns.

During his sophomore year, Belanger worked as a counselor at an Alfred dormitory. He was barely a year older than the freshmen he counseled. They asked him for advice about joining a fraternity. Vague rumors about hazing at Klan Alpine and Delta Sig circulated on campus, and many students were afraid. One story was that someone had straddled a blindfolded freshman and shoved a weiner in his mouth to harass him. Hell Week was a particularly bad time in the dormitory. The sinks, toilets, and floors in the bathroom were often brown with vomit. Belanger used to feel sorry for the cleaning lady. Every so often he would hear moaning, help a student wash up, put him to bed.

One night Belanger himself had been drinking at a party. From a deep sleep, he heard someone scream his name. At first he thought it was a fight that he needed to break up. Naked, he hurried into the shower and saw a huge freshman on the floor. The boy was bluish and appeared not to be breathing. Belanger and the boy's friends cleared the youth's throat and blew air into his lungs. The student came to and eyed Belanger. Fearing that he would be reported, he pleaded and promised. "Please, I'm fine, I'm fine," he said. "I'll never do it again."

Belanger, in his words, "made a very bad judgment." He promised to say nothing. He had never told Chuck that story. Would it have made a difference? he asked himself. Or once Chuck began to slide down that slippery slope would he have hit bottom no matter what?

Steven Peterson, the new Klan Alpine advisor, was watching the late news in Buffalo the day after Chuck's death. The mention of an Alfred fraternity death alarmed him, and he rushed to the store the next morning to purchase a copy of the Buffalo *Courier Express*. The lead story was the death at Klan, accompanied by a photograph of the fraternity house.

Klan Alpine students had asked the young professor to advise them three months prior to the fatal Tapping Night. He took on the responsibility, he says, primarily "because the Klan had always had kind of a bad name, and yet the individual students I knew from Klan always seemed so nice." Among those he regarded as topnotch people were Scott Sullivan, the president, and Rocky LaForge. "I said, 'I'm not really comfortable with certain aspects of fraternities and so on, but this group seems like a bunch of nice individuals,' so I said, 'what the heck.'" Other Alfred faculty members had turned Klan down. Peterson was paid nothing for his services. He had no special training to become a Greek advisor, not even the minimum training session that the dean's office required all resident assistants to attend.

A self-described student of politics, Peterson admits that his knowledge of sociology and human behavior was "not very sophisticated." His awareness of small group social psychology was limited to the concept that "Individuals start accepting group norms when, if they were outside, they'd probably say, 'This is kind of dumb.' . . . It's the sort of thing where collectively you just lose your common sense when you're in an organization." While Peterson did seek assurances that no men would be discriminated against for their religion or race, he failed to give much thought to other aspects of the pledge program. "I just thought it's kind of dumb to put people through Hell Week and not let them sleep and so on. From my point of view, silly as [hazing] is, it's not necessarily harmful as long as people understand that they're going to be penalized in their classes and so on. . . . I hadn't even thought to ask about hazing; it just didn't occur to me that it was an issue. I remembered that in the [early] seventies there had been a wave of hazing deaths and accidents. I had, foolishly in retrospect, assumed that it was over—that standards had been tightened and that fraternities had recognized the difficulties. Silly, silly me."

Peterson, a slender man with rumpled hair and a gentle demeanor, says he experienced a feeling of emptiness after reading that first newspaper article about Chuck's death. His first thought was, "Oh, my God! Some poor kid is dead." Although Peterson was out of town on Tapping Night, he says that he wouldn't have attended the ceremony at Klan Alpine had he been in Alfred. Like Don King and Eileen Stevens and ex-Klan advisor Robert Heineman, he would have learned about the tragedy via a ringing phone. After the tragedy, he attached reins to his young charges as best he could. "What the devil will you be doing this year?" he asked Klan members. They assured him pledging would be on "a much lower key." But, without his knowledge, limited mental hazing was still conducted in the late seventies.

What was on Don King's mind in the days following Chuck's death? Heineman recalls that King was concerned about damaging the college's public image. King admits that the negative publicity and preparation for a trial sapped his energy and misaligned his focus until well into the 1980s. He says that his family was harassed. "The most difficult part of it was that we would get irate calls at home or letters from all over the country; some of them were really obscene," says King.

Letters from people who had read interviews with Eileen Stevens disturbed him. "They would respond to say, basically, 'How could you permit this to happen?'" says King. "Even though I think we dealt with it pretty well, you question your own integrity. . . . It's not that I condoned this because I was infuriated and as irritated as anybody."

The Sunday following Chuck's death King met with Scott Sullivan and advisor Steven Peterson, as well as other officers of the fraternity. The meeting lasted approximately ninety minutes. The next day King met for much of the day with Sullivan. Except for chatting with people in his unofficial campus information network, of which he often speaks with pride, these meetings form the essence of the investigation he promised Eileen. Of his meeting with King, Sullivan recalls, "He wouldn't look me directly in the eye. He was shifty-eyed. He looked at the side of my forehead — his eyes only had peripheral vision."

Three Klan brothers interviewed separately have the same impression of the Sunday meeting with King. They had told him the truth, the three say, and the impression King gave them was that the university was representing their viewpoint in the tragedy. Sullivan insists that King gave them strict instructions. "As long as this is under investigation, you're not to comment on this incident," Sullivan says he and the others were told. As a result, Sullivan told the brothers to remain silent. Rocky LaForge stood like a monument in the doorway of Klan Alpine to chase away reporters.

Whether the silence was a conspiracy, as Eileen Stevens charges, or simply the prudent heeding of legal advice depends upon your viewpoint. It is common for both hazers and pledges either to refuse to talk about hazing they have witnessed or to lie about it. The family and friends of hazing victims find it hard to accept that hazers feel that they face an impossible dilemma. By speaking the truth frankly, they break faith with a group that has tremendous importance to them at this stage of their lives. Whether it is a hockey player in a high-school hazing, a pledge or brother in a fraternity hazing, a neophyte about to enter some important adult secret society, or a serviceman in a military hazing, being a snitch or whistle-blower carries a terrible stigma in our society. At the same time, if hazers lie and say that hazing did not occur, they may still suffer tremendous guilt. Witnesses are in a no-win situation that must be recognized by anyone trying to interrogate them.

Perhaps the best example of how difficult it can be for those in authority to get to the bottom of what goes on in a hazing is the case of Douglas MacArthur. When he was a "plebeian," or "plebe," at West Point at the turn of the century, MacArthur found himself in a hazing controversy. In his book *Reminiscences* he tries to look at hazing in its best light, saying that it "was practiced with a worthy goal, but with methods that were violent and uncontrolled."

Young MacArthur, like dozens of West Pointers, was commanded to testify at a congressional court of inquiry ordered by President William McKinley in December 1900. The hearings had two purposes: to deduce whether the unwritten code of hazing had caused the recent death of a young cadet named Oscar Booz of Bristol, Pennsylvania, and to determine if hazing was a significant problem at West Point. The court of inquiry doubted whether Booz's death could be blamed on West Point cadets who undoubtedly had harassed and even beaten him. However, when that special committee had finished its report, there was no doubt that the United States Military Academy had a serious hazing problem.

The importance of this study, in retrospect, is the striking similarities revealed between many latter-day hazing practices and the West Point abuses. These similarities raise the possibility that military academy dropouts introduced hazing practices into the colleges they later attended and, thus, played a leading role in the history of hazing on American campuses.

The select committee was made up of six distinguished members of the House of Representatives: Charles Dick, chairman (Ohio), Irving P. Wanger (Pennsylvania), Walter I. Smith (Iowa), Edmund H. Driggs (New York), Bertram T. Clayton (New York), and Major H. A. Kasson (Ohio), Sergeant-at-Arms. It met during the fifty-sixth Congress, second session. The committee concluded that cadets who were the descendants of famous military men—including Douglas MacArthur, Ulysses S. Grant, and Philip Sheridan, Jr.—were particularly subjected to ridicule and harsh hazing. Sheridan, for example, was ordered to make a mockery of his famous father's victory at Winchester, yelling "Turn, boys, turn, we are going back," while riding a broomstick down a company street.

As a teenager, General Arthur MacArthur, Douglas's father, served under Phil Sheridan, Sr., in the Civil War. After the war, Douglas's father gained fame in remote American outposts for his role in squashing the warring Indian tribes and other heroics. Only one year before young Doug entered the military academy, his father, the brigadier-general, had become a household name for his leadership in the Philippines during the Spanish-American conflict.

Douglas himself would become one of the most famous and controversial generals in history, but during the congressional inquiry into hazing he was a not-so-robust kid facing an inquisition. His testimony reveals many sides of the future general. He was scared but plucky, arrogant yet polite, defiant and cooperative by turns. Previous testimony by those who knew him in the old "beast barracks," where the plebes began their service, established that Douglas had been so brutalized by hazers that his body had gone into convulsions and that he had ordered a comrade to stuff a cloth into his mouth should he cry out, lest he be viewed as weak or his ordeal be discovered by officers. MacArthur denied that a cloth had been stuffed into his mouth.

While giving testimony, MacArthur—ranked number one in his class by his superiors—steadfastly refused to name the upperclassmen who had hazed him, yet he tried to appease the select committee by giving them the names of several men who had already quit West Point for one reason or another. He downplayed the convulsions he had experienced after being seriously hazed, and he most certainly lied on the stand when he said that he could name with certainty only those hazers who had already left the service academy, a Mr. Dockery and a Mr. Barry.

Over the years his testimony has been echoed by thousands of hazed young men in less august hearings at other schools. Reports of his hazing had been "very much exaggerated indeed," MacArthur said. MacArthur admitted that he had never reported being hazed and that he had refused to testify against his hazers during a previous similar interrogation conducted by a West Point officer.

As the testimony wound down, MacArthur was presented with a list of hazers and a list of fifty-nine "methods of hazing" that had come out in the testimony of cadets and former cadets less willing to maintain silence at all costs. "Those are all I know of," said MacArthur after viewing the list of hazers. "Those are all I can remember; yes, sir," he said when shown the fifty-nine methods of hazing. Many years later, in *Reminiscences,* MacArthur recalled what a quandary he had been in while testifying to the select committee. "My father and mother had taught me those two immutable principles—never to lie, never to tattle. But here was a desperate situation for me. If the court insisted and ordered me to reveal the names, and I refused to obey the order, it would in all likelihood mean my dismissal and the end of my hopes and dreams. It would be so easy and expedient to yield, to tell, and who would blame me?" he writes.

The turning point came during a recess, writes MacArthur. As he tried to regain his composure, a note was pressed into his palm. It was from his mother. She had written him advice, in verse, that encouraged him to remain silent about what he knew.

MacArthur's mother made his decision easier, but his solution points out how difficult it is for school administrators, the courts, and law enforcement officials to learn the truth about hazing. He would not blab; he would deny, deny—and let the select committee get what it could from those who had quit West Point for one reason or another. He left the court, expecting expulsion for his actions, but the committee didn't dare expel a victim—the son of a war hero and the proud possessor of the best academic record at West Point in decades. Douglas MacArthur returned to West Point as a superintendent following World War I, and he outlawed some of the worst hazing practices that had persisted since his student days. But not even MacArthur could completely eliminate the ritual at the United States Military Academy.

7

A campus memorial service for Chuck Stenzel was held at eight-thirty
P.M. the same Sunday that Don King conducted his investigation. The Klan
brothers attended en masse, many of them looking uncomfortable in
jackets and ties. Although a letter to the student newspaper complained
that students who disliked Klan Alpine had stayed away, the chapel was
packed. Chuck's yellow slicker had been as visible on campus as Dick
Tracy's trenchcoat. President Rose told the assembly that no individual
could be blamed for Chuck's death, a highly premature announcement in
the midst of supposedly impartial investigations by the school, village
police, and district attorney.

Melvin Bernstein, a longtime Alfred faculty member and head of the
B'nai B'rith Hillel Council, addressed the congregation. He said, "Tonight
we are a church, we are a congregation." Don Gallup, a friend of Chuck's,
said he hoped the audience would leave with good memories of "constantly
helpful" Chuck, not memories of his death. One of the young women who
had transported the Stevenses during their campus visit told the audience
that Eileen hoped students would learn that "Drinking will not be taken
lightly." Her meeting with King had led Eileen to believe that the university supported her in that wish.

Chuck's wake lasted three days. "Three days is too long," Eileen wrote
in her journal. Her agony was prolonged. But three days was also too
short. At the end of that time, she knew, she would never see her son
again. "Who wanted to remember him this way?" she wrote, this quiet
stranger lying in the coffin with his name on a placard. Suzanne was
aghast when she saw him. "Oh, Mom, his hair," she cried, when she saw
how the autopsy had ravaged the wheat-colored locks.

At times during the wake, Eileen fought anger toward Chuck. "How
could you, you foolish, trusting kid?" she thought. "But I can understand,"
she wrote later. "You saw the good in people. How often you admonished
me for being impatient, critical, or short-tempered with anyone! You hated
gossip and pettiness."

At night she went to Chuck's room, fondled his possessions. She
lamented the loss of a box that held, among other things, Chuck's trade-
mark red hat. It had either fallen off the truck or been stolen from the
truckbed during Belanger's drive back to Long Island. She stroked the
navy down coat, the workman's boots. She hauled out awards Chuck had
buried in a drawer and hung them on the wall.

She read sympathy cards that said Chuck was at peace, with God, a part of the universe. She wanted to believe every comforting word, that Chuck had found an enchanted harbor in which to dock for eternity.

But it was hard. He died without last rites, after all— "a derelict in the street gets them!" she wrote bitterly. No, the comforting words didn't help. She wanted him back.

The thick snow outside the window was no comfort either. In her mind's eye she saw Chuck trading snowballs with Scott. Razzing Sue's artistry with snowmen. Playing hockey with Billy Vollmer and the biggest kid in the neighborhood, Mr. Vollmer.

Jimmy Arnoux and Mike Shivers had taken flights from the West Coast. Scott Doty, Jimmy Schildt, Billy Vollmer, and Belanger stood with them: an impenetrable group, their faces rigid, but none daring to break down. They had to be strong for Chuck, Arnoux had told the gang of six at his house while his mother set out hot coffee and plates of food. The gang approved of Chuck's burial outfit, his stepping-out clothes: a yellow shetland pullover sweater, dark brown corduroy Levis, a blue shirt with its button-down collar open. Chuck's grandmother—Eileen's mother—had insisted on washing the pants and shirt although they were clean. It was her final act of love.

Already troubled at learning from Roy's brother Bill that Chuck had been placed in a car trunk, the Stevenses were also disturbed to see that his knuckles were badly bruised. The family assumed those bruises came from knocking to get out of the trunk. But a Klan member insists that if the bruises happened in the trunk, it was because pledges and brothers were yelling back and forth to each other in a spirited, but not hostile, manner. Eileen and Roy also heard a rumor here, a comment there, from some of Chuck's Alfred friends that there was more to the Klan Alpine night of drinking than just an ordinary party.

Although she was touched by a beautiful floral display that Klan sent, Eileen was disturbed that Chuck's fraternity friends didn't come to the funeral. Scott Sullivan says that many members wanted to attend but didn't because King had advised them to have no interaction with the family for fear of legal reprisals.

People that Eileen would never have expected came to say goodbye to Chuck. A member of her church who had once shared a hospital room with Chuck offered condolences. Chuck had kept in touch, the man told her. Knowing that the man loved shellfish, he had dropped off a bushel of clams once or twice.

Not until his death did Eileen learn that all the shoveling Chuck had routinely done for the neighbors had been for free. She had assumed that money was his motivation. As the bad press about Chuck filled every area newspaper, Eileen took comfort in one of the few positive paragraphs about him. *Newsday,* the Long Island paper, interviewed a Sayville neighbor who said Chuck "never failed to show up" after a snowstorm.

At the wake and for months after Chuck's death, Eileen heard from women who had dated Chuck or been his friend. He had loved the company of women more than she had known, Eileen learned, but not only in a sexual sense. Nanci Lunati, his longtime friend, said that Chuck was always the one to spot an unattractive girl, alone in a corner at a party, and talk to her.

Lunati's sister, Maria, had dated Chuck seriously the previous year. Greg Belanger and Scott Doty always felt that Chuck would marry the beautiful, quiet Maria and that Jimmy Arnoux would marry petite, vivacious Nanci. The friends thought that in an ideal world the two couples would live on the same street in some oceanside town. Maria—whom Chuck called 'Meezzy' after he learned that's what she'd been called as a child—was devastated by his death. She and he had had a spat and only reconciled by mail the February he died. "Thank God, or otherwise that would have been burning at me, too," she says. "There was a time that we didn't [write] for a long time—a scorned woman I guess I was. We were going to get back together as friends when we got back together in town."

The Lunati sisters used to wait for Chuck and Arnoux to dock their clamboats before going out on the town to listen to live music at a Sayville hotspot called the Parrot. Maria and Chuck occasionally drank illegally, she says, but she swears it was never excessive and that they never had hard liquor. She hates the image some people in Sayville later had of Chuck as a drunken alcoholic stumbling along.

Jimmy Arnoux and the Lunati sisters were all set back by Chuck's death. Arnoux returned to California for several months, and Nanci quit school to join him. When they returned to Long Island months later, Arnoux dealt with Chuck's death in the only way he could. He stepped aboard his clamboat and worked, worked, worked. Neither Lunati sister talked to the other about Chuck until 1989. "I guess we wanted everybody to think we were okay," Maria says. For a long time, she refused to let Chuck's death enter her mind. To keep her concentration on her college studies, she pretended that the funeral had been only a bad dream. "I made everything look like it was fine," she says. "[But] it wasn't fine; it wasn't fine."

With Eileen, she shared memories of Chuck in a wet suit, washing her car, and of how he had played like a kid with Suzanne. At night, alone, she recalled holding hands. His hands were big, always sore and sporting horned calluses.

Many letters and short notes came from the Alfred area and from parents who had children at the university. "I first met Chuck when he first came to Alfred last year," wrote a female student from Rochester. "He really knew how to live and make people feel that they were beautiful too. He called me "Sunshine," but if anyone was sunshine it had to be him." The parents of the pledge who had been in Rocky LaForge's room with Chuck wrote to say, "Our prayers are with you." A boy from Chuck's dormitory wrote anonymously to say that he had experienced some emotional problems and that Chuck was the only resident "who cared enough to help me." According to the letter writer, when some bullies harassed him, Chuck intervened. Moreover, because the letter writer lacked a ride home, Chuck gave him a lift in the blue Ford. "When I tried to thank him, he just brushed the issue aside like he was only doing what any decent human being would do and didn't deserve thanks," he wrote. "Chuck meant a great deal to me. . . . He cared when people hurt inside and went out of his way to help them."

Few Alfred faculty took the time to write, but the handful of letters Eileen did receive were important. In time they softened her bitter feelings toward Alfred, and in conversation she makes a distinction between the school's faculty and its administration. Besides President Rose, one administrator who wrote was Dean John R. Foxen. He and his assistant, Fred H. Gertz, wrote, "The death of a young man has a profound effect on his student friends and those who were his teachers. [We] want you to know that we share in your sorrow." Another came from his English professor, Elizabeth M. Sibley, who wrote, "I mourn his death."

But the most sensitive letter came from uprooted Oregonian Stuart Campbell, who had seen something noble, special, promising in Chuck. "Last year your son Chuck was a student in my class in Western Civilization," he wrote. "I came to know him well, and I admired both his personal character and the quality of his mind. He was a fine young man, very able, intelligent, filled with elan, and obviously well raised. . . . His death came as a terrible shock and was a horrible tragedy. Words are ultimately inadequate to the sadness of the occasion. As a parent, I can understand the depth of your loss. As Chuck's friend and teacher, I also share in it. If there is anything I can do to help you in this difficult time, please do not hesitate to contact me."

Before closing the casket, the family said their goodbyes. Eileen took his rosary and kissed him for the last time. A few days later, she cursed herself for not cutting a lock of his hair. Suzanne, in her turn, approached the coffin. She wanted to make certain that Chuck didn't forget what the family looked like. Eternity is more than an adult can fathom, let alone an eleven-year-old. With her mother's permission, she placed Chuck's favorite pictures of the family beside him. The funeral was at ten A.M. the Tuesday after Chuck's death. A photograph of four family friends bearing the casket into St. Lawrence the Martyr Church was published in *Newsday* on February 28. The cutline chilled, humiliated, and saddened the Stevens family with its starkness. "Stenzel . . . died Friday night after excessive drinking at a fraternity party at Alfred University."

Although Eileen thought the service beautiful, it unnerved her. She saw Chuck in every pew. Over there he received the sacrament of Confirmation. There he knelt all his years as an altar boy. There he proudly received his eighth-grade diploma.

The officiating priest had similar memories. "I first met Chuck when he assisted me as an altar boy right on this altar," said Father William Logan. "During my years at St. Lawrence we often met: in the classroom, the schoolyard, at basketball games on the court. Chuck was energetic, bright, and had a smile and helping hand for everyone. It is difficult for us to smile today. Our hearts are heavy, and we are full of confusion and questions. Why did this happen? Why Chuck?"

At the end of his talk, the Reverend Logan turned his attention to the mourners. Perhaps he feared that it might be in a friend or mother's heart impulsively to join Chuck in death this grey day. "Remember, he loved life and would want us to go on with ours. Chuck is with God, and our faith promises us that we will meet again."

The family wanted Teresa, Eileen's sister, to speak even though Catholic funeral masses don't normally include family eulogies. She was only twenty, Chuck's age, and she said only a few words before the congregation dissolved into tears.

Jimmy Arnoux also spoke. Eileen watched closely, afraid that he might break, but his weatherworn face was a mask he dared not drop. He and Chuck had been brothers in every sense that fraternity brothers claim to be. They had clammed together, had traveled the breadth of the country. Greg Belanger and the other clammers also studied Arnoux with concern. "I remember he was so strong that it was amazing," says Belanger. "I would have been in pieces up there. His message was, 'Life goes on— Chuck doesn't want to see a lot of people ruining their lives with grief. Chuck would want things to go on.'"

Eileen heard Arnoux's words, too, but, unbeknownst to her, her former life had departed as surely as Chuck had. "I had a lot to learn," she wrote some years after the funeral. "I had been insensitive, unresponsive, selfish, self-centered. . . . I had to learn the hard way."

Outside the church, there was the roar of Chuck's truck engine turning over—followed by the sound of other trucks starting. Sayville neighbors looked out their windows to see the hearse followed by dusty trucks, not the black Cadillacs and Lincolns they were accustomed to. Somehow it didn't matter to Eileen what her friends or neighbors thought of the procession: Chuck's blue pickup truck, driven by Belanger, and a puffing, grumbling procession of similar trucks, their beds laden with more than one hundred floral arrangements, followed by more conventional automobiles. "Chuck would have loved it," Eileen says defiantly. If she could have strapped Chuck to his clamboat to wander the seas forever, she would have. She could not be bothered that some Sayville citizens were offended by the parade of pickups. Let them call the affair a freak show or circus, she decided. This wasn't their funeral. It was her boy's.

The trucks lined the small cemetery where Chuck was to be interred. Big, burly clammers, some in washed work clothes and others squeezed uncomfortably into dressier attire, came to pay their respects to a fellow seaman. These were plain working stiffs who knew how to outlast unfriendly winds, tipped skiffs, and brutal storms. They were men who judged you by what you did and who you were, not by the club you belonged to or the thickness of your wallet.

Don King, fearful of a lawsuit, never contacted Eileen Stevens to give her the results of his investigation. The day after the funeral, however, the Stevens's phone rang in the evening. The caller, according to three Klan Alpine brothers, Don King, Eileen Stevens, Gary Horowitz, and two newspaper accounts, was Joseph F. (Joe) McCaffery, Chuck's roommate.

Eileen considers McCaffery's phone call a heroic gesture. The Klan members had agreed to keep silent after Scott Sullivan talked to King, and Eileen has since been told that his breaking of this unwritten oath went against what members of a group would ordinarily do in such a situation. "I couldn't see you when you came to the campus—I was too upset," said McCaffery, according to Eileen. "Forgive me for not coming to the funeral; I couldn't deal with it." McCaffery went on to say that he had pledged Klan Alpine the previous year and had touted the merits of the organization to Chuck, telling him it was Alfred's "oldest and strongest fraternity."

The phone conversation went on for several minutes, and Eileen took notes on a greeting card she still has. But from this point her account and McCaffery's vary.

Eileen went to *Newsday* with what she said she had learned from the roommate and Roy's brother, a Nassau County police officer. The thrust of the resulting article was that something untoward had befallen her son in the trunk of a car. Eileen maintains that her basic recall of the conversation with McCaffery is sound, but she acknowledges that he used several fraternity terms that she had never heard, including *Tapping Night, Hell Week, big brother,* and *pledging.* She insists that while it is possible that she may have misunderstood specific terms, she did not misread his substance. She says that he did not make light of the trunk incident. "I can imagine Joe McCaffery omitting things that would make me feel horrible," she says. "But I can't imagine Joe McCaffery not saying things that would be comforting."

McCaffery's alleged admission that Chuck was "out of it" when he left the trunk is a specific point of dispute. Eileen mistakenly took "out of it" to mean "unconscious."

All hell broke loose on the Alfred campus after *Newsday* printed Eileen's account of her conversation with McCaffery. Papers in Buffalo, Alfred, and Rochester jumped on the story, publishing claims by the Alfred administration that Eileen had distorted the information. The Klan brothers confronted McCaffery when once again they were in the news. "How could you say anything?—we promised not to," people asked McCaffery.

Greg Belanger, in his role as a staffer for the student paper, quoted McCaffery as saying that he had given Eileen what was "exactly true," but that his words had become twisted in her mouth. Don King also adheres to that explanation. Joe Bachman, an acquaintance of McCaffery's, says that Chuck's Klan Alpine roommate always told the truth. Bachman believes his version. But Eileen's version might have been what McCaffery told her. Scott Sullivan says that he and others used to tease McCaffery for occasionally getting facts mixed up in his stories. "We called him a fountain of misinformation," says Sullivan, laughing. Greg Belanger had heard from another *Fiat Lux* editor, Nancy Cushing, that McCaffery was a decent person, bruised by Chuck's death and subsequent media coverage. "He won't talk to friends; he won't talk to anyone about this," says Belanger. "That's what I've been told."

McCaffery's call certainly triggered strong suspicions in Eileen. After speaking to the roommate, she no longer trusted the Alfred administration. More importantly, she resolved to find out about this thing called hazing that had killed her son and to fight it with all her being.

Eileen also learned the identity of Chuck's big brother and talked to him by phone while he was still in Klan Alpine. She preserved her notes on that conversation as well. She asked him if it was fair that Chuck died. The big brother said, "What's fair, Mrs. Stevens?" He said that he hadn't killed her son. When Eileen again tried to talk with him, she received an angry letter from his wife, demanding that she stop contacting him. Kevin LaForge, the big brother's roommate, says, "I know for a fact" that his roomie was emotionally torn up by the Stenzel incident.

One weekend after Chuck's death, a professor who showed movies on campus for a second income decided to cancel the film he had booked, according to Martha Mueller, an Alfred University associate librarian in Scholes Library of Ceramics. But he allowed Mueller and about nine other movie buffs to see it in a discreet private screening. "It had impact on all who went to see it," says Mueller, another neighbor of Klan who collects beer cans and other trash deposited after parties to sell to a recycling outfit.

The movie was *Fraternity Row*, a film loosely based on the 1959 death of Richard Swanson, a Southern California student who gagged on a fist-sized piece of liver that Kappa Sigma members ordered him to swallow.

The adverse publicity generated by Chuck's death quickly reached Klan Alpine alumni living in the Northeast. Elsewhere in the country, the death received minor coverage. Out of a tragedy most saw as senseless, Rich Sigal made intellectual sense. His letter to the *Fiat Lux* ran on March 20, 1978:

> In sociology we refer to "rites of passage," the culturally different rituals symbolizing movement from one status to another, in this case, from that of non-fraternity member to Klan Alpine pledge.
> The initiation itself seems rather crude. What is ultimately proved by one's ability to drink and either

"hold it well" or "blow one's lunch"? Pragmatically, nothing.

Symbolically, in fact, it becomes quite meaningful given the society in which it occurs. . . . Like it or not, America is a drinking society. Drinking and overdrinking become the norms at fraternity initiation rituals. Such frivolity is an expected part of events imbued with anxiety.

Thus, at Klan Alpine fraternity, a tapping night ritual, the roots of which date back some fifty years, ended in tragedy. The climax of anxiety-filled weeks, the reinforcement of brotherly solidarity, and a need for the expression of virility combined to result in the death of one young freshman and the hospitalization of two others. "Tapping" symbolized the beginning of a period of socialization created to instill those feelings of solidarity existent among brothers. While outsiders might easily view the overconsumption of alcohol as behavior characteristic of adolescents attempting to reaffirm their manhood, there nevertheless exists the very real fact that the tradition serves to reinforce important, socially approved values. Intense feelings of loyalty [cement] support for, among other beliefs, nonsectarianism . . . a highly valued American ideal. Somewhere between my years in Klan and the present, the ritual in which I had so often participated both as pledge and brother evidently underwent a change. The ceremony known to me consisted of simply the awarding of pledge pins and the downing of innumerable mugs of beer. Hazing was non-existent.

I grew a lot in Klan Alpine, possibly more than during any other four-year segment of my adult life, and so now there is pain that such tragic events as this have occurred, could have taken place during such a meaning[ful] moment of revelry. Should the tradition be changed, when so many others before have participated without fatal repercussions? Is there available another, less dangerous initiation ritual capable of satisfying the same needs?

In the weeks after the funeral, Eileen was a woman possessed. The three hundred thank-you notes she had ordered were inadequate. In the end she used nine hundred. She labored hours, often going to bed after two A.M. She wanted each person's kindness repaid. Several friends had sent books, including *On Death and Dying,* by Elisabeth Kubler-Ross. Eileen felt she had to let people know that their gestures had been noticed. To repay Belanger's kindness in driving the blue Ford to Sayville, Eileen sent him packets of pictures of the old gang.

Eileen's grieving sister Mary also wrote letters, but of a far different tone. She took Alfred to task for her nephew's death. She wrote President Rose to tell him how Chuck had worked on his blue truck to make sure it would be sound for the trip to school. She told Rose that neither Chuck's family nor Alfred University would ever be the same. Her letter to Klan Alpine was equally harsh, demanding that the fraternity disband.

Each day Eileen and her mother, Rose Hurney, drove to the cemetery. Her mother stayed a week, preparing special meals, doing the wash, and, most important, listening. The women shared long talks, longer cries. When Eileen couldn't answer the phone or the doorbell one more time, her mother substituted. Friends and neighbors continued to bring cooked food all that first week, too.

Despite comforting assurances from those who loved her, guilt began to assail Eileen. Chuck had enjoyed his semester away from Alfred. She had nagged him to go back, reminding him how important his education was. "Get back now," she told him. "Don't postpone it."

Had she sent him back to die?

By March 2, 1978, Chief Tiny Jamison told newspapers that no charges against Klan Alpine were contemplated since he had found no indication of foul play. The Alfred *Sun,* which said the investigation was to be "continued through this week," did not explain how that determination had been made so quickly. But Jamison told another paper that "anything can happen by the time we're finished" with the investigation.

The mayor of Alfred, Gary Horowitz, echoed statements by President Rose. "We view this death as part of our larger problem with alcohol," he told a *Newsday* reporter. "There is a great deal of it on campus. There is a sense of disbelief on the campus, a sense of tragedy. But it is a national problem. It could happen to any college kid on any campus." Horowitz defended the character of the young men involved. "Klan brothers are not a bunch of derelicts," he said. The mayor also denied that the administration could have prevented the death, saying it "was something the university cannot control."

Greg Smith, the *Fiat Lux* business manager, disagreed. He said, "The school has to do something to clean this up and make sure it doesn't happen again. It was not an isolated instance. . . . The people at Klan just went a little too far this time." However, Smith agreed with Horowitz that the death could have happened on any campus.

It may be true that Chuck's death could have happened anywhere. But during the next decade and beyond, Eileen Stevens was to see that sentiment used repeatedly to rationalize tragedies that occurred on other campuses. The year after Chuck's death an accident that attracted only sporadic national attention occurred at Harvard University. For many years certain Ivy League school organizations ended their initiation ceremonies with a wet and wild time called "Sink Night"—so termed because new members would sink into debauchery. "There might be an inch of beer on the floor before it's over, and someone might get hurt," a Dartmouth student told *Newsweek*. "But I won't say it's bad to swim around in beer."

Harvard's Paul Callahan might not agree. Following his initiation into Pi Eta, a campus eating club, he followed the local tradition of disrobing, running from the clubhouse to Harvard Library to check out a book, then racing across Harvard Square to purchase a candy bar. One year earlier, a naked student had been injured when he accidentally streaked through a plate-glass window while hurrying to comply with tradition. Callahan, a one-time Harvard basketball player, celebrated his initiation by wrestling on a beer-coated floor. Something went wrong, and he was paralyzed during the match. "The whole tragedy is that people are pinning it on Pi," a friend of Callahan's told a local newspaper. "It . . . could have happened anywhere."

An announcement by Don King on March 6, 1978, angered Klan Alpine members, who thought they had been betrayed. The dean withdrew recognition of Klan, failing to stipulate whether the penalty might last a week or several years. He said—and would say many times over the next decade—that the action marked the limits of the university's authority over the fraternity. The statement contradicted another he had made to *Newsday*, one that appeared on March 6 as well. In that statement King had said that one option was the expulsion of Klan Alpine members and the permanent withdrawal of school recognition. Such stern measures "in effect, would kill the fraternity," King assured reporter Steve Wick. King's failure to ban the fraternity permanently saddened Eileen Stevens.

Flash forward to 1989. If conceding that one might have been wrong is a sign of courage, former Alfred president Richard Rose is a courageous man. Unlike the Alfred administration, which has defended its actions in the Stenzel case to this day, Rose has gained a perspective since leaving Happy Valley. A grandfatherly man whose conversation invariably reveals strong religious beliefs, Rose has come to recognize how the incident might have been more humanely and responsibly handled.

"If I had to do it over again, I would have been personally involved with the family," says Rose, "even though the lawyers said, 'You say nothing.' . . . That's one time where advice from lawyers was ill-advised. The family was devastated, as you can imagine. Their first utterance was that they were going to sue everyone in sight. [Eileen denies saying this.] Well, that's kind of normal. The advice I got was 'Don't have anything to do with it.'

"Well, you had to have something to do with it. I was there. It was a small college. I regret not having personally met with the family. Our counsel felt that that would just [make] liable the institution and myself. I don't think that would have been the case. . . . Well, I took their advice. I'm years more experienced as a college president now, and I'm not as likely to follow advice; I'm likely to follow my personal instinct. My instinct is to behave like a father. In that case you're angry at the loss of a human life. . . . My feeling really was that it was a tragedy. As an institution we tried to take appropriate steps, [but] I'm not so sure we did all the things we could have done. Personally, I wasn't as involved as I would choose to be."

Asked whether Klan should have been permanently eliminated, Rose says, "I think so." He had no desire to punish former Klan members, but the situation could only stay raw and inflamed. "By keeping Klan there as a symbol — even though they'd been there a great many years as a social entity — Klan continued to exist. By continuing to exist, it kind of sent the message — in my judgment — to the rest of the students that, well, that was unfortunate, even a tragedy, but life goes on. Klan almost became a negative symbol, if you will. And so I think we'd have been further ahead, looking back at it in hindsight, not to have had it. I don't know how we could have done it. We couldn't just close them down. But maybe we could have worked with public officials and done something."

But in 1978 the university avoided the Stevens family, and Eileen took as another negative symbol an azalea plant sent belatedly by Rose "from your friends at Alfred." She wanted direct contact with him, nothing less. Rose's "message" to alumni in the April 1978 newsletter loudly echoes the sentiments of attorneys. "Our subsequent decision to disassociate the University from Klan Alpine was based not only on the tragic event, but on a pattern of increasingly disruptive behavior over the past several years," said Rose. "This action (the extent of our legal rights) does not mitigate our collective sense of shock and sadness. . . . We all know that prohibition [of alcohol] is not feasible. It does not consider the constitutional rights of young people." Rose acknowledged that he had received mail on the Stenzel incident. He asked alumni to stay true to their alma mater. "We count on you to recognize, despite this tragedy, what remains excellent and worthy of your respect."

The memory of the big, strapping pledge who nearly perished in the dormitory shower kept eating at Greg Belanger in the days after Chuck's funeral. Finally, he wrote an account of what had transpired — leaving out the name of the boy he had saved and his fraternity (not Klan Alpine) — and published it in the Alfred student newspaper on March 13, 1978.

Surprisingly, Belanger's letter sank without a ripple. Not one administrator called him on the carpet: not Dean King, not Provost S. Gene Odle, not President Rose. Nor did faculty members raise a fuss although many months after the incident the *Fiat Lux* reported that the assistant dean of student living had informed the Greeks that she wanted no pledge activities in the dormitories. Worse, the letter attracted no student reaction in subsequent issues of *Fiat Lux*.

The lack of a university response of any kind adds strength to Eileen's contention that the university simply wanted the episode to evaporate. That the university had hired a resident assistant who knew mouth-to-mouth resuscitation is admirable; had any of the Klansmen with Chuck those last fading seconds known the technique, he could conceivably have lived. Not so admirable is that the university failed to take advantage of

Belanger's attack of conscience to investigate and at least try to stop young people from drinking themselves to death in order to gain admission into social organizations. Shouldn't the administration have demanded answers from the former resident assistant? What fraternity was involved? What was the occasion? Who was the pledge, and who was with him that night?

How can the Alfred administration justify its failure to launch an investigation in the wake of such a serious allegation? The failure to investigate this incident calls into question how motivated the institution was to get to the bottom of Chuck's death. Had a full-scale investigation of Belanger's charges been conducted then and there, the university might merit public sympathy. But with two serious incidents in the space of one year — one of which was neither punished nor investigated — Alfred University is lucky to have received only minimum public censure from Eileen Stevens and the press.

As another letter writer to the student paper back then pointed out, excesses at Alfred University in the late 1970s had become so common that some lost their fear of consequences. "Every day in this town people play with fire under the illusion that it is perfectly safe. Be it liquor, drugs, or sex, people are convinced that nothing is ever going to happen," wrote Mary Bliss, a member of the Class of 1981. "People around here are going to have to realize that when you play with fire you get burned."

Don King's attitude toward the Stevens family is evident in a letter he sent to Roy on March 16, 1978. Written three weeks after Chuck's death, it has the warmth of Nome winters. The dean makes it clear that if Roy has other questions, he should take them elsewhere — to the treasurer of Alfred University.

King had one other communication with the Stevens family. He wrote "Mrs. Roy Stevens" on April 18, noting that a Sayville student had relayed Eileen's request to be sent news clippings. She had received some from friends and strangers but realized many more articles had to have been published. King sent two clippings, a fraction of the dozens of articles about the incident published by Buffalo, Rochester, Alfred, Hornell, and Wellsville newspapers. Nonetheless, King's letter declared that he was unaware of additional newspaper coverage. He closed by offering his assistance if Eileen were to need anything in the future.

On March 22, Eileen stopped at the John Esposito Memorial Company and purchased a monolith made of select Barre granite. Her instructions were simple. She wanted a small cross only; Chuck would have hated gaudy symbols. The inscription was brief:

Charles M. Stenzel
1957 - 1978

Eight days later she phoned the memorial company. The inscription bothered her. Not even his teachers had called him Charles.

"Is it too late to make a change?"

No, she was told.

Eileen said that she wanted to add a word on the line between her son's name and the dates.

The representative asked her what it should say.

"Chuck," she said. "Just Chuck."

After all the thank-you notes were done, Eileen began writing letters to anyone she thought might show an interest in banning hazing practices. She was inspired by her sister Mary, who had written letters to educators, legislators, and journalists.

Family and friends were Eileen's strength as surely as Chuck was her inspiration. Mary helped Eileen take a concept and mold it into an organization. Roy did his part on weekends. He took Suzanne and Mary's two children to the park while the women worked. Their tasks mystified him, and Eileen's passion frightened him, for her sake. To him she seemed to be chipping away at an approaching glacier with an icepick, and he feared the glacier would run right over her. Nonetheless, he carried piles of hazing clippings to his office to photocopy, filed letters on Sundays, and, most important, he paid the bills.

Chuck's death coincided with Roy's success in the business world. Sadly, at a time when he might have been taking Eileen on the wonderful trips they had planned when they were younger, he was pouring money into photocopies, airline tickets, postage stamps. Time the couple could have spent together can never be reclaimed. But Roy never complained. Moreover, he wouldn't let his three children complain when he was around either. "This is a lot better than paying for a shrink," he told them.

One Sunday afternoon Roy brought home a couple of misfit file cabinets that he'd rescued from the trash. They were brown and battered; Eileen hid them in the laundry room, but they did the job. Many's the time a victim's attorney would ask Eileen's "secretary" or "staff" to send him clippings or copies of past legislation. She wondered what the lawyer would think if he could see her smacking her head against Roy's underwear drying on a line as she yanked files out of her junkyard cabinets.

Unlike Eileen, Roy never adjusted to fraternity jargon. The subtleties of terms such as associate pledges, conclaves, interfraternity councils, and rites of passage escaped him. What Roy knows best is the tool and die business. One day he volunteered to help Eileen bring some order to her files. They worked from early afternoon until early the next morning. Both were punch-drunk without sleep. Roy tossed a bunch of clippings aside in mock disgust. "Sigma what? Alpha who? Beta which?" he shouted. "How do you keep them all straight, Eileen?"

Roy Stevens internalized his grief about Chuck. Years later, Eileen would say he took the loss the hardest because he needed to be strong for everyone else and thought he couldn't show his grief. In Roy's mind the breadwinner threw back his shoulders and never complained. In those first months he didn't talk to Eileen about how he felt about losing Chuck, and it irritated her because she feared—irrationally in retrospect—that Roy didn't care. Roy thought he was showing love by putting on a good face for his wife and remaining children. If he broke down, he reasoned, how much worse would he make the other family members feel? Grief can do you in, but only if you let it, Roy believed.

So while Eileen tried to unload her emotions by verbalizing how she felt, Roy buried himself in his work. Eventually, she and Roy were able to talk about their loss and have many times. Eileen says, "Chuck's death strengthened us as a couple, but it definitely was the greatest test any marriage could go through." Roy cooperated all he could, but the world Eileen had entered was foreign to him. At his factory, kidding with the men and talking shop, he could relax and be himself. When he came home, he never knew if he were going to find a reporter, a student, or a trained kangaroo usurping his chair. In addition, the odds against Eileen's getting her message about hazing out to the public seemed hopelessly stacked. He feared that her work might come to naught, and the setback might be more than she could endure.

Eileen felt otherwise. "I won't fail!" she wrote in her notebook. "I'll make them listen. I'll persevere if it takes every bit of strength I have. It is helping me survive."

Scott Stevens played all sports. Basketball was his love, but baseball was his passion. Spring training at his high school began a few weeks after Chuck's funeral. All winter Scott had talked about lettering in baseball. One day in March he approached the coach. He told him that he couldn't go out for the team. The coach was upset. "Why?" he asked. Scott told him that his grades had slipped and that his parents forbade him to pick up a glove. The coach offered to intercede with Roy, but Scott begged him not to. The decision had been made and that was that. Had Scott's last name been Stenzel instead of Stevens, the coach might have grilled him. Chuck's name, after all, had been splashed all over *Newsday* for weeks. Scott left the coach, sad but relieved, and his mother didn't learn about the duplicity until 1989.

"I couldn't play," he told Eileen. "I couldn't face people. I was afraid I'd get upset." Scott for a time donned an impenetrable shell. At the time his parents asked him why he hadn't gone out for the team and accepted his explanation that he had changed his mind. Scott might have gone back to the coach if his parents had asked him to rethink his decision, but sadly neither did. Both were caught up in their own grief. Chuck would have been crushed that Scott sacrificed his varsity baseball chances. He had been his brother's biggest supporter. Later that year Scott came home holding his yearbook. Eileen flipped to the basketball section and was proud to see him pictured. "Look in the stands," Scott told her. She did. There was Chuck cheering his brother on.

Suzanne had problems getting herself ready for classes. She dragged herself into health class one afternoon. The teacher told the students that they would discuss alcohol poisoning and how the body shuts down after an overdose. She talked about what happens to vital organs, the nervous system, and other body parts. Suzanne kept an implacable face until the teacher used Chuck's recent death as an example. Again and again, she said his name. Each time Suzanne recoiled. Once again a teacher failed to connect the name Stenzel with Stevens.

Eileen's heart pounded when her daughter relayed the story, but she tried to give calm advice. She told Suzanne it was good, not bad, that her teacher had highlighted Chuck's name as an example. But nothing she said took away her daughter's pain, nor that of her sons. In mid-June 1978 one of Eileen's sons mailed a letter to Klan Alpine bitterly informing the members that this would have been his brother's twenty-first birthday. According to Klan's Carl Pelcher, the members posted the note for all to read.

An essay that Chuck had written on Kurt Vonnegut's novel *Slaughterhouse-Five* investigated the book's color imagery. Reading the paper, Eileen saw that her son had been fascinated by the power of blackness as a literary concept. The paper said that Vonnegut used orange and black to create an atmosphere. The darkness of the boxcar emphasized the gloom of prisoners being transported inside it, wrote Chuck. "Another time this blackness is emphasized is after the Dresden bombing," he said. "The whole city was virtually destroyed, as were 130,000 lives."

One hundred thirty thousand lives! Against all that death and destruction her son's demise must seem insignificant to historians. Certainly it seemed insignificant to the fraternity alumni who wrote her, saying she was blowing the issue of fraternity deaths out of proportion. She wondered, in turn, if her critics had sons.

The deep snows of 1978 quickly covered Chuck's grave. Friends called the Stevenses to say that they could not find the burial spot. Roy said nothing to Eileen. He went into the garage and began working. With his own hands he fashioned a cross out of wood. When it was done, he carved Chuck's name into it. He cried as he worked, but nothing stopped him. What he carved was much like him: nothing fancy but it did the job. He and Eileen drove to the cemetery. Roy cleared away the snow and drove the cross into the frozen ground. Eileen watched, silent for once.

The brothers of Klan Alpine sent their alumni a letter to inform them about the circumstances behind the death of Chuck Stenzel. Scott Sullivan cites the correspondence as proof that the brothers were not trying to conceal the facts of that evening. He also readily says that the addressing of the envelopes was done by Alfred University, courtesy of a member's connection to an employee, a gesture that shows that school and fraternity were not quite as separate as the administration wanted the public to believe.

One of the brothers who received the memo, David Hoff, penned a letter of his own, printed by the *Fiat Lux* on May 8, 1978. It read:

> I do not consider myself an active alumnus of Alfred but ironically enough I sent a pledge [of money] to the university about a week prior to "Klan" tapping night.
>
> I preface this letter with that statement more to justify writing it than for any other reason. I . . . received correspondence from the University and from Klan Alpine and felt a need to respond. I am both an alumnus of Alfred and a brother of Klan Alpine. I have fond memories of both institutions. One of my not so fond memories is of a tapping night in 1968, my tapping night. Yes, I chugged beer from the Loving Cup and vomited innumerable times as did pledges before and since. I looked at it then and still do now and say, "for what?"
>
> I look back fondly at the days on the football field as a member of "Klan" and the party weekends, the meals at the house, house meetings and the bull sessions at the bar. The only problem, the only inconsistency is, "What price does someone have to pay, what are the limits?"
>
> This is not to say that I was not as crazy as all the rest because I was. Having been a part of Klan Alpine's history does not justify Chuck Stenzel's death. Thank God I don't have to live with that memory hanging over my head.
>
> I think that Klan Alpine was headed for February 24 for 60 years. I know that it must be difficult for the brothers at a time like this because "Klan" seems so important. I respond to their correspondence: "No, closing Klan Alpine will not bring back Chuck Stenzel, and neither will keeping it open." It's a double bind, and I can't say that I won't miss 61 North Main Street, but I can't justify a human life for a fraternity. I applaud President Rose's decision, although it is with sadness. As a former college professor and administrator I have feelings in many directions. The death of an institution is sad, but the death of a human being is much worse.
>
> David F. Hoff
> '71

When she realized that the Alfred administration had cut itself off from her, Eileen began accumulating information from a network of people in Allegany County. Don King suspects that one of her local sources was Grace Jillson. The widow of an axed Alfred professor, Jillson freely admits as much. Other sources of information were Alfred students, citizens from New York's Southern Tier, and at least one professor who considered himself a victim of the so-called reforms at Alfred.

Henry Kissinger used to say that academic fights are so bitter because the stakes are so small. Alfred University's dismissal of many faculty members was no doubt well intended and perhaps economically necessary. But as with the Stenzel incident, the administration failed to deal with an unfortunate situation as humanely as it might have. Aging Dave Jillson and other professors were hurt, humiliated, and financially strapped. In tiny Alfred, they stood out as unpleasant reminders that the entire faculty had stood trembling, watching others in the herd go down. Professor Dmytro Sich wound up, for a short time, as a janitor; he had been an excellent teacher of Russian, according to Gary Horowitz. The stigma of being canned was disastrous even though it was no fault of his own. Alfred University did, however, prove victorious in a civil suit filed by Sich.

President Rose came across as a hangman in the career executions, and in this respect he took undeserved heat for doing what had to be done to reverse an alarming drop in standards at Alfred. Rose's predecessors had gotten sloppy about tenure, too often allowing it automatically without regard to merit, according to Horowitz.

Other than Sich, nearly all the fired professors took their dismissals quietly. But not Dave Jillson. Inspired by his pepperpot of a wife, he filed an age discrimination suit. Grace Jillson became Alfred's most persistent critic and seized the Stenzel incident as one more example of perfidy in Alfred. An energetic and tireless woman, she was fueled by bitterness and great love for her husband. She made it her business to become a full-time critic of the Alfred administration. She materialized like one of the Furies everywhere, cornering citizens to fry their eardrums with her accusations. Even after leaving Alfred she never stopped being vocal.

King suspects Grace Jillson of spearheading a publicity campaign called the "Committee Against Wasting Tuition" aimed at discrediting Alfred. He may be right. If Jillson did not lead the movement, she certainly was a key figure in it. A scathing eight-page anti-Alfred pamphlet produced anonymously by "C.A.W.T." was mailed in October 1980 from the same Boston post office box that Jillson used for personal mail after her permanent departure from Alfred. "This report is a result of investigation of Alfred University, Alfred, New York; it brings out negative aspects," said the brochure. "If you are a superintendent, a principal, or a headmaster, please reproduce this report and give copies to all guidance or counseling personnel who are dealing with pre-college students."

According to Eileen's 1979 diary, she had misgivings about dealing with people who had an ax to grind. But she had gone to the Alfred administration first and been rebuffed. Much of the information Jillson gave Eileen ultimately proved true. For example, Jillson informed Eileen that Rose had interviewed at Rochester Institute of Technology in September 1978. Revenge against Alfred may have been Jillson's primary goal in helping Eileen; the faculty wife likely saw the Stenzel incident as an opportunity to avenge her husband's dismissal. But that explanation doesn't tell the whole story and doesn't do justice to Jillson. Without wavering, she provided ongoing moral support and solace at a crucial time when Eileen thought she was alone in her crusade. Had revenge been Jillson's sole motivation, she would have dumped Eileen when her lawsuit against Alfred University fizzled. But Jillson came to love Eileen Stevens, and that love became reciprocal.

Eighty-plus years have not tempered Jillson's bitter feelings toward Alfred. Now living in Boston, Jillson charges her former neighbors, Klan Alpine, with several obscene, distasteful, and dangerous wrongdoings (holding pledges' heads down in human waste, etc.) that Klan's Rocky LaForge, outraged, terms not only untrue but "satanic." Jillson can't recall where she heard these allegations.

The main source may have been Will Archer, the neighbor who recanted his rumors about Klan in a sworn statement to the police. Archer admits spreading rumors but insists that he got them "from students," that he didn't originate them.

In many ways, whoever started the wild rumors did a disservice to Eileen Stevens, to Klan Alpine and its advisors, to Don King, to Alfred University, and, for a short time, to Tiny Jamison's investigation. The rumor-mongering made it seem as though Chuck's death was caused by sinister young men. That sensationalized the case and detracted from its truly terrifying aspects.

Properly viewed, Chuck's demise was significant because it was caused by an initiation ceremony involving liquor and because that ceremony was not isolated. It was a premeditated, common rite of passage. The hazing incident that killed Chuck Stenzel was as American as a sick joke, a racial slur, a nasty prank, as American as a celebratory, falling-down drunk on the town.

The young men of Klan Alpine were not cold-blooded sadists looking for innocents to snuff out like a flame in the wind. The members, the majority of them anyway, were upstanding kids very much like Chuck. "What happened is bad enough without . . . dramatizing things," says Steven Peterson. "I mean, it was just an ordinary thing where, if you're a kid, you'd think there would never be a problem. I think that what really happened is worse, in some ways, than how [Eileen Stevens] described it. It was so ordinary."

To be sure, the Klansmen deserved whatever punishment the legal system could throw at them for their culpability that night. They were to escape all liability because a district attorney chose not to prosecute them. They did not, however, escape the damning insinuations spread by a handful of Alfred citizens who made them out to be monsters they had never been and never would be. They did not deserve to be slandered by these neighbors. They did not deserve to be used as surrogate whipping boys for retrenchment moves at Alfred.

Chuck Stenzel got a raw deal at Alfred when he died and when the administration tried to place the entire blame on him. So did his mother.

So did Klan Alpine. So did Don King when he became a scapegoat for all the wrongs of the Alfred administration and, by extension, those of a dysfunctional educational system that allows hazing to flourish in this country. So did Grace Jillson when her husband was axed a few years before retirement. All these people were points on a compass, a circle without beginning or end.

Jillson admits providing Eileen with her version of what transpired that fatal night at Klan Alpine. She knew several Klan members personally. "I used to type papers for them," she says. "Once in a while I'd ask them to do something for me because my husband was ill. If I couldn't move a big thing, I didn't hesitate to say, 'Hey, guys,' as they were walking by, 'would you come and move something for me? They'd come in and do it, and I'd thank them and that would be the end of that. I simply needed their muscle, and I used it, you know what I mean? . . . I was good to people when I was young, and I feel it's all right for me to have a little help now and then when I need it."

In the end many unhappy people in Alfred helped Eileen by sending her clippings from the *Fiat Lux* and other newspapers, letting her keep up with what was going on at the university. Unfortunately, they also hurt her by sensationalizing Chuck's death, making it seem as if cold-blooded killers were responsible. His death was all the more tragic in that it occurred in conditions created by young men who would become educators, corporation presidents, lawyers, ceramic engineers, and healthcare professionals.

Worse still, his death can become meaningful — if such senseless nightmares can be so termed — only if the Big Picture comes into focus. The root causes of hazing must be recognized and eradicated at all levels of society — not only in college fraternities and sororities. "I'm frightened. Of us," says Ralph in *Lord of the Flies* after participating in Simon's bloodshed. The ultimate lesson of Chuck Stenzel's death is that we should all share that fear.

PART TWO

8

The investigation into Chuck's death by Allegany County District Attorney George F. Francis lasted five weeks. Francis still refuses to say precisely what constituted his investigation although he did talk to both King and Rose. It is also possible to establish that his office did not interview certain people:

■ The membership of Klan Alpine fraternity. Scott Sullivan, president at the time of Chuck's death, is unaware of any brothers' being questioned by the district attorney or his representatives. Certainly, neither Carl Pelcher nor Rocky LaForge — who discovered the dying Chuck Stenzel — was ever questioned by George Francis.

■ J. J. Cosgrove, the state trooper, on the scene after the fatality.

■ Robert Heineman, the former Klan adviser, also on the scene after the fatality.

Eileen Stevens did get one phone call through to Francis. She remembers it as a very brief exchange. She expressed her concern about the bruises on Chuck's knuckles. Francis told her that he had taken a note on the matter. Then, according to Eileen, he cut short the conversation, saying that he was working on an important case but would call back. He never did, she says, and his secretary always told her that he was unavailable.

During the five-week investigation, Francis said he could not comment on an ongoing case and sidestepped questions from the press. He refused to return phone calls and ignored reporters when they cornered him. "I have no comment on any case where an investigation is pending," he told the Buffalo *Courier Express*.

Not only did Francis refuse to reveal what would ordinarily be the public's right to know, but he demanded that at least one other public official remain silent. He ordered Allegany County Coroner Dr. Irwin Felsen not to reveal the results of Chuck's toxicology tests. In fact, the coroner was not to tell the press whether he had even seen the results. "I think it's foolish, and I think you have the right to know," he told a *Courier*

Express reporter, "but I cannot tell you. What can I do?" More than a decade later Felsen says that, in his opinion, Francis acted like a "shithead."

About Francis, one of the state troopers at the scene of Chuck's death says, "I didn't care for the man." He adds that other troopers hated to work with the former district attorney because Francis had a reputation for prosecuting primarily sure-thing cases. On the other hand, Gary Horowitz, the former Alfred mayor, says he liked the DA.

On April 4, 1978, the district attorney announced that his investigation had ended. "I found no evidence of criminal activity or wrongdoing," he said. "No further action is contemplated." But he still refused comment on details, and he continues to maintain that silence.

The last five words of his statement—"No further action is contemplated"—crushed Eileen and her family. So did Don King's clipped statement to the press: "The case is closed."

On April 28, 1978, Francis wrote Eileen to apologize for his delay in contacting her and to advise her that he could not yet provide all the information she desired. He attributed the delay to pressing and urgent matters, saying that he had no help with day-to-day business, perhaps merely overlooking the assistant district attorney who worked with him. Moreover, he added, his secretary had been on vacation. He admitted being unable to give Chuck's case the time it deserved.

He did, finally, release the autopsy and toxicology reports. He also promised Eileen another letter explaining the circumstances of Chuck's death.

According to Eileen, that April 28 letter was her first and last written communication from Francis; she never received the complete and accurate report he promised—perhaps because she had complained to the press and a state legislator about the DA's handling of her son's case. Had she known that sometime later Francis's file on her son would disappear from his office, never to be seen again, Eileen might have been more insistent about holding the attorney to his agreement to provide her with specifics about Chuck's death.

After five months had passed, Eileen still refused to get rid of Chuck's possessions. She did give Jimmy Arnoux Chuck's favorite coat and some clamming wear but later learned he couldn't bring himself to wear his friend's things.

In the weeks and months following the funeral, Eileen lived by rote. She longed for her dead son as she never had longed for anyone or anything. She spent hours pouring over scrapbooks, placing loose photographs of her son under plastic sheets. She made enlargements of several favorites and rejoiced when someone gave her a picture from the Doane yearbook. Her wall display of photographs of a smiling Chuck gave friends such as Nanci Lunati the willies for years afterward. "Look at him looking at me," Lunati said during a 1989 visit to the Stevenses. "He's saying, 'You don't know what you're talking about, Nanci!'"

Eileen learned to subdue her talk of Chuck around her family. While she ached to talk about him, they ached to forget the pain of his loss. Silence enveloped them like new skin over burnt flesh.

One day she stood alone in her darkened garage on a mission. With no one to mock her or to sympathize, she stood barefoot in Chuck's work boots. She had decided to discard them. They were unsuitable even for donation to a thrift store as mildewed as they were. She knew that. Steve could wear them, but they hardly fit his suave image. Scott would have worn them to please her, but, though he would one day grow into a young moose, for now his feet floated in them. The boots had to go. But before they rattled the trash can, Eileen wanted to put her feet once more where Chuck's had been. They were so much a part of his blue-collar identity; he hated razzle-dazzle shoes. There, in the dark, with no one to see, she allowed herself another cry. This one actually brought relief. Few had. She crossed a threshold by tossing away a part of Chuck that no longer had meaning to anyone but her, and she knew it.

Getting rid of another talisman proved next to impossible. Chuck's pickup sat parked in the driveway save when Roy or Scott started it up to keep the battery from going dead. To Roy, a self-professed "bit of a fusspot," it was an oil-dripping nuisance. Eileen regarded it as an icon, a memorial-at-hand. That truck had been Chuck's pride, like his clamming boat. Sometimes even he hadn't known which came first in his heart. When Roy took the truck out on some errand or another, hearts stopped in the neighborhood. The Vollmers, Chuck's second family, got boulders in their throats. In time, this great big ghost ship filled with memories became an unwelcome sight to all but Eileen. Everything about it suggested Chuck, from the fat, expensive tires to the Alfred University parking sticker. The family could not even step outside without thinking of the youth who would never drive that truck again.

Roy brought up the subject of getting rid of the thing once or twice, but his wife's stricken look silenced him. Although she knew the truck pained everyone else, and certainly her at times, she would sooner have sold five quarts of her own blood than part with it. Eventually, though, even she understood that this bold blue reminder of better times had to go.

"You can sell the truck," she said one day to Roy. "But not to anyone local."

One weekend a buyer came to the house. Roy handled the transaction. Eileen kept a stoic face while her husband went outside to start the truck. She retreated to the couch in the downstairs den where Scott was sitting.

The two looked at each other, and dams broke. Eileen had tried to contain her sorrow in front of the children and, for the most part, had done well. But this time she couldn't hold back. She let go. That truck had been Chuck. He'd toiled hours to clean, scrape rust, sand, and paint. Something on it always seemed to break, so he poured the fruits of his clamming labor into the beloved gas-burner.

I wish I'd burned it rather than let someone else take it, Eileen thought while she cried.

Roy returned a few minutes later, pleased to be rid of a painful memory and an eyesore. He came bounding down the stairs with a wad of cash in his hand. Perhaps he expected praise. Instead, two pairs of hurt and unfriendly eyes bore into him. Roy stood there, a man of action rendered helpless, while Eileen and Scott held each other, sobbing as if Roy had sold Chuck's soul.

Eileen never saw the truck again. That was as she had wished. But sometimes on the expressway, when a bold blue truck appears in her mirror, she has to concede that in her heart of hearts she still longs for one more glimpse.

Selling Chuck's last treasure was equally painful. Scott Stevens tried hard to love clamming as his big brother had, but he and clamming mixed like oil and water. He lacked all natural aptitude for the job. And he certainly lacked Chuck's zest for the Great South Bay even in its cruelest seasons. When something went wrong with the old clamming boat, Scott felt frustrated and guilty over his frustration. The boat required time and maintenance that interfered with his own dreams and pursuits, such as playing baseball. Roy again said little to Eileen. He continued to pay for new fiberglassing and fixing sprung leaks, as well as for all the required engine maintenance. Twice the boat sank, once when Scott's girlfriend was with him. The two scared, embarrassed kids, neither a good swimmer, had to be rescued from the strong current.

That episode frightened Eileen and mortified Scott. But it took yet another incident to make her realize that she was honoring her dead son at the expense of her live one. One day she nagged Scott until he agreed to take her for a boat ride. The water was peaceful, but passing clamboats and a ferry kept disturbing Eileen's thoughts. Each time a boat passed, its skipper would ring a bell or blow a horn and wave. "This is ridiculous," Eileen complained. "Why do they do that?"

Scott's lip quivered. "Oh, Mom," he said. "They know this is Chuck's boat. They're saluting him."

Even before the boat returned to shore, Eileen knew that it had to go. Nonetheless, when the moon is right or the day sunny, she still visits the bay. The roll of the waves and the sharp salt smell stir something primeval in Eileen, as they had in her seafarer son.

As Chuck's things vanished, so did the hope that anyone from Allegany County was going to take a personal interest in his family. The waiting irritated Eileen. Results of the investigation Don King had said would be forthcoming were never published. A part of Eileen had wanted to confront King at their initial meeting, but something about the woman she was then stopped her. Academic titles would never stop her again, she vowed. She would evaluate the person, not the pedigree. "I'm sorry,

Chuck," she wrote in a journal entry. She felt that she had let him down by not knowing how to conduct her own probe.

Over time Eileen did her homework on hazing. She paid for a New York *Times* computer search on fraternity hazing and was shocked when it uncovered forty-three items. She would have been even more depressed had she had the research expertise to look up hazing incidents under other headings, deaths caused by freshmen versus sophomore class scraps, initiation injuries not termed hazings, and the wide variety of other hazing abuses practiced in society from grade school to the Masons. She read what she could on fraternities and saw all the movies she could locate. In time, when her pounding heart could take it, she saw *Animal House,* the release of which coincided with an alarming rise in the number of fraternity tragedies in 1979 and 1980. She saw the movie only because so many reporters had asked her about it. She found nothing redeeming in the Hollywood, fast-buck portrayal of fraternity life inspired by writer Chris Miller's own fraternity days at Dartmouth — experiences that he would continue to milk as late as 1989 in sensational pieces for *Playboy.* A line in the movie chilled her. "You fucked up," says Otter, a character played by actor Tim Matheson. "You trusted us."

An author's representative sent her a copy of a horrid novel about a father who gains bloody revenge against a fraternity that has killed his son in a hazing incident, as well as against an insensitive college dean who gets bumped off in a grisly, climactic scene. The writer wanted her to endorse the book. The letter said that the author, David R. Slavitt, had been inspired to write *Cold Comfort* in part by Eileen's work. The implications disturbed Eileen, who felt that the revenge depicted in the novel was more despicable than the hazing death itself. Yes, when she first heard of Chuck's death, she remarked to Scott and a handful of close friends that she ought to blow the whole fraternity house up. But she would no more have done that than blow up her son's grave. She ignored letters from young men offering to join fraternities in order to expose their hazing practices. In her mind, no amount of good could justify such deception.

Three weeks after Chuck's death, Eileen returned to her job at Town Squire, but her mind was on correspondence, not corduroys. One day a neighbor phoned Eileen at the store to ask her if she knew that Suzanne was going to the cemetery from the school bus every day. She drove there in the rain the next day, and, sure enough, her daughter was sobbing over her brother's grave.

"I need to be home," said Eileen, and she bid her boss goodbye.

Having quit, she felt free. She could spend time with her family yet still perform the tasks required by her fight against hazing. Until she quit, and occasionally even afterwards, there was strife in the Stevens household. Five people under one roof had a private hell in common, but each reacted differently.

* * *

By August 1978 Eileen knew that she wanted to found an organization. Rather than fight to close down the fraternities, she decided that her best chance to save other young men was to work within the fraternity system. Her message was simple and self-explanatory. "I am anti-hazing," she said over and over, "not anti-fraternity." She also began defining hazing as "a preconditioned activity to join an organization," thereby eliminating long and cumbersome definitions except when the media, legislators, and administrators asked for specifics.

The organization seemed even more real once it had a name. Doreen Stenzel was adamant. "C.H.U.C.K. has to be its name," she insisted.

"But what do the letters stand for?" Eileen wanted to know.

Doreen couldn't be bothered with details. She told Eileen something would come to mind. A longtime friend of Eileen's, Dianne Donaudy, came up with the organization's incorporated name: C.H.U.C.K. — Committee Halting Useless College Killings. After a few months, Eileen decided that Committee to Halt Useless College Killings had a better sound to it. She continued to capitalize the word CHUCK to distinguish the organization from her son, but she eliminated the periods in the acronym.

On August 6, 1978, Eileen would write in her on-again, off-again journal that expenses for CHUCK "are unbelievable." Like Thoreau at Walden Pond, she listed them:

typewriter	$179
postage	90
stamp (address)	10
stationery	35
calls	84
stamps	36
supplies	118
paper	21.

The only money she had to finance the organization was the refund of Chuck's tuition from Alfred. The money for postage came from dutiful Roy and from her younger brother Michael, who gave her a roll of stamps weekly. A high-school girl used the typewriter for forms and letters for CHUCK. Eileen pounded pavement, not keys.

Without a home office, Eileen worked at her dining room table. There she nested, blurry-eyed and fuzz-mouthed from lack of sleep. Many of her letters dropped into a black hole. She wrote all the national fraternities and received no responses whatsoever. They ignored her. It took her three months, but she wrote at least one letter to every New York senator and state representative, getting polite responses, at least, from many of them. She sent letters to many college presidents and news bureaus, hoping to verify hazing deaths that reached her attention. A little more than one-third responded.

Many of the letters she received from administrators showed her that she knew more about hazing deaths at their institutions than they did. "We have not had a hazing death in the history of the fraternal system," wrote Albert S. Miles, a University of Alabama vice president for student affairs, in 1979. He was apparently unaware that Glenn Kersh died there in 1923, following a fraternity initiation.

Eileen continued to make supper for her family, but her mind was always racing, eager to finish a letter or pursue a new tack to get the attention of congressmen. She knew she wasn't giving Roy and the children the attention they were used to, but she felt they had to understand her compulsion. To a point they did, but this hard-driving stranger in their midst sometimes overwhelmed them, too.

Eileen's success has astounded some, but Greg Belanger says that he should have realized that she had always had something that made people respond to her. "She always had a strength in her that was attractive to young males like me," he says. "The rest of us felt you could always talk to her about a girl problem or something like that. She just took that strength and made it public."

Big, quiet Billy Vollmer supported her, too. "I was on Eileen's side because I didn't want to see it happen to anybody else," he says. "He was my best friend. I didn't want to see it happen to somebody's else's best friend. But I don't think she ever dreamed of getting into it with the force that she did."

When the organization was only a few months old, the Stevens family was embarrassed by Eileen's notoriety and dropped hints that she needed to come back to her senses. Later, when thousands of letters sat in mailbags in her makeshift office, her loved ones were baffled by how a homemaker at her dining room table could have touched such a national nerve. Certainly, Don King had never envisioned such a crusade when he sat in his office the day after Chuck's death, trying to talk to Roy and avoiding Eileen's eyes. A sportsman like King should have known that underestimating an opponent can be deadly.

Eileen's mind, once so stagnant that she hardly knew how to write Chuck a zippy letter, bristled with ideas and alternatives. Each morning she awoke filled with purpose. What congressmen should she write today? What radio or television show might do a small segment on her organization? She couldn't type the way her sister Mary could—her hunting and pecking brought giggles from the family—but she could handwrite one helluva letter. Chuck's death had tapped a creative well. Words poured out. Dozens of letters soon turned into hundreds, eventually thousands, most written in her neat, crowded, distinctive script. Years after beginning CHUCK, she attributes part of her success to the personal touch her letters imparted. She rarely made grammatical mistakes and had even fewer spelling errors. When Chuck was alive, she teased him about his spelling, including his bugaboo, the word *course,* which he consistently spelled with two *c*'s and no *s.*

Over the years she received hundreds of letters from concerned parents, nearly all supportive. Several came from mothers of former Alfred students. One wrote to complain about the treatment of her son Bill, a former Alfred football player, when he was having difficulties in school. "On numerous times I called student affairs and whoever I could," said the Connecticut letter writer. "I found everyone 'cold' and 'standoffish.' I got the feeling that they did not want me to be concerned. . . . The whole time I spoke with everyone there, I got the feeling no one really cares up there. Now we are so happy he left." The mother of an Alfred sorority president, class of 1974, praised Eileen for her work, saying "You are approaching a very heartrending problem in a sensible, logical manner." A former Fairport, New York, resident wrote from Florida with another Alfred fraternity horror story from the 1960s. "We were awakened [at] four A.M. with a phone call from the hospital," wrote a parent. Her seventeen-year-old son Terry had had to drink shots, one purchased by each member of a fraternity she didn't name. "Terry was lucky," she wrote.

Eileen never knew what she ate or drank anymore. Roy was worried. She saw it in his face. But he kept quiet for the most part, his instincts telling him that Eileen's work was the only way he could keep a second member of his family from being destroyed. She couldn't mend her broken heart, he knew. But she could strengthen the pieces by helping others who needed her strength.

One by one, friends and relatives dropped out of the original CHUCK organization. There was only Eileen. The long hours, the workload, and the grimness of the subject drove them away. Unlike Mothers Against Drunk Driving (MADD), CHUCK has never attracted thousands of members. It was and is essentially a one-woman organization. Eileen, never one to delegate well, became the organization's chief executive officer, secretary, public relations person, and file clerk. Several times in the early going she let the mother of a victim talk her into opening a chapter, but the move was always a disaster. Most mothers of broken pledges could not accept Eileen's basic premise. She wanted to change the attitudes of fraternities and sororities; they wanted to abolish Greeks or punish them.

One mother from the Midwest showed up at a fraternity's national conference. She identified herself as a representative from CHUCK and insisted that the moderator let her speak. She even phoned the staff at *60 Minutes,* again saying she was from CHUCK and insisting that she needed to talk to Mike Wallace. Fortunately, for Eileen, the woman never got through to him. After a final debacle in which the woman wrote insulting and possibly slanderous letters to some university administrators on CHUCK stationery, Eileen asked her to resign. "What you do in your state is your business," she said to her. "When you use my organization's name, it's my business."

Since that episode, she has crusaded alone although many people who support her work are loosely associated with CHUCK. The organization has no dues, meetings, or committees. If you are opposed to hazing and want to be a member, you are. Your name goes into Eileen's bursting-at-the-seams address book, not into a computer's memory.

"Hazing has been permitted and insufficiently punished by collegiate authorities far too long," an anonymous "American Mother" wrote the New York *Times* on November 22, 1903. Her letter could have been written by Eileen Stevens three-quarters of a century later. Nothing had changed in all that time. "By what right shall the student or company of students so maltreat one of his comrades that insanity or lifelong disfigurement or even death shall follow and suffer at most expulsion from college? . . . Public spirit should rise and protest vigorously against the continuance of this practice. Let the full penalty of the law follow murder or assault or misdemeanor in the ranks of the college as it does in civic life; and hazing—often a misnomer for cruelty—will become but a hideous memory."

The mother's closing exhortation is poignant as the nineties give way to the twenty-first century. "Let this twentieth century witness the end of this barbarity," she wrote.

During the nineteenth and twentieth centuries, at least a half-dozen parents have vowed to fight hazing by fraternities or—prior to the 1920s—by college upperclassmen determined to put lowly freshmen in their places. None of them have known the odds they faced.

They didn't know that the custom is rooted in American culture. They didn't know that many faculty members and administrators once considered hazing a good way to discipline freshmen. Besides, it gave the frosh a natural enemy in the sophomore class; that lessened the chances that the students would harass the faculty as they did routinely at such institutions as the University of Virginia in the 1800s. In 1845, for example, the school had a major riot. Students—many on horseback and armed with pistols—shattered glass, battered doors, and frightened the citizens.

Another thing parents hadn't counted on was that hazing and other barbaric customs are often defended as good, clean fun by those who think such "traditions" build school spirit. One of the most addlebrained traditions occurred at the Colorado School of Mines in Golden. On "Sneak Day," costumed seniors rounded up professors and categorized them from "Super-Stinker" to "Fragrant," temporarily incarcerating them in a mock jail labeled "Trash." The Colorado professors—apparently willingly—were squirted with beer, splattered with eggs, endured mock hangings, and were covered with fire extinguisher foam. *Life* covered the outrageous custom in 1949.

Before Eileen, the best-known crusader against hazing was a Mrs. George Steinmetz, who drew headlines for a short while in Chicago and Indianapolis in 1929. Steinmetz charged that Delta Chi's "rough initiation"—the era's equivalent of hazing—had contributed to the death of her son George, an Indiana University student, from lung disease. The school, which already had been trying to ban rough initiations, and the fraternity both supported Steinmetz in her fight. Perhaps believing that her job was over, she promptly vanished from public view.

Eileen never discovered Steinmetz or any of the other historical battles by parents to outlaw hazing. She thought her idea was original. She is the first mother to achieve ongoing national success in highlighting the nasty practice. Without guidance, without even a long-term plan, she put on her flashing red beacon and tore down the highway. Those in her way had to pull over or lock bumpers.

9

Thirty miles from Reno, under a star-drilled desert sky, a lone pickup truck ground to a halt alongside the Pyramid Lake highway. Three young men slid out of the cab and ambled to the back of the truck. All wore black hats adorned with a yellow patch that depicted a setting sun. The three grinned at the sight on the truck bed. Five youths, their clothing flecked with vomit, were sprawled across the floor like cordwood.

The trio ordered them to get out. Four struggled to comply, easing down from the tailgate to the road. But one remained motionless, a dark-haired giant with a thick Fu Manchu mustache. The three youths with hats were amused and clambered aboard to wake him. Laughing, they shook him, believing he had passed out.

Finally, one of them tore open the limp young man's coat and put an ear to his chest. The laughter ceased. They heard the whistling wind bending back the sagebrush.

The dead youth was John Davies, a twenty-three-year-old University of Nevada-Reno football player. His death on October 12, 1975, concluded a three-day drinking spree required for admission into a suspended but still active campus organization called the Sundowner Club. In sixty-five hours, Davies and four other pledges were forced to consume eighteen quarts of hard liquor, sixteen gallons of wine, and vast quantities of beer. Photographs taken by Edd Lockwood, a freelance photographer and member of the school yearbook staff, show a Sundowner pouring alcohol into the mouth of inebriated initiates. The setting? A lot across from the campus.

When Davies's body simply gave out from what the coroner termed "an acute alcoholic overdose," his blood alcohol count was .42. A second pledge suffered complete respiratory arrest, ceased breathing, and was kept alive with specialized hospital equipment. Had he not made it to Reno, he too would have died. A grand jury investigating the case determined that the five pledges had been pummeled, ridiculed, cursed, and intimidated "by approximately ten of the [thirty] Sundowner members . . . with the apparent encouragement of the membership." All five had been forced to consume flaming glasses of Everclear, a 190-proof grain alcohol. One, unable to swallow the substance properly, had suffered chest burns.

Nonetheless, the Washoe County grand jury "in a courage-lacking rationalization," according to the Reno *Evening Gazette,* "failed to properly discharge its duty by taking no concrete action." The grand jury let the Sundowners off the hook because it believed that Davies, in effect, had himself to blame, saying "if an initiate had made a decision to stop drinking at this point in the initiation rites . . . he probably would have been allowed to do so." The *Evening Gazette* further criticized the grand jury, saying it was unlikely "those under the brutal coercion would be of a mind to withdraw, if, in fact, with that quantity of alcohol being consumed one can even talk in terms of rational or mindful thinking."

Also drawing the paper's scorn was the district attorney, Larry Hicks, who agreed with the grand jury and sealed the case as tight as Davies's coffin. "A district attorney, proving no courageous leadership, abdicates," said an editorial. The story inflamed the campus, particularly after Lockwood sold one-time photo rights to Nevada-Reno yearbook editor Bob Horn, who printed the photographer's disturbing images despite bitter opposition from the school's publications board. Horn printed them without comment, allowing yearbook readers to make up their own minds about what had transpired. He said that the photographs were not objectionable in themselves; readers had the option of reacting as they saw fit.

Some years after Davies's death, Eileen Stevens traveled to Reno to speak at a fraternity conference. There she met Billie Davies, John's mother, who eventually lost a wrongful death suit. Their meeting had tremendous significance for Eileen. Here, at last, was a fellow traveler, someone who knew her torment. Davies shared with her the agonies that she, her husband, and her daughter had felt. After their son's death, her husband had sat for hours, looking off at nothing in particular. The story of his grief reminded Eileen of how hard Charles W. Stenzel, Chuck's granddad, had mourned.

Billie Davies was the first of many grieving parents Eileen was destined to come into contact with. The young men lost in fraternity initiation deaths and alcohol-related deaths, as well as the young women killed in sorority escapades (none a clearcut case of hazing, despite rumors), forged a grim bond among these parents. Their children had become a metaphorical Lost Chapter. Eileen realizes how valuable a release her crusade has been for these people, providing, among other things, a means for turning bitterness into constructive action.

Everywhere she traveled, year after year, the details were different, yet the story was the same. Always another family shattered, another school trying to pretend that hazing deaths were accidents, another district attorney or grand jury unwilling to put away nice-looking young men with futures their victims would never enjoy.

She met Joan Cerra, a feisty woman from Eagle River, Wisconsin, whose son Rick—a short but powerful wrestler—had died in 1981 while pledging FEX, a fraternity at the University of Wisconsin-Superior. A reporter from the Washington *Post* gave Cerra Eileen's phone number. Her son collapsed while performing strenuous calisthenics required by the membership. Actives forced him to wear heavy winter clothing from boots to ski mask despite temperatures in the high forties. Once he collapsed, instead of taking him directly to a hospital where he had a chance of being saved, the members took him back to their headquarters, "hoping he'd come out of it," says Cerra. His body temperature reached 111, destroying major organs. Members argued that they were merely following a tradition that had been around since 1919, but those who testified under oath knew so little about their fraternity's history that they couldn't say with certainty what FEX stood for.

Cerra had already adopted the CHUCK philosophy. "It's not my idea and it's not Eileen's to do away with fraternities," she says. "The original conception is a wonderful idea if they just did not have this aspect of hazing with them."

Fraternity spokesmen always blame the press for sensationalizing hazing deaths. But as Eileen heard story after story from the lips of parents, she began to see that these incidents were indeed sensational. On the telephone she talked with Dorothy Flowers, a New Jersey mother whose son William became a victim in a 1974 Zeta Beta Tau initiation at Monmouth College. William had to dig a six-foot grave alongside the Atlantic Ocean then lie in it. It collapsed. He smothered before his brothers and a passerby could save him. "I was blown away by her tragedy," Eileen says. "Her son's death had been so awful."

Another grieving family hailed from eastern South Carolina, an area of sweet-scented pines noted for weekend barbeque huts and porch swings. One morning Maisie Ballou arrived at her job at a local bank only to be whisked inside a van by several concerned bank officers and fellow workers. While her mind raced with a thousand awful possibilities, she endured the short drive to her house. Her husband, Ray, was waiting for her in the driveway. The bad news was about the younger of their two sons, a handsome boy with dark features.

"Barry's gone," he said quietly.

His wife went crazy. She has some recollection of tearing her lawn out by the roots. Later she and her husband learned that Barry, like Chuck Stenzel, died from an alcohol overdose. The school was the University of South Carolina; the fraternity, Sigma Nu. The accident happened on campus, in a dormitory-like building on Fraternity Row, a short walk from the school infirmary.

Following the incident, Eileen and the Ballous communicated many, many times by phone and letter. But, like most parents of Lost Chapter members, Ray and Maisie Ballou have never met Eileen in person. Nonetheless, they consider her "family."

Nearly all fraternity deaths have a pattern. At first everyone at the school and offending organization expresses sorrow and regrets. But soon afterward the tendency is to trivialize the death or to blame it on the victim. Klan's Scott Sullivan believes it is natural for those who participated in fraternity deaths to do some rationalizing to maintain their sanity and sense of self-worth.

In the months after Chuck's death, Eileen experienced anger and disbelief when some students tried, in her opinion, to make light of her son's death. An Alfred source sent her an editorial that appeared in the

Fiat Lux on October 16, 1978. The campus paper chided her for "placing blame where it is unwarranted" on Alfred University and Klan Alpine. "There is . . . such a thing as misdirected anger," the paper said. "It is respectfully suggested that Mrs. Stevens focus more closely on the society which formed a generation's behavior, rather than on the small fragment of that society known as Alfred. Alfred is comparable to any university in its social orientation. It should not be made to pay for an act of chance."

For a time, until a lawsuit was imminent, Don King continued to present Alfred University's view of the incident to the press. But he refused to discuss Klan Alpine's involvement in prior misdoings with reporter Barbara Kreisler of the Suffolk County *News,* saying that he didn't "think it is in the best interest of the fraternity or the college to go into a discussion of their previous behavior." He told Kreisler that Alfred did not allow hazings and that the assumption that it did was incorrect.

King denies that he could have foreseen a tragedy on Alfred's Tapping Night. "We assume that induction ceremonies aren't going to be harmful to anyone," he insists. "I'm not sure what was involved in the Klan's induction ceremonies in the past because they are secretive."

The more Eileen learned about hazing, the more disturbed she became about the fraternity system's downplaying of mind games. "It's only mental hazing," she was told again and again—by fraternity alumni and leaders as well as undergraduates. She wished these misinformed advocates of "mental hazing" could meet some of the disturbed young men and women who had contacted her after seeing articles on CHUCK. These pledges had been truly broken. They had the uneasy, ready-to-retreat look of kicked or tortured puppies. Some cried uncontrollably when they talked about their ordeals; afterwards they experienced shame and anger because they perceived their tears to be signs of weakness. One frequent caller stuttered; others harbored killing anger. *Only mental, indeed* Eileen would snap whenever someone gave her the standard line.

Over the years, Eileen has collected examples of "mental hazing" to use in her talks. For her these mind games include sleep deprivation, lineups in which pledges are shouted at or asked unanswerable questions, pseudo-ceremonies in which pledges are falsely told they have been black-balled or accepted as members, interrogation sessions in which pledges are made to reveal their sexual histories and other intimacies, lying to pledges to humiliate or confuse them, isolation tactics, ostracization, and labeling pledges with demeaning personal nicknames.

According to the Chicago *Tribune,* blindfolded pledges at Miami University of Ohio had to volunteer a testicle while a whirring chainsaw was held close to their bodies to intimidate them. Syracuse University pledges traveled their campus with dead fish tied around their necks. Other Syracuse pledges leaped onto a four-inch "nail" sticking out of a board. The nail turned out to be aluminum foil. During the late seventies Klan Alpine had pledges jump into a pile of "broken glass," which was really only corn flakes.

One of the earliest recorded episodes of mental hazing occurred at Brown University in 1922. "Now upperclassmen are substituting mental torture by methods learned in psychological courses instead of by the time-honored custom of paddling," said a New York *Times* front-page article. "Two of the leading fraternities have adopted the new system and are pronouncing their work good. Others are expected to follow, as the results are declared to leave the initiated in a much more tractable state of mind and imbued with a 'proper sense of his unworthiness.'"

Eileen came to know every inch of the New York State Capitol. An imposing structure that would be more at home in Chartres than in Albany, this white, domeless building towers over the Hudson River like a beached white sturgeon. Architecturally, it is a mongrel of many influences, but Eileen finds it a beautiful, although intimidating, shrine.

Her friend Dianne Donaudy, who has a better-than-average grasp of how a bill is passed, was an important ally for Eileen. Again and again, while the legislature was in session, Eileen and Donaudy drove to Albany. Her ebullient nature made Eileen a star lobbyist. She converted her speech to college students to a thirty-second pitch given over and over again. After these intense outings in Albany, spent scurrying along the Capitol's august halls and stairs like a lab mouse in an experiment, Eileen returned to Sayville emotionally drained and fatigued.

At first she fought only against dangerous hazing practices. But she grew more intolerant of all hazing after coming to understand that many fatalities and injuries are the consequence of activities that start as so-called good, clean fun. To ask hazers to draw their own lines is foolish and unrealistic. She came to see that all hazing is inherently wrong. No rationalization can justify it.

Legislator Paul Harenberg and his assistant John Longo were impressed with her grasp of how to go about changing the law. Eileen was taking on an entrenched establishment — lawyers and district attorneys and educators — and had the unenviable goal of persuading them that the criminal code trivialized the deaths of hazing victims.

Eileen trusted Harenberg, a former teacher at Bayport High School in Long Island, who was the one legislator to respond to that squadron of letters she and the original CHUCK crew had mailed. His image was that of a reformer. He won as a Democrat by fewer than four hundred votes in a heavily Republican district in 1974, the Watergate era. He and Longo — his former student — looked for injustices that they could right rather than polls that could tell them how to vote to please the public. Longo was a stocky young man, not much older than Chuck would have been had he lived, and he looked as if he might be more comfortable in a country-western bar than in the state capital.

Longo was impressed with Eileen's drive and the support she had from Roy. "He was a saint," says Longo. "He was so incredibly patient. . . . But she impressed me more. She went from being a housewife to a national figure, almost overnight. . . . Any lesser person, it would have gone the other way. But she had the stamina to tell her story, and then stop, and then talk about the broader implications of it. She didn't continue to dwell on me, me, me, me. . . . Her story became, as time went on, a smaller part of it. . . . She would talk about the bigger problem. . . . I saw her grow from the mother who was grieving to the national figure who could talk about the issue, and talk about what's being done, and why it should be done."

In Longo's mind Eileen's strongest virtues were her persistence and willingness to learn. He and Harenberg perceived that this enthusiastic housewife's ability to convey the Big Picture made her the best lobbyist available for the anti-hazing cause. Harenberg helped raise the New York legislature's awareness of the problem, but when it came time to solicit sponsors for the anti-hazing bill, he and Eileen both contacted legislators in person, by phone, and by mail to seek or clinch support. "Eileen's lasting tribute is her ability to grow as a spokesperson for what wasn't at that time a very popular opinion," says Longo. "Fraternity members often wind up in high places." And they are unafraid to use their power and authority to protect their own. In Georgia, for example, a Democrat from Decatur named Frank Redding, Jr., once unsuccessfully proposed an amendment in the state legislature that would exclude his fraternity, Kappa Alpha Psi, from an anti-hazing bill.

One of those high places was the New York District Attorneys Association. "While recognizing the serious adverse consequences that can befall those who are the subject of 'hazing,' we are constrained to recommend disapproval of this bill," said its representative. Many other groups either opposed the bill or said they had no interest in it. Deputy attorney general Charles J. Hynes wrote a letter to discourage passage. "I do not see any utility in this bill, except perhaps as a warning to students, a job best left to school officials," said Hynes. He was not alone in his opinion. "We are not aware that, other than the incident that motivated this bill, hazing is so prevalent a problem as to require the rather draconian punishments here prescribed," wrote Robert M. Schlanger, New York Division of Criminal Justice Services. "It should be remembered that basically it is college students who would be prosecuted thereunder—hardly a group generally noted for its criminal proclivities. On the whole, we believe that this bill is an overreaction to an unfortunate accident arising from puerile behavior."

On CHUCK's side, activist Nancy Coughlan helped rouse the New York State Congress of Parents and Teachers to back the bill. Other support came from administrators from twenty-three colleges who welcomed the bill. "I am in full accord and support your endeavor," wrote David H. Huntington, the president of SUNY College of Technology at Alfred. "Our first commitment, like yours, must be the protection of life," said Seldon M. Kruger, the acting president of SUNY Agricultural and Technical College at Delhi. "Cornell University is firmly against hazing in any form," wrote President Frank H. T. Rhodes. "It is demeaning to the individual and has a detrimental effect on the reputations of the fraternity and sorority systems."

Eileen solicited friends and acquaintances to hit the streets seeking signatures in support of the legislation. A nun from Queens who had known Chuck as a tyke sent a package stuffed with signatures. "I taught Chuck and I loved him," she said in a note.

Co-sponsoring the hazing bill with Harenberg was Caesar Trunzo, a Republican from Bayshore. Not only did he live down the street from the sister of Thomas Fitzgerald, a young man who was slain with a knife blade during a senseless ritual involving a St. John's ROTC club called the Pershing Rifles, but he himself had been physically initiated into the Knights of Columbus. Trunzo, however, was typical of many anti-hazing proponents. He thought that others who hazed were wrong, but at the time he saw his own experiences as mere participation in a harmless initiation. Trunzo was in favor of the law to control hazing, not eliminate it; he was one of many lawmakers who argued that hazing deaths could be prevented by common sense measures. "Hazing is as old as apple pie, but is completely uncontrolled," he told one reporter. "The thing that is most disturbing about the two cases [Fitzgerald and Stenzel] is that nothing is coming out of them. The ROTC is content to let it wash away, and Alfred University seems to be shoving the whole matter under the rug."

Many colleges chose to ignore the anti-hazing bill, fearing government intervention in academic matters, a common misgiving among college administrators. "Nothing [is] so fatal to inspiration as excessive legislation," said a Harvard lecturer on the topic of university reform in 1866. "It creates two parties, the governors and the governed, with efforts and interests mutually opposed; the governors seeking to establish an artificial order, the governed bent on maintaining their natural liberty."

Many Alfred University adminstrators and students were skeptical that the Harenberg legislation would accomplish what Eileen hoped. The administration spoke out against hazing but refused to support the bill. A Lambda Chi on campus told the *Fiat Lux* that the law "wouldn't curtail activity, just cool it down for a little while." Eileen knew that the opposition had some justification for its conclusions. She knew that passing a law wouldn't stop hazing deaths any more than drunk driving regulations had halted drinkers from slaughtering innocents on highways. But it was a deterrent, she insisted, and it gave administrators and national fraternity executives something tangible to hold over the heads of offenders.

No bill ever comes to fruition without crises and compromises, and Harenberg's was no exception. On one occasion, a tough but respected legislator named Dominick DiCarlo tore into the legislation like a hungry shark. He not only criticized the bill, he stomped it, kicked it, spat on it, and concluded that it wouldn't serve its purpose. Harenberg was stunned when DiCarlo finished his diatribe. He gestured to Eileen. "Any words?" he said.

Eileen stood up and took a breath. She smiled at DiCarlo. "Thank you for your expert judgment," she said. "Now will you help us fix it?"

The legislator was stunned. But miracle of miracles, he said he would. Eileen didn't have time to gloat, however. There were other corridors to walk, more stairs to climb, many more DiCarlos to win over. DiCarlo later told *Newsday* that Eileen had been a dogged lobbyist. "She's gone about it in an eminently fair way," he said. "She's doing it objectively, not emotionally."

On September 29, 1978, Harenberg wrote George Francis a curt letter, asking why the "initiation rite" wasn't prosecuted under 240.25(4) of the New York Penal Law. The state lacked a strong, specific anti-hazing law. But under this statute any person in an "institution of learning" could be found guilty of harassment for hazing. Harenberg requested an immediate reply "so that other lives need not be lost as a result of further hazings."

Francis received the letter but failed to reply. On December 18, 1978, Harenberg wrote a highly accusatory letter to Governor Hugh Carey. Alfred University was the area's largest employer and in 1979 contributed twenty million dollars to a thirty-mile geographic area surrounding Alfred, according to the *Fiat Lux*. Harenberg wanted assurance that the district attorney's refusal to charge Klan Alpine with at least a violation—which would have given Eileen valuable information for her civil suit—was devoid of political motivation. The assemblyman's letter read in part:

> Repeated calls to Mr. Francis from Mrs. Stevens, her lawyer, and from members of the press went unanswered. It appeared that Mr. Francis, for whatever reason, was unwilling to discuss the outcome of his investigation—if there was an investigation.
>
> It appears to me that the Allegany County District Attorney is attempting to cover-up or conceal from the public the full story of the events of February 24. Clearly the school wishes to avoid negative publicity for itself, but the District Attorney is not paid by the public to serve the University. Their "image" should not stand in the way of a full investigation into Chuck Stenzel's death, which clearly is essential to the public interest.
>
> There are many questions still left unanswered. For example: Why did the local pathologist term this death "manslaughter"? How did the deceased get bruises on his head, hands and knees? What were the findings of the secret "investigations" by the District Attorney and the University administration? Why were no charges for hazing [Penal Law 240.25(4)] brought against the students involved?
>
> The District Attorney, in response to a subpoena issued on behalf of Mrs. Stevens, now says that he will not respond to any inquiries into the case, because it is "under investigation" by his office. We seriously doubt that. It is more and more clear

that this is nothing but a legal maneuver designed to conceal the truth and protect the University's reputation. I am convinced that a legitimate investigation into Chuck's death will not result if left to the authority of the local District Attorney. The people of New York State deserve and require a higher standard of justice than is obtainable through that local office. I ask therefore that you call upon the State Commission of Investigation, or whatever agency you deem appropriate, [to] assist us in obtaining a credible and thorough investigation.

In November 1978 Alfred University received notice that it had received an eighteen-hundred-dollar grant for an alcohol-education program. That same fall Richard Rose announced that he would no longer continue as president after January 1, 1979. The beleaguered administrator said he planned to move upstate to accept the presidency of Rochester Institute of Technology, a respected technical college. He said that he was leaving because he no longer enjoyed the trust of the shell-shocked faculty after the controversial axing of twenty-two full-time employees. Another factor, he admitted, was flak he had taken following the Chuck Stenzel "hazing." Its report on Rose's announcement is one of the few times that the *Fiat Lux* referred to the incident by that term. Rose said that Eileen Stevens's campaign had brought "negative publicity" to Alfred. "The number of Long Island freshmen has fallen off considerably," he added. "I think the parents of prospective students reacted very strongly to what happened." Rose departed for Rochester, leaving behind his school-owned Checker Marathon and a parting shot: "Alfred is a far better school than is recognized in Alfred." The university promptly ordered the Checker, a symbol of Rose's troubled presidency, auctioned for charity.

"I shall never forget 1978," Eileen wrote in her diary on January 1, 1979, "a year of sorrow and pain as I've never known." Nineteen seventy-eight changed her life. She couldn't know on that New Year's Day that 1979 would shape its future.

Eileen and Roy finally began going out again. When the Vollmers invited them over to see home movies of Chuck and Billy, they went eagerly. But the movies froze them. It was too painful to watch young Chuck swimming, playing in the water, cavorting with Billy. Roy and Eileen excused themselves early and walked the half-block home in mutual silence.

More and more Eileen used her diaries to unload. One member of her family had chastized her, saying she was "overdoing" her grief. "Not many want to hear me lately," she wrote. "I can't help it. I have to express myself and those who don't understand just bug me. I want to scream and say, 'What if it were your son?'" At the same time, she lacked sympathy when friends complained about minor things. She wished that she could give them her perspective for one minute.

Early in 1979 *People* magazine scheduled a story on Eileen. An inter-viewer came by the house to ask questions and seemed sympathetic. "Great," Eileen wrote in her diary. "Let 'em rot," one of the few hostile comments about Alfred to be found in her personal papers.

People's photographer visited. Eileen cut her hair for the occasion and was relieved that Roy liked it. The magazine wanted to photograph Eileen by Chuck's grave. She resisted. The cemetery was her private place to grieve. The idea was morbid. The photographer insisted, and in the end she went along on a rainy, gloomy day. She convinced herself that there was nothing wrong with readers seeing a headstone and realizing a young man has died needlessly. Nonetheless, she agonized over the photographs, terrified that the magazine's readers might think her sleazy or tasteless. "It was very draining and hard on all of us, especially the kids," she wrote in her diary. "Oh, I hope it's OK. I hope we've done the right thing. I pray so." The photographer left Eileen with the names of some media contacts. She spent that evening writing to them.

Steven Stevens departed for college in Florida. After the *People* inter-view, he quietly but firmly rebelled. He could no longer be part of a public campaign. From then on, reporters made the sensitive young man fly off like an owl caught in daylight. He took another part of Eileen's heart when he departed. "I let him down," she told her journal. "His mother was forever changed." She wished the Alfred administration and Klan

Alpine could see the domino effect that Chuck's death had had on her once-happy family.

Eileen hated the snows of late January and February, hated the approach of February 24. She could not know—in fact, would have thought it unfathomable—that several Klan members too grew uneasy as that date drew near and would for years to come. "Snow makes me sad," Eileen told her diary. "It has become synonymous with Chuck." No sooner had Richard Rose settled into a routine at RIT than he demonstrated that he would no longer tolerate fraternity abuses. He reacted swiftly after the Theta Xi fraternity there incurred thirteen hundred dollars' worth of damage at a Valentine's party at the Americana Hotel in downtown Rochester. RIT booted the fraternity off campus for several years for showing, according to a school announcement, "a pattern of behavior problems and character out of keeping with the standards of student life at the institute."

In January Eileen received an invitation from the producers of Phil Donahue's talk show. She accepted but feared that she would be a basket case. No one wants to look foolish on national television. Naturally she was intimidated.

To present a balanced program, the show's producer had also phoned Don King. When King demurred, Donahue himself picked up the phone and tried to persuade the dean to present Alfred's side of the controversy. King says that Donahue spent fifteen minutes on the phone, but he turned him down. He had received word from the Stevens's attorney of a summons, his notification of a pending lawsuit, and Alfred's lawyers advised him not to appear. Once again Alfred University violated the Gary Horowitz rule of good PR. Nobody, but nobody, was telling anything.

In the green room at the *Donahue* taping, Eileen huddled with Dorothy Flowers, the woman whose son had perished in a sandy grave. Flowers recalls that her emotions were ready to crack. "I told Donahue that I would cry, and I know he didn't want me to cry," she says. "It was very difficult, very."

Flowers was so frightened of strangling on tears that she failed to observe that Eileen was also terrified. "Eileen was well prepared," she remembers.

Eileen says that her concern for her fellow panelist calmed her. Flowers, even in 1990, cannot discuss her boy's death without losing her composure. "I guess I just can't talk about it," she admits. Her grief has been a pacemaker regulating her life.

Donahue can be a relentless interviewer. But the host eased Flowers and Eileen through the program. Eileen, who in her diary had disparaged herself as "an emotional cripple who cries at the drop of a hat," had no idea how she might react on stage with Flowers. Hindsight suggests that, had Eileen proved unable to control her emotions on *Donahue,* Alfred University might well have been forced to tack a "For Sale" sign on its front lawn. Her grief would have shattered America's picture tubes.

Keeping her composure on the show was a major step for Eileen. She had lived through what James Dickey has called "the fast and sudden part" of grief and was ready to experience what the poet names "the long, slow part of sorrow" for the rest of her life. She was not yet the self-assured woman whose appearance and bearing turn heads in airports and restaurants, but she was no longer a simple Long Island housewife either. "Mom, you are two people," her children kidded her after seeing her emote like an actress on television. "That I am," she once shot back. The truth of that statement surprised her as much as it did them.

After *Donahue* she began to contact other parents whenever she read about a pledging-related death. She sent a card to the parents of Richard Fuhs, the Rutgers University student who died in a one-car accident after attending a "voluntary" early-morning drinking session for Delta Phi. Dick and Clara Fuhs sent back a heart-wrenching note:

> We saw the *Phil Donahue Show* that particular day you were on. . . . Because of having seen the show, I tried to tell my son to be so careful during "Hell Week." Being a normal boy of 20, he thought we were just overexcited, over-worried parents, but as it turned out one day of his "Hell Week" was his last day.

Eileen's appearance on *Donahue* gained her the enmity of many Alfred students and faculty members. One of the young men who appeared on the show with her was an Alfred dropout who had written to tell her about hazing abuses on campuses. Administrators and faculty say Eileen lost credibility by that connection. She defends herself, saying that he was one of only two students with Alfred connections willing to appear on the show. "They asked me to supply Phil Donahue with a list [of possible students]," she says. "He chose the guests; I didn't."

People hit the stands in mid-February. Eileen had the odd sensation of going into the local supermarket and flipping through an issue with her face, and Chuck's, on the inside.

February 24, 1979, was a day of torment for all the Stevenses. The pain for Eileen had lessened only slightly by the anniversary. "Can it really be one year?" she asked her journal. "So many days and nights without Chuck. How have I kept my sanity? I have wished to die many times [to] be with him." She no longer absently set the dinner table for six, but in her mind she still saw him at the table making Sue giggle.

The changes in Eileen were apparent to everyone in the family. Roy discussed her crusade frankly with his children several times while she was lobbying in Albany. The woman her children had known was no longer a resident; she was gone forever. Eileen herself was both sorry and pleased about her former self's departure. Sometimes she missed her; sometimes she wondered how she had tolerated her. But she could no longer be what she had been. Her work focused her and gave her priorities that she hadn't needed before.

Oh, to be sure, when in doubt, she still vacuumed. Her house was still the neatest on the block. But her compulsive nature had shifted its attention to social change. Hazing would be stopped in her lifetime — period. Blessed with Irish-Italian dark beauty, she no longer cared how she looked. Although she didn't realize it at the time, her meetings with reporters and legislators probably saved her looks. They forced her to pay some attention to her appearance.

The hours she kept were frightening. When Roy insisted that she come to bed at midnight, she complied to save an argument. But she listened to his breathing and slipped back out to the dining room table to address envelopes or write letters when he was in deep sleep. She was to achieve success, but along the way her public persona threatened to obliterate her private self.

On the morning of the first anniversary of Chuck's death, she rose early to attend a Mass in his honor. Friends had given donations for dozens of Masses, and she drove all over Long Island to attend them. The donors could not know how much comfort they brought her. "I've loved every one," she told her journal. But almost all were said that first year. After that nearly everyone's grief, save hers, had subsided. "He was cheated," she wrote in her journal. "He was so swiftly taken. . . . Can't he have another chance?"

On the anniversary Eileen's calendar was dotted with appointments to visit colleges and high schools that had contacted her about speaking on hazing. The schools had little to lose. She offered to pay her own expenses, not daring to presume that what she had to say could be worth meals, airfare, and a room, let alone a fee.

The first college to invite her to speak was St. Bonaventure University, a Catholic school in New York's Southern Tier, located a short drive from Alfred. No one in the audience knew that minutes before her speech a panic attack almost paralyzed her. A nasty voice in her head said, "You're not intelligent enough, you're not educated enough."

As she waited in the wings, a dean grabbed her arm. "Eileen, I don't know if I should tell you this or not, but a busload of Alfred students just pulled up."

Her intestines were already tangled. "What does it mean?"

"I don't know if they're going to jeer you or what it means."

Once on stage Eileen leaned on the lectern. Her eyes darted this way and that, looking for Alfred sweatshirts. I'll give it a shot, she thought. It's in God's hands. If I make a fool out of myself, I'll make a fool out of myself. She spoke. The audience was receptive, although somber. When she finished, she invited comments.

A young man raised his hand. "I represent a group from Alfred," he said. "There are thirty-five of us."

Here it goes, she told herself, ready for whatever she had to say or do.

"We're here to support what you're doing. That fraternity has brought bad publicity to our campus. Chuck shouldn't have died."

Eileen bit her lip, an unconscious reaction whenever something surprises or pleases her. She rattled off a thank-you. Her adrenaline supply went back to normal. She felt like a ship's captain who has steered past an iceberg.

Another aspect of Eileen's work had begun. About this time she moved her office into a small room in the house and began decorating it with pennants she purchased at the schools where she lectured. In time, every inch of wall and ceiling space would be covered not only with souvenirs but also with plaques and framed certificates of appreciation.

By March 1979 the negative publicity generated by the Stenzel incident, the dismissals of longtime faculty members, and a flap about a nearby landfill rumored to be a health hazard had the Alfred administration antsy. Rather than solve the problems, the university relations office tried to clamp a lid on the faculty. H. Martin Moore, the director of public affairs, sent a confidential in-house memorandum to all faculty and administrators. He advised them not to talk to the media without talking to him first.

Following Eileen's television appearance, some four thousand letters and postcards came, all of which she or her dwindling CHUCK crew answered. She knew it was unnecessary, but she felt an obligation to respond personally. A friend printed form letters, but Eileen wound up writing personal notes on them. She was surprised to receive many supportive letters from Alfred townspeople. The daughter of a longtime Alfred store manager wrote to say that she found Eileen's work "very commendable." Moreover, she said that she routinely attended fraternity parties as an underage high-school student, although not Klan Alpine's. "Klan had a very bad reputation," she wrote. A former Alfred University employee wrote from South Bend, Indiana, to offer encouragement and a deteriorating view of the school's fraternities. An Alfred resident wrote to blast the school. "If this is the way the administration has dealt with this, I have no respect for them," she said. Another Alfred resident at the time of Chuck's death said, "I speak for a lot of people at Alfred when I tell you many people were shocked, and then further revolted by the actions or I should say lack of action on the part of the university in the aftermath of the tragedy." He said that he was a Navy veteran and called Klan's parties "as bad as anything I had ever seen at some of the worst seaports in the world." Still another writer wrote to praise her work but begged her to stop her vendetta against his alma mater.

Eileen's letters also included several written by grown men who defended the hazing they had done. A Malvern, Arizona, man said that paddling was rather harmless, not realizing that what he said was an affront to all pledges who have suffered kidney damage or cracked vertebrae from misplaced swings. One letter that shook Eileen was from a

Long Island man who attended Cornell University from 1971 to 1975. He said the responsibility for Chuck's death "lies upon his own shoulders and perhaps yours." He downplayed the role of peer pressure and a young man's desire to belong:

> I think the young men in that house didn't act in good judgment. But many others [hazings] are done for fun and also to create unity among others and new pledges. For example, the [dead son of the] woman who appeared with you on the show. Digging a hole and lying in it seems to me to be a harmless thing. The fraternity may have been doing this thing for . . . 50 years or more. The fact that in this case the grave caved in is freakish and accidental. . . . My house had a beer fight where people shook up beer cans and sprayed each other. This too could have caused the loss of an eye, serious cuts, etc. (By the way, it never did.) But again the point I'm making is that these activities are potentially dangerous but most of them are not very much so. If we all thought that each thing we did would lead to serious injury or death we would live our lives inside of the proverbial plastic bubble.

A Texas man wrote to say that hazing, when controlled, established bonds. Over and over Eileen heard the same attitude expressed until she wanted to grab the speakers and shake them until their eyeballs collided. The basic attitude was that someone else's hazing was horrible, but you just can't know the extenuating circumstances behind our hazing, lady. "I feel our frat was an exception to the rule," said the letter writer. "We were not forced to drink except once—a hot Jax with a raw egg in it, and the most that happened was someone threw up. We were taken on 'walks'—but when anything physical was involved—it was [only] exercising until you dropped." Another letter came from a Rapid City, South Dakota, alumnus of a state school. "I participated in some of the most rigorous initiations allowed from both sides of it. It is unfortunate that you cannot understand the purpose of hazing; but, having never done it you probably never will." The writer concluded that the only people hurt in initiations are those "who have not been able to stand on their own two feet." He ended on an equally sarcastic note. "Keep up your crusade!" he said. "Perhaps before long everyone in the country will be protected from everything and not required to be responsible for themselves at all."

At a substance abuse panel on which Eileen participated, a male student confronted her. The gist of his attack was that he'd been hazed, but he was glad. "It made me a better person," he said. "I don't perceive hazing as something negative." Other members of the panel and the audience buzzed, but Eileen was unshaken. "I'm not liking what you're saying, but I think you're speaking for a lot of people," she said. "You are courageous enough to speak what other people are feeling. If your best friend were injured, or you were, maybe you'd feel differently."

Eileen and her CHUCK friends had written to several journalists. A few responded. The most influential was James J. Kilpatrick, who was a student at the University of Missouri in 1940 when a classmate, Hubert Spake, died during a drinking marathon sponsored by a sub-rosa fraternity. Kilpatrick, a member of Sigma Alpha Epsilon, wrote Eileen two letters and delivered a strong commentary on WDVM-TV, the Washington, DC, affiliate of CBS, on September 23, 1980. "[Hazing] is, quite literally, a sophomoric business, but it is something more: it is a kind of sadism, verging upon the criminal, that cannot possibly be defended or condoned," he said. "The practice is stupid, degrading, unfunny, and unforgivable. College presidents, I submit, ought to begin by expelling those who haze, and continue by closing the offending fraternity houses for good."

Eileen had less success getting executives from the fraternity world and college presidents to respond to her. Out of that barrage of mail and phone calls after *Donahue* came only a few responses from academics and fraternity people. Not all offered positive comments. The first college president to respond positively was Georgian James E. Walter of Piedmont College. "I thought you would like to know that Piedmont College discontinued all hazing, physical and mental, in 1950," he wrote. "As President I could not assume the responsibility for the general welfare of our young people and permit the customary practices of hazing. My absolute position on this matter was not a popular stand." Walter said that it took the much-publicized 1956 death by drowning of Thomas Clark—an MIT pledge from Delta Kappa Epsilon who had been given a "one-way ride" into the country— "to convince our faculty of the foolishness and non-intellectual hazards of this kind of sadistic activity."

Walter's activism first came about as the result of an October 1949 incident at his school in which a freshman named Donald Smith was abandoned in unfamiliar woods while wearing only his sneakers and shorts. Smith took sick and eventually left the college without a degree, and the president blamed his leaving, in part, on the effects of the hazing. Later, Walter would say on a WCON radio broadcast that the Smith drop-off caused him to act. "I said to myself, 'How can the innocent rattlesnakes at Mount Yorah or Brasstown Ball know that the . . . young men at midnight are only looking for a way home, rather than looking for a way to step on slumbering snakes?' . . . One single rattlesnake bite would cause a tragedy. So I reasoned to myself, 'Why should I wait at home for the inevitable loss of a young life on a nearby hill or farm? Therefore I outlawed this kind of horseplay among intelligent and alert young people at Piedmont College. The decision was not popular, but it was right."

The first fraternity leader to contact Eileen was a history professor from Columbia who phoned to say he backed her crusade. The caller, Frederick D. Kershner, told her that he had been fighting fraternity hazing for years, but with only so-so success. "Maybe they will listen to a parent," said Kershner, a member of Delta Tau Delta. He sent Eileen articles that he had written on the history of hazing as well as on more positive fraternal matters. He is an opinionated man, who has a theory that the growth of hazing in fraternities can be linked to the influx of college athletes into them. He explained to Eileen the difference between initiations, which he considers a useful rite of passage, and hazings, which he finds reprehensible.

"I hope you'll consider working within the system because you'll have much more impact than working solely from the outside," he said.

"Well, I'd like to," said Eileen.

"I can't defend us on this, but this [hazing] is not the only thing we [fraternities] do."

Over the years, Kershner has shared his ideas with Eileen. He wanted to launch a fraternity-subsidized professional journal, to be called the *Journal of Student Life*, not to be limited to studies of the Greeks. He told fraternity leaders that unless they sponsored this or some similar publication, there were few outlets for anthropologists, sociologists, psychologists, historians, and educators to publish serious studies on Greek life and, thus, few scholars would concentrate upon research in that area. Unfortunately, he was rebuffed, and the idea has gone begging; but he hasn't abandoned hope that it can be revived.

Eileen always looks forward to meeting Kershner at various Greek functions. He has a boyish enthusiasm but is solemn about the need for fraternal reform. "We've got to return to the benefits of fraternity, the kinds of things we used to have," he likes to say. "We should be cooperating with the administration and getting leadership experience on campus [by getting involved] with other student groups. The only way [we] will beat this hazing thing is to work on alternative interests and make them so attractive that you get those kids [to pledge] who want to get the most out of the college experience."

This one encouraging soul from the fraternity world buoyed Eileen's morale. He told her that CHUCK was needed and that in time the fraternity world would see her criticism as constructive. "Heaven's sake, this woman is reasonable enough," Kershner says he decided the first time he saw her on a television talk show. "I don't see why the fraternities couldn't support her quite freely. It's really the same thing they're telling their kids, but from a different angle."

"He just believed in me," she says, and "gave me a tiny bit of hope." Kershner is different from the business-oriented fraternity members she so often meets, a brilliant man who doesn't want the term "fraternity ideals" to become an oxymoron, nor the homes of fraternities to become known as houses of ill repute. He looks at hazing with an academician's eyes. He served on the dissertation committee of a young Columbia Teachers College scholar named Thomas A. Leemon, whose study was eventually published as a book, *The Rites of Passage in a Student Culture*. Leemon argues that pledging involves complicated rites in which "ritual systems with their processes and structures [are] substituted for those characteristic of the social relations in other systems in which pledges and members participated." Pledges, Leemon suggests, must repudiate "their pasts through ceremonies, oaths, ritual purifications and the acquisition of symbol objects—[pledge] badges." Furthermore, he says, pledges are "required to display a qualitative disassociation from their past by maintaining a look of expressionlessness or a symbolic loss of memory at these events, by repeatedly being punished for their responses while being shouted at and by being physically worn down through extensive exercise."

Through Kershner and the kindness of a handful of other academics who sent her doctoral dissertations and scholarly papers, Eileen began to see that hazing was both commonplace and—to many people—a reasonable part of the process of bringing new members into groups such as fraternities, sororities, the military, high-school clubs, and adult secret societies. The body of literature on hazing was pitifully small, she learned from Kershner. His theory is that the Greek system has been overlooked "as a veritable laboratory" for sociologists, archaeologists, educators, and psychologists. They are ignoring a scholarly diamond mine in the midst of academia. Few scholars take the subject seriously enough to give social clubs a tumble. Yet these organizations have been around in one form or another since America emerged from colonies to nation. Many studies on group behavior ignore fraternities, but their findings apply to them.

In a study of hazing published in the *Journal of Abnormal and Social Psychology,* authors Elliott Aronson and Judson Mills claim that an initiate who endures a severe ordeal is likely to find membership in a group all the more appealing. Aronson and Mills write that the commonplace behavioral theory of cognitive dissonance can explain why initiates put up with so much from hazers. The cognitive aspects of the pledges—specifically, how they perceive themselves fitting into the world they live in—need to be satisfied regularly. If not, frustration and stress—dissonance—occur. Once the initiates envision themselves in the Greek world, the military, a sports team setting, or wherever, they feel dissonance if they believe something might deprive them of the opportunity to be a part of the group. Hence, they do what they must do, accept what they must accept, to gain entrance. The initiates believe the group to which they aspire has value. Therefore, what the members ask them to do cannot be so unreasonable. Besides, didn't the members all go through it?

What is more, says Frank W. Young in his *Initiation Ceremonies,* a social group that already possesses high solidarity is likely to formulate the most dramatic rites-of-passage ceremonies.

Sociologist Milton Glenn Walker, in his dissertation on fraternity hell weeks, compares the group solidarity that arises from fraternity hazing with that of a military boot camp. He cites an anonymous article from the *American Journal of Sociology,* "The Making of an Infantry Man," that says: "It is out of the agonies of training that [the infantrymen] develop pride in having done what they believe many of their former friends could not have done and which they themselves never thought they could do."

Walker maintains that "rites of passage [that] often include unpleasantries and ordeals, both physical and mental," must not be "mistaken for negative sanctions." For example, says Walker, "paddling during an informal initiation is not necessarily done just for the enjoyment of the harasser, nor is it necessarily used as a punishment for misbehavior; sometimes it is a test of loyalty and self-control, and sometimes it is used simply to increase the stress."

Ball State University professor Paul Biner, now in the beginning stages of studying hazing in the workplace, says that hazing expected of all new members of a group should be differentiated from similar actions used strictly to punish the new people on the block or, significantly, to drive them away so that they don't become a part of the group. An example of the latter behavior would be when military cadets at West Point decide to "cut," or ostracize, a plebe and refuse to speak to him or her.

Pledges who desire entrance into fraternities and sororities aspire to wear Greek letters, which are highly symbolic. Those Greek letters have an almost mystical appeal for neophytes. They symbolize a group that has an image the initiate finds appealing. They symbolize a group that attracts a certain type of the opposite sex. They symbolize a group whose members make up a society that the pledge feels is worth joining.

Eileen learned that the foolish and dangerous practice of hazing was more complicated than she had at first suspected. She began to hope that once hazers and the hazed came to understand their behavior, they might adopt safe, undemeaning alternatives.

Fred Kershner's worth to Eileen Stevens cannot be overestimated. She had sent letters and copies of her newspaper clippings to many national fraternities and to the National Interfraternity Conference. She received no replies. She didn't know what to think of the Greeks. Did they think she was a threat, a bitter mother, a nuisance — maybe all of the above? She had no way of knowing. Kershner, a sturdy, bespectacled man with a cherubic face, understood her message to mean that she believed hazing, not the Greek system, ought to be ended. She avoided the temptation to ally herself with anti-Greek individuals and was dismayed that many fraternity and sorority leaders perceived her to be anti-Greek. Kershner agreed with her that bad-actor chapters, particularly those where serious injuries or deaths occurred, ought to be punished severely. She also vehemently objected to disgusting anti-female elements in the pledging requirements of a few fraternities in which members were required to prove that they had gotten sexual favors from women in order to improve their status with members. Kershner had been the voice of reason in the Greek system for years, though too often the leaders of the fraternity movement patronized him instead of heeding his advice. "A letter from someone like him who understood I wasn't being negative was so encouraging to me," says Eileen.

Quite often in her community college classes, Eileen wrote papers on fraternity-related topics. "You can't tell me that your founders had hazing," she was fond of telling students. "I've done my homework, and I know that's not true. The founders would hang their heads today." She charged that those who hazed were perverting their very principles and constitutions. Hazing is like the chestnut blight that plagued this country early in the twentieth century. Brought here from another country, it has thrived remarkably and rotted its hosts from without and within. Over and over, Eileen heard the same tune and similar lyrics: Don't highlight our bad side, the Greeks said, highlight our good side. But she believes that the dark side must be illuminated before it can be eliminated.

As much as she would come to appreciate what was good and decent about fraternities, the vision of Chuck's death kept her from making compromises that violated her organization's founding principles. Hazing is, for Eileen, a mad troll the Greeks keep chained in their collective attics; she wants the beast tamed. There can be no compromise in her mind.

The rituals are beautiful, as are the reasons for the founding of these organizations, Eileen says. The founders — usually young men themselves — had broken away from established fraternities in much the same way the colonists broke away from established religions during America's youth. Several began because hazing, among other abuses, was loathsome to them.

European harassment of students wasn't called hazing, Eileen learned from Kershner. Early in the fifteenth century a system known as pennalism flourished on the continent. By the seventeenth century, master's degree students needed to obtain a document that affirmed they had gone through the equivalent of a Middle Ages hell night. Under the system of pennalism, older students regarded newcomers as savages who needed to undergo hardships to prove themselves worthy of admission into the company of educated men. Veteran students extorted money from the younger men, abused them physically, and forced them to dress in odd garb. One such French custom that emigrated to our universities was the cap or beanie that American freshmen and many Greek pledges routinely wore for a term or a year. (The custom still exists on a voluntary basis at a few American colleges, including Phillips University in Enid, Oklahoma.) The system of pennalism, fortunately, disappeared from the continent, but not before many young men were humiliated, injured, and killed.

From Kershner, Eileen also learned about the English aristocracy's practice of fagging, which flourished in prep schools and was occasionally practiced at Cambridge and Oxford. Fagging was defined in *The Spectator* in 1891 as "the right exercised by the older boy to make the younger do what he likes, and what the younger one generally dislikes." *The Spectator,* in an article defending fagging, said that human nature — not corruptness — makes boys in groups behave abominably. "Boys, even when honest and honourable, are very queer cattle," it said. "A boy may still be as honest, as good, as simple-hearted, and as loveable as the day that he left his mother's side, and yet the little wretch will bow his little knee in the temple of custom, and be found aiding and abetting his small school-fellows in malpractices that at home he would have considered criminal."

Each new student was to learn humility and etiquette by becoming a fag, or man-servant, to an upperclassman. The newcomer did chores, ran errands, cleaned digs, or quarters, and anything else that came into the upperclassman's mind. The senior men physically abused and mentally harassed their fags. Suicides, serious injuries, and deaths sometimes resulted. The practice, condemned by the poet Percy Bysshe Shelley as "brutal and degrading," wasn't stopped at Britain's celebrated Eton until 1980. American colleges had a form of fagging although anti-British sentiment during the eighteenth century prevented the word's being used. Vocabulary distinctions notwithstanding, Kershner found that freshmen at Harvard, for example, were expected to run errands, refrain from sauciness, and never use the upperclassmen's privy.

The practice is occasionally found today in high-school athletics in the United States. Some coaches have rationalized that fagging is good if it is supervised. In 1985, for example, the Manheim [PA] High School head football coach and the assistant athletic director sent parents initiation policies in writing for a football camp they planned to hold at Juniata College. According to the document, the arrangement teamed sophomores to seniors in a so-called little brother-big brother relationship, but in practice there was nothing to distinguish this system from fagging. Among other duties, sophomore boys were expected to carry team equipment and the seniors' luggage, cart food on trays for big brothers, and bring a food package [no more than five dollars] to camp for the big brother.

Another practice at Oxford University in England during the 1600s was called salting and tucking. An upperclassman would scrape the skin off a younger lad's chin with a knife just before a traditional drinking ceremony, according to a *Smithsonian* article by Michael Olmert. The young man then chugged a schooner of salt water. The water that spilled from the vessel stung the youth's exposed flesh.

Olmert also quotes Martin Luther as he initiated new students to Wittenberg in 1539. Luther made neophytes wear silly "yellow bills" (horns) on their heads and basted them in wine to wash away, symbolically, their pasts and "former unbridled natures." Said Luther, "You'll be subjected to hazing all your life. When you hold important offices in the future, burghers, peasants, nobles and your wives will harass you with various vexations. When this happens don't go to pieces. Bear your cross with equanimity and your troubles without murmuring. . . . Say that you first began to be hazed in Wittenberg when you were a young man, that now that you have become a weightier person you have heavier vexations to bear. So this test is only a symbol of human life in its misfortunes and castigations."

By about 1850 hazing was common on Eastern campuses, perhaps spread by young men who had quit West Point and Annapolis to attend public and private colleges. The jargon of hazers varied from campus to campus. At one time the practice was called dibbling at West Point. During the late 1860s, the most serious form of hazing was a practice known as yanking, which occurred when upperclassmen picked up the blankets upon which a cadet was sleeping in order to do mischief to him. Fraternity hazing was not a major problem during the nineteenth century at public and private universities although it was hardly nonexistent, as some Greeks have claimed. The most serious hazing arose from class rivalries, particularly those between freshmen and sophomores. These took the form of battles royal, known as scraps. Often there was a form of warfare called the cane rush, in which the two classes vied with each other to get the most hands on a cane. Many college presidents and faculty members deplored the practice, but others condoned it or looked the other way, believing it built school spirit and class unity.

Kershner and others trace the beginning of American fraternity existence back to Phi Beta Kappa in 1776 (although it has even earlier social antecedents). The original purpose of this literary society was to give students a forum of their peers to express their views at a time when America was breaking away from British rule. Thus, the original concept of fraternities had both an intellectual and social appeal; later, its leaders would add a system of noble and worthy values. One Phi Beta Kappa rule that was subsequently lost forever was a ten-shilling fine for drunkenness. The so-called "Union Triad" (so named because they were popular at Union College) of Kappa Alpha, Sigma Phi, and Delta Phi flourished next. Writer Stephen Birmingham has noted that fraternities then spread across America and parts of Canada like wildflowers. In time fraternities broke with other fraternities, and young men visited other colleges with the zeal of Mormon missionaries to form new chapters. Kershner says that these forebears of the fraternity movement thought nothing of taking a six-hundred-mile train ride to visit another chapter or school. When there were sufficient chapters, national associations were the result, and fraternities in time became a successful business.

Fraternal hazings became more common by the 1880s. The University of Georgia's Zeta Chi, for example, tossed pledges high in the air on a quilt held by members; one heavyset pledge was shaken up when a quilt split in two, dropping him on his buttocks. On another occasion Georgia Zeta Chi brother Donald Fraser played a practical joke on his fellow members. The candidate he had been instructed to bring to an initiation backed out at the last second. Fraser donned the mask and quilt of the candidate and entered the initiation ceremonies. The members were clad in sheets; a single candle barely illuminated Phi Kappa Hall. The supposed initiate was introduced to the mysteries of the brotherhood, docilely submitting to some absurd hazing practices until a voice ordered him to stick out his tongue so that it might be branded. The members tried to force him to comply, and the jokester whipped out a pistol. Unknown to the membership, the gun contained blanks. Fraser took aim at the panicked Zeta Chis. Two men jumped out a window, dislocating their ankles in a fourteen-foot fall. Others were bruised or suffered wrenched arms. What happened to the prankster when his game was discovered is unrecorded.

Significantly, Kershner found that hazing was slow to take hold on the Pacific side of the Mississippi, possibly because Westerners despised a custom they saw as typical of effete schools back East. The University of Colorado student paper boasted in 1893 that the institution "has never had a case of genuine hazing." But in 1895 the attitude at Colorado flipflopped when the school hired Eastern professors who decried the lack of school spirit in their new students. By 1899, says Kershner, the student paper at Colorado said hazing was "a natural part" of student life, so much so that the faculty unsuccessfully tried to abolish it in 1900.

The word *hazing* has a colorful history. Kershner has written that the term was used by English sailors to honor a man's first trip across the equator. Another popular use of the term was on the American frontier. Old timers frequently subjected greenhorns to hazing in the form of cruel pranks and verbal abuse. The term *hazers* also came to be used by Western ranchers to refer to men on horseback who used quirts as they cornered a horse they were trying to break.

Hazing deaths occurred during the nineteenth century. Eileen Stevens's CHUCK files contain a letter from a woman who claims that her ancestor, John Butler Groves, died in an 1838 hazing at Franklin Seminary in Kentucky. Since all school records were lost in a fire, the claim cannot be easily refuted or affirmed. Without doubt the first hazing death to receive extensive newspaper coverage occurred in 1873 at Cornell University. A pledge, Mortimer N. Leggett, the son of the U.S. Commissioner of Internal Revenue, was blindfolded and taken for a long walk in the country by members of Kappa Alpha. Two members eventually took off his blindfold, and they all tried to return to campus in the darkness. Unfamiliar with the terrain, the three plunged down a slope to the edge of a cliff. Leggett died of injuries sustained in the fall.

As if to prove Eileen Stevens's contention that few people are aware of what constitutes hazing, the death was ruled an accident. The Kappa Alpha members testified that there had been no drinking or hazing. They argued—successfully since no charges were placed—that the death was the result of an initiation rite. The father of the dead youth, General M. D. Leggett, accepted initiation into the fraternity in place of his dead son.

In 1899 the Kappa Alpha fraternity at Cornell again required a pledge to walk through unfamiliar terrain near Geneva, New York. Edward Fairchild Berkeley of St. Louis perished when he accidentally fell into a canal. By 1912, according to *The Literary Digest,* a London *Morning Post* correspondent wrote that "Death at a fraternity initiation" or "Seriously injured while being initiated" were almost standing headlines in American newspaper offices.

Hazing dropped drastically during World War Two (as it had during the First World War) when fraternity membership plummeted as college men went off to war. Following the war, many veterans would not tolerate being hazed by fuzz-cheeked kids, recalls Mark Steadman, now writer-in-residence at Clemson University. But ironically these same vets introduced strenuous physical hazing that gave some fraternity pledge programs a boot-camp aura. When fraternity membership boomed during the late forties, hazing also increased dramatically on many campuses. Instances of freshman hazing and cadet hazing in service academies also rose during this era. Hazing "had become worse than it had been for the last ten years," a Texas A&M dean complained to the press in 1947. The school blamed hazing for a whopping forty-eight percent dropout rate of dormitory students after a single semester.

11

Like Eileen, Greg Belanger underwent some positive changes after Chuck's death. He drank less, for example, and he helped convince the sponsors of an annual spring fair to make the event booze-free. The sponsors thought it might flop. Instead, it drew more people, and those attending actually remembered their fun. Moreover, encouraged by his advisor, Stu Campbell, he assumed the co-editorship of the student newspaper. A continuing activist in nuclear issues, Belanger questioned a university research project on the suitability of glass for storing nuclear waste. Some students and professors took such behavior as further evidence that Belanger was a genuine radical.

Belanger and the other activists in the People's Campaign decried the apathy they found on campus until Three-Mile Island shook more complacent citizens. Suddenly, more people started showing up at the films, speaker events, and forums sponsored by the People's Campaign. Even some of Greg's detractors participated.

Campbell motivated Belanger although the professor had no direct involvement. "He was such a tremendous inspiration to me personally and to others in the group," says Belanger. Campbell's lectures in his "Europe Since 1848" class often encouraged students to address the issues of their own time. Belanger and the People's Campaign saw him as having a moral commitment, a characterization the essentially secular Campbell would hate. Clearly, though, he was the catalyst for the students' taking positive action. Belanger also became interested in other issues, such as poverty, concerns that persisted in his work as a reporter with the New Orleans *Times-Picayune*.

Covering the one-year anniversary of Chuck's death for *Fiat Lux* was difficult for Belanger. He had divided loyalties. On the one hand, he loved the freedom that Alfred administrators and professors gave students to grow and be all they could. He felt—and feels to this day—strong allegiance to the institution. His love for Alfred rivals Don King's. The school afforded him educational opportunities and challenges he might have missed at a large college. But, on the other hand, he lost his friend there. He could not understand how such a caring institution "could behave so callously and poorly" toward Chuck's family. In the end he accepted the university's explanation: that King and Rose had simply been cowed by the threat of litigation.

Not a few students and Alfred citizens were angered by the strong possibility of a suit against the institution by Eileen Stevens. "There would have been a lot less resistance within the legal institutions in Allegany

County if the university wasn't on trial," says Belanger. Klan Alpine had little campus support at this time, and many in the community would not have minded seeing the fraternity swing from a tall cottonwood if Eileen hadn't also attempted to drop nooses over Don King, Steven Peterson, and Robert Heineman.

The situation made Belanger an angry young man. "It was murder as murder can be," says Belanger. "I've always believed that. Chuck was not — one single bit of him — suicidal, or even masochistic. If he knew what was coming, he would not have done it. That's the bottom line. . . . It couldn't have been that important."

Klan Alpine members, in turn, blast Belanger.

Scott Sullivan calls him the fraternity's worst critic. Gary Horowitz remembers others saying that Belanger hadn't given his friends Chuck Stenzel and Jimmy Arnoux the time of day the semester both were at Alfred. Belanger says, in his own defense, that he thought his two meetings with Chuck in February 1978 had brought them back together. "I felt that we might not share the same sphere of friends every day, but in a sense we [had] a bond that's deeper, because it [was] a childhood friendship," he says. "It's very natural for childhood friends to grow in different directions — even more so . . . because I had come to Alfred two-and-a-half years earlier."

One of Belanger's first editorial decisions was to run a special issue on Chuck's death. He devoted four full pages and parts of two others to the incident but included no first-person account of their friendship. Eileen's appearances on *Donahue* and *Today* had scandalized the campus. While sororities experienced a reduction in pledges, the fraternities perversely benefited from the bad publicity. Klan Alpine, proving that dissociation was hardly the punishment it was meant to be, enrolled twenty-three pledges in its 1979 class — more than twice the number in Chuck's group. Rocky LaForge says Klan had to blackball "curiosity seekers" or the pledge class would have been even larger. "A lot of guys who pledged Klan this year are out to prove something," one president of a rival fraternity told the *Fiat Lux*. "They want to go home and say they joined the fraternity where someone died."

Klan outlawed physical hazing, but mental hazing apparently still went on in 1979. No alcohol was consumed on Tapping Night, however. As for Klan's parties, advisor Steven Peterson told the *Fiat Lux*, "They're rowdy but not more rowdy than the other fraternities," hardly a ringing endorsement under the circumstances. Moreover, although enrollments from Long Island dropped, the press about Alfred's problems with booze and parties actually attracted some students. Applications for the 1980-81 freshman class were thirty-eight percent higher than the previous year. "It seems to show that the public is extremely unpredictable," a university spokesman told the Rochester *Democrat and Chronicle*.

King refused to label the Stenzel incident a hazing, but he did send out a memo to all fraternities before Tapping Night reminding them that Alfred forbids hazing. He went on to define the term. Nonetheless, hazing remained alive on campus with the avowed exception of two fraternities, Alpha Chi Rho and Lambda Chi. The Alpha Chi Rho chapter claimed its members never hazed, calling King's memorandum "a slap in the face." Lambda Chi purportedly had ended hazings months before Chuck's death at the request of their national organization. But Alfred's Lambda Chis were almost the last chapter to adopt the associate member program developed by the national office as an alternative to pledging. One Lambda Chi member said in *Fiat Lux* that hazings existed at other houses because "everyone's hung up on tradition." The president of Kappa Psi Upsilon told the student paper that his fraternity still hazed, playing "mind games" on pledges. He rationalized their tendency to "go to extremes," saying, "That's the way it is overall in fraternity houses." The president of Theta Theta Chi sorority gave a statement that showed she was unaware of the definition of hazing. "Hazing is like forcing individuals to do certain acts," she said, discounting the deadly persuasion of peer pressure. "Never have we forced anyone to do anything," she concluded, echoing Klan members' statements after Chuck's death.

Eileen had been disturbed by a *Fiat Lux* editorial even though it panned the administration for its handling of the incident. "We cannot . . . sanction the actions of the administration," said the unsigned editorial. "If it had been more open with Stevens, the distortions and negative publicity surrounding the event might have been prevented." The editorial writer concluded, however, that the administration must be held blameless and laid responsibility for the death directly on Klan Alpine.

In the special issue Belanger elected to print a letter from Eileen dated October 30, 1978. The letter had been ignored by his predecessor. Eileen argued that the issue of legal responsibility was for the courts to decide, not student editors. "If there is no legal or moral responsibility on the part of the University, why did they disassociate themselves from Klan Alpine after Chuck's death?" she wrote.

She intended to expose the legal fiction that Alfred University and many other institutions hide behind when a hazing tragedy occurs. In her view, universities enjoy the benefits of the Greek system, which attracts students, but when a hazing disaster occurs, the schools disavow all ties to the offender. Alfred argued that it had no responsibility because it contributed no staff or money to Klan Alpine's operation. "Fraternities are individually incorporated, have their own financing, their own officers and advisors, and are self-regulating and self-perpetuating separate from the University," said a university statement to alumni.

Eileen interpreted the high-sounding words to mean that local fraternities at Alfred were a bunch of college boys doing what they pleased without guidance and control. That the fraternity had a faculty member as an advisor didn't count, in the administration's opinion, because advisors at Alfred were essentially volunteering their time. Nonetheless, the university allowed faculty members who advised fraternities to list that accomplishment under "service to the university" for tenure and promotion considerations. Such service, however, had little weight compared to factors such as publication, teaching evaluations, and research achievements.

That all the fraternities followed rush guidelines set by King and a Greek council didn't seem to count either. Nor did it matter that the fraternities were listed by name in the catalog, had their plaques on the wall in the student union, often began their Tapping Night initiations in school dormitories, and had faculty members on their rolls as honorary members.

If fraternities did things that endangered potential members, why hadn't the school informed her and other parents? Why hadn't it published a disclaimer in the catalog, telling prospective students and their parents that fraternities at Alfred had no legal connection to the university and that students were put on notice that they were joining these groups at their own peril?

Finally, Eileen considered the administration's contention that Alfred "should not publicly be held liable" wishful thinking on its part. For one thing, she argued, since the administration had knowledge that Tapping Night was traditionally a night of drunken excess, it had a moral and ethical obligation to police the fraternities on this night to prevent a death, knowing that young men might be in trouble—the pledges' own possible contributory negligence notwithstanding.

The public's reaction to *Donahue* and other television shows was overwhelming in its support of Eileen's battle against Alfred. Moreover, since newspaper coverage of her campaign has been heavy, constant, and mostly supportive since 1978, the university administration has hardly helped its public image by maintaining its posture into the 1990s.

The bottom line, as both Eileen and the press saw it, was that her son died at Alfred University in a fraternity rite of passage. The school's decision in 1979 not to endorse the Harenberg anti-hazing amendment unless it were specifically requested to do so meant a lost opportunity to reverse negative public sentiment. That decision seems especially puzzling in light of King's acknowledgment that the school supported the bill's spirit even in cases that did not result in death. When the *Fiat Lux* asked King whether "the negative publicity and general misunderstandings" would have been prevented if the administration had better informed the Stevenses, he said the paper would have to judge that.

The special issue of the *Fiat Lux* carried a lengthy statement by the university, that included King's version of Chuck's death. Belanger printed the complete university account, hoping that readers would spot "the inconsistencies and implausibilities," he says. "The best thing journalistically I could do [was] print it verbatim for everybody to see and to compare it against what they already knew." Belanger felt he had to print both sides. "As a journalist you evaluate your source. Here on one side is a grieving mother, and . . . her taciturn husband, and it doesn't seem like they're going to lie. And you've got this kind of bureaucrat who's in the hot seat, and that's how I looked at him. In the differing accounts, I believed Eileen's account. But I wrote both [versions]."

* * *

Despite support from Fred Kershner and a handful of other Greek executives, Eileen had to admit that her attempts to reach fraternal executives had been mostly futile. Least receptive of all to her anti-hazing efforts, according to newspaper sources, was Jack L. Anson, the NIC executive director, who told reporters that Eileen's attempts at legislation were doomed. "The general feeling is that legislation is not the solution," he said. "We think education against hazing is the best answer."

Eileen admits that she was frequently discouraged by her early failure to rally NIC and national fraternity executives behind her cause. Her calls were not returned; letters went unanswered. Those executives who did pick up the phone were evasive and noncommittal. Still she persevered, believing that fraternal ideals as explained to her by Kershner were worthwhile. She kept trying to convince Anson and the fraternity world that it was in their best interests to have legal recourse for victims of hazing in the form of a New York anti-hazing law.

When the Greek world ignored her calls or patronized her, she buried her frustration. The only way some good could come out of Chuck's death would be by defeating hazing. He had always liked making a difference in the lives of others. She felt certain that he was on her side.

Kershner's Delta Tau Delta was not the first fraternity to hear Eileen address a convention. Another group, Phi Kappa Tau, phoned her a few weeks after Kershner had invited her to appear at his group's national convention. Their convention preceded Delta Tau Delta's by ten months. Phi Kappa Tau, one of several national fraternities founded in Oxford, Ohio, has been in existence since 1906.

Eileen worked and reworked her speech. As with every other talk she gave—even to state legislators in the august halls of the Capitol—her notes were handwritten on legal paper. Her diary reveals her genuine fear about taking the podium at the fraternity's forty-fourth convention, to be held at a Knoxville, Tennessee, hotel. "I'm nervous about Tennessee," she wrote. "My God, how can I speak to 500 or more men & boys—about my experience—my efforts—my lonely crusade? I'll never do it. . . . But today plane tickets arrived. It will happen and I must go through with it [despite] my vocabulary, my diction, my lack of experience speaking. Eileen, you're up to your ass this time! And on your own. . . . No Roy—nobody to help."

A few days later the housewife-turned-activist again revealed her terror of public speaking. "Will they leave—or resent my words?" she wrote. "I'm scared. Would Chuck approve? I think he would—he valued life and its gifts."

In mid-August 1979, one year after CHUCK had its name, Eileen addressed her first fraternity. Her preconceptions were way off base. The young men and national executives of Phi Kappa Tau—perhaps sensing the depths of her anxiety—were gracious, solicitous, and supportive. It was only her second trip to Tennessee. The first she made as a pregnant seventeen-year-old to visit her first husband. Then, as on the day of her speech, the temperature soared above one hundred degrees. *Deja vu,* she told herself as she wilted in the heat.

Her speech bore shadowy resemblance to later talks she would give when she possessed "more pieces to the puzzle." Because of her absolute lack of reliable information, that first speech—reprinted in Phi Kappa Tau's magazine—had many inaccuracies. She thought Chuck died roughly forty-five minutes before he did. Unable to envision her son putting a bottle of booze to his lips, she believed that Chuck and his companions had been given shots of alcohol in paper cups "to psyche them up." She thought the pledges were unconscious when the car stopped in front of the Klan Alpine house. And she repeated the misconception about Chuck's last night that she had gleaned from Joe McCaffery—one that members of Klan Alpine still believed as late as 1990—that Chuck might have lived had he vomited before passing out. Eventually, enough young men who *had* vomited would die from alcohol poisoning for Eileen to see the foolishness of this bit of fraternity folklore.

But some of her perceptions were quite astute, given the limited information and the misinformation she had gleaned from sources here and there. She understood that there was something very wrong about fraternity members asking pledges to give them blind trust, then abusing that trust by requiring them to drink until their bodily organs absorbed alcohol like blotters. "It wasn't that long ago he was sitting where you are sitting, planning his future, deciding on a major," she told her listeners. She said that if all players in the horrors of hazing—the fraternity, the pledge, the parents of fraternity members and pledges, and administrators—cooperated, "we've got a chance."

"I am not anti-fraternity, absolutely not," she promised. "I am anti-abuse. I am not vindictive. . . . I don't feel that would accomplish anything. I just feel we should take a tragedy, learn from it, share it, and perhaps prevent it from happening again."

She thanked the group. The men gave her a standing ovation. They didn't cheer. They were too subdued. But they clapped, hard. "The convention was exhilarating and wonderful," she wrote in her diary when she returned home. "I know they listened—their reaction was overwhelming. I feel I am doing a worthwhile thing. I prayed so hard—it worked. They clapped forever it seemed. It went so well! What a relief."

Paul Harenberg, the idealistic high-school teacher who had entered politics, succeeded where all the reporters from Buffalo, Rochester, and Long Island had failed. Harenburg's letter to Governor Carey provoked a response from DA George Francis. On March 8, 1979, Francis wrote a four-page letter to Harenberg and Paul L. Gioia, the assistant counsel to Governor Carey.

He apologizes for failing to respond more promptly to Harenberg's first letter to him, saying that he realized his silence had raised suspicions about the investigation of the Stenzel case. He denies the allegations against him made by Eileen Stevens and criticizes her decision to slam him in the media.

Francis goes on to say that he is reluctant to disclose the confidential findings of his investigation because media attention could influence the resolution of the case — a puzzling position since he had closed the case nearly a year earlier. Had he done further work since? If so, whom had he interviewed? What leads had he pursued?

Francis claims that he didn't prosecute Klan Alpine individuals under the provisions of Section 240.25(4) of the New York Penal law for several reasons. First, based on the evidence at hand, he found its enforcement questionable. Second, he lacked proof of any Klan member's guilt, making conviction doubtful. Third, he says he didn't want to charge anyone with a minor crime for fear that double jeopardy would prevent future prosecution for a more serious crime. Finally, he says that minor convictions would trivialize Chuck's death. Those responsible would be guilty of nothing more than a "violation," and the maximum sentence could be no more than a $250 fine and fifteen days in jail. Francis's reasoning bears examination. Point one is particularly compelling in terms of the bill that Harenberg was trying to introduce. Francis says precisely what Eileen had been saying: that the New York law was ineffectual to combat hazing. Point two, the problem of proof, is also worth considering. Precisely how many witnesses to the Stenzel incident did the district attorney interview? Why hadn't he interviewed the officers of Klan Alpine who, if their pretrial depositions can be believed, never had a visit from the DA? Why didn't he interview the state troopers who were present at Klan Alpine after Chuck's death? Or did the district attorney simply read the depositions obtained by the Alfred village police, trusting that Chief Jamison had done a proper job? Point number three raises the question of what, if any, more serious crime Francis considered prosecuting. Point four is presumptuous in that Francis assumes that Chuck's family would prefer no fine and no jail time for those involved rather than a token penalty, which Eileen believes would have served as a deterrant to future hazing crimes.

On page two of his letter, Francis first denies not returning calls to Eileen Stevens and her attorney, then hedges slightly by saying that calls were not intentionally not returned. Francis acknowledges that many, if not most, calls from the press were not returned. He goes on to say that he considered the case "open," contrary to the implications of his terse statement to the press the previous year. He also says that he doesn't think the media a proper forum for the investigation of a serious crime.

Francis attacks Harenberg's letters, which, he believes, wrongly cast slurs upon his character. He denies efforts to cover up evidence and justifies suppressing some facts because an ongoing investigation must, by law, be kept confidential. He denies being an advocate for the university by allowing the school's image to stand in the way of an investigation and expresses his conviction that a thorough investigation was most certainly in the public interest.

Francis does, however, defend Alfred University in the letter, a curious turn after having denied serving the institution's interests. He also challenges Harenberg's assumption that full disclosure about the incident would put the university in a bad light.

Francis attacks Paul Kolisch for calling the death manslaughter during his encounter with Eileen at the morgue, suggesting that Kolisch spoke informally, without legal foundation or full grasp of the facts.

"In short," says Francis on page four, "I believe I am acting responsibly, both in the investigation of this matter and in my insisting that the results of my investigation to date, my motives, and my plans remain confidential. . . . There is still no reason for Mrs. Stevens, Mr. Harenberg, the national press, magazines, TV, or the Governor to reach the conclusion that I have done, or am doing, less than my duty."

The investigation remains confidential. Francis has no comment on the case.

Eileen has always credited her religion with getting her through the difficult first year after Chuck's death. She donated vestments to a missionary in her son's name, and she corresponded with several priests and nuns who had known him. "If I didn't have my faith or a relationship with God, I would have probably thrown in the towel long ago because there've been very dark days," she says. Because she has strongly conservative Catholic views, she was all the more distressed about the reserved way a priest from Alfred treated her. Father Paul F. Stengel, a tall man with spectacles, was chaplain at St. Jude's in Alfred and the pastor at St. Brendan's in nearby Almond, New York. The Reverend Stengel spoke at the memorial service for Chuck, telling the crowd, "It's never easy to face tragedy." He also sent a notice that Klan members had purchased a Mass to be celebrated on January 3, 1979, at five P.M. Pleased, Eileen wrote back. He answered cordially on January 20, 1979, to tell her that Klansmen had donated money in Chuck's name, a gesture that touched her, and she was pleased to hear that the priest had said a second Mass for her son, as well as purchased a sanctuary lamp globe and stand in Chuck's memory.

In his letter the priest revealed that he not only had been in contact with certain unidentified Klan members, but had also talked with some parishioners who were part of the emergency response team that came to Chuck's aid. The parishioners had painted a picture of chaotic confusion that night. Therefore, he dismissed the fact that Chuck had failed to receive Last Rites, blaming the omission on all the confusion. The Reverend Stengel did offer one comfort. He said he was certain the rescue team would share with Eileen what they remembered about the night of Chuck's death. She wrote back immediately, pleased that at last an ally had emerged to fill in some blanks for her.

Once again someone from Alfred dashed her hopes. He had spoken out of turn, the priest responded, and the rescue members would not talk to her for fear that their comments might be given to the press.

* * *

Eileen continued to promote her organization, but not all talk show hosts embraced her the way Phil Donahue had. She accepted an invitation to appear on *Good Morning America*. David Hartman, then the host of the show, greeted her and Roy warmly in the green room. He told them that as a father his heart went out to parents who suffered such a loss. But Hartman was not the interviewer on that segment. Eileen feels the subsequent interview with Sandy Hill was a flop. Off-camera, following the segment, Hill asked Eileen, "Do you think you'll get anywhere with this [crusade]?" If she hadn't convinced her interviewer of CHUCK's worth, Eileen thought, what conclusion had millions of viewers reached?

Her visit to the *Today* show went no better. Tom Brokaw warned Eileen to keep her answers brief. Before the show Jane Pauley told her that she had been in a sorority at Indiana University and had never experienced anything such as Eileen was claiming. On the show with her was a young man representing Beta Theta Pi fraternity. Eileen told herself afterward that he had come off better than she. He had been well coached, was articulate, handsome, a walking advertisement for the Greek world.

Eileen had gone too soon to the major networks with her message. She needed seasoning and, in retrospect, might have improved her delivery had she first gone on the circuit of regional talk shows. On the other hand, her failures helped her, too. She watched her performances on videotape, more critical than a drama coach of her gestures and facial movements. In a matter of months, she came across polished and composed on the screen, expressing complex ideas in ten-second chunks for television. By the time she traveled to Boston to appear on the *Joe Oteri Show,* she was beginning to feel comfortable on a program set. When one of Oteri's guests, author David Halberstam, praised her performance, she hung on every word.

His peptalk sustained her when she appeared on Tom Snyder's *Tomorrow* show in April 1979. She wasn't prepared for this energetic man with the booming laugh. He addressed the topic with feverish gusto and expressed his own strong opinions. During a break, the show's young producer, Andy Friendly, slipped a mailgram to Snyder. The host read it and told Eileen that it was from Alfred University. Snyder, never a predictable man, waved the telegram in his hand and castigated the institution, asking why it was giving explanations to him and not to this woman who had lost her son. Snyder's words flew like punches. No more mailgrams came from Alfred when Eileen appeared on television.

But even as Eileen drove her runaway plow into public places to create awareness in those who would listen, she also endured some losses. On July 17, 1979, Governor Carey vetoed the anti-hazing bill and sent it back to assembly. Despite Francis's refusal to slap even a minimal violation on Klan Alpine brothers and despite dozens of historical incidents that had similarly been kept out or thrown out of court, Carey argued that "the conduct covered by the proposed new crimes is already covered under existing penal law provisions." He also said the bill insufficiently defined hazing, and he thought it failed to provide "constitutionally required notice as to the precise type of conduct prohibited." Further, he argued—despite Alfred University's inability and possible unwillingness to provide Eileen Stevens and the public with written specifics of Don King's investigation—that school administrators should be the ones "enforcing rules related to hazing."

Paul Harenberg believed that Carey's view of hazing was misguided. "Whatever hazing may be, it certainly is not an accident," he said. "Accidents occur spontaneously. Hazings are planned, premeditated acts which have sadistic implications." Other strong criticisms of the governor's action came from Caesar Trunzo and Norman J. Levy. They said they feared that the Greek system would get the message that they could haze without fear of suffering criminal penalties. "We owe it to all those students who have been victims of senseless hazings to see to it that stiffer penalties are imposed," Levy told *Newsday*. "Otherwise the number of unpunishable deaths and serious injuries will continue to increase."

Once again Eileen and her friend Dianne Donaudy trudged back and forth between Sayville and Albany. One strong roadblock was a certain New York senator. "This bill is unconstitutional, to say the least," the senator's counsel told her. He tried to explain why in legal terms that cooked Eileen's brain. Nonetheless, she persisted and tried to explain how her own situation demonstrated that some sort of protective law was necessary. The counsel sympathetically told her that if the senator could see that the public mood was behind such a bill, perhaps a compromise could be arranged.

"What do you suggest?" asked Eileen.

"Letters and cards would help," said the attorney.

Donaudy and Eileen conferred in the hall. "I've got an idea," said Eileen. "How about all those people who wrote me after *Donahue*? They're all asking what they can do. Let's send them postcards."

Eileen bought five hundred postcards with postage and addressed every one of them to the senator. They wrote notes to five hundred *Donahue* viewers asking them to write the senator urging his support of the bill. Weeks later Eileen returned to Albany. The senator's secretary pointed to a wire basket bulging not only with postcards, but also with letters and mailgrams from states as far-flung as Texas, Missouri, Alaska, and California. "Those wonderful people not only wrote postcards," Eileen told Donaudy, "but they asked their friends to write also." Representatives from three other states wrote Eileen to request information about the pending New York legislation. Their constituents had demanded that a similar bill be passed in their home states.

Still, some of Eileen's optimism had been destroyed. Publicly, Harenberg tried to stroke the governor, telling the press that Carey had made valuable suggestions that he had incorporated into the new bill. Privately, he and John Longo warned Eileen that there was a strong chance that the governor would veto the bill every time it crossed his desk.

* * *

Roughly nine months after Eileen's organization had a name, she and Roy attended a dinner party held by the mother of Chuck's friend Jimmy Arnoux. Several other couples attended, including the parents of a girl Chuck had dated. Eileen had been grateful for the invitation. She hoped to hear some news about Jimmy, who was still in California and had been joined by his future bride, Nanci Lunati. Jimmy hadn't talked much to Eileen since she started her campaign. "It made me uncomfortable," he told her with his characteristic directness.

During the evening, the hostess—whom Chuck had called his second mother—confronted Eileen in front of the other guests. "When are you going to get back to normal and start taking care of your husband and other children?"

Eileen swallowed hard. Normally glib, she could not get the words out this time. She could not say "none of your business" to a woman who cared for her and was only trying to shock her into giving up what she considered a mad crusade. "Well, I think I'm taking care of everyone just fine," Eileen stammered. "Everyone's okay, and I'm doing what's okay for me."

The mother of one of Chuck's former girlfriends, away now at college, attacked next. "I'm not comfortable with you writing my daughter either," she said. "She needs to forget him. All you're doing is reminding her."

Eileen found an excuse to leave. Once she was alone with Roy in the car, she cried until she reached Marion Street. The people whose support she wanted most could not give it to her.

Oddly, she accepted their censure. They believed that she was keeping a wound open. She thought she was preventing new wounds by saving the children of other mothers. She never considered giving up her friends. Nor did they abandon her. She loved them and decided that she had to understand that they loved her enough to tell their version of the truth to her face.

Eileen hated it when others thought they knew how to turn off her grief. CHUCK had achieved slight success, but the price was costly, Eileen's diary reveals. While her immediate family tried to stow their doubts and help her with CHUCK, believing it kept her sanity intact, many friends and neighbors drifted away or castigated her. Many who had known the old ebullient Eileen found her preoccupation with her dead son morbid, her moroseness irritating. They did not accept her explanation that CHUCK "was about life, not death." She saw the looks too many times to mistake them. *Enough, enough, Eileen,* they said with their eyes.

After Chuck's funeral, other lives resumed. Maria Lunati dated and eventually married, as did his other loves. Other friends and family members tucked his death into their private storehouses; they latched mental padlocks on the windows of their minds. Jimmy Arnoux has difficulty expressing his feelings about Chuck's death. The surviving members of the gang of seven have never had a heart-to-heart talk about what happened to their friend.

But for Eileen public speaking proved a wearying, wonderful chore because talking about Chuck's death released some of the smoldering fury within her. She loved the young people she met, as well as fraternity leaders and educators who shared her passion for students. Her job exhausted her, but she wanted nothing less than complete immersion. Otherwise, she might become like other parents of Lost Chapter members, taking to bed much too early, staying in bed much too late. Always there was another stage, another podium, another audience of young people. She poured her heart, guts, and message into these kids, shaping and reshaping her lecture at every performance. The weariness in her voice at the end of every presentation was too natural to be feigned. She was, after all, keeping a schedule that would have flattened her prior to Chuck's death. She became addicted to the elation she felt when her message was greeted with standing ovations, becoming so commonplace that it jolted her when an occasional audience sat on their hands. She often wondered if her words kept some young man or woman from being the cause of broken pledges, but of course she never knew for certain. "That's the thing about preventive medicine—you never know what you're preventing," one fraternity man told her.

But while her public saw a strong, unbreakable Eileen, her family saw a preoccupied, saddened husk. They might have been more worried had they known that occasionally she succumbed to urges that even she couldn't explain. Once she paged Chuck Stenzel in an airport, experiencing bittersweet satisfaction at hearing his name on the public address system in a way not associated with his death. Often she tried speaking to him in the dead of night. While Roy—dead tired from immersing himself in work—slept heavily beside her, she extended her arms into the emptiness and prayed that God might grant her a miracle. She wanted Him to let Chuck take her hand, but she had no otherworldly experiences. Her connections with her son were entirely of this world: his letters, his schoolwork, the memories his friends shared from time to time. She reexamined every mark in his textbooks, pining for history books she had impulsively given Greg Belanger, and saw new meanings in every notation, particularly those that dealt with death.

Often in weak moments Eileen had tiny kernels of doubt that what she was doing had any purpose. For a brief period one of Chuck's Sayville buddies wavered, sending out the cards to congressmen at her request yet telling her he could not see the "ultimate importance" of her work. She tried to tell him that she knew passing laws wasn't the only solution—or even the best solution—to ending hazing. Her experiences had taught her intuitively that somehow societal norms and values had to change. Yet, even as she worked, one of the fired faculty members at Alfred wrote her in confidence to tell her that yet another fraternity man had had a close call with alcohol.

Criticisms from her college-educated friends particularly shook Eileen's convictions. How dare she, this housewife from Sayville, confront educators and fraternity leaders to join the fight against hazing when she lacked even an associate's degree? Yet when Greg Belanger, for example, told her how his alcohol consumption had plummeted after Chuck's death, she had hope. If Chuck's sad example could have a dramatic effect on one young person, why couldn't it have the same effect on others?

Nonetheless, the confrontations wore her down. At the supermarket she ran into a woman who had known Chuck as a child. "I saw you on television," she said, after Eileen's appearance on *Tomorrow.*

"Oh?"

"Why don't you let him rest in peace?"

Eileen felt the familiar squeamishness. "He is resting in peace hopefully."

"Oh, let this go, Eileen. Chuck would be furious with you."

"I don't believe that. I don't believe that he would want it to happen again to somebody else. I think he would feel good about it."

"No, you're wrong. You need counseling." The woman wheeled away and put as many aisles between herself and Eileen as possible.

The Alfred administration, even in the blackest days after *Donahue,* certainly thought that Eileen would cease this campaign after making her point, but they misread her intentions. The mood on campus, Greg Belanger recalls, was amazement that here was this revenge-bent woman trying to wreck the university. If revenge were part of her motivation at first, that quickly evaporated as she began to perceive that what had happened to Chuck at Alfred was occurring to a greater or lesser extent at many schools in the country. Moreover, from the mail and phone calls she received, it soon became apparent that hazing was not restricted to fraternities. She realized that hazing was also a problem at high schools, in particular, but also in college clubs, bands, and sororities, as well as in some adult secret societies. Hazing was part of a larger social problem, in her opinion, and she became attuned to the larger implications of her son's death. On the other hand, she had a scenario in her mind about what had happened to Chuck at Klan Alpine, and she wasn't going to be satisfied until she had some answers.

In July 1979 Eileen received an air-freight package. Because she had been receiving so many media tapes, books, and packages of clippings, she opened the package from Paul Kolisch without thinking. Inside were the glass slides from Chuck's toxicology report. Kolisch sent them to verify his finding that carbon monoxide poisoning had not been a factor in Chuck's death. Eileen looked at the slides and realized that she held her son's flesh and blood. She had to steel herself against a sudden, irrational impulse to rub the tissues all over her face. Instead, she took them to a trusted advisor, who thought them grisly and disgusting. They were reviewed a second time by a pathologist, who also found nothing significant, says Eileen. Nonetheless, she again had cause to bless the gruff little man from Friendship, New York. His actions showed her there was decency in Allegany County.

12

As Eileen lectured at school after school, she began to perceive fraternity members as victims. They were caught up in a type of behavioral slavery that was bigger than any one fraternity, bigger than all men collectively. *Science Newsletter* claims that hazers are "reenacting rites performed by primitive people for hundreds of years," citing widespread initiation practices among primitive people that are as "bizarre as any hazing customs that college boys of today can think up." Michael Olmert theorizes in *Smithsonian* that fraternal paddling is a reenactment of a primitive custom "in which [the initiates'] former evils and their immaturity are transferred into the wood." Thus, Eileen's sense that certain fraternity practices are "barbaric" is, apparently, grounded in anthropological fact.

Activities called hazing today were also part of early civilized societies. St. Augustine, while a student at Carthage, was connected with the naughty Eversores. Hazing also existed at ancient seats of learning such as Berytus and Athens.

Fred Kershner theorizes that hazing in contemporary life is the result of the trivialization of chapter life. The emphasis on partying smothers fraternal ideals. Kershner concedes that fraternal hazing reflects society as a whole but says fraternity leaders cannot justify it that way. "Fraternities are not supposed to be satisfied with reflecting society as a whole," he says. "It's supposed to be not average or below average, but the leaders, the better people. If we can't keep that—which is where we started from—we ought to go out of business."

While Eileen sympathizes with fraternity members, she remains true to her original purpose. She can forgive hazing transgressions but insists that legal sanctions against hazers are necessary to deter others and to punish those who haze—to show that a crime has been committed. Because her emotional stake with Greeks at the workshops she leads is not as strong as with Klan Alpine, she deals with admitted hazers as coolly as a social worker. Grief and resentment wash away whenever she addresses rooms filled with young people who truly listen to her message. She sees in their eyes the need for direction, for an authority figure to tell them that what they intuit as wrong *is* wrong.

Looking out into audience after audience, she realizes that she knows only a fraction of what goes on in Greek life and in other secret societies and select groups. She meets with smiling people putting on their best faces. They treat her with courtesy and respect. But what goes on behind closed doors once she heads for the airport? Why can't she get more young people to buck group thinking and confront their peers? On more than one occasion students have revealed to her that pledges get extra punishment because of her visit. Year by year she has added file cabinets to hold all the hazing articles in CHUCK's records. Coverage swells when a new name joins the ranks of the Lost Chapter, but a death in Texas never means that hazing goes down in Florida. "Yeah, sure, another accident," she said bitterly to Roy when the 1980 death of Lex Batson, a Phi Kappa Psi pledge at the University of Missouri, was ruled "horseplay" instead of hazing.

A rite of passage robbed Eileen of a child, and, hence, she looks for and finds Chuck's lost youth in the faces of the young men and women she meets during her travels.

Eileen has a story to tell, and she tells it from the heart. "Why am I standing here?" she says to audiences of young people. "I am standing here because I have a responsibility. I would not want your mother nor your family to go through the pain and devastation that we have. . . . I think I've heard most of the excuses for why hazing persists. In my travels I'm told that it unifies the pledge class, it strengthens the bonds of friendship and brotherhood, it builds respect, it builds character, it is a tradition, we have always done it that way, we have to make them prove themselves, and the worst, the saddest reason of all, 'I went through it — now it's their turn.' They are all the wrong reasons as far as I'm concerned. There is nothing anyone could ever say to me that would convince me in any way that there is anything positive about hazing in any form. You can certainly achieve friendship, brotherhood, and strengthened bonds through something positive, constructive, and useful. You are not going to get respect from pledges by demeaning or degrading them; you are going to have to earn it."

She has certainly had the power to trash the fraternity system. She could have summoned journalists into her living room every day of the week. She had the right to hate, but who would gain? Chuck wouldn't have wanted that. He had died because something in him wanted the company of Klan Alpine as brothers. In fact, some years after her life started to settle down again, Eileen began to realize that had Chuck lived and joined Klan, she might have had a different tragedy to face. Had Chuck become a brother, he might have hazed. In so doing, he might have sacrificed some other mother's son.

Instead of ripping the system, sharing the stories of her dead son and other broken pledges became Eileen's road to peace. Instead of waging a vendetta, she tries to educate. "The young faces in my audience didn't kill Chuck," she once said. "They were in junior high school at the time."

Not all her talks bring standing ovations or even loud applause although a high percentage attract both. A few young men, sensitive to fraternity bashing from other speakers, have left the room or baited her during the question-and-answer sessions following her lectures. "If we want a pledge bare-assed on his hands and knees pushing an egg across the floor . . . who are we hurting?" a member of Sigma Alpha Epsilon asked during Eileen's visit to Northwestern University. An alumnus of Phi Kappa Tau at a convention in Knoxville, Tennessee, told her to "stick with Barbara Walters" rather than share her stories with his group.

Most fraternity and sorority members listen and give her a fair chance to express her views. When Eileen talks, occasional sighs or sobs go off like bombs. Her listeners transpose their own mothers' faces onto Eileen's. They envision the pain their kin would feel should they die or be involved in someone else's death. Many hazers squirm while she talks, aware they're hearing someone else's truth even if it isn't theirs. "You can't fool students," she often tells administrators baffled by her success. "They can see I'm sincere, and they respond."

She speaks without the skills of an evangelical preacher. She never raises her voice, and she doesn't scold. Her accusations against the Alfred administration and Klan Alpine are matter-of-fact, not shrill. She comes across as what she is: an ordinary housewife in an extraordinary fix.

After her talks, when young people crowd around to confide hazing horror stories, she tells them to make a difference in their own systems. "Look at me," she says. "If you believe enough to do something and you have the guts to try, you can do it. Plus, you'll like yourself better for the effort." Slowly, one organization at a time, a few national fraternities have become her allies. Alpha Tau Omega printed business cards for her. Sigma Alpha Epsilon published an informative twelve-page booklet called "Death by Hazing" that has been distributed to libraries (including Alfred University's), fraternities, and sororities across the country.

Eileen's attorney refers to her work as a "labor of love" while others call it an obsession. Again and again she has promised Roy and her children that she will ease up. But then the phone rings with another parent's sad tale, or an advisor inviting her to yet another college, or legislators inviting her to their state to speak on behalf of another hazing bill—at her own expense. In her journal she expresses amazement that people thank her so profusely. "Thank me?—me!—what I have done or am doing is a blessing to me. With God's help, somehow I have the strength to continue. At times I've felt my heart was buried [along] with Chuck. . . . The tears don't come as often, but the pain—the void—remains." Roy continues to tease her for never being satisfied with all she has attained. "She always wants better achievement," he says.

The scenario after every road tour is the same. Roy meets her at the airport, lips ready for a kiss. He always asks how she did. She always replies, "Well, all right, but it could have been better." If ninety-nine people give her a standing ovation, she recalls the one who walked out. If Lambda Chi, Sigma Alpha Epsilon, and Alpha Tau Omega make her feel like a queen, she agonizes over Delta Kappa Epsilon and Sigma Tau Gamma, who have never invited her to speak.

Nonetheless, some of the fraternities that originally mistrusted her now schedule her for summer conferences and hazing-awareness programs. Unable to say no, she overextends herself. What if she failed to give a talk that might have saved someone? Roy sometimes chides her for letting her dinner get cold to take a phone call—often collect—from a fraternity or sorority pledge trying to deal with hazers. "I can't just tell them no," she says to him. "What if someone had been able to help Chuck that night?" Roy's own awareness has expanded. He once paid the fare of a teenage drunk who had been thrown off a ferry boat and drove the youth home to make sure nothing untoward happened to him in his helpless state.

Early one morning, shortly before two A.M., Eileen dragged her sore feet into the lobby of the Fairmont Hotel in New Orleans. This was her seventh convention in seven days. Yet she couldn't stop. She felt woozy with lack of sleep. The lobby looked like it probably looks on a Super Bowl Sunday. Everywhere she glanced she saw fraternity men in tee-shirts adorned with Greek letters. Ordinarily she'd have been eager to find a familiar face, but now—although she hates hotel rooms—the thought of clean sheets inspired her. She longed for her king-sized bed and the body of her king-sized husband alongside her.

The noise level was so high that she shut it out of her consciousness. A night on Bourbon Street is a fantasy many student vikings wait all year to enjoy. Many were tipsy and boisterous. Some had downed hurricanes at Pat O'Brien's pub. "Part of me enjoyed seeing the relaxed air of fun and partying," she later admitted. "But most of me—the mother—wanted to say, 'Please! Be careful. Don't drink to excess.'"

She fell onto a lobby chair and dug through her purse for her reservation. Looking up, she noticed six young men stalking her, stupid grins plastered across their infantile faces. Drooping eyelids indicated they were only a drink or two from calling it a night.

Eileen figured them for spontaneous greeters, out to wish her well in her talk in—oh, Lord—a few hours. She wondered how they recognized her. She smiled at the ringleader. He returned a crooked, dimpled grin to hide his uneasiness. He thrust a wad of bills at her.

"What do you charge?"

Baffled, she could only stare at the proffered cash.

The ringleader frowned. "There's more where this came from."

Before Eileen could speak, a bell captain swooped down on the youths. "Sorry, ma'am," he said. "But an unescorted woman is sometimes misconstrued as a lady of the night."

Amazed at her thickheadedness, Eileen reddened. But she roared aloud when she reached her room. The next day, when she faced her audience of five hundred or so, she heard a distinct moan when she gave a special thanks "to the Sig Eps who welcomed me in the lobby."

Roy enjoyed this story. "You didn't take the cash?" he said in mock indignation. "CHUCK could have used the money."

Between lecture stops, Eileen again pushed for passage of an anti-hazing bill in New York state. "If it were anybody else but Eileen, it would have died there," says John Longo. "That would have been the end of it. But she wasn't willing to give up." Backed by Longo, she begged, cajoled, and reasoned with Paul Harenberg to start the fight afresh. The pressure that Eileen and her supporters put on the governor with letters, signed petitions, and mailgrams was tremendous, showing that there was public sentiment against hazing. She met individually with appropriate committee members and legislators from both parties. She talked with them in their offices, met them for coffee, and in one case buttonholed a rising star named John Dunne who said that she could talk to him while she walked him from his office to the elevator.

While Harenberg tried to reason with the governor's counsel, Eileen went for Carey's throat. She threatened to plant the next New York death on the governor's doorstep.

Predictably and sadly, another death did occur — at Ithaca College, another small school in New York's Southern Tier. In April 1980 a former first-string linebacker from Fordham Prep in the Bronx, eighteen-year-old Joseph Parella, Jr., died of hyperthermia while performing fraternity calisthenics in a steam room. As happened in the aftermath of John Davies's death, a grand jury investigating Parella's death failed to recommend that charges be brought against the offending fraternity, Delta Kappa. (The grand jury's not bringing charges is perhaps an indication of what might have happened in the Chuck Stenzel case, had George Francis elected to bring his evidence before an Allegany County grand jury.) The school kicked the group off campus, but the members voted to continue operating as a sub-rosa fraternity, accepting new pledges.

However, in an unusual move, the grand jury recommended that New York pass criminal legislation. In a statement, jury foreman H. Ernest England said that a law was necessary "to deal effectively with a situation which we the Grand Jury feel continues to be an imminent danger to the health, safety and welfare of a large number of students who seek membership in fraternities, sororities, and other voluntary associations with secret pledging and initiation procedures." The grand jury emphasized that "no fact emerges from this investigation more clearly than the fact that the fraternity brothers were completely undeterred by college rules and warnings and criminal laws." Moreover, it chided Ithaca College for making "little or no attempt to communicate the illegality of such practices to fraternity members." The grand jury recommended that some sort of punitive action be taken against colleges that failed to submit adequate plans for the supervision of fraternity initiation practices, inquiring whether denial of state aid might be one such measure. The grand jury found that "existing criminal laws are so inappropriate to this situation as to make their applicability almost impossible. . . . We find the law to be wholly inadequate in this area and we further find it to constitute almost no deterrent to the conduct of those who every day conduct pledging and initiation exercises on the campuses of colleges across the country."

The grand jury's conclusion criticized Ithaca College. "Joseph Parella did not go off to war. He went off to a placid campus in a very safe upstate community. . . . In seeking membership to a college fraternity, however, no deaths are necessary, and even one is far too much. This Grand Jury is convinced that Joseph Parella was in a real sense murdered. He was murdered by collective stupidity, collective insensitivity, and collective irresponsibility."

As she had threatened, Eileen demanded that Governor Carey take some responsibility for Parella's death. "Perhaps if that bill had passed last year, someone would be held accountable for the student's death at Ithaca. But instead the governor's veto signaled fraternities to go ahead and continue their dangerous and potentially fatal hazing practices," she said. Eileen notified Harenberg the day of the tragedy, and he promised to see the governor's counsel. "I intend to write a personal letter, but I don't know if it'll ever reach his eyes," she said. "If this tragedy makes him think more about the dangers of hazing, so be it."

The new version of the Trunzo-Harenberg bill was introduced the same week as the Parella death, and this time state senator John Calandra and many other lawmakers needed no prompting to trumpet its virtues. "Apparently the taking of a life is of no concern to this governor," grumbled Calandra. The legislation attracted forty-five Assembly and twenty-five Senate sponsors. Moreover, Eileen received many letters of support from key figures in the fraternity world. The fraternity system itself was to become increasingly pro-active in the fight against hazing. "We have the support of national fraternities now," she told the Buffalo *Courier Express.* Another nice surprise came from Alfred. A spokesman gave the bill a statement of support that might be labeled lukewarm. "If this legislation focuses attention on the problem, it may be of some value," H. Martin Moore, executive director of university relations, told the *Legislative Gazette.* "We have never tolerated hazing [but] we can't control and often don't know about hazing activities."

The key provision of the revised bill was that a victim's consent was no longer a defense. To overcome the governor's contention that the law was too vague, the bill also defined hazing: "Hazing means a method of initiation into a student, fraternal or similar club or association, or a ritual engaged in with respect to such a club or association which is perpetrated by a member or members of such club or association upon an individual in a manner which submits the victim to indignity, ridicule or humiliation."

This time, the governor was overmatched. He signed the bill without a public protest. In Albany, Harenberg stood in the assembly chambers and smiled at his colleagues. He moved that the bill go on record as the CHUCK law. He introduced Eileen to the distinguished gathering. The assemblymen stood to applaud the housewife from Sayville.

Klan Alpine alumni made a pilgrimage to the university in 1981. A 1961 graduate then living in Virginia had spent many hours contacting Klan members from the fifties and sixties. "Let's get back to Alfred and see if we can shake that house up" is how he put it to them. About forty percent of those contacted agreed that a reunion was a good idea.

"Responses from past brothers varied, running the gamut from those feeling a sense of loss, to others who could care less," recalls Rich Sigal.

He didn't know what he would find in Alfred. Would the white, three-story Victorian house to which he had such a strong emotional attachment be boarded up? Had it been sold? What condition would it be in?

Sigal and the others who came to the reunion were those who believed most strongly that Klan Alpine had enriched their lives. The ideal of nonsectarianism had bonded them, and many admitted they had been unabashedly idealistic about the possibilities of brotherhood. For the reunion they brought their families and arranged to stay on campus.

Their first glimpse of the house disheartened the insiders-become-outsiders. "Everywhere were signs of deterioration," says Sigal. "Rotting steps, a leaky roof, holes in plaster walls, filth, and disarray." The group had no need to ask about Klan's new image. The stench of beer and vomit and urine that assaulted their noses told them. "All [of us] were shocked," says Sigal. "Everyone agreed there was work to be done."

Nonetheless, both Sigal and his former pledgemaster, Richard Klein, say that the reunion with former members who came from as far away as California was one of the most fulfilling experiences of their lives. "[There] was this tremendous rapport," says Klein. "It was so natural to sit down and talk to these people and find out what was happening to them in their lives. It was just a wonderful, wonderful experience — very positive."

At the reunion Klein gained a better understanding of what Klan had actually meant to him. The group had helped him develop a closeness to people that had been restricted to his family before he went away to college. He learned that he could count on people and trust them. "They are not always going to behave the way you would like them to behave," he says. "But when push comes to shove, they could be counted on to be there for you. That's a most valuable lesson." He came to believe that greater good could come from team than individual effort. The members' joint ownership of the Klan house taught him to be proud and respectful of his property. His relationships with men matured as a result of his membership, he says, and he came to see himself as responsible, to a degree, for the welfare of those with whom he lived.

Before coming to Alfred, Klein had been a high-school fraternity member at Valley Stream North High School on Long Island. "There was hazing in that fraternity, but not a lot of it — certainly not as much as I experienced when I went to college," he says.

Sigal, Klein, and another Klan brother revived their band, the Klan-tones. They could no longer carry a tune in a bucket, but the old enthusiasm remained.

Following the songfest, the alumni met with Don King. They were stern and polite but hardly amicable. Their arms were folded; their smiles, stiff. They saw themselves as an enlightened bunch even though King didn't. King laughs when he's asked if he thought these brothers were different from the Klan members of the seventies and eighties. He doubts there was much difference while both groups were in school. Nor does he believe that the house was better maintained or smelled less vile than it does today. "It's the same smell," he says.

King believes the brothers when Chuck Stenzel pledged were good people on an individual basis, too. "But it's like a pack of dogs," he says, offering an analogy. "You get one dog alone [and] it's fine—the dog's not any potential harm to anybody. But you get a group of dogs together, and it creates a whole different atmosphere. I think it's the same thing with a fraternity. . . . Provide them with alcohol, adrenaline, and all that, it's a very different situation."

Sigal says that King told them that Chuck's death was only one of a series of incidents involving Klan, "and [that] the membership failed to respond effectively in policing its own." Moreover, King maintained that he had presented a proposal to the Klan undergraduates designed to get the group back into the college community but that the membership's actions failed to merit reinstatement.

Sigal and other Klan alumni doubted this last statement, saying that it was unlikely the school's legal counsel would permit Klan to be recognized until some of the public clamor died down. Sigal says that the Klan membership in 1981 felt that the university wanted the fraternity to fold. "They sensed no encouragement to shape up their act," he says. The members believed that the university had pressured faculty members not to associate with Klan Alpine. The house was in disrepair, the young Klansmen told alumni, because banks refused to lend money with rumors rampant that Eileen Stevens planned to file a multimillion-dollar lawsuit against the fraternity. In fact, the alumni themselves feared that word of their visit might leak out and somehow embroil them in litigation.

"We recognized that we had some responsibility for whatever had gone on," says Klein, "which I thought was a perceptive notion on our parts. They were different from us, but somehow what we had done, the seeds that we had sown, had led to this. Therefore, we had some responsibilities to make it right."

Many of the young brothers didn't want the university's supervision. The fraternity's desperado image continued to attract large pledge classes. One member at the time of Chuck's death says Klan members acted like outlaws because outsiders and the administration began to treat them like outlaws. In many ways, King couldn't win no matter whom he tried to please. After President Rose left, the dean became the sole point man on the situation. He had Eileen shooting him in the front, Klan Alpine knifing him in the back, and the press dropping grenades onto his head.

Eileen, working alone in the dark, never knew that both Klan Alpine and King were, for different reasons, experiencing some of the same stress she endured every day. The Klan alumni at the reunion became impatient with their heirs. One older member nearly belted an intoxicated student who had the poor sense to approach an alumnus's wife, recalls Sigal. By the end of the reunion, it was clear to Sigal at least that the generation gap might be too wide to overcome.

During the early sixties Klan member Joel P. Moscowitz wrote a short speech to convey what the fraternity meant to him. That letter was read to new pledges during the rest of that decade to acquaint them with the ideal of nonsectarianism and to demonstrate that Klan Alpine was a group with values despite all exterior evidence to the contrary. During the course of the reunion, with emotions running high, Sigal read that letter with all the power and passion he puts into Eileen's letter to Ann Landers in his classes:

> It's not the house or the food, or our athletic prowess, or even our social life — it's the Klansmen. It's that imperfect college student, who'd like to live in a house where no one gives a damn if you're colored or Jewish or Catholic, or if your parents are millionaires, or if you just arrived in this country. That's what makes Klan Alpine — "The Klan." Sounds idealistic — well, it's the truth, and any Klansman will tell you so in no uncertain terms. We're not perfect; in fact, we're far from it. I've seen Klansmen drink. I've seen them neglect their studies. I've seen them do a lot of things that would make me a little ashamed to say they're my fraternity brothers. Sure, I've seen them do a lot of things. I've seen Klansmen drive twenty miles on a winter morning to help a brother out of a snowdrift. I've seen Klansmen stay up all night trying to help a brother pass an exam. I've seen Klansmen work together cleaning up their house. I've seen Klansmen put their brothers to bed — and I've seen them work together like brothers should.
>
> Klan's a funny place. We like to say we're individuals — yet we're all brothers — it's a house of contradictions. It's a house of differing principles, beliefs, and ideals. Yet, it's a good house — it really is: and more important than that it's my house. . . . Most important of all, I'm a Klansman.

Reaction to Sigal's reading was intense in the alumni, not-so-intense for current members. The older men sat there in tears; the younger ones tried not to look embarrassed. "That's right," an alum said, "that's what it was like."

Sigal himself was struggling with powerful emotions. He had relinquished his house to these young men, and, to be honest, he didn't like them. The house smelled like "ground-in barf," recalls Sigal, "years of it." The furniture was tattered. The rooms were pits. Even worse, in his mind, someone had taken the Klan Alpine symbol, a crest, down from the big tree outside where it had proudly hung for many years. In its place, the house had hung a surrealistic, threatening painting. What that sign alone implied to Sigal and the returning brothers was that these kids needed rules, were perhaps even crying out for them. Klan Alpine was disaffiliated. Klan Alpine was floundering. Klan Alpine had become an outlaw sect, and it was behaving like one. Sigal realized that he had to say his piece to the new brothers. His voice became parental.

"Okay, as I see it, this is your choice," he said. "If you're going to get reaffiliated, you're going to have to do the following things." At this point, he and other brothers set some ground rules. They freely offered their financial help as well as advice, but they attached conditions. They wanted Klan reunited with Alfred University. They wanted the house restored to good order, and they wanted that sign taken down. They wanted a new image. There were some objections, but the old-timers were adamant. Unlike the new brothers, they knew the Klan's constitution, could cite chapter and verse. "One of the things that you don't realize is once a brother, always a brother," Sigal warned the younger men. "We always have a vote. If we want to, as a bloc, we can decide to vote you out of existence. We can vote to disband the whole house."

The new brothers agreed to the demands. A couple seemed even to welcome them, to realize that they needed clear-cut norms to survive. Parameters had become vague, starting in the mid-sixties, even earlier at schools such as Columbia and Berkeley. "Drugs, for example, were nonexistent," says Sigal. "It wasn't anything we had to contend with. The drug [scene] cannot be counted out for setting the tone for a lot of other things that are going on, including . . . partying for four-five days in a row and never knowing when the party's over. . . . As an analogy, there was a lot of joy in walking my date back to the dorm and watching the doors close after her—the night was over. It had a beginning, and it had an end; I knew when it was. The boundaries were there; they were clearcut."

At every senior prom in the early sixties, the Klan members enjoyed hearing joyful squeals as one young woman or another became engaged. Relationships were defined. An engagement was, as Sigal says, clearcut. A marriage was clearcut. People generally didn't shack up together. Today, he claims, relationships are no longer clearly defined. Male and female students stroll into the same dorm at night, often into the same room. The symbolism of rings and pins and lavelieres is gone. "When we don't know where the boundaries are, when we only have the vague outline of a horizon to shoot at, we become anonymous," insists Sigal.

The 1981 Klan Alpine meeting was a successful reunion. But in the end it failed to alter the behavior of the contemporary Klan members. "I don't think the meeting got things done," says Klein. "That was a frustrating experience." The Klan alumni felt they were trying to fight a mountain of Jell-O. They pushed in a certain area and met no resistance. But when they got through, the other side of the mountain was still there.

What the alumni tried to do, of course, was to persuade strangers to alter their behavior. "That's hard to do," says Klein, a distinguished-looking man whose white hair makes him look a decade older than Sigal. "Something having to do with hazing is deeply ingrained in us."

* * *

Eileen's lectures brought her several unexpected benefits. She never knew who might show up and help. Once she lectured to a scant forty people at Middlebury College in Vermont. But among the group was the education editor for the New York *Times*. The column he wrote brought her the most mail she had received since *Donahue.*

Another benefit was that her lectures put her in touch with a handful of young men who answered some of her questions about what had happened to her son that dismal night.

Eileen met Lambda Chi Alpha's longtime executive director, George Spasyk, at a 1979 talk she gave at her own expense. She liked Spasyk's optimism. "Hazing is a problem, but for every problem there are hundreds of problem solvers," he told her. She understood from a frank discussion that Spasyk had expected not to like her because the anti-Alfred student on *Donahue* had been a Lambda Chi. But the two immediately captivated one another and have ever since. Spasyk's acceptance of Eileen was as significant as her acceptance of him. His national organization flew her to its 1980 convention in Denver, Colorado. As always, Eileen rose early, and Roy drove her to Kennedy airport after a quick breakfast at her parents' house. She wore Chuck's confirmation ring around her middle finger for luck and packed the rosary she had taken from his coffin.

Lambda Chi Alpha is one of the younger Greek organizations, founded in 1909, but it has become one of the stronger and larger groups. Lambda Chi alumni include Harry Truman and several United States senators. During the seventies, Lambda Chi was one of the first nationals to use the term associate member instead of pledge. In an ideal Lambda world associates would have many of the same rights and responsibilities as members.

Following her speech, a member asked what Eileen thought had been on Chuck's mind the day of his death.

"I might be able to help answer that," said a voice in the room.

Eileen studied the speaker, a young representative from Alfred University named Mark Matar. He said he had attended Lambda Chi's Tapping Night the same evening that Chuck died. He had lived in Openhym, Chuck's dormitory.

"I was in the room with his girlfriend when she found out about it," Matar said at the convention. She became hysterical, he added. "I decided I'd have to call her mother. There wasn't anyone else who could help her."

Matar says that everyone on campus was aware that tapping nights at Alfred revolved around alcohol consumption. "Klan, in particular, was the hardest-core fraternity on campus," he says. "It had the craziest parties and most drug use in addition to beer use — a lot of hard alcohol." The hard drinking, Matar feels, put brothers in danger of becoming alcoholics.

He described a mood of shock on campus, particularly at Openhym where people who knew Chuck were "significantly . . . upset."

Eileen listened with a heavy heart.

"At Alfred on pledge night, you just hoped you'd be able to find your way home," said Matar. "You really expected to drink a lot." Matar's father knew about fraternities. On pledge night he talked to his son about what to do if his fraternity required him to drink too much alcohol. "He told me to take a sip and to spill the rest of it," said Matar.

Troubled, Eileen stood at the podium. Maybe Chuck would have spilled the booze that helped kill him, she thought, had only she or Roy known to warn him.

She thanked Matar and managed to continue. It was a tense moment. But she was a professional now and managed to address the remaining questions before collapsing on her bed.

In 1980, Eileen's work was praised in the *Congressional Record* by Mario Biaggi, then the ranking member of the House Education and Labor Committee. "By educating the public at large about the risks associated with this kind of activity, we can help to bring an end to unnecessary deaths of our young people in such tragic fashions," said Biaggi.

Eileen visited Doane College with Sue Cantwell, the girl Chuck had dated there. On a hot, humid day, she met Ed Watkins, the counselor who had befriended her son. They became old friends instantly over a dinner of corn-fed beef.

The college was much more beautiful than Chuck had said. The grounds were serene and lush, prettily landscaped with flowers, calm ponds, and trees. The campus, deserted in summer, seemed surrealistic. "I can't believe I'm in Nebraska," she said to Sue. It was so eerie to be with a girl Chuck had cared for, walking the paths he had walked, visiting his dormitory. As discontent as Chuck had been, Eileen felt comfortable. She did an interview with local television reporter Rick Sullivan. He turned out to have taken Chuck to the state fair.

Eileen also met Lila McVay, whose son had been injured in a hazing incident. Doane's fraternities, all locals, routinely engaged in pranks that constituted hazing, Eileen learned, dispelling another myth she had created to imagine a different fate for her son: that he would not have been hazed, would not have died, had he stayed at Doane.

On January 28, 1981, Alfred University presented a Bergen Forum on the campus Greeks. Bergen forums were Stuart Campbell's brainstorm. He named the intellectual debates in honor of a dead colleague.

Greeks at Alfred at that time numbered more than four hundred, and the fraternities' combined annual budget was around $400,000. At the forum Don Koglmeier, a former president of Alfred's Inter-Greek Council, discussed the goals of Greek student organizations.

The meat of the forum, however, was the question-and-answer session, which focused on hazing. One speaker referred several times to the suspension of Klan Alpine, saying that it could not be lifted while litigation was in process. The forum demonstrated that hazing was alive on campus despite Chuck's death three years earlier. "Hazing has not been abolished," Koglmeier said, "but hazing practices are limited to meaningful tasks." A speaker asked how hazing could continue at Klan after the administration had ordered it to cease. "Klan has its reasons for not giving in to the university on this point," he said.

Koglmeier stirred up the gathering when he defined hazing as "physical and mental discomfort," and argued that "hazing is a necessary initiation rite."

"Is physical and mental discomfort necessary for membership to the houses?" asked a woman.

Koglmeier told her that he thought everything in life contained some degree of hazing. "Hazing [is] justified by its definition," he said.

Another young woman then attacked the speaker, saying that a friend who was a sorority pledge had been blindfolded by members and dropped off in Hornell during the middle of the night to find her way home as best she could. She wanted to know why such practices were tolerated.

Koglmeier allowed that such things shouldn't be done, stressing that hazing was forbidden by all national Greek organizations. He suggested that an alternative was for actives to assign two to three times as much schoolwork as a normal load to develop a pledge's "stamina" as a student. The audience, polite and well-mannered, as Alfred audiences tend to be at such events, burst into a collective giggle.

Don King was in the audience but said little except to clarify certain points. He made no attempt, however, to halt the participation of the well-represented, "unaffiliated" Klan Alpine members in the audience.

Eileen's argument that supervision of Greeks at Alfred is worthy of public scrutiny can be documented by examining incidents that occurred after her son's death:

■ On March 28, 1979, Alfred police issued Alfred Village Court appearance tickets to two Klan members, one of them a senior, on charges of third-degree assault and harassment. The charges were made by a neighbor who claimed the two had attacked him.

■ In 1982 the dissociated Klan Alpine again brawled with another fraternity. Five Klansmen were arrested on charges of disorderly conduct and unlawful assembly. King again refused to outlaw the group permanently. But he did say, "This type of incident doesn't help their cause."

■ On September 20, 1985, Alfred University's Delta Sigma Phi fraternity brawled with Alfred State College's Gamma Theta Gamma shortly after two A.M., sending one person to the hospital with head injuries.

- On October 11, 1985, nine "little sisters" pledging Zeta Beta Tau were injured during a pledging custom when an automobile plowed into them. Three women suffered fractured legs (one of them had both legs fractured), one suffered a lost tooth and fractured palate, the others suffered miscellaneous bruises. "Don King stated that no alcohol was apparent at the accident," said the *Fiat Lux*, but he did not comment on whether he thought the incident violated the state law on hazing. A local newspaper made no mention of the accident's being fraternity-related.

- On January 26, 1986, a Delta Sigma Phi senior named Bryan Karl was paralyzed when he participated in a well-known and often dangerous college stunt called stair-diving. King told the campus paper that the game involved "a person standing at the head of the stairs, diving and attempting to break his fall." Karl, a varsity soccer player from Friendship, New York, was treated by Dr. Paul Kolisch, the pathologist who assisted at Chuck Stenzel's autopsy.

  "I'm not treating him," says Kolisch today. "I'm carrying him."

  Said King in the *Fiat Lux*, "The community and his peers are greatly shocked."

- In 1989 Gary Horowitz learned from a Kappa Psi Upsilon mother that her son had been burned in a pledging incident in which a Bunsen burner was a prop. The injured young man suffered scars. The incident was not reported in the campus 18,30paper, nor was it ever investigated by King because the fraternity hushed up the affair. The young man, Eric Twiname of Langhorne, Pennsylvania, will give only a terse statement regarding the affair. "There is no reason to blame the members," he says, terming the incident an accident. "I lit the Bunsen burner and loaded it; it was my own fault." Asked how hazing incidents might be prevented, Twiname gives a sarcastic response. "It's pretty easy—don't haze."

Until Chuck died, Eileen had never gone anywhere without Roy. After she had become an accomplished crusader, traveling mostly alone, her husband escorted her to receive an award and has kidded her ever after. "I know now why you come to these things," he said in mock anger. "We've only been here ten minutes and already you've been hugged by a dozen handsome men."

Roy consistently stayed on the sidelines, content with running the Jem Tool & Die Corporation that he and some other workers bought with their savings. Started in a garage, it is a small operation that retains a family atmosphere. The former owner was always donating something to Eileen for CHUCK, most notably a copier.

But while Roy is in Long Island, he is never far from Eileen's thoughts. He has backed her organization, defended her from more attacks than he can count. For months after Chuck's death, he held her through the nights, the one time when she didn't have perpetual motion to protect her from her grief.

The two continue to have a marriage that the survivors in the gang of six envy. Roy wires her flowers too often to count. They write each other love notes. "You are overwhelmingly in my thoughts this moment," she once wrote him while thirty-seven thousand feet over Louisiana. "For some unexpected reason I feel compelled to tell you a few things other than the usual. Have I told you lately that I'm proud of you? Your achievements and recognition in your work have surpassed all of our youthful expectations. Your support, love and patience [with] my 'plight' since CHUCK is something I'm so grateful for. Without it I'd be lost. You must know that . . . your talents, your devotion to me, [and] your stability are things (qualities, strengths) I admire and cherish. Especially of late when I made my decision to 'go fight' you supported that."

Rich Sigal had been permitted to drink at eighteen in his native New York state, but he has another perspective now as a father and teacher. Although an avowed protector of human rights, he had no regrets when New Jersey authorities took the "right" to drink away from eighteen-year-olds. Yes, these youngsters were old enough to vote, old enough to die for their country, old enough to own and operate a fraternity house. But he nor they could dispute available research. New Jersey auto fatalities plummeted when authorities raised the drinking age to twenty-one. Not even young people unhappy with the change could deny that the population of college-age kids includes far too many heavy drinkers likely to self-destruct if left entirely to their own devices in the use of alcohol.

When his son was three or four, Sigal was working in the backyard on a summer day and had set down a cold beer that he planned to enjoy on his next break. Josh Sigal was in the middle of a game with friends. Although his throat was dry, he didn't want to interrupt his fun by going into the house for water. Sigal watched him grab the beer. The boy took a slug and ran back to where the real action was. All their lives the Sigal children learned by their father's example that you drink beer to quench thirst.

But when his children reached adolescence in the eighties, he feared that peer pressure might supplant his example. He of all people knew that youngsters can ignore every warning. He and his wife had tried to mold their children's behavior, not wait to change it after drug or alcohol dependency wreaked their havoc. The Sigals refused to leave instruction up to the schools. After all, how many kids have heard the local lawman's anti-drinking pitch in class and viewed the smashed-up cars on the school lawn, hauled there as examples, then gotten drunk that very weekend and blotted their young lives out on a concrete wall?

It was only a matter of time before Sigal and his wife had to confront their teenage daughter. "We hear there's a lot of drinking going on at the high school, Brynn," Sigal said.

Their daughter, a soccer player now attending a topnotch eastern college, studied them. Wanting to be honest with her parents, she admitted having a beer now and then. Both parents' backs stiffened, and they braced themselves. She went on to acknowledge being drunk once, Sigal says, but said they had always trained her to be cautious with drinking and to know what she was doing. She said that if she were in a situation with beer around, she might take it and might not. The upshot of the heart-to-heart was that the high-schooler had been to plenty of parties where she declined the beer on ice and had a Coke or nothing. "But I've been to some parties where I felt like having a beer, so I had a beer or two," she said. "That's the way you raised us."

Alone, Sigal and his wife discussed the problem. They faced the dilemma of all parents in this wacked-out, turned-on, turned-inside-out half-century. On the one hand, their hearts were totally with her, and they blessed her for her honesty. On the other, they knew drinking was against the law. What if they had to take a phone call in the middle of the night? The Sigals knew how they would feel if a caller informed them of a bust of minors, an alcohol-related smashup, or lord-knows-what involving their sweet scholar-athlete.

Nor were they any less worried about their son. He had told them that he had plenty of opportunities to drink. He was on an island in the Caribbean for six weeks when he was fifteen, the guest of a buddy whose family was from South America. At night everyone goes to a disco, he told his parents. The kids are on one side, the adults on the other. Everybody drinks. The only ones who consistently get drunk are American visitors—be they adults or kids. Young Sigal watched the South American kids buy a drink and sip it all night. He saw the gringos barf in the streets.

Sigal once cornered another South American friend, Keith, who was from Guyana. "Just between you and me, what's really going on here in the United States with alcohol?" he asked him.

Keith shook his head and started laughing. The American rites of passage with alcohol struck him as a colossal joke. "In Guyana if you drink to excess and you show it, you're less of a man," he said. "Here, you have to vomit on the floor every weekend to prove your manhood."

On her birthday in August 1982 Eileen reflected in her journal on how special occasions were still hard to take. At Easter memories of Chuck coloring eggs taunted her. He had never failed to wake up early to hide eggs for his sister to find when the family returned from church services. Halloween had been one of his favorites. Strangely, what he loved best about the day was getting to dump candy in the bags of the costumed neighborhood kids when they came to the door. Thanksgiving reminded her of how he'd eat like a boa constrictor. Christmas reminded her of a time when he was six. He had peeked in his grandfather's shed, where his presents were hidden, and been shocked when someone told him Santa probably wouldn't bring him anything. To head off the calamity, Chuck penned Santa a note, apologizing for snooping and hoping that he would still get his gifts.

Appearing on television and talking to state senators came naturally to Eileen now. But she realized how much she had really changed when she and Roy accepted an invitation from Billy Vollmer's dad to travel to Chuck's beloved Moose River. While she used to dread spiders and crawly things, now she observed them. Holding hands with Roy, she took walks that Chuck had taken and rode a canoe in the river he had loved. She gloried in the night sounds made by insects, owls, and animals. "I'd never listened before," she says. "I was listening now." Vollmer made steak and potatoes, and they tasted better than anything she'd eaten at the hundreds of hotels where she had stayed. Late at night, still chuckling from Vollmer's nonstop patter, she curled inside a sleeping bag. She imagined Chuck giving her his full-toothed grin at a sight he never saw. "Another lesson learned, Mom," she envisioned him saying. Then she enjoyed one of the best sleeps of her life.

Eileen continues to attend legislative hearings in other states whenever legislators invite her to testify. She pays for the trips out of donations to CHUCK or the occasional honorariums that the Greeks offer her for speaking. Her friends back home in Long Island frequently ask why she remains involved since the New York law has passed. Why put yourself through a multi-cycle washer every time you address a new group or fight a bunch of legislators with their minds dead set against having an anti-hazing law in their states? But she tells them her goal is to have laws in fifty states. Even after statutes are passed, she fights to get laws strengthened, including successful amendments in New York. With exceptions in New York, Texas, Ohio, Georgia, and Maryland, most anti-hazing bills still bite with gums, not teeth.

"What do you care if there is a law in every state?" her friends ask her.

"But I do care" is her reply.

College humor can be black, grim, tasteless. Sigma Alpha Epsilon fraternity incurred a two-year suspension from the University of Cincinnati after the group demeaned Martin Luther King's birthday with a racist theme party. The fraternity issued fliers bearing a photograph of assassin James Earl Ray. The invitations urged partygoers to bring a canceled welfare check, your father (if you know his identity), and a radio bigger than your head.

At Alfred University, Lambda Chi threw an Air Florida party one week after a plane hit a bridge in Washington, DC. The members couldn't understand why Don King was furious. During the Attica prison uprising, a Lambda Chi brother thought he was being funny when he said, "Let's have an Attica party—everybody come with smashed heads."

"It's total stupidity, but not really meant viciously," says Gary Horowitz.

Thus it happened, that, after the Harenberg bill passed, Eileen met a young chapter consultant from a national fraternity that had a chapter at Alfred. The consultant, an Idaho resident, told her that he had attended a party at Klan Alpine a couple weeks after the bill passed. Uncomfortable, he told her that a student viking from Klan had jumped up on the bar to propose a toast.

"Fuck the hazing bill, fuck Eileen Stevens, and fuck Chuck!" the Klan member shouted.

Roy Stevens recalls how the story deflated his wife's joy over the bill's passage. But by 1990 she was able to look at it in another light. She says, "That young man probably had been terribly hurt by all the attention that had been given Klan Alpine, and that was just his way of expressing it."

Courtesy Elms (1968)

Author Hank Nuwer (2nd row, 3rd from left) pledged Sigma Tau Rho at State University College at Buffalo.

Courtesy United States Military Academy Library

As a West Point plebe, Douglas MacArthur stonewalled a congressional investigation into hazing in 1901.

Branch McCracken quit Indiana University's Sphinx social club to protest so-called "rough initiation." He later became the Hoosiers' basketball coach.

Courtesy University Archives, Indiana University

Turn-of-the-century hazings at Gettysburg College involved hoods, blindfolds, masks, and paddles — all still common in hazing rites.

Courtesy Special Collections, Gettysburg College Library, Gettysburg, Pennsylvania

Gettysburg College, early 1900s.

Time *magazine covered an
Alabama high-school hazing and
a fraternity hazing at the
University of Minnesota in the
early fifties.*

Courtesy Kanakadea (1978)

The imposing gothic architecture of the Steinheim Building (1875) at Alfred University reflects the beauty and love of tradition typical of the campus.

Courtesy Richard Sigal and Kanakadea (1962)

Richard Sigal (front, left), a member of Klan Alpine at Alfred and now a sociology professor, and three other Alfred students performed as the Klantones in the sixties. They sometimes shared the bill with Robert Klein, another Alfred student, who aspired to a career as a stand-up comic.

158

Chuck Stenzel, of Sayville, Long Island, New York, died at Alfred University of an alcohol overdose on Tapping Night, the traditional initiation ritual of Klan Alpine fraternity, in 1978.

Eileen Stevens's children (1964): (left to right) Scott Stevens, Chuck Stenzel, Suzanne Stevens, Steven Stevens.

Eileen and Chuck on the day of his confirmation (1969).

Eileen and Chuck in January 1978, only weeks before his death.

A message painted on the walls at Alfred University by a person or persons unknown captures the institution's darker side.

The Klan Alpine house, where Chuck Stenzel died.

The sign outside the Klan house celebrates its history as Alfred's oldest fraternity.

A candid photo of a Klansman vomiting from the porch of the fraternity house captures the emphasis on drinking to excess that has often been part of life in the brotherhood.

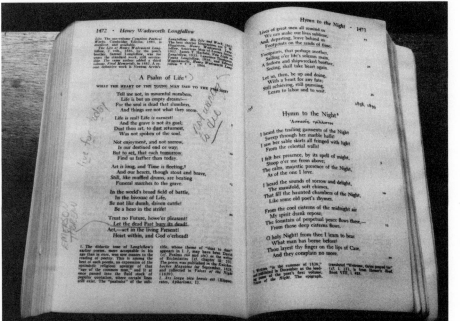

Chuck Stenzel's annotations in his English textbook reflect his interest in literature, particularly nineteenth-century American literature and its fascination with death and darkness.

Richard Rose was president of Alfred University at the time of Chuck Stenzel's death.

Don King (left) was vice president of student affairs at Alfred when Chuck died and was in charge of the university's investigation. He is pictured with Gene Odle, another Alfred administrator at the time.

Gary Horowitz was a history professor at Alfred University and the mayor of the village of Alfred in 1978. Today he is advisor to Klan Alpine.

History professor Stuart Campbell served as a mentor for Chuck and his friend Greg Belanger while they were Alfred students. Chuck had decided to become a history major shortly before his death.

Klan Alpine brother Rocky LaForge first found Chuck's body on the night of his death.

Greg Belanger, Chuck's friend from Sayville and a fellow Alfred student, became a critic of Alfred's handling of his friend's death.

165

Once a housewife and part-time sales clerk who'd never left home without her husband, Eileen Stevens now barnstorms the country as an award-winning antihazing advocate and founder of CHUCK (Committee to Halt Useless College Killings).

Barry Ballou was a high-school athlete before his hazing-related death at the Sigma Nu house at the University of South Carolina.

Ray and Maisie Ballou, Barry's parents, won their civil suit against Sigma Nu.

166

One thousand people turned out to mourn the 1984 hazing death of Jay Lenaghan, a student at American International College in Springfield, Massachusetts.

Rick Cerra perished after fraternity brothers at the University of Wisconsin-Superior forced him to perform calisthenics.

In 1989 Joel Harris died in a fraternity hazing at Morehouse College in Atlanta, Georgia.

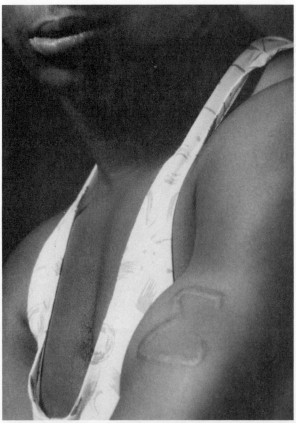

Photo by Scott Lightfoot. Used with permission of *expo*.

Members of black fraternities, including this Ball State University student, frequently show pride in their organizations by being branded with the group's Greek letters.

First-year students in the School of Forestry at Lakehead University in Thunder Bay, Ontario, were initiated by immersion in ditchwater filled with cow manure, fermented wheat, and sawdust.

Photo by Andy Hueton.

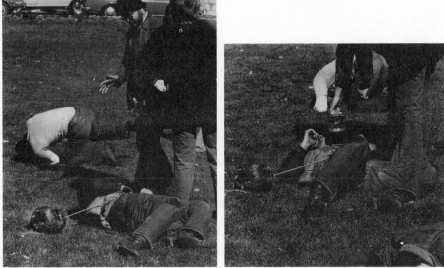

The Sundowners at the University of Nevada at Reno forced members to drink massive quantities of liquor.

Bondage is a recurring theme is many initiation rituals. Here a pledge of Phi Delta Theta at Arizona State University permits himself to be bound to a lounge chair suspended in mid-air.

13

Richard Rose was succeeded as president of Alfred University by Howard R. Neville, who came to the school from the University of Maine. Neville died after serving only a short time. The search for his successor ended in 1982 when Edward G. Coll, Jr., was appointed to the post. Coll told the student paper that the university's role in its approaching lawsuit with Eileen Stevens would be to prove "the independent nature of a fraternity on a college campus." He also said, "I think the fraternity . . . has a role of defense which it must protect in terms of justifying the activities and traditions of Klan Alpine."

Such thinking, so far as Eileen was concerned, indicated that Alfred had hired a leader who believed fraternities should solve their own hazing problems. That news story further alienated Eileen from Klan Alpine. In her view the interviewer let the president-elect's comments slide. To what Klan traditions was Coll referring? Drinking on Tapping Night? Hazing to achieve unity? Stuffing pledges in cars?

Eileen could not know, of course, about prouder Klan traditions: remaining brothers long after leaving Alfred, loyalty to the alma mater, accepting brothers without regard to race, religion, or class status.

In an interview Coll said he had talked with Bill Clements, the current Klan Alpine president, and had taken a liking to him. Coll hoped a recently appointed committee of administrators, students, and faculty would recommend that Klan be "reinstated." If the committee hadn't been a rubber stamp prior to that comment, its members no longer had to guess at the president's wishes. "I personally would not like to see [Klan] die a natural or unnatural death," said Coll.

Did Klan deserve to be brought back? Coll admitted they did not. The fraternity's conduct had been unacceptable from the day it had been dissociated. "I'd been here only a short time and had a major confrontation with Klan at the St. Pat's parade," said Coll. "I'm still not sure who was right or who was wrong, but it personified to me the dichotomy between the Klan and the campus. . . . I get dismayed from time to time with the activities of Klan, which doesn't reflect the kind of responsible leadership I see in the president of Klan."

Coll went on to say that Clements hadn't received proper backing from brothers regarding deportment. "I think some of their actions have embarrassed him tremendously, both in his relations with the University and with the community leadership. . . . I've seen him in a couple of embarrassing situations where he's made commitments to certain people, and then had to come back within forty-two to seventy-two hours and apologize for the house's breaking those commitments. . . . [Bill's] the first to admit that he has a difficult time in convincing all of the brothers of the worthiness of what he's trying to do. There are certain Klan brothers who really don't care whether they're reaffiliated with the university or not."

Near the close of the interview, Coll mixed his metaphors in a revealing way. He said that he preferred to have too much play in the steering wheel rather than display a heavy hand. His image ignored the fact that the loose steering wheel had come off in the hands of Klan members on February 24, 1978. Chuck Stenzel was killed in the process. Ignoring the reservations he himself had expressed, Coll insisted that Klan was once again fit to drive.

Don King, Steven Peterson, and the Klan Alpine brothers named in the suit gave pretrial depositions in 1980. Eileen attended many although they were excruciating to sit through. She heard new things about Chuck's death, but she was suspicious of almost everyone involved. She didn't know who or what to believe.

The suit against Robert Heineman was withdrawn after he gave his deposition. Eileen's attorney saw no reason to continue legal action against the former advisor. This was fortunate for Heineman since the Alfred administration had decided that it would provide an attorney for King and Peterson, but not for him. Heineman, an Alfred village justice, says he felt that distinction was "unfair on the university's part." The university's treatment of Heineman sent a clear message to other campus advisors as to what they could expect in a similar situation. Heineman had stepped down as advisor in the first place because "the group had gotten too large to control." Pressed by civic and academic duties, he "couldn't constantly be working with them."

The strain of the pretrial hearings was unbearable to Eileen. A mother who had lost her son at Lehigh University in a pledging fatality that was ruled an accident told her to "back off — settle with the fraternity if you can."

Rocky LaForge described Chuck's last moments in one hearing. Eileen saw pain in his eyes. She couldn't stay silent and left the room in tears. LaForge, whom she regarded as a good kid, reminded her of Billy Vollmer. "He started to cry — he was breaking," she recalls. "I got upset and broke the mood." The pain in LaForge's face disturbed and angered her although he couldn't have known that. The heartache written all over the small-town boy tugs at Eileen's heart to this day.

Steven Peterson, the Klan advisor, recalls how the brothers felt in the aftermath of the death. "Just listening to these people talk about it, you could see how badly they felt," he says. "In some ways I'm not sure that should be terribly relevant — they were part of a stupid ceremony. But, on the other hand, they're human beings. You could see they were really affected. Some of those people [have been] really affected since then." One of those is Peterson, who admits having trouble talking about the death even now.

Heineman, who went back to the Klan house the afternoon after Chuck's death to console the young men, recalls that they were "crazy" with grief . . . "in pretty rough shape."

LaForge took the tragedy especially hard, in Peterson's opinion. He questions his former student's career choices in the wake of the accident. Although LaForge now works in the family excavating business in Wellsville, New York, and is hardly ready for the public dole, he has the intellect and educational background to be successful in a less physically demanding job. Chuck may not have been the only man in that house to be deprived of his dreams. Before the death Peterson had written recommendation letters for LaForge's admission into prestigious graduate schools. "He had been a really topnotch student here," says Peterson. "Some of his fellow brothers from the area said [Chuck's death] was eating at him over time. . . . In some ways that lingering effect still exists."

In the same way that a defense lawyer blames a victim for a gang rape if she consents to have sex with one fraternity member and the rest pile on, so too would Alfred and Klan's attorney be forced to blame Chuck, the victim, for what befell him. Eileen's attorney warned her that the opposition would "crucify" Chuck if it could. The school's attorney would have tried to prove that Chuck had started drinking earlier that afternoon, according to Don King. Edward Hammond, an expert on the issue of school liability, would have testified that he didn't think the administration was liable for Chuck's death. Ironically, Eileen had heard of Hammond. His secretary had once contacted her for some articles on hazing deaths. Her boss wanted to use them for an article he was writing.

Eileen wasn't the only one having problems in the pretrial proceedings. King did not perform well on the stand. He had occasional difficulty completing his sentences. His speech pattern is such that he adds many qualifiers and digresses often, making himself occasionally difficult to understand. While testifying at his pretrial hearing, he made a crucial, inadvertent slip of the tongue. He said the pledges had been taken from the residence hall, "given something to drink and put — asked to go into the trunk of the car." The slip might have been innocent and accidental, but Eileen saw it as evidence of collusion between the administration of Alfred and Klan Alpine. She saw them as allies, having no idea that the Klan brothers were barely containing their anger against the administration at this time, and vice versa. Klan Alpine and Alfred University shared the same attorney (with the exception of Carl Pelcher, who obtained his own counsel), so the two groups had been forced into a temporary truce.

Eileen learned some important facts from King's testimony. Alfred University, he said, had no stated definition of an advisor. He also admitted that, during his investigation, the Klan witnesses gave him "not a lot of detail probably." He also admitted that his investigation didn't even produce the name of the big brother who picked Chuck up from the dormitory. Only after the investigation ended did King say that "in passing" he had learned that brother's name. It also turned out that King himself had not summoned Klan members to the meeting. He left that up to the judgment of Scott Sullivan. No pledges were present at the investigation, he admitted. This called into question his statement made after his meeting with Klan in which he insisted "the pledges knew beforehand that the car rides and drinking were part of the fraternity's initiation process." King never managed to explain how this supposedly secret car ride—known to Klan members as a kidnapping—was made known to the pledges, nor why the fraternity would have deviated from tradition to inform them about what was to take place ahead of time.

Eileen also learned that, for whatever reason, King's memory of that night was blurred. He could not even recall the weather with certainty. "I am not sure if it was a snowy night, but it was winter," he said. Nor could he remember if the big brother had attended the investigation that night. He could not recall if his investigation took place on a Sunday or a Monday. When asked by Eileen's attorney if he had ascertained the identity of the brothers in the car, King testified, "I don't remember if I did or not." He could not remember if he had discovered in whose car one of the other hospitalized pledges had been placed. Nor was he prepared to address Eileen's assertion that Chuck had been placed coatless in the trunk. "I assume he was clothed," said King. Finally, he conceded that he had not even learned at his investigation which brother had given Chuck the bottle of liquor.

King also said that no other Alfred University administrator or faculty member had conducted an official inquiry. He said that he conducted no other investigative sessions with group members as a whole. The dean made no attempt to contact any law enforcement officers to obtain details on the incident except "just that evening when it occurred." He conceded that he never wrote an official report from his notes. Yet after his February 26, 1978, meeting with Klan members, King told a reporter that he had taken "depositions from students attending the party." King's testimony made it clear that he had only listened to statements; he took no depositions. The one official who actually obtained depositions directly after Chuck's death was Alfred police chief Tiny Jamison.

The dean talked only once to George Francis, "when he came to see me," said King. "I am not sure exactly the time, but it was within the first couple of weeks after the accident." To King's knowledge that was the first time that the district attorney came on campus to investigate. He was certain he had no telephone communication with the district attorney prior to that meeting. He was certain the district attorney never requested a follow-up meeting. He didn't even know if the district attorney had met with President Rose. "I imagine they might have," he said.

During the pretrial hearings, King also had trouble answering a few specific questions asked him by Eileen's attorney. Some of these were:

Question: Did he [a hospitalized pledge] tell you whose car he was in?

King: No, I don't remember.

Question: Did he tell you who his big brother was?

King: No.

Question: Did he tell you who gave him the alcoholic beverages?

King: No, I don't recall.

Question: Did he tell you if he was alone?

King: I don't recall that either.

Question: Did you ask him those questions?

King: Yes, I did.

Question: Do you know if any of the young men, the members of Klan Alpine, gave statements to the district attorney or his representative?

Answer: I am not aware of that.

Despite King's stumbling on the stand, he believes today he and the university would have won the suit. "I'd hoped it would go to court," he says. "We wanted to go to court, but the insurance company wanted to settle." King reveals that Alfred's terms of the settlement were that the school, Steven Peterson, and he were taken off the hook financially. "Even if it were five or ten thousand dollars, she would have exploited that, I believe, to say that we were responsible. To this day I don't think we were responsible," says the dean.

Others in the Alfred community don't agree. Will Archer, for example, says that King could count on him as one of his staunchest supporters ("he's a wonderful person"), but that he thought the administration didn't do enough beforehand to prevent a tragedy. "The university to a large extent was responsible for what happened because they knew what was going on," he says. "They had full knowledge of what was going on there — the [Klan's] lack of regard for almost everything. I'm sure they had many complaints; there were complaints from the neighbors. . . . They were nice kids. With the proper leadership it would never have happened, simple as that — from the university and within the fraternity itself."

When State Supreme Court Justice John Broughton closed the case on October 25, 1982, Eileen settled for an undisclosed amount of money. One newspaper account estimated it at slightly over fifty thousand dollars, attributing its figure to an unidentified Hartford Insurance spokesman. King and Eileen say that they promised as terms of the settlement that they would not reveal the amount. But Eileen does say that the payment came to less than twenty thousand dollars once lawyers' fees and expenses were paid. She insists that the lawsuit was to produce answers, not dollars, citing her refusal to ask for a speaking fee as proof that she has not tried to profit from the tragedy. "I don't know if there would have been a lawsuit if I had seen the investigation," she said at the time, emphasizing that Francis refused to reveal why he had not charged Klan members with a violation. "For four-and-a-half years I've had many unanswered questions," she told a reporter at the time of the hearings.

James Kehoe, the attorney for the defendants, also refused to comment on the terms of the suit. "We took a vow of silence so we can't really say what's included in the settlement," he told reporters. "Like most lawsuits that are settled out of court, we had to weigh this and weigh that and make a compromise that was fair. Both sides had to give a little."

Thus, Eileen's sixty-four-million-dollar lawsuit against Alfred University and Klan Alpine ended undramatically on the courthouse steps. She says she agreed to the terms after Francis promised she could read the supporting depositions. "The purpose of my lawsuit was to obtain all the information connected with my son's death and to have some long-unresolved questions answered," she told reporters. She also told friends privately that she had settled rather than "put my family through the whole thing again."

Had it gone forward, the case might have had crucial legal implications. Certainly Eileen has chastised herself a thousand times for settling. The issue of precisely what a university's legal responsibility is to off-campus students is the topic of much lively intellectual debate. Certainly the liability issue is a concern of administrators, particularly when they are personally named. Two aspects of the Stenzel case would have been watched with interest by attorneys and academics alike: 1) Could Alfred University be liable because it did not sufficiently publicize and enforce rules regarding drinking and hazing? Alfred yearbooks, for example, clearly demonstrate that Tapping Night was a long-standing drunken tradition on campus; and 2) Was Klan Alpine, as a private corporation, responsible for its own behavior even though it was a school-sanctioned fraternity listed in the college catalog?

Significantly, Alfred's problem might have been that it gave too much supervision, not too little. "A school's failure to enforce unrealistic or intrusive regulations is a far more likely basis for tort liability than its failure to adopt such rules in the first place," the law firm of Covington and Burling advised the American Council on Education in 1987. Despite the admittedly limited supervision that Peterson, and Heineman before him, had given Klan, the school still provided more guidance than do some universities.

The University of Michigan, for example, has absolutely no connection with fraternities other than putting on awareness workshops. Perhaps as a result of that lack of supervision, Michigan fraternities have occasionally found themselves in hot water. The most publicized incident occurred in 1980 when members of Alpha Delta Phi strung up its house's cat, "Bad Kat," or "BK" for short, cut off its paws, and set it on fire.

While many parents would consider such lack of university responsibility deplorable, there is no doubt that Michigan, by such a stance, has less chance of being found liable in an alcohol or hazing death than does a low-involvement school such as Alfred or high-involvement schools such as Indiana University or the University of Texas. Nonetheless, as president of Fort Hays State University, even liability expert Hammond (who was to have testified had a trial been held) prefers "to be involved" to satisfy himself that he has taken every precaution to protect his students.

The issue of liability, suffice to say, merits as much thoughtful consideration as does hazing itself. Administrators who put their necks on the lines for their students insist that they shouldn't be guillotined in court. Such administrators have long hoped that the judicial system can write a good samaritan law to protect them in exchange for high involvement that may safeguard students. Otherwise, who can really blame King for saying, "We cover ourselves now in many ways not to expose ourselves legally." He and Peterson know what it is like to face the possibility of a sixty-four-million-dollar judgment. Peterson jokes now that he and his wife didn't have quite that much in their checking account.

For many years colleges supposedly functioned as parents under the *in loco parentis* system. King says that he believes Alfred and other institutions still do, despite assertions to the contrary. But many educators believe parents shouldn't expect universities to serve as a home substitute. One Harvard educator had this to say on the subject in 1866:

> Professors should not be responsible for the manners of students, beyond the legitimate operation of their personal influence. Academic jurisdiction should have no criminal code, should inflict no penalty but that of expulsion, and that only in the way of self-defence against positively noxious and dangerous members.
>
> Let the civil law take care of civil offences. The American citizen should early learn to govern himself, and to reenact the civil law by free consent. Let easy and familiar relations be established between teachers and taught, and personal influence will do more for the maintenance of order than the most elaborate order. Experience has shown that great reliance may be placed on the sense of honor of young men, when properly appealed to and fairly brought into play.

Nonetheless, the nineties are almost certainly going to see more high-dollar suits against high schools and colleges should hazing persist. In 1986 an Oregon circuit court awarded $325,000 to a former University of Oregon member of Kappa Sigma for injuries he suffered during his initiation. In 1987 former pledge Jeffrey Furek won thirty thousand dollars in a state of Delaware superior court suit as a result of burns he suffered when Sigma Phi Epsilon members dumped lye-based oven cleaner on his head.

With the legal proceedings over, Klan Alpine was eligible for reinstatement. One committee member, librarian Martha Mueller, fought that. As a neighbor of the fraternity, she was more aware of their parties than were her fellow committee members. She had called the police four, maybe five, times after midnight, but only when she had an appointment the next day and the fraternity blasted "the kind of music you don't want to hear." When Chuck died at Klan Alpine, she wasn't surprised. "The general feeling here was that Klan would be the one it happened to," she says.

The conditions for reinstatement, says Mueller, were that Klan had to satisfy the school academically, perform community service, and meet certain good-neighbor standards. Klan invited the committee to an open-house inspection. Mueller didn't notice the scrubbed floors. She could see only the "broken-out windows with pillows stuffed in them to keep the rain out," she says.

The committee overrode Mueller's dissenting vote.

Klan was back.

According to the terms of the settlement, Eileen sat in a small room to read the "general supporting depositions" from Klan Alpine members. "I agreed to disclose statements of the fraternity brothers, neighbors, and ambulance personnel," Francis told the Hornell newspaper. He said that he had released only that portion of the files that he believed would have been subject to court scrutiny during a trial. An officer of the court stood nearby while Eileen read. She recalls feeling overwhelmed by anxiety, depression, and frustration. After reading the material, she tried to write down all she had read, only to discover that little had lodged in her head. While she does not have photographic recall, she does usually have an exceptional memory for details, names, dates, and faces. But, somehow, the trauma of reading the depositions erased everything except the image of Chuck standing in the bathroom after his shower with foam or fluid coming out of his mouth.

At one point, the supervising officer looked out a window with his back to her. Eileen had noticed that the file inadvertently contained two photocopies of Scott Sullivan's deposition. On impulse she stuffed one of them down the front of her bra. From it she learned only that Sullivan thought that Chuck had thrown up after his shower, a detail that conflicted with what others had said.

"What little I received in court was [worth] nil," she claims. She resigned herself to knowing that in this life, anyway, she would never discover everything that transpired on Chuck's last night. "Perhaps it's better that way," she said in her journal. She also asked a rhetorical question: "I wonder if they [Klan men] have sons of their own now." Whether they fear sending a beloved boy to college, only to receive a phone call in the middle of the night. The Klan men had given a terrible new meaning to the phrase "Brothers to the death," she concluded in her journal entry.

One of Eileen's favorite fraternity leaders has been Maurice (Mo) Littlefield, executive director of Sigma Nu, one of the largest Greek systems in the country. He has the reputation of being the hardest-working, most "hands-on" leader in the Greek world. Thus, she had mixed feelings when her equally valued friend Ray Ballou called her to say that he was looking forward to seeing Sigma Nu members go on trial in the 1980 death of his son Barry. A county coroner's jury had exonerated Sigma Nu, calling the death "an unfortunate accident caused by an overdose of alcohol."

"I'm going to bury Mo Littlefield," Ballou promised her.

"Ray," she said, "you're not going to believe this, but you're going to love Mo Littlefield."

Eileen again experienced divided loyalty when she agreed to speak at a Sigma Nu convention in Utah. A nervous group of young men shuffled up to her, identifying themselves as Sigma Nus from the University of South Carolina. Eileen greeted them, realizing that some of them could have been part of the ritual that led to Ballou's death. The young men said that they hadn't been principals in the Ballou case; nonetheless, they knew Barry or knew of him. "He was a good guy," they told her.

She listened to the words spill from their young mouths. Everything they said echoed what she had heard directly or indirectly that the Klan Alpine members had said about her son: *We never thought he would die. No one meant for it to happen. Lots of us had been through it before.*

She felt on the verge of vertigo while they talked. Here were the "bad guys," not three feet away from her. They were no different in appearance from the athletic young men who had shared Chuck's last hours. A shock of recognition overcame her. She had been so busy trying to get the members of the Greek world to change their minds about her that she never realized until that moment that they had somehow changed her mind about them.

Yet she could not deny that the University of South Carolina chapter of Sigma Nu was a reckless carbon copy of Klan Alpine. In one tragic night the fraternity's tradition of viking behavior turned the house into a veritable legion of dishonor.

Four months before Barry Ballou's death Sigma Nu had been charged with a violation of university rules against drinking and was rebuked by the USC dean of student affairs. Hazing was a routine part of Sigma Nu's pledge program. Members, for example, soaped and wet down a floor and required the pledges to slide across it on their fannies. They required them to break up a coed party by running drunkenly through a rival fraternity house in their underwear despite cold January temperatures.

In 1988 Eileen again attended a Sigma Nu convention, this time in Arizona. Roughly one thousand undergraduates, advisors, alumni, and executives of the fraternity sat in the hotel's grand ballroom. Every partition had been thrust back to accommodate the throng. The center of attention was Dave Westol, a district attorney from Kalamazoo (in 1989 he became executive director of Theta Chi), who traveled around the fraternity circuit to put on a program called "Hazing on Trial." His program provided an inside look at what it is like for a fraternity to go on trial for a hazing death. Westol, as he always did, played the prosecuting attorney, Eileen played the mother of a dead pledge, Mo Littlefield played himself, and some Sigma Nus played fraternity men charged with hazing.

Eileen felt as if she were in a real courtroom, not on a stage. In fact, at a subsequent enactment of "Hazing on Trial," she forgot the name of her fictitious son and said Chuck, taking everyone in the audience aback.

The young men chosen to play the defendants squirmed in their seats. No one in the audience cracked jokes to break the tension. The atmosphere was much like live theater. One by one, the Sigma Nus traipsed to the chair: chapter president, treasurer, social chairman, rush chairman. On the stand they hardly resembled big men on campus. They looked small and shriveled, terribly young and conspicuous. With their right hands on the Bible, they were little boys in the principal's office, nobodies on a job interview. They glanced at the jury, a Greek chorus as it were, who stared back at them as if they were scum, criminals, a tribe of ants. One by one, Westol confronted the ants. This one he cooked. That one he fried. Those he parboiled. The walls in the room closed in on the tribe.

Perhaps the toughest moment of all was when Littlefield took the stand. To the Sigma Nus, Littlefield is God himself come down to earth in a strange disguise, their shaman. The young men respect, fear, like him. But here he was, clearly out of his element, being grilled like a weiner over a bonfire. As the questions flew, he sizzled, popped, and looked in danger of falling into the flames. His hard-earned reputation as an educator was for nought. His longtime battle against hazing was as if it had never existed. The cherished name of Sigma Nu was worth no more than a steaming pile of manure. For ninety minutes every brother felt guilty. For ninety minutes every Sigma Nu was guilty. If any student in that room, with his new knowledge of what a trial entails, returned to his chapter and continued to haze, he deserves a penalty harsher than a thirty-day jail sentence.

The room was ominously silent when the mock trial ended. The judge, as if he were a priest reciting an antiphon, addressed the gathering. He told them that this was only play-acting. But in reality a bright young man from the University of South Carolina was dead. His parents' lives were unglued. The Sigma Nus in that chapter were forever shamed. The national fraternity had been disgraced. The young delegates had a new bit of fraternity trivia to ask their pledges to learn — information that might save young lives.

Barry Ballou was from Johnsonville, South Carolina, a tiny town. But Johnsonville's people care. They comforted Ray and Maisie Ballou after their boy was found face down, dead in his own vomit. So did Eileen Stevens. Throughout the ordeal of Barry's death and the subsequent suit, she phoned and wrote the Ballous to assist them in ways no one had been able to help her. "Please keep up your work," Mrs. Ballou wrote Eileen. "You have touched so many, many people. Just knowing you [has] helped me."

Lawyers for Sigma Nu underestimated the determination of the country couple from Johnsonville. They offered the Ballous a ten-thousand-dollar settlement and additional moneys for a Barry Ballou scholarship fund at the University of South Carolina. Mr. Ballou, an Andy Griffith look-alike, told the lawyers that not only was he not settling, but that Sigma Nu could stop suggesting how the Ballou family should run its affairs. With the financial resources of a national fraternity stacked against them, the Ballous bent like a pine in a hurricane. But they refused to crack or topple.

They froze their faces while Sigma Nu's attorney blamed their son for his own death. "He had drunk before, and I don't want you all to get the picture of a young man who is off in the so-called big city for the first time," said the attorney. "He had been drinking before. He had drunk heavily before. But, again, I want to put this case in its proper perspective and let you understand that young Barry Ballou, with a history of drinking, knew how to handle his alcohol. He went to a party that night, said to a friend of his that afternoon, 'I am going to get bombed.'"

But the Ballous' attorney expertly used the testimony of the Sigma Nu brothers themselves to elicit the truth. Like many of the Sigma Nus, Barry had been drunk on occasion, but he was hardly a hardcore drinker, certainly not an alcoholic, definitely not trying to kill himself with booze. Certainly he had never before drunk enough to have his blood alcohol level reach .46 — the same as Chuck Stenzel's. His would-be fraternity brothers performed miserably on the stand. The jury listened to the words of a Sigma Nu drinking song taken directly from a fraternity publication. The night of Barry's death, the members roared that the pledges should "drink, drink, drink" and "drink, drink, drink" some more.

Mo Littlefield, as Eileen had predicted, proved himself a man of character. In the end, the Ballous deleted Littlefield and two USC officials from the lawsuit. But the proceedings also made clear Littlefield's lack of power to stop any of the 180 chapters then under his supervision from hazing once the individual group decided to do so. Moreover, Littlefield's testimony demonstrated that when he arrived in Columbia the day after Barry's death, the membership gave him a distorted sense of what had occurred. The hard lesson for the public in Littlefield's testimony is that a chapter willing to mislead and stonewall its executive director is also quite likely to treat a police chief, a district attorney, a dean of students, a faculty advisor, and the parents of the deceased brother in the same way.

Littlefield testified that he learned from all the members and one alumnus that the party that killed Barry Ballou was merely a "typical social function." He also noted that university officials concurred. "I was clearly informed that there were no initiation activities of any form," said Littlefield under oath.

According to his testimony, he was never informed that pledges were segregated from the party for the expressed purpose of hazing. He didn't know they had been forced to play games with names such as Air Raid and Flood. He wasn't informed that pledges had been required to drink from a cup of truth until three years after the incident, and then his source was a newspaper clipping, not the Sigma Nu membership. He didn't know until the trial that pledges had been required to strip to their shorts. He didn't know that an alumnus had been master of ceremonies the night of Ballou's death.

Littlefield also testified that "it never surfaced" that Ballou had died in a hell night initiation. He said he had intended to attend Ballou's funeral, but that the president of the University of South Carolina, James B. Holderman, advised him not to. "He himself would not be attending but would have a representative and [recommended] that I should do the same," testified Littlefield. The president was concerned lest someone from the national fraternity or USC chapter attend the funeral in a less-than-desirable emotional state and perhaps compound the tragedy.

One by one, the attorney for the Ballou family gunned down the Sigma Nu brothers, forcing them to substantiate the things Littlefield hadn't been told about at the time of Barry's death. He mowed down witness after witness, convincing the jury that the Sigma Nus at USC had fudged, deceived, covered up truth. Ray and Maisie Ballou learned that several members and pledges had been concerned by Barry's bluish skin and general appearance. At least one member suggested taking their son to the infirmary not two hundred feet from where he lay. But, after managing to rouse him, they decided to let him sleep it off, lest he be embarrassed.

Sigma Nu member Robert Preston Parker—by then a high-school teacher—was cross-examined by the prosecuting attorney. Parker's testimony showed that Dave Westol's "Hazing on Trial" drama was very close to the truth:

Question: Do you recall one of the jurors at the inquest asking you some questions?

Answer: I don't totally . . . but they may have. But I don't remember.

Question: I hand you this [document] and ask you if you recall a juror asking you "Did it look like he"—referring to Barry—"chugged a pretty good bit?"

Answer: I guess I did.

Question: Do you recall he asked you that and what did you tell him?

Answer: It says, "It looked like he probably drank anywhere from a quarter to three quarters of it. I wouldn't say he drank the whole thing."

Question: It was more than a little sip, wasn't it?

Answer: Yes, sir.

Question: You mentioned that you were tested as a part of your pledgeship, Mr. Parker. Barry likewise took the same test, didn't he?

Answer: Yes, sir.

Question: Do you recall on one of your tests being asked the question, what were the objectives of the pledge?

Answer: Yes, I think that was on one of the tests.

Question: What were the three objectives of [the] pledge that you were asked?

Answer: I couldn't recall and tell you right now.

Question: Would it sound like silence —

Answer: Secrecy and obedience.

Question: That is what you were taught and that is what you were told — that you were told to act . . . as one of the brothers?

Answer: . . . You weren't told to do anything, you make your own decisions.

Question: . . . You were told that that was the object of being in that fraternity, and that is the way you would conduct yourself, weren't you?

Answer: No, you don't get molded by anybody. You, you are expected to be yourself.

Question: Did you talk to Mr. Littlefield when he came down here?

Answer: When, today? No.

Question: No, when he came down here after Barry's death.

Answer: I probably recall speaking to him.

Question: . . . Aren't you the person who found Barry dead?

Answer: Yes, I am.

Question: Do you mean that Mr. Littlefield came down here and did not talk to you, knowing that you found this boy dead in the fraternity house?

Answer: I don't see what that has, the big deal is, I mean —

Question: You don't think it is a big deal that one of your brothers died on hell night in the fraternity house?

Answer: No, that wasn't the question. I said I don't think it is a big deal if [Littlefield] personally comes and speaks to me.

Question: When he came down to make an investigation as to what happened, didn't he?

Answer: Yes.

Question: And you are the person who found the body and identified it to the university police?

Answer: Yes.

Question: And you did talk to him when he came down here, didn't you?

Answer: I said I probably spoke to him.

Question: You spoke to him? But you didn't tell him about the hazing?

Answer: We didn't talk about it.

Question: You did or you didn't?

Answer: Did not.

Question: You did not. You didn't tell him about the air raids?

Answer: No.

Question: You didn't tell him that Barry had been forced to strip down to his underwear.

Answer: I wouldn't say anybody was forced.

Question: You were told to do it, weren't you?

Answer: Yes, but that don't mean you have to do it.

Question: . . . You talked to Mr. Littlefield, and you talked about honor and truth, and you didn't tell him any of the truth about what happened the night Barry died, did you?

Answer: I wasn't asked any questions.

Question: You mean to tell me Mr. Littlefield didn't ask you what happened to cause this boy's death?

Answer: I don't recall even talking about the incident.

Question: You don't recall what?

Answer: Talking about the whole incident with him.

Question: Well, did you talk to him or not?

Answer: Probably, probably spoke to him, socially [to] speak.

Question: Just socialized while [the Ballous] were having Barry's funeral?

Answer: No.

Question: Did you not consider this was something official from Sigma Nu [when] the top man in the organization comes down? You didn't consider that important.

Answer: This was important.

Question: This wasn't a social visit by Mr. Littlefield, was it?

Answer: No.

Question: He came down here to try to find out the truth and he didn't get it from Robert Parker, did he?

Answer: I reckon not.

Question: . . . You told the police the party was given by the active brothers for the pledge class as a part of their activation?

Answer: Is that my statement?

Question: Yes, it is.

Answer: Can I read it?

Question: Yes, sir. Look at the first line and read it.

Answer: It says, "The party was given by the active brothers . . . for the pledge class as a part of the activation."

Question: A part of the activation. You also said the party included the drinking of various types of liquor, of alcohol, including liquor?

Answer: Uhhuh [nodding yes].

Question: And you knew at that time that liquor was being served in the fraternity house, that it was in violation of the regulations of the university, didn't you?

Answer: No, I wasn't paying any attention to that part at the time.

Question: You weren't paying any attention to it but you knew it was a violation of a regulation?

Answer: Yes, I guess it was in violation.

Question: They weren't supposed to have the liquor in the lounge, were they?

Answer: Nope.

Question: And you also made the statement to the officer that "to the best of my knowledge Barry drank a combination of the alcoholic beverages that amounted to about two pints"?

Answer: What's in the statement, that's—

Question: You made that statement and you signed it and you swore to it, didn't you?

Answer: Yes.

Question: You also made the statement that he drank the two pints which was not anything any more than anybody else who passed out. You made that statement?

Answer: Yes.

Question: How many did pass out?

Answer: Three.

Question: Or possibly four?

Answer: Or possibly four.

Question: They were all lying on the sofas down there . . . when you left, weren't they?

Answer: Yes.

Question: But you noticed, Mr. Parker, that there was a substantial difference in Barry than any of the other three, didn't you?

Answer: I wouldn't say that I noticed that.

Question: You wouldn't say that you noticed that?

Answer: He was lying, lying on the couch passed out.

Question: I ask if you made this statement? "12:15 A.M. I checked on Barry as well as three others who were also passed out on the couches. They were all OK, but one thing I noticed about Barry was that he felt as if he was unconscious." Did you make that statement . . . ?

Answer: Yes, I made it.

186

Question: You made that statement. And Barry was in substantially worse condition than the other three, wasn't he?

Answer: I reckon so.

Question: Did you tell any of the active brothers "Let's do something for Barry"?

Answer: No, I didn't.

Question: Did anybody say, "Let's do something for Barry"?

Answer: I remember others checked on him.

Question: It was obvious that Barry couldn't do anything for himself, wasn't it?

Answer: Yes.

Question: He couldn't sit up, he couldn't stand up, he couldn't even talk? Isn't that true?

Answer: I didn't try to get him to sit up, stand up, or talk.

Question: Did anybody try to get him to sit up, stand up, or talk?

Answer: I think two other people did try to get him to sit up. I wasn't there when it happened, but from what they said—

Question: Did you hear the discussion about taking him to the hospital?

Answer: No.

Question: Did anybody discuss taking him to the hospital?

Answer: Not while I was down there.

Question: You picked him up off the floor and put him on the couch, didn't you?

Answer: Uhhuh (indicating yes).

Question: And you said he was already unconscious at that time?

Answer: Yes, he was lying on the floor propped up against the—

Question: Did anybody do anything during the night to try to help him?

Answer: I don't understand what you are asking.

Question: When you went back down the next morning and found him dead, wasn't he still lying there in about the same condition as you saw him when you left?

Answer: He was still lying face down.

Question: Still lying face down on the sofa dead?

Answer: Uhhuh.

Question: Is that right?

Answer: Yes, sir.

In both the Barry Ballou and Chuck Stenzel deaths, a fraternity's rites harmed someone the brothers were duty-bound to protect. Both groups created pressure to drink to dangerous levels. Both failed to take ordinary, reasonable, and necessary precautions to protect their victims after contributing to their intoxicated states. Even if the Klan Alpine attorney *had* been able to prove that Chuck contributed to his own death, the Ballou case established that a pledge's actions do not necessarily bar recovery of damages by the plaintiff. The South Carolina court ruled that while Barry Ballou participated in the drinking rite, he did not "as a matter of law freely and voluntarily with full knowledge of its nature and extent incur the risk of dangers created by the fraternity's action of promoting extreme intoxication." The Ballou case went all the way to the Supreme Court and Court of Appeals of South Carolina. The original verdict was affirmed. Among other things, the court found that Sigma Nu's contention that the South Carolina chapter was "totally devoid of any suggestion of recklessness or willfulness" on the part of the fraternity was "manifestly without merit."

The Ballous received $200,000 in actual damages and fifty thousand dollars in punitive damages. They haven't spent a dime of it. Eventually it will go to their grandchildren for their educations. "Money is not what I'm interested in," says Mr. Ballou, adding that he and his wife wanted to demonstrate that the fraternity's actions contributed to Barry's death. "I'm interested in justice. . . . When we found out that an alumnus conducted the whole . . . ritual, and they sit back and lie and lie and lie, that's when I got a little upset. . . . It's mighty low to think that a person loses his life for brotherhood, and not a soul turned a hand to save his life. . . . These kids got to live with it. Every day they wake up, they got to think about it. Whether you like it or not, things like that don't go away." He adds that he thinks fraternity members ought to be nailed on conspiracy charges every time they are caught hazing. "They are conspiring to commit a crime," he charges, saying that parents get all sorts of answers after a death but that they don't get "straight answers," only those that have been "rehearsed."

The Ballous' victory heartened Eileen Stevens. She was as pleased when they won the appeal as if she had won the case herself. In some ways, the Ballou case became, overnight, the landmark for others to study. "If they have any litigation against any type of hazing, they [will] look up *Ballou v. Sigma Nu*," says Mr. Ballou.

* * *

One of the aspects of Barry's death that troubled the Ballous was that hazing had touched their lives previously, but they had not been alarmed enough to tell their son that the practice could be dangerous. Barry endured hazing as one of few freshmen on the Johnsonville High School varsity football team. Barry and his fellow frosh had to drink cheap beer, strip, and run buck naked around the football field. Barry's older brother was on that team, and he pushed his kid brother as hard as anyone else did.

According to Connie DeCamps, a Ballou family friend who has lived in the area for more than forty years, hazing has been a problem in some South Carolina schools. "Even in middle school the children expect to be initiated," she says. "They put them in the trash can or something like that." She also says that the Ballous had a difficult time deciding to pursue the case against the young men who hazed Barry. "The Ballous felt bad for the young boys involved," she says. "They really felt for them because they're the parents of young men. . . . [The Sigma Nus] didn't intend to kill Barry by any means."

Thanks to the tenacious efforts of the Ballous, a state law against hazing was passed. But hazing continued to be a problem in a South Carolina secondary school east of Johnsonville. At Loris High School in Loris, South Carolina, bizarre initiation practices were required for admission into the National Future Farmers of America (FFA). Two Loris students, seniors Sammy Graham and Scott Causey, spoke freely about the rites of passage into this supposedly pre-professional society at the November 1989 FFA convention in Kansas City. A verbatim transcript of their conversation shows that the Ballous' concerns about high-school hazing in their state were justified:

Question: Tell me, what type of initiation rituals do you have?

Causey: Well, we have different stages we set up and send them through. Like one stage we'll have 'em sittin' in a five-gallon bucket of ice-cold water. Then we'll put 'em on their stomach and crawl under electric fences, and we'll take the sticks and "accidentally" lay 'em down on their tails.

Question: Take the sticks? What kind of sticks?

Causey: Just any kind of little brown stick that's dead. That way we won't get shocked.

Graham: Tobacco sticks. They crawl up under the wire and the wire's lit up with juice and then they get up under it. They're already wet so you touch any part of their body and the whole body's going to get fried.

Causey: Kind of fries 'em a little bit.

Question: Now, you say you have three stages—

Causey: —we have several different—

Graham: —we have a bunch.

Question: Is this like over a period of months, or is it in one night?

Graham: This is one night—all of it's mind-boggling. You tell 'em that you're gonna put [them] through all this stuff, and they get real scared and everything. And then after they go through it and take their blindfolds off, then watch everybody else go through it—then they laughed.

Causey: What we're actually doing is playing mind games with 'em.

Question: So this all happens in one night. What else do you do in that one night?

Causey: Well . . . last year we played musical chairs with 'em, and we had wooden chairs and had nails drove through the bottom—and had wire wrapped onto it and running to a little small lawnmower motor. And we set 'em in the five-gallon bucket, and we set 'em down in the chairs. There's three chairs and four people. [We] told 'em that when the music stopped the one that didn't get to sit down had to drink prune juice. So the ones that sat down, they thought it was going to be all right; so when they sat down we flipped a switch, and they come jumping up. . . . They was set up like little electric chairs.

Question: So you have a chair hooked up. Now tell me how this hook-up works again?

Causey: We have the chairs back-to-back.

Question: Like what kind of chairs? Just a wood chair?

Causey: Yeah, those little wood chairs—

Graham: —with nails in 'em. . . . And you just play it and they just go one round. Then we have this big ole mixture of baby food and all kind of stuff like that and prune juice and then we take the blindfolds off just enough to see it so they think it's something real bad. And they say, "The loser, who don't get to sit down, has to eat this." And then if you sit down, you get to go on to the next stage with everyone. And then they sit down and they get fried.

Causey: They get shocked. We got the nails sticking just a—

Graham: —the head of the nails—

Causey: About a quarter of an inch.

Question: So the nails are hammered into the chairs?

Causey: Yeah.

Graham: Yeah.

Question: How does the electricity get into it? You got just a wire hooked up to the nails?

Causey: You got wires hooked up to each nail. Then there's the wire that runs off to the lawnmower motor. And we got the motor hooked up to where we can plug it into a light socket. And we got a regular little switch, a light switch to work it. So when they sit down, and we turn it on, the motor comes on and it shoots electricity into the nails, which is [while] they're sitting on the nails.

Question: So this all happened the same night the crawling under the wires happened? Then what happens?

Graham: OK. Another stage is, we have a goat, right? And before initiation we tell 'em that they're going to take their finger and stick it—now you can imagine, OK? In the goat's—

Causey: —in the goat's tail.

Graham: Anyhow, we have this goat here, and we take their hand and let 'em rub the goat and everything like that. . . . They still have the blindfold. . . . Anyhow we have an old Mason jar with a piece of carpet over the mouth of . . . the lid.

Question: Piece of what?

Graham: Mason jar with a carpet over the mouth of it, so it's getting furry—you know, feels like fur. [It] has a hole in it. And in the jar we have molasses and all other kind of stuff—

Causey: —sardines to make it stink real bad.

Graham: Anyhow, we take and rub their hand across the goat, and then we just take a finger and run it in the Mason jar and they just—it's so hilarious.

Question: So that's the third thing that they've gone through this night?

Causey: We've got a toilet sitting up, and we got it filled with—I believe we fill it up with Mellow Yellow or Mountain Dew or something like that. Then we take Baby Ruth candy bars and drop 'em all down in it. And [we] tell 'em there's an apple or a piece of candy or something at the bottom of it, and they got to bob and stick their head in the toilet and get it. And we let 'em. We pull the blindfold up just enough that they can see the commode down there. And they get all worried about it.

Question: Now this is in the bathroom? This actually happens in the bathroom?

Causey: We stole a commode. We got it set up in the shop.

Question: So this is the fourth thing they've done this same night. What else do you do?

Graham: Another thing we have, we have this big ole board. It's just filled full of flour. [It] has this big ole mountain of flour on it—on the very top of it. We have two students take their blindfolds off. . . . We put a cherry on top of the mountain of flour. And then we say, "Go!" No, first we say, "If you don't get the cherry, you have to go in and get it with your mouth." You got two of 'em going in at the same time. And if you don't get the cherry, we tell 'em, "You have to go back and do the whole thing again." But we don't make 'em go through it again. We say, "Go and push the cherry all the way to the bottom." You have to go through all this mouthful of flour after flour and then get a cherry. So you have a real dry mouth at the end. At the same time they're doing that, we're taking syrup and pouring it in their hair.

Causey: Breaking eggs and all kinds of stuff in their hair.

Question: So this is their last stage?

Graham: Syrup, molasses and that in their hair.

Question: And that's their last stage. And then what? They're an FFA member?

Causey: They're in the organization.

Question: They're an official member? Who's present at this night? Is it just members? All the current members?

Graham: Second year on up. Students get to do it on the first-year students—[the] second-, third-, and fourth-year students.

Question: Does the advisor know about it?

Graham: Yes.

Causey: Yeah, he's there; he's in on it.

Question: He's there?

Graham: He makes sure that we don't no nothing against school policies or nothing like that. . . . We don't do nothing to harm 'em.

Question: What's your advisor's name?

Graham: Benjamin Hardee.

Question: Benjamin Hardee?

Graham: Yes, sir.

Question: Do you do anything with . . . the Greenhand [first-degree of FFA membership] ceremony? We hear about that. Where they make the people paint the hand green and walk around—

Causey: Greenhands. We make 'em—they have to cut out a hand out of a piece of board or cardboard or whatever they want. They have to paint it green and hang it around their neck. They have to walk around with it around their neck for about a week. They have to get officers to sign it and then [they] have to have at least about twenty signatures on it.

Question: Twenty FFA signatures?

Graham: Yeah.

Causey: And then we'll have 'em—it'll be farmer day and they have to come dressed up in their little plaid shirts and overalls and all kind of stuff. Some days [they] have to come with a bucket.

Question: So this happened before this other night?

Graham: This is the week of that night.

Question: Now, Scott, you went through this initiation.

Causey: Oh, yeah.

Question: What did you think about it? What were you thinking when you were going through this?

Causey: Well, I couldn't tell ya'. I was too busy trying to dodge eggs.

Question: I mean, were you mad about it?

Causey: No, it was fun.

Question: You didn't sense there was tormenting? There was emotional anguish or anything?

Causey: No, 'cause everybody's getting messed up just like you are. So everybody just laughs at each other.

Question: What about you, Sam?

Graham: It was pretty scary. Then after you go through and everything, you watch other people go through. You about die laughing and everything. It was so funny.

Question: Has anybody ever been hurt bad at your school or anything?

Graham and Causey: Nah.

FFA advisor Benjamin Hardee confirms that these events had occurred but promises that such initiations will be stopped. He regarded the use of electricity in the ritual as harmless, claiming that it was no worse than a kid touching his tongue to a low-voltage battery. "We weren't frying people," he says. Hardee insists that the initiation was mild compared to the hazing he endured for initiation into an agricultural society at Clemson University. "Way back yonder it was rough," he says. For example, he was forced to chew tobacco while eating a sandwich. Hardee believes the initiations were intended "to get us closer together, and it did, I can honestly say." He says that he regards his students "as my family," claiming "they are as close to me as my young-uns. Say what you want about me, but I don't want anybody saying anything bad about my kids." Hardee doesn't want a book to give an impression that "we were dumb southerners down here trying to kill somebody." He promises to have a field day as a substitute for hazing. He demonstrates, however, that he has little knowledge of what constitutes hazing by one of his choices for a field-day activity: having students move a manure pile with a spoon.

Historically, the FFA has had problems with hazing, particularly at the entering Greenhand-degree stage, when initiated students are mainly freshmen. "Hazing is a sign of immaturity in an organization," University of Illinois professor Lloyd J. Phipps writes in a 1952 edition of *Agricultural Education Magazine*. "It is a barbaric practice which indicates the immaturity or insecurity of the members. It may also indicate a lack of proper guidance by an advisor and by parents." Phipps goes on to cite several frightening things that had happened to FFA youngsters who had been hazed. He mentions a nervous young man who so feared his initiation that he boarded a train out of town and was not located for days. "Many instances could be cited of boys receiving broken arms and legs or sprains in hazing activities," says Phipps. "Often a . . . hazing or initiation ceremony . . . backfires in the enthusiasm of the moment and produces physical violence."

Prior to the revelations of Graham and Causey at the national convention, FFA director of information William (Bill) Stagg said he knew of no educational studies of hazing conducted by his organization. Neither does the organization encourage hazing, he added.

Stagg listened to the story of hazing at Eastern High School in Green County, Indiana. Joe Bill Shields, an alumnus of the organization, says that bananas were stuffed into his nose until he bled during his FFA initiation. His wife, Debbie, is now concerned because the couple's son, Joey, has been initiated under the same advisor. Blindfolded and forced to eat spaghetti, Joey was led to believe he was swallowing worms. Advisor Garry Heshelman says that he had recently ordered limits for initiations because of public concern, but he also says that he notices more group cohesiveness when "harassment-type" activities are conducted.

After hearing the Shieldses' story, Stagg articulated the FFA's position on hazing in a letter. "The National FFA Organization does not condone, encourage or accept hazing practices injurious to our members as a part of initiation ceremonies," he says. "The FFA has a strong and long-standing commitment to developing leadership, cooperation and citizenship among its members, and hazing practices are inconsistent with those priorities."

Interviews at the 1989 convention indicate that many FFA chapters, according to their members, do not haze. Emily Bucher of Pipestone, Minnesota, says that in her chapter, "We like to make new members feel really important." Other chapters do haze, however. Among the schools with past or present questionable initiation practices are:

■ Cissna Park High School, Shabbona, Illinois. Junior Joel Prestgaard says that on Greenhand Day candidates must wear official dress. "If they don't wear official dress, we dip both hands in green paint," he says. "If you wear official dress, you got to have your one hand dipped in green paint. You got to wear it around school. It shouldn't be something to be embarrassed about."

His advisor is Ron Lynch. "I don't let them get out of hand," Lynch says, adding that students' hands are dipped in green food coloring, not paint.

■ McLean County High School, McLean, Kentucky. Sophomore Robert Bishop says that around their necks new initiates had to wear a scratchy corn cob on a grass string. Their hands and arms are painted green. They carry toy tractors. Two students say the initiations have gotten lenient since their parents experienced theirs. They used to make initiates pull down their pants and sit on a block of ice for five minutes, claims David Bell, the president of the McLean chapter. Advisor Carl Atherton says that the corn-cob initiation had not been done "for three or four years." He says students no longer are required to carry a toy tractor. Initiates do continue to have their hands painted green in the early morning before school starts, says Atherton.

■ Pierce City High School, Pierce City, Missouri. Upperclassmen vote on "humiliating things" to do to new FFA members, says Eric Hartley. Initiates are placed in a dark room while a spotlight is aimed in their faces, for example. Hartley and Maynard Moudy say upperclassmen put pudding or applesauce in a bowl and wafted fresh cow dung in front of the initiates' noses. Initiates put their hands in the food, thinking all the while they are mashing the manure. They say advisor

Jeff Martin supervises the initiations so that "the upperclassmen will stay under control." Hartley says that he was first initiated when he was a sixth-grader passing into the seventh grade. Upperclassmen will "take a guy and kind of get him in touch with a flagpole," says Hartley. They "get on either side, spread your legs and arms and run them into a tree or flagpole," says Hartley, "I did it to my best friend. I didn't mean to hurt him, but that's life." Jeff Martin says that FFA initiations had formerly occurred but had now ceased. "Yeah, they used to do that here, but not any more," he says.

■ Williamsburg High School, Warren, Kansas. The FFA upperclassmen "made us [blindfolded freshmen] eat stuff that wasn't the best thing," says Jay Dee Weers. "They made us eat onions and squirts of toothpaste and drink Sprite behind that." Jay Dee played football and says Coach Chuck Lee had a firm policy forbidding initiations. Principal Pat Happer says that he forbids hazing in all student organizations. He says that he would be "disappointed" if he found the allegations to be true.

■ Nodaway-Holt High School, Graham, Missouri. Student Andy Sportsman says new members are required to wear a painted green hand around their necks. "Yes, we did that," says the school principal. "But we didn't call it 'initiation,' though. It was more a celebration of the FFA." He says the students wear the hand for one day out of a one-week celebration.

Not all victims of hazing die. Many must go on living with the effects of a few minutes of stupidity. Such is the case with Mark Maddy of Brownsville, Texas, a long-time correspondent of Eileen's, whose sister Faith advises Greek students at Washington University in St. Louis. On August 28, 1982, Mark, an upperclassman, agreed to watch the belongings of freshmen participating in the sophomore's annual dunking of freshmen in a creek on the campus of Phillips University in Enid, Oklahoma. Three students decided to throw Mark into the creek for fun, but he landed improperly in the water. In that split second he seriously injured his vertebrae, paralyzing him from the chest down.

Mark returned to school and sued the university, eventually settling for an undisclosed sum. "The general climate toward me was fairly cold," says

Mark. "They thought I was out to destroy the university. . . . I must say I learned an awful lot about who my friends are and what it takes to be a friend and how you should treat other people." As a result of the Maddy case, says Dan Seim, vice president for student affairs, initiations have been made voluntary. Students are no longer allowed to throw anyone into the creek, and other activities are supervised, he says. The initiations provide "the freshman class a greater opportunity for cohesiveness," says Seim. "We also emphasize the traditions and heritage of the university." Nonetheless, he says that he cannot guarantee that students have stopped dangerous initiations. "Students are going to be students," he says. "Spur of a second events are difficult to control."

Lyle Payne of Broken Arrow, Oklahoma, was more fortunate than Mark Maddy. Lyle recovered from a senseless incident at the University of Oklahoma that could have killed him. Now a policeman, Lyle cannot tell his story without resentment in his voice. In 1983 he had been one pledge in an initial class of approximately forty-five men. With a class that big, the brothers of Phi Delta Theta thought they could afford to lose a few pledges who couldn't take the heat. They never figured they would nearly kill one along the way.

Lyle Payne was a wiry but muscular eighteen-year-old. He had built himself up by lifting weights and pushing himself during workouts. Unlike some of the pledges, he had the sense to get around some of the ridiculous requirements. When a brother poured Tabasco sauce on his cereal, he just threw it away. He hadn't been all that eager to join a fraternity in the first place. A neighbor from back home was a member, and he asked Lyle to join. That's all there was to it. The first time he heard about hazing was during rush. The brothers gave him some literature from the national headquarters of Phi Delta Theta that said there would be no hazing. "I had seen stuff on television where they paddled, but I don't believe anything I see on television anyway," says Lyle.

Despite the literature's protestations, he was hazed from the beginning. Members rang his dorm room at two A.M. and ordered him to come to the house. They told pledges "to line up" and kept them there while they screamed at them for two to three hours. But Payne claims the mental abuse didn't bother him. "I can pretty much take any kind of mental abuse they can give me," he says.

The physical harassment didn't begin for many, many weeks. The pledges endured an entire term of abuse, but the brothers told them another term would be required because they were such screw-offs. "By that time I said, 'Shit, I've done this much, and I'm not going to give up now,'" says Lyle. He continued to clean the house every Friday at midnight and memorized five facts about every Phi Delt in the chapter. Since then he has tried to figure out what motivated the members and has concluded that they simply want to assert authority over other men. "It's like a power trip," he explains. "That's like some cops. Some cops get the badge and that gun, and they try to beat the shit out of everybody they pull over."

Payne's "opportunity" to join the Lost Chapter occurred after a rare heavy snowfall in Norman. The members revived a tradition called the "Phi Delt Border Crossing." One group of pledges had to make huge piles of snowballs and bring them into the house. Another group had to run back and forth across an open area while brothers, many of whom had been drinking, blasted them with snowballs. The parquet floor grew slippier and slippier as the snow melted. When the accident occurred, Payne was the fifth pledge in a line of men the brothers compared to clay pigeons.

"Pull," a brother would yell, and a pledge had to race down the hallway to the other side while snowballs broadsided him. Payne's turn came. "Pull!" he heard. But as he ran full-speed across the hallway, he saw a member step from behind a pillar. Things happened fast, but the upshot was that Payne tripped or was tripped and landed hard on "two little steps." Organs crushed into vertebrae. "I mean, BOOM!" says Payne. "I just started throwing up."

Members ran to help him. "It's okay, it's okay," they told him. Payne pulled off his shirt, and his skin started to discolor almost immediately. The pain increased, if anything, and he couldn't breathe. A brother dropped him off at the infirmary, and he sat there alone, not realizing that his liver had been severed. In the meantime a brother called Payne's mother to tell her that the pledges had been horsing around and that her son had tripped on a curb. (Later, as Payne bitterly recalls, the brothers would claim that he and the pledges had started the snowball "fight.")

It took nearly four hours for doctors to ascertain that Payne had been critically injured. A doctor later told him that he was lucky to have come in when he did. Had the members simply put him to bed, bile and bodily secretions would have spread through his system. Peritonitis would have occurred. After performing exploratory surgery, doctors removed part of his liver. His stomach and pancreas were also bruised.

When Payne got out of the hospital, the brothers initiated him immediately. They even made him scholarship chairman of the new pledge class. But when the fraternity wanted his parents' insurance to cover the mounting medical bills, Payne turned on the group and sued, settling for more than fifty thousand dollars from the organization and the member who had tripped him. The only redeeming part of the whole incident, he says, is that one member was contrite and apologized.

But Payne has no affection for his fraternity. About the same time he was injured, the Oklahoma chapter of Beta Theta Pi found itself in trouble for dropping a naked pledge off a long way from the fraternity house. According to Payne, the Phi Delts proposed having a commemorative "Strip and Trip" party to mark the anniversary of the two incidents. "That really ticked me off," he says. "They were trying to make a joke out of the whole thing. . . . They just mocked it."

PART THREE

14

While a Black Forest of paper has been reduced to pulp for articles and congressional investigations into hazing at the military service academies, few twigs have fallen to the investigation of abuse, dehumanization, and tawdry hazing among the rank-and-file in the armed forces. In Vietnam, for example, elite fighter squadrons held initiations that ended with new men groveling in the mud to prove to the veterans that they were worthy. In today's Coast Guard occasional hazings are as frightening and senseless as anything fraternity boys can dream up.

Hundreds of pages of Coast Guard documents, generated by a congressional inquiry, prove it. Senator Richard Lugar of Indiana was the main force behind the inquiry, assisted by then-Senator Dan Quayle, also of Indiana. They were concerned about the hazing of Joe Branson, a young enlistee. The Coast Guard promptly looked into Branson's case. A single investigator relentlessly questioned the crew but failed to exhibit equal diligence with the top brass aboard the CGC *Mesquite*. In the end, although a man's life may have been permanently altered by hazing on board the ship on November 11, 1986, few perpetrators were punished — none seriously — and no top-brass heads rolled.

Documents make clear that the Coast Guard command felt Branson had brought many troubles upon himself. On the other hand, a psychosocial assessment performed on him by the Michigan-based Woodland Counseling Centers concluded that without the hazing incident, "there is nothing in Mr. Branson's history that would lead one to believe that he would not have . . . made an adequate adjustment to the Coast Guard." According to that assessment, "He had a normal, happy childhood, made a good adjustment in high school, got along well with his peers, and did well in boot camp and there was nothing up until the time of this outrageous treatment to indicate that Mr. Branson had emotional problems. Since this trauma, Mr. Branson has been in numerous incidents which I believe are directly related. This is very similar to a rape victim who has been blamed for being raped or an abused child who is punished for fighting, lying or stealing, which are all acting out behaviors due to that abuse."

One disturbing by-product of the investigation into Branson's case is the conclusion that this particular hazing was less intense and less brutal than many past Coast Guard initiations aboard ship. The Coast Guard and the Navy are known for their initiations; both have practices that certainly could and should be termed hazings. According to one source, a

Navy fireman, last assigned to San Antonio, Texas, seriously injured his back during an initiation and was mustered out of the service as a result.

The Navy's best-known initiation ritual, the "Order of Neptune," occurs when a sailor (a "pollywog" or "landlubber") crosses the equator for the first time and is initiated by veterans known as "seafarers" or "shellbacks." According to a study by folklorist Keith P. Richardson, the equator ceremony requires pollywogs to wear ridiculous costumes, sample an inedible breakfast, perform silly or demeaning tasks (impersonate a cigarette girl, for example), and crawl on a deck covered with repulsive substances.

Like the Navy, the Coast Guard has initiations to accompany the promotions of officers. In the Coast Guard one such ceremony includes a mock branding in which the initiated man must drop his trousers. According to information obtained by Coast Guard investigator G. P. O'Brien, an initiation for crossing the Arctic Circle has also been used. In it, the neophytes become slaves to veterans. The hazing lasts two days and includes calisthenics, the wearing of silly costumes, a kangaroo court, the smearing of faces with grease and soot, a hosing down with a fire hose, and a ride down a garbage chute in a life raft.

After talking to Branson, Eileen Stevens concluded that only a congressional hearing can end hazing in the Coast Guard and possibly the Navy. The Branson investigation was flawed. The investigator did not confront the ranking officers aboard the *Mesquite* to the degree that impartial members of a congressional hearing routinely would. The officers may indeed have been innocent, although Branson contends otherwise, but their guilt or innocence, he maintains, should have been determined only after a thorough investigation.

Still, incomplete though it may be, a review of the official Coast Guard investigation, combined with Branson's own comments, provides a chilling look at a hazing at sea.

A new commanding officer, Lieutenant Commander Thomas M. Conlan, reported to the *Mesquite* on June 23, 1986. He was briefed by the outgoing commanding officer on most matters of concern. But not on one: the initiations of new men that had become a tradition on this ship in the seventies. Second- and third-class petty officers ran the hazings, and many enlisted crew members joined them. In August 1986 Conlan was approached by two veterans on the *Mesquite*. They asked permission to hold a kangaroo court, which they described to him as "similar to a chief's initiation." What they didn't tell him was that since 1984, the initiation "rites" included nudity, sexual innuendo, and simulated oral sex. Conlan had no reason not to take what the two spokesmen said at face value since he regarded them as two of the most outstanding seamen on board. Both, in fact, had been recognized as Sailor of the Quarter. Nor had any new initiate on the *Mesquite* registered a formal complaint although the commanding officer had to admit that he was "vaguely aware" of what was happening during those initiations.

Conlan heard no grumblings from initiates on that occasion, so he had no problem with a request to hold a second ceremony on the evening of November 11, 1986, while the *Mesquite* was under way from Charlevoix, Michigan, to Sturgeon Bay, Wisconsin. Earlier that day, initiates had satisfied the first demand of the kangaroo court by donning outlandish costumes. Branson wore his T-shirt and underwear over his outer garments. Another initiate modeled a bra and panties over his uniform. A third's uniform-of-the-day was a garbage sack for his torso and a paper bag over his head. A fourth had to don a makeshift rat costume, complete with ears, tail, and whiskers; a fifth was a whale. A man wearing a "Lick Me" sign was licked on the face by petty officers during the work day.

The ship's log registered temperatures mainly in the mid-twenties. Cumulus clouds predominated. Winds blew up to fourteen knots. Waves were calm part of the day.

Between 1800 and 1900 hours a message piped over the public address system announced the beginning of the initiation in the crew's lounge. "Better hide," the speaker warned the initiates. Branson took the ceremony seriously. For days he had heard rumors of what went on. "We're gonna get you," said a half-dozen men. After the announcement he concealed himself in a locker in the crew's berthing area. A friend slapped a lock on the locker's door. Another man hid in the weather entry from the buoy deck. But no one else was the least bit afraid. They reported to the lounge and were taken directly to the head by second- and third-class officers, who asked the initiates to remove all their clothing and wait their turn. One man at a time was led into the mock courtroom. When a man was about to return to the head after his ceremony, a guard ordered his still-uninitiated peers into the toilet stalls so that they couldn't observe his condition.

While the first initiates addressed the court, a posse stalked the ship, quickly finding the man in the weather entry but unable for the longest time to locate Branson. They grew angrier as minutes passed into an hour, but at last they found him. "Your ass is mine," one of them yelled, pounding on the locker. The search party used bolt cutters to extricate him.

They took him to the head, where they stripped and blindfolded him. Two men, one on each elbow to keep Branson from bolting or injuring himself, led him through a passageway outside the crew's lounge. Three men spat tobacco juice on the prisoner as he stood blindfolded waiting his turn.

Finally, they hauled Branson into court to face trial and sentencing at the hands of the Prince of Punishment. "People were pretty wound up," the so-called prince later admitted to an investigator.

Charges were read. Branson was tried and convicted. The Prince of Punishment sentenced him to be shoved into a tub of ice water filled with refuse from a spittoon. Branson, like those who preceded him, was to stand and sit inside it for ten or fifteen minutes. To add to his discomfort, crew members clamped his hands to an electrical device called a megger. The device, the Prince of Punishment told him, was the "lie detector machine." A medical corpsman stood in the crowd in case his expertise was required, but he made little or no protest to stop these proceedings. And Branson didn't know of his presence until after the events had transpired.

The hazers—judge, prosecutor, defense attorney, bailiff, and jurors—rattled off inane and demeaning questions. They jolted Branson with an electrical current whenever they didn't like his responses, and several men sprinkled breadcrumbs atop his head. The sensation from the shock was like touching a nine-volt battery with wet fingers or walking into a charged fence on a farm. At first the shocks tingled, but after enough repetitions they began to smart. The shocks "felt like ants on your fingers," an initiate would later say.

During the interrogation each blindfolded initiate was required to bite deeply into the Apple of Truth—an onion. Crew members took rolls of toilet paper and wrapped length upon length around the prisoners, making scatological references all the while. The sailors had a seemingly unquenchable thirst for sadism. They squirted Branson with a syringeful of warm water and coffee. "Oh no!" someone yelled in mock horror. "Don't piss on him." Later, a crew member would swear that one man got carried away and did actually urinate on Branson.

Branson was not the only one to take abuse. A shutter-happy camera bug clicked away, supplying incontrovertible evidence that could have hanged the crew, had the Coast Guard been so inclined. The hazers dipped carrots into axle grease and stuck the vegetables between "a couple" of the initiates' buttock cheeks. Click, click went the camera. They squeezed liquid soap until it spattered against the bodies of six men. "He came on you, he came on you!" roared the crew. "Here's some donkey come," one man was told. A crew member stuffed his palm with butter-flavored Crisco. "Eat it," they urged him. He did.

The group made certain that no trouble-making bystanders would try to stop their fun. A crewman was ejected by the merrymakers for demanding that they "give the kid a break."

One initiate heard the sound of scissors snapping shut next to his genitals. "Don't move, it's really close to your cock," he was told. The scissors cut a swath through his pubic hair.

"Where is your dick?" they screamed at Branson, pretending it was too small to see. "Did you bring your pecker?"

"How many times a day do you jack off?"

"Do you give good head to guys?"

"Are you a homosexual?"

The sailors had no mercy. They accepted only answers that demeaned the initiates.

"You can't have sex with a woman, can you?"

"Yes sir, I can." Jolt. One thousand volts pricked an arm or a leg.

"What's that, faggot?"

"Yes, I can." Jolt, jolt, jolt. Branson's arms jerked involuntarily. "No sir, no sir."

When he answered "correctly" — "No" — they called him a faggot, but they stopped shocking him until the next question came. In the midst of the mock trial Branson's blindfold slipped, and he saw the rocking, gyrating band of tormentors, including the man working the voltage device.

After Branson "admitted" having sex with men, the kangaroo court presented him with a sausage. Several initiates before him had been given carrots carved in the shape of a penis. "Give it head," the men shouted. "Stroke it, stroke it."

Branson was forced to simulate oral sex. When he wouldn't oblige the crew, one of the revelers grabbed him by the back of the head and pumped the sausage rhythmically, into his mouth and out, in and out.

"Don't use so much teeth," someone yelled.

"Looks like you've done that all your life."

"Deeper, deeper! Faster!"

"Which officer do you like the best?"

"Like to have sex with the CO?"

Branson's nightmare went on and on. They sprayed his genitals with purple surgical dye. His pubic hair was discolored for two weeks. They packed black bearing grease into his ears, hair, and genitals. That disgusted even some of the sailors.

Next, like the others, Branson was given a choice of punishment: an egg to eat or some "grog," a mixture of Worchester and hot sauces from the galley. He chose the former. Someone jammed a whole egg in his mouth.

"Jump up and down until the egg breaks," he was told. "Jump, jump! Now chew it, chew it," they ordered. He did. Another initiate was hit in the jaw until his egg spattered. "Cluck like a chicken!"

To wash down the egg, the crew had another surprise.

"Want something a little sweeter?" they shouted. "Give him Tom's Mom's cookies." The "cookies" were globs of shortening and sugar laced with Tabasco sauce or chewing tobacco.

Throughout Branson's session, the sailors yowled and howled, enjoying the sport until Branson started feeling ill. Taking whatever revenge he could, the initiate repeatedly jammed his fingers into his throat until he vomited the egg and the shortening and the Tabasco sauce onto the floor, a display that even these men could not take. Branson heard their cries of disgust, and he laughed aloud, taking pleasure in the only revenge available to a blindfolded prisoner.

The Prince of Punishment kicked him out of the court. Because Branson left "early," he was spared another indignity. The others had been required to tie a line of string to their penises or testicles. One neophyte refused, and a crew member did it for him. A five- to eight-pound shackle was already attached to the other end of the line. "It's the Shackle of Truth," the initiates were told. Crew members ordered them to throw the it.

The string had been cut although the bearers didn't know that. Each grimaced as he threw down the rock.

When the initiation was over, Branson and the other five were ordered to clean up. "Congratulations," the Prince of Punishment informed them. A jury vote had been held, and five of the initates — including Branson — were told that they had done themselves proud. "You're now part of the crew." One man got a thumbs-down.

Eileen Stevens listened to Branson's cleaned-up version of what had occurred. Her lips were pursed during much of their phone conversation. She paced her kitchen. Just when she thought she had heard it all, someone always came along and showed her new horrors that men were capable of inflicting upon other men. Branson said he felt less a part of the crew after the ceremony than before. He felt disgraced. He was angry. He believed his shipmates had betrayed him. He had tried to accept the premise that it was all done in fun, but his strict Catholic upbringing wouldn't let him sell himself the falsehood.

He told Eileen that he didn't report the incident immediately. Instead, he became depressed and irritable. He got into serious fights with fellow seamen. He threw ice at crew members. He began to drink. He cried in public, so hard that his six-foot frame shook convulsively. His superiors threw the book at him, calling him a troublemaker and putting him on report. He began missing appointments and even fabricated a story about his bunk's being invaded, hoping to nail some of those who had violated him. Even his friends began to shun him. All he could talk about was the night they wanted to forget.

Finally, he told an officer why he was so troubled. The commanding officer canceled all future initiations. The crew members were incensed.

"Snitch," they called him. "You big pussy."

The abuse aboard ship increased. One crew member in his mid-thirties devoted all his extra time to making Branson miserable. His most annoying trick was to pick his nose and flick boogers on Branson's food.

Branson's offenses increased. He could no longer prevent himself from striking out blindly — even when he knew he was on the verge of being drummed out of the service. He talked to a district bigwig in the Coast Guard but received no sympathy because this man had himself survived an initiation. Branson's chief executive officer denounced him for "always making a big deal out of everything." Later, a Coast Guard investigator would look into the situation and concluded in his report that Branson's immaturity, antagonism, and poor attitude contributed to the seaman's problems with his shipmates. No one could or would admit that the initiation had thrown him into an icy skid. He couldn't stop hitting everything that came into his path.

"On top of everything they've made me feel so guilty," he told Eileen.

"They're the ones who should feel guilty," she replied. "You didn't do anything — they did."

15

Addressing a new audience is always exciting for Eileen Stevens, but few invitations have meant as much to her as her first to speak before a black fraternal organization.

She arrived at the tiny Charleston, South Carolina, airport at two A.M. The waiting area looked surreal in its emptiness. Soldiers from her plane were greeted by loved ones. Young men fresh from boot camp racing into the arms of eager mothers always prick Eileen's heart with sadness, a sense of loss, but on this particular evening the ache was especially strong as she stood alone and watched the joyful reunions.

Soon the soldiers had been whisked away, and the airport was silent. Lights dimmed. No other flights were due till morning. Eileen had to beg a surly custodian to let her remain in the closed building. Had she mixed something up? One time, completely exhausted, she had slept right through a connection and had to reverse her course. She called her host, Charles Wright of Phi Beta Sigma, at his hotel and woke him from a sound sleep.

He thought she was his wake-up call. He had decided to grab a few hours sleep, but the desk hadn't bothered to ring him. He was on his way, he promised. Within minutes a stretch limousine pulled up in front of the airport. Three extremely handsome black men, all with the step and self-assurance of professional athletes, came in and took over her bags. The custodian's jaw dropped. Eileen would have forked over a twenty-dollar bill then and there to read his mind.

She ducked inside the limousine, and Wright introduced his associates. Despite this bumbling start, Wright would come to be one of the fraternity leaders who gives Eileen hope that hazing *can* be put to an end. But this night, all she knew was that she wanted to kick off her heels, brush her teeth, and flop into a firmer-than-firm hotel bed. Her watch showed three A.M. already, and she was addressing scores of young black men for the first time in six scant hours.

Eileen, Wright, and their companions approached the hotel desk. Dressed to the nines, she was striking, and all three men could turn women's heads with their good looks. The four got the desk clerk's attention in a hurry.

"I'm sorry, madam," he said. "Your room reservation was canceled when you failed to show up."

Wright and his companions looked worse than Eileen, who looked extremely ill. Isn't there anything? the four asked all at once. Well, said the clerk, there was a suite that had been cleared away to serve as a conference room. But there was no bed, he cautioned, and a meeting was scheduled there at eight A.M.

Hey, beggars can't be choosers, Eileen thought. At this point she would have curled up on a lobby couch and gone to sleep.

Wright, an attentive and fastidious man, was upset, but Eileen tried to reassure him. The fraternity men bid her good night, and a bellman showed her to the conference room. Inside were a conference table, a collapsible table, a bar, a dining table, six swivel chairs, and two television sets. She phoned the desk. "Can I at least have a cot?"

"I'm sorry, madam," said the clerk. "The convention people have taken every last cot."

Eileen looked at the floor, the tables — ruling out the collapsible one — and the swivel chairs. The chairs won. "Sleeping in one is an experience," she wrote in her journal.

The wake-up call came at seven A.M., but Eileen didn't need it. She stumbled over to the television and watched Lady Di marry Prince Charles while she dressed and made herself up. She wanted to cry. How did this blasted woman on television have the nerve to look glamorous when she was frazzled and weary? For years she had been hoping for an introduction to the world of black Greeks, and here she was, a bone-tired, wilted wreck about to address a roomful of men she didn't know. Worse, as she dressed, early shows for the eight A.M. meeting in her room kept knocking on the door.

At eight she swept it open and marched past a startled assembly of conventioneers. Wright was waiting in the lobby with his associates. They escorted her to the Civic Center downtown, the only site large enough to handle the Phi Beta Sigmas here, in part, to listen to her speech. She was as nervous as she had ever been.

Wright tried to reassure her. They had met earlier at a conference in Bowling Green, Ohio, where he impressed Eileen as few other speakers have. "I'm crazy about Charles Wright," she says.

Wright has held many important offices in Phi Beta Sigma, including national president. When he confronts a roomful of young men to offer his no-nonsense opinions on hazing, he becomes a one-man forest fire. He attacks the standard defense that somehow branding, walking together "in line," hardcore physical beatings, and shaving heads are a part of black culture and heritage. He tells them that black tradition is not only important but essential to uphold; nonetheless, brutality is *not* what his race is all about.

Eileen admired Wright's courage to say — to bellow, if necessary — that hazing is wrong. His speech at Bowling Green had given her goosebumps. She admired the sheer power of his passion. Looking around at the Ohio crowd, she had seen with dismay that other, more conservative executive directors didn't like Wright, or at least they didn't like their shortcomings shoved down their throats. But no one dared confront this burly, athletic man who looked so self-confident. With his tailored designer suit, his fur coat, and his leather briefcase, Wright looked every inch the successful role model that these young men who hazed said they were hazing to become. All that flamboyance, combined with the oratorical skills of an old-time preacher, kept his audience tame as doves while he spoke.

Eileen wrote in her journal that the vastness of the Charleston Civic Center, the electricity of twelve hundred black men buzzing when a woman — a white woman at that — walked into their midst, and the fear that she might let Wright down drove the sleepiness out of her. Wright, his associates, and a few young members gave her encouraging looks. No one dared smile, least of all Eileen. Some of the older members — she judged a couple to be in their seventies — looked at her with unfriendly eyes and challenging faces. The old fear of failure hit her. It was the same terror of public speaking she had experienced on *Donahue,* at St. Bonaventure, and meeting with her first fraternity group. In her journal she later wrote: "I was scared! I prayed for it to go well. Please, God, let me reach them. Let them listen!" Wright had been honest when he invited her, telling her some members would be resentful. Having a woman at a national convention was itself setting a precedent. He told her, however, that he was sure they would lower their defenses and embrace her message. Hazing, if nothing else, was an equal opportunity evil. It existed as a threatening specter in both white and black America.

Wright took the stage to introduce her. Once again, she admired his ability to mesmerize an audience with the sheer fury and power of his belief that hazing was a vile curse upon the land. Eileen had learned from Wright that some black fraternity members argue that they are clinging to tradition, not hazing. They feel that when laws are passed against hazing it's just another case of whites trying to take away their culture.

Eileen took the stage and launched into her talk as if it were her first. She poured her spirit, her love, and her very being into those men, young and old. They responded. She saw a friendly nod here, a relaxing of folded arms there. Soon they were repeating her words at the end of a phrase. When she made a particularly strong point, someone said "Amen." And when she finished, the applause was like a drum roll. She looked over at Wright, able to smile at last.

Wright, now at Coppin State College in Baltimore, won't compromise on the issue of hazing. His fraternity officially ended pledging in 1988, and all other national black fraternities have since followed suit. Their new goal is to eliminate it from renegade Phi Beta Sigma chapters. Wright says that he believes that those who compromise give the young men and women who haze an excuse to cut themselves more slack. He opposes the idea of giving a list of hazing offenses to students. In the wink of an eye they will come up with a hundred demeaning, dangerous acts not listed. Wright himself was brutalized as a pledge, and no members gave him quite so fierce a whipping as did alumni from his chapter. In black fraternities, unlike their white counterparts, alumni chapters are often stronger than undergraduate chapters. Nor do black fraternities have a trained national field staff to deal with hazing problems. Regional directors are volunteers, as are chapter advisers—mostly faculty or graduate students.

Wright has been the most vocal black leader on branding. Almost without exception, the leaders of the major black fraternities have backed away from the issue. Since the fraternities have ordered no branding until men are fully accepted as members, they have been able to skirt the connection between branding and hazing. Fraternity leaders have said that they could no more stop a member from getting a brand than they could stop him from getting a tattoo if that is the individual's choice. The issue of peer pressure has been completely glossed over, according to Eileen.

In a winter 1987 interview with *expo,* the student magazine at Ball State University, a member of Wright's fraternity, Kenny Gholar, talked about his brand. He had almost decided against it, but the sight of his fellow pledges getting theirs convinced him. "Three seconds more—I wouldn't have gotten it," he admitted. "I was losing nerve. . . . The pain isn't intense. You just smell your skin burning and you hear it crackling. To some, that might be enough to drive them crazy. You can't move because they'll make a mistake. Once you move it's hard to correct the mistake." To him members who think a brand is worthless are "not worth Phi Beta Sigma."

Errors are blotted out with an *X,* as if on a letter to a friend instead of human flesh. Then the procedure begins anew on some other part of the anatomy. The branding irons are merely wire hangers bent in the shape of the desired Greek letter. The procedure is repeated as often as necessary until the brand forms a thick scar, known as a keloid. Traditionally, the black brothers get their first brands on their left bicep because that's the one closest to their hearts, but it's not uncommon for members to get five or six brands on different parts of their bodies, including the buttocks, legs, and chest.

Wright, now the vice president for institutional advancement for Coppin State, notes that branding has no part in Phi Beta Sigma's ritual. "It's forbidden," he says, "but the argument is that we do it because it shows pride in the organization." He called such reasoning "nonsense," "animallike," "of no value."

Historically, the black Greeks have accepted branding, and for a time some also got tattoos of their Greek initials. Even a few sororities branded women as part of the ritual, sometimes on the inner thigh, according to Wright. His flesh-and-blood brother, also a member of Phi Beta Sigma, was branded three times because the first two didn't take. Wright watched his brother be branded, but he was opposed to the practice even as a pledge in 1966. He refused to bend to peer pressure. However, ninety percent of his chapter elected to participate in the ritual. "It's a macho, I'm-a-man, I-can-take-the-pressure mentality," says Wright. Supporters of branding disagree, saying it is a gesture on the part of members to show devotion to the fraternity.

Wright, as an undergraduate, was a cruel and unreasonable hazer. "My best friend, who happens to be a fraternity brother, tells me all the time, 'I just cannot imagine you being on this anti-hazing kick because when I pledged, you were a demon,'" says Wright, who believes he has "blacked out" his own hazing.

Wright didn't become an anti-hazing activist overnight. He first became aware that hazing had its bad points when his chapter started losing good men who refused to put up with abuse. Phi Beta Sigma was losing the pre-meds, the brains, the student body president, the yearbook editor, and the top athletes. "My fraternity brothers would die if they heard me say this, but we're going right down in the gutter," he says. "The good students don't want to be part of it. We've got to maintain numbers . . . so we just dig down, get anybody left over. Twenty-five years ago we wouldn't have even looked at them." He says that he wants a fraternity of individualists, not clones. "I don't want us to be all alike," he says. "I want an athlete, and I want a scholar, and I want a community activist, and I want a writer, and I want a student government leader—I want a heterogeneous membership."

He became passionately involved as an anti-hazing activist after a nationally ranked boxer, a member of a black fraternity, was told to retire by a medical committee because of an inflammation in his spine caused by abuse suffered during his pledging. This case convinced Wright that someone's future might be stolen from him because of hazing abuses. He says that Phi Beta Sigma's founders seventy-five years ago got along quite well without hazing; he wonders why contemporary members believe they can't. He says that it is incomprehensible while blacks in South Africa are fighting for freedom that blacks in this country are dropping pledges off in the country (a practice called "Jericho" in the black fraternities), shaving heads, and forcing them to wear ridiculous outfits. He even objects to making pledges walk in line. Anything done without direct bearing on a pledge's contribution to the organization is, in Wright's opinion, hazing.

Wright sees no evidence that an ability to withstand hazing makes a member a more valuable brother. To him being branded is not as significant an expression of love for the fraternity as refusing to subject the group to abuse that lowers its esteem in the public's eye or, worse, bankrupts it with a lawsuit. "You want the faculty off your back about the fraternity experience?" he asks audiences of young men. "Don't have [pledges] fall asleep in the front of class."

Wright accuses white school administrators of being soft on hazing because they fear being labeled anti-black. "I don't think universities are doing enough," he charges. "With white organizations the administrations sometimes look the other way. But they definitely look the other way with black organizations because the black man says, 'You don't understand us,' 'We're unique,' 'It's part of our history,' and the administration doesn't want to be called racist or reactionary." He also condemns administrators—be they presidents or deans—who let a fraternity off the hook because they themselves belonged to a Greek organization in college. It's even worse if an administrator is a member of the fraternity in trouble. Giving that group a slap on the wrist is nepotism, Wright believes.

He also blasts critics of hazing who say that too much has been made of a small number of deaths. "One death makes it a major problem," he snaps.

The number of incidents involving predominantly black fraternities is as appalling as the number for primarily white fraternities. The four major black fraternities were founded on noble principles. Omega Psi Phi, for example, has four cardinal principles: manhood, scholarship, perseverance, and uplift. However, with increasing regularity after 1975, hazing scandals have obscured the noble goals of black fraternities:

- During the late seventies members of Omega Psi Phi at the University of Florida engaged in a repeated pattern of brutality. Members were whacked in the head with boards, beaten with fists, and hit with bricks. A confidential University of Florida report lists twenty-four separate incidents of abuse. There was also severe mental hazing.

- In 1979 a Tampa-based member of Sigma Gamma Rho sorority, a line queen for a black fraternity, charged that she had observed line brothers being forced to drink large amounts of alcohol and to use drugs as a condition of pledging.

- In 1981 a Long Island district attorney charged that hazing practices had gone on at Old Westbury College of the State University of New York. Among the charges, DA Denis Dillon said that pledges were forced to eat dogfood. He charged Omega Psi Phi and Phi Beta Sigma with abuses.

- In 1983 Vann Watts of Tennessee State University died after what was described as an Omega Psi Phi hazing party. He had a blood alcohol level of .52 percent, and his body had been beaten with switches. The drinking began to celebrate the induction of pledges as brothers.

- In 1989 a member of Omega Psi Phi claimed that he and his line brothers had sold drugs to raise money for their fraternity at a large, predominantly black college.

* * *

Another black fraternity man who has strong anti-hazing feelings is Steven Barkley Jones, who halted his studies for the ministry in 1990 to begin a book on black hazing practices. A tall man with spectacles and a boilermaker's build, Jones looks every inch the man of God except for his cigarette. Jones has had an experience that he hopes his future teenage parishioners won't ever have to go through. He is one of very few men ever to do jail time after a fraternity hazing incident. His time in prison changed his life. "It turned into a religious experience for him," says Eileen Stevens, who met Jones on a TV talk show. "He found God, and it made him a better person."

Newspaper clippings from 1986 and 1987 tell a story that is only partially true, says Jones. They say he alone perpetuated a hazing horror at North Carolina Agricultural and Technical State University in Greensboro. He was only twenty in April 1986, when he made the front page of the Greensboro *News and Record*. The charges were serious: four misdemeanor counts of assault with a deadly weapon, two felony counts of assault with a deadly weapon, two counts of hazing, and assault and battery. A&T officials suspended Jones's fraternity for a minimum of four years, its second suspension for hazing.

The story reads like something out of a sensational tabloid. Supposedly, seven Omega Psi Phi pledges allowed a berserk Jones to beat the living hell out of them with a two-by-four. One had a head wound that couldn't be closed with stitches; another's head wound required seven stitches; a third's head wound resulted in a blood clot. Another line brother, said the reports, suffered a scarred chin when his beard was set afire. In April 1987 a North Carolina superior court justice told Jones, "I think you need some time in prison." He was sentenced to two years, followed by five years supervised probation.

By 1989 Jones was ready to speak out, hoping to save some other fraternity member from the degradation and trauma of prison. But he was also speaking out for another reason: to set the record straight about himself.

He alleges that some members of his Omega Psi Phi chapter acted with him in the physical mauling and degradation of pledges. He doesn't want to excuse his own behavior, but he does want to explain it. Jones says that his particular chapter wasn't a fraternity. "We were a gang," he insists. During his stretch in prison, Jones—an educated man among thugs—had time to reflect upon his own version of the Big Picture. He deduced that he and some other Omegas— "Que Dogs" as they were informally called—had been, for all intents and purposes, a cult.

In this respect his conclusion is precisely the same as that of Long Island physician and intellectual Mark Taff. Taff, an acquaintance of Eileen Stevens, has studied Chuck's death and was himself a fraternity member at the University of Maryland when pledge Brian Cursack perished performing exercises. He says that he has observed many similarities between fraternities and cults.

Jones has come to believe that Omega's intense, semester-long mental and physical hazing was akin to brainwashing. "Any time you allow your mind to be played with it's a dangerous thing," he says. Even before he became a line brother, he spent a semester in an Omega interest group that fortified his desire to become a member. As a line brother he spent eleven to twelve hundred dollars for fraternity-related expenses, including a magnificent sweatshirt that cost him nearly six hundred dollars.

Pledges believe so strongly in the fraternity that they are willing to go into court and lie, willing to lie to a dean of students even if they have been physically injured, and willing to sell one fraternity member down the river if it means preserving what's left of the former good name of the group, claims Jones. He says that alcohol has always been a part of the tradition in his chapter. He alleges that the pledge class, previous to the beatings, was forced to consume thirteen liters of wine, plus punch spiked with Everclear.

He blasts the practice of branding. He says that it is part and parcel of a cult-like mentality. "If you really look at it, branding's what we do to cattle—that's what we [did] to slaves," he says. National Omega leaders have said repeatedly that they are powerless to stop branding because it always occurs after initiation. But Jones alleges that he received his brand "the night before I went over," which would make it a serious hazing offense. Jones says that he had to consent to the branding "or I wouldn't have been initiated," and he explains that whether members receive a brand before or after initiation varies from chapter to chapter. "If you didn't get a brand in my chapter you were an outcast," he says. "You go to the beach any given day in the summer, and you'll see all these brands on all these proud chests [proclaiming] 'I achieved something.'" He also says that anyone refusing to get a brand after initiation would be regarded as "an outcast" or, at the least, a "lower caste" member.

Part of the cult-like nature of the fraternity, says Jones, is for one line member to emerge as the so-called "honcho" of the pledge class. "The honcho gets double of everything," he says. "If we got four paddles, he got eight. But he was guaranteed the presidency the next year." Jones doesn't think the honcho idea is significantly different from what some pledges in white fraternities do to impress the group. Given his limited knowledge of Chuck Stenzel's situation, Jones believes that Chuck might simply have been trying to show the Klan Alpine members that he was the best, most macho member of his pledge class.

Because he was Omega Psi Phi's dean of education and, thus, responsible for the pledge process, he willingly set himself up as a scapegoat to spare other members. Not until he realized that the judge planned to send him away did he frantically try to refute the story that he and some fraternity members had concocted, Jones alleges.

Jones isn't trying to absolve himself of wrongdoing. He admits participating in severe physical hazing of pledges. He has also, in his eyes, paid a stiff penalty for that lapse in judgment. But he insists he compounded his mistakes by accepting the blame for abuse he didn't do.

"My mother said 'It wasn't until the judge slammed that gavel down that you snapped back into reality, Steven,'" says Jones. On the stand he felt he was fighting for his life. "You don't get a chance to answer the way you'd like to," he says. The voice of the prosecutor drilled him again and again. "Stick to the question," he heard time after time, "yes or no." Thus, when the prosecutor asked him if he had "participated" in the beatings, "of course I had to say yes." But he believes that every other alumnus and member who hazed should have gone on trial with him.

Jones credits his prison experience with strengthening him. Living among hard-boiled thugs toughened him mentally and spiritually because he could rely on no one "but me and my God." He now believes the judge did him a favor. But he feels that he was a sacrificial lamb, punished as an individual for the injustices of the fraternity system.

He also thinks he wouldn't have gone to jail had he not been black. After all, white fraternity members involved in the deaths of Chuck Stenzel, Joey Parella, John Davies, and on and on, have never done one day of jail time. Therefore, Jones can't help but see his penalty as racially motivated, given his prior clean record. He thinks that record merited at least the option of a pretrial intervention program. "Here I was a young man who had never even gotten a traffic ticket at that time," says Jones. But he concedes that the judge might have wanted to make an example of his case.

To Jones newspaper portraits of him as a berserk madman acting alone in an isolated incident missed the Big Picture. The journalists failed to dig hard enough, failed to show that administrators at A&T were not as blind to hazing as they claimed to be. Much of the Que Dogs' abuse did take place indoors, but enough was out in the open to alert deans or faculty members, had any of them sought the truth, he says. "I'm not trying to paint a picture that they were all wrong and not me," says Jones. "Yes, I went through the motions. . . . I would never tell anyone I was justified in what I did. But I just want to be clear on what I didn't do. That's most important."

Jones makes some serious allegations against his Omega Psi Phi chapter. He says that a line brother was slammed so hard in the face that a tooth popped out. That he himself has a lump in his chest from an injury suffered during pledging when a member leaped onto him from a dresser. That he and his line brothers were forced to "lay there like a holocaust scene while they just jumped on us." That the Omegas burned matches between line brothers' toes and fingertips.

That they took a piece of fiberglass and beat a pledge severely on the buttocks, resulting in an infection. The young man refused to tell anyone, according to Jones, because his dad was also an Omega, and he didn't want to let his father down.

That, as dean of education, Jones went to a professor to ask him to change the pledge's grade so the young man's grade-point average would be high enough to get on line. Did the professor do it? "Yes, he did it—he did it," alleges Jones. "He was a member of the fraternity." That he himself had held a pledge down while a member slugged a line brother in the face with brass knuckles.

During his stretch in prison Jones tried to figure out why he turned his back on the strong religious principals his mother taught him. His conclusion? He demonstrated clearcut cult-like behavior. "I . . . believed what some members of the fraternity were saying," he says. "'We're going to support you, Steve,' 'We're going to back you up,' 'We love you, Steve,' 'You take the rap for us and nothing will happen to you, Steve.'" The bottom line was that some of his brothers told him that they feared the school or the national fraternity would yank the chapter's charter unless the incident could be made to look like the isolated lunacy of one member.

While testifying, he was still "brainwashed in a sense." He says, "I had this mentality where I wouldn't go to jail. But as you get closer and closer and see that this thing is for real—my God! It jolts you, like an earthquake, back to reality." His attorney tried, without success, to argue that his client had been a scapegoat for the entire chapter.

As a result of doing time, Jones has concluded that there is nothing redeeming about the physical abuse required for membership in some predominantly black fraternities. "I can't see anything justifying it," he says. "Our parents didn't whip us like that. Why the beatings? Why, at that time, did [I] allow them?"

He hasn't decided yet whether fraternities can be a good thing for young men. "That's a hard question," he says. "Just as God made good, he made evil. We've got to admit that there are [both] forces in our society. I think there is the potential for any person or any group to be corrupted. . . . Most members of the fraternity who still affiliate, they live a lie. They're under the illusion of a false sense of brotherhood. I always say now my true brothers are in the church."

Whether Jones is telling the truth or simply talking to save the vestiges of his reputation may soon come out in court. He has been involved in two civil suits with former pledges, notes North Carolina A&T vice chancellor for student affairs Sullivan A. Welbourne, Jr. The vice chancellor says he's satisfied Jones alone committed mayhem. "All the information leads to Jones," he insists, adding that he believes Jones's accusations against administrators and fellow fraternity members are unfounded.

Omega Psi Phi completed its suspension in 1990. The university has required an annual summit since 1986 to stress its opposition to dangerous hazing practices. During the 1989-90 school year there were no major hazing incidents on campus, and Welbourne has hopes that A&T's fraternity problems are over. Nonetheless, the university still faces a legal battle in a suit brought against it by a pledge injured in the Jones incident.

"If you're not black, you can't understand": that's the message on sweatshirts some young black Greeks wear.

Adrienne Harris knows that saying is untrue. Were she to wear a shirt with a message, it might read, "If you're not bereft, you can't understand."

In October 1989 her son, Joel, died after alleged hardcore physical abuse by members of Alpha Phi Alpha, a prestigious, predominantly black fraternity. He was one of nineteen line members in his pledge class at Morehouse College in Atlanta, the alma mater of many black leaders, including the Reverend Martin Luther King, Jr. Joel, her only child, had a history of heart problems, but he had been active in sports nonetheless.

Newspaper reporters asked Harris if she planned to start an anti-hazing campaign. "No, that's a house divided," she said. "I just hope to get with Eileen Stevens and help with her campaign. She has the expertise that will help me get through my mourning."

Harris lives in a comfortable middle-class neighborhood in the Bronx, in a high-rise apartment at the top of "Cardiac Hill," as the local kids refer to her street. She has not yet had the energy to dismantle her son's bedroom, a compact space with a view of the Hudson, distant cliffs, and nearby tennis courts where she plays to keep in shape. A poster bearing the slogan "Free South Africa" hangs on one wall. Photographs keep him alive for her: Joel at the high-school prom, Joel on a bearskin rug, Joel with his grandmother, Joel on horseback. On his dresser is a copy of James Agee's *A Death in the Family,* along with a two-dollar bill, his button collection, his *GQ* magazines, and his swimming trophies. There's also his fraternity cane, the one he used for summer practice on the fancy footwork necessary for the choreographed steps that black fraternities require.

In the living room a color television set is tuned not to network programming but to a video of a memorial service. Morehouse College sent the tape. Harris watches intently as the camera lingers on Leroy Keith, the college's president, himself a member of a black fraternity. He tries, with only partial success, to keep his hands still during the service.

The invocation is given by Joseph Robinson, a friend of Joel's. His face is tortuous to behold, twisted in a grimace as he forces his words out while struggling to hold back tears. The camera pans the audience, dressed in Sunday finery for the most part. Many of the young people have on sunglasses to hide red eyes.

"Here one day, and gone the next," intones Robinson. "Pain, anguish, grief. Adrienne Harris is screaming. [Joel's girlfriend] is moaning. A brotherhood is screeching, and a college campus is yelling! Death has struck. And our wills will not accept it. Our minds don't want to believe it. And our hearts are too weak to bear it. Why, God, did you have to take him? Lord, on this day, help us to understand that this is not about Alpha, this is not about pledging, this is not about lines, this is your will! And you can see us down here, pointing the finger—blaming and pointing, blaming and fighting, blaming and scheming, trying to clear our names."

Speaker after speaker takes the microphone. The music in the background is lovely but mournful, particularly when a man with a rock-bottom baritone sings a beautiful song called "I'm Building Me a Home." The camera finds the members and pledges of Alpha Phi Alpha. They are stiff, silent, holding onto their emotions to keep from wailing.

The entire congregation tries to hold its emotions in check, but no dam could hold such grief. The waters soar and roar when Joel's best friend takes the microphone. He explains how he and a friend convinced Joel to come to Morehouse. "We had some real good times together in Hugo Hall," he says. "I can remember Joel and I—we would come out in the hallway at three o'clock in the morning. We would have on our step boots, and him and I, we, would just step all night, singing. . . . We just— I just loved him. We would just sing and step all night 'cause we were on Hugo Hall's step team together last year. Joel would always talk to me about how he wanted to pledge Alpha. He said he would do anything to join the fraternity. I'm sorry he had to lose his life because of the fraternity."

Harris turns off the set at the end of the service. The last frame had shown young men and women, their arms crossed across their bodies, holding hands with their neighbors to either side. "That's what brotherhood is all about," she says in a low, nonaccusatory voice. She walks into her bedroom to be alone with her thoughts for a few minutes. When she returns, she is her smiling self—a radiant woman in many ways the mirror image of her late son.

She begins with yesterday's news. The papers reported that attorneys for the young men involved in her son's death were fighting their expulsion by the college, arguing that their clients had futures to consider. Harris notes, quietly but firmly, that Joel, too, had had a future. "His grade point average was 3.4," she says.

The school acted hastily to placate the press and public. A legal door temporarily opened for the students' return when attorneys proved that due process had not been followed. Morehouse had to give proper notice to the hazers before finally expelling or suspending them in a way that stood up in court. Harris admits that she was disturbed that the college didn't handle the situation so that the students could not come back to Morehouse. She emphasizes that she is not vindictive, that she prays for the "children" present when Joel died. She adds that she empathizes with the families of those boys as well. Nonetheless, she believes expulsion is essential to set an example for other fraternities.

Had the situation been reversed—had Joel been a member and someone in his care had died—she says her son would have left the school. She would have helped him rebuild his self-worth, but he would have had to show appropriate remorse and atonement. "That these young men would even want to return," she says, demonstrates that "they're still thinking about themselves. . . . They never got the message. We need to look into ourselves and our children. We need to give them more guidance and role modeling."

Adrienne Harris hadn't wanted her son to pledge. She knew too well what fraternities were all about. When she was younger, she ran for queen of Kappa Alpha fraternity's pledge line. She had frequently gone to fraternity parties. The fall before his death Adrienne and Joel had a discussion at dinner.

"Mommy, I want to be an Alpha," Joel said. He told her that becoming a member would put him among the top black men living and among the best of those still to be born. He said that no matter where he went, he would have a brother. He argued about networking and connections.

"Fine, Joel," she said. "But why don't you wait until your junior or senior year? Right now the most important thing is your studies."

"No, Mom, I want to do it now."

In the end she consented. But she told him that she disliked the idea, and she refused to give him the seven hundred dollars he needed to get through pledging. She had seen the so-called dog lines where members walk in step. Had heard about the brutality. Witnessed how tired the line brothers looked. Knew some had to eat dogfood, unbelievable amounts of crackers, dry cookies, dried fruit. She thought it "ridiculous" what members of black fraternities demanded of young men who would be brothers.

"I know these young people—they get carried away, Joel," she told him. "Why don't you suggest to your big brother that during the pledging period that each one of the candidates choose a child in the area?" She reminded him that Morehouse is situated almost in the middle of a slum and all around its outskirts are low-income homes and families. "Why don't you suggest to the brothers that each pledge take one child, and work with that child, for the six weeks or eight weeks of pledging?" she said. "Each pledge tells what they're going to try to accomplish with this child at the end. If that child could read a book, if that child could do a math problem that he could never do before—at the end of the six weeks, if there is a change in the child, that is your going over."

"Mommy, that is an excellent idea," said Joel. "I promise you that when I become a big brother, that's the way I'm going to stress pledging."

Her son went back to Morehouse. Their last telephone conversation was about pledging.

"How are you, Joel? You sound tired."

"I am, a little. I have to get up every morning and run at 6:07."

"Run for whom? Yourself?"

"No, for the pledging."

"Why 6:07? That's such a strange time."

Joel said they met at six because none of the pledges on line had a class at that time. The seven honored the seven jewels of the fraternity, the organizers of Alpha.

"How much do you have to run?"

"Oh, it's not too bad, Mom. Just waking up is the hard part."

"Joel, take a little time for yourself. If you're tired, just sit down. If it gets to be ridiculous, like I told you before, forget it. Do it some other time or never do it. But you sound tired to me."

Her last words to him were "I love you."

His last words to her were "I love you, too."

Nagged by things she should have told him, she sat down to write him a letter. Like Eileen's last letter to Chuck, hers was returned unopened.

In the wake of his death Joel's cherubic face appeared on the front pages of papers across the county. His mother was inundated with letters and flowers. She was overwhelmed by the public's response but too wise to think that those in high places might actually be encouraged to action that might save other young men.

By terrible coincidence, Joel graduated from the same Bronx preparatory school that Joey Parella had attended, Harris says. His classmates, some friends from Morehouse, and hundreds of strangers crowded past Joel's bier. She knows such attention won't prevent the deaths of more Joels, Chucks, Barry Ballous, Joey Parellas, of more Jay Lenaghans, Rick Cerras, Stephen Calls, of more John Daviesses, more Vann Wattses. "'Oh, the family, the poor family,' they say, and forget after that," says Harris. "Until it touches home you don't know the pain those families have gone through. That's what happens with this incident with Joel. Everyone looking at the newspaper, the TV coverage, says 'Poor child, poor family.' In two weeks they won't even remember his name [or] what school it happened at. . . . But God forbid it happens to one of theirs. Then it all comes back to you. No one should have to go through that. This is a dumb thing. Death is sad anyway. We all realize we have to die. That's a given. But to bring the children this far, and then to have them leave you because of foolishness—that hurts."

She also castigates the fraternity leaders—the executive directors. "I feel the elders in these fraternities have let the children run it," she charges. "My son's passing I compare to this: You take a six-year-old. You ask that six-year-old, 'What do you know about a car?' The six-year-old will say, 'There's a wheel, there's an accelerator, there's a brake, and there's a hole for the key.' Now with just that knowledge the six-year-old most likely could drive the car. . . . An adult . . . gives the six-year-old the keys and says, 'Start it. You know where the accelerator is, you know where the brake is, you know where the wheel is.' The six-year-old drives off. If there's a tragedy that occurs with this car, who do we blame? The elder that gave the keys to the car. That's who I'm really attacking: the elders in these fraternities. They've given the keys to these young men, and they gave them the gas." Harris has concluded that fraternity elders must take the keys away. She says, "They know they've been lax." She wants them to deal responsibly with the consequences of their leniency.

Two months after Joel's death Harris took a brief vacation in Jamaica. There she ran into filmmaker Spike Lee, whose *School Daze* is a damning portrayal of black Greeks.

"Mr. Lee, I just wanted to shake your hand," she said. "My name is Adrienne Harris."

Lee looked her full in the face. "Joel Harris's mother?"

They talked briefly about her son's death. In February 1990 Lee visited his alma mater—Morehouse College—to receive an achievement award. "During this past semester, a young man . . . died," he said. "I think we should abolish fraternities from Morehouse College."

16

Five years after Chuck's death the statute of limitations for charges against Klan members ended. In November 1984 Eileen's attorney wrote James E. Euken, George Francis's successor as the district attorney of Allegany County. He told Euken that Francis had indicated he would honor Eileen's request for a copy of supporting depositions in case index number 18613/78, *Eileen H. Stevens, as Administratrix of the Estate of Charles Stenzel v. Alfred University.* He assured Euken that his client wanted to fill in gaps about what had happened that night in February 1978.

On November 5, 1984, Euken responded, informing Eileen's attorney that his secretary, Deb Cook, had "searched our cabinets unsuccessfully for a Stenzel file." He asked if there were any "other names besides Klan Alpine, Alfred University, and Charles Stenzel where we might look?" Euken also sent a carbon copy of his letter to the Honorable George F. Francis in Buffalo.

Eileen's attorney thanked Euken on November 16, 1984, for responding to the request "of ordinary people like Mrs. Stevens." He could only repeat what he had said in his last letter, however, "not knowing the filing system that was in effect when George Francis was the District Attorney." He said he doubted the file could be under any other name.

Euken failed to respond. Eileen's attorney wrote a terse note in January 1985, saying that his client was "totally perplexed as to how these statements could have gone astray, especially when they had in fact existed as they were reviewed personally by myself and the former District Attorney Francis."

The district attorney fired back an equally curt reply. "I will once again direct my secretary, Deb Cook, to scour through the old files and look for the above. I will advise when we locate the file."

Cook dutifully searched but once again found nothing. A new complication surfaced in 1985, when a Hollywood film studio representative, Arthur Kananack, contacted the district attorney independently in an attempt to locate the Stenzel file. The studio had approached Eileen, expressing a soon-to-fade interest in a film on Chuck's life. Euken wrote Eileen's attorney on June 19, 1985, to inform him that a contact had been made by the studio.

Eileen's attorney responded cordially, thanking the district attorney for the information and for promising to send Cook on a third expedition into storage. "I realize your office is not unlike many other offices . . . that occasionally misplace a file," he said. But, if this search proved fruitless too, he could only conclude "that the file was not misplaced but had been removed from the office or that the file had been destroyed." The letter concluded with an implied warning. "These perceptions are not difficult to arrive at either by the undersigned, Mrs. Stevens or by the general public."

The third search again failed to produce the file. In 1989 the district attorney's office verified that the file was still missing. Through a secretary George Francis refused a request for an interview on the Stenzel case. He did allow the secretary, Paulette Jankowski, to make an official statement for him—the only comment he would make about the incident.

"The judge remembered that the mother's lawyer had asked to see the files," says Jankowski. "After that, he hasn't seen the file over there. He knew that the attorney had read it. Mrs. Stenzel's [sic] attorney had read the file but since then, he didn't know anything about it, the judge didn't. But he did know it was missing."

The Stenzel file was not a thin folder that might somehow fall through a crack. It was thick, involving at least three folders, according to newspaper accounts at the time of Eileen's suit.

"I don't understand how a file disappears," says pathologist Paul Kolisch. "Allegany County is one of the most lawless places—absolutely lawless," he adds. "And if you do insist on some respect for the law, you're a son-of-a-bitch."

Nonetheless, Kolisch does not think Francis had anything to do with the missing file. "George is one of the less lousy attorneys I've dealt with," he says. "I do not think he was patently dishonest." Kolisch does, however, think the missing file may have significance. "There's so much cover-up here it's incredible," he says.

As Chuck's friend and as a journalist, Greg Belanger is outraged about the file's having vanished. "The whole Chuck Stenzel court file is missing?" snaps Belanger. "The biggest publicity case they had in probably twenty-five years! I can't believe it." Belanger doesn't speculate about who might have taken the file, but he does think whoever took it probably got rid of the incriminating evidence. "I'm sure it doesn't exist now," he says.

Eileen never pursued the missing file. She realized how difficult it would be to prove guilt if, in fact, one individual had acted alone to destroy or remove it. However, she did write Allegany County Clerk Joseph Presutti to ask for another copy of the coroner's autopsy reports. That office returned her four-dollar check. The unsigned response was presumably handled by a deputy clerk. It said, "We do not find a report on file in this office under that name."

Eileen jammed the reply back into its envelope, thinking someone ought to teach Allegany County a better filing system—among other things.

Year after year some new mention of Eileen's work appeared in print, occasionally stirring the curiosity of Alfred undergraduates. In 1986 a *Redbook* article "A Fraternity Ritual Killed My Son" caused a "big fuss," according to an article in the *Fiat Lux* on February 7. King told a student reporter that the incident "keeps resurfacing," but that he wasn't worried about its affecting admissions. "It didn't really affect us when the case was in court, so I don't expect it to now." The reporter misidentified the dead youth as Chuck Stevens.

But the *Redbook* article drew an emotional response from a member of the Class of 1980 that revealed many things about Chuck and about Alfred's perennial problems with booze.

"What is the big fuss about?" wrote Linda Carl in a subsequent issue of the newspaper. "Well, first of all, the student's name was Chuck Stenzel, and not Stevens. Secondly, he died from alcohol poisoning in Klan Alpine. . . . And thirdly, the biggest irony was that Chuck was joining Klan because he enjoyed the 'brothers' and not for 'all the beer he could drink in one semester.' Chuck was not a drinker for alcohol's sake, which is probably why his body reacted to, and tried to reject, the mass quantity he had attempted to consume that evening. Chuck was not some little wimpy freshman who couldn't hold his booze, nor was he the stereotypical all brawn and no brain Klanimal. He was a hard working, down-to-earth person. . . . Chuck was . . . starting his second semester at Alfred when he died. Even though he wasn't a full-year student he wanted to put down some roots in Alfred and he felt that pledging Klan would be the answer."

Carl said she had talked with Chuck that fateful day, and at long last she provided a simple but plausible reason for his decision to join Klan Alpine:

"Chuck, of all the guys I know, you are the last one I expected to be joining a frat," I said to him that day.

"Yeah, I know," he replied, with a twinkle in his eye.

"Why are you doing it?" I asked.

"Because I like the guys," he said.

Carl then offered her view on what happened that evening. Her comments, for any Alfred student or faculty member who caught their significance, demonstrate that actions have consequences—for the actor and for others. As Klan learned the hard way, a fraternity better make sure that the image it projects is the image it wants because that's what it ultimately becomes. "Unfortunately the guys didn't care enough about him and the other pledges to provide a more humane way to initiate them," wrote Carl. "There was nothing accidental about what happened to Chuck. He drank too much, and it killed him. The real miracle is that more have not died. And not just from pledging. When I was at Alfred, it seemed like 95 percent of the social activities focused on alcohol. That was OK with me because I'm an alcoholic. However, in the past sixteen months since I had my last drink, I have grieved over the things I lost due to alcohol: a large quantity of brain cells affecting my memory and my ability to reason, the respect of my family, friends, fellow students and professors; my reputation, my self-respect, a lot of money, and a friend called Chuck."

In 1986 Rich Sigal again returned to Klan Alpine for a reunion, this one sparsely attended. Sigal found himself unable to communicate with the latest generation of Klan. At one point he and his former roommate looked at each other and said, "That's it." There would be no more reunions for them; there would be no more donations to Klan. Sigal believes that his fraternity's values have become dangerously shallow, and he didn't see any way to reverse the downhill tumble.

For him Klan is emblematic of fraternity houses across the country. "Unless society goes through a broad, high-level, structural change in terms of its values, I don't see on . . . the fraternity level that anything real [positive] will happen," he says. "What do I mean by a social structural change? . . . A war? A famine? An AIDS epidemic? A real depression?"

Sigal has concluded that fraternity members really want the symbols that the media have convinced them have value. "Dammit, they want a Porsche; that's all they care about," he complains. "What kind of a society is that? They want a Porsche and they want to party."

Sigal has observed the same valuelessness in adults. For years he has lived in Sparta, New Jersey, in part because he believed his children would get a quality education. Sparta is an upper-middle-class, white-collar community, a flagship town in Morris County, one of the country's most affluent areas. "We have to stay on [our children] and talk to them on a regular basis to let them know what our values are," says Sigal. "Most parents don't do that. Most parents aren't there at breakfast. Most parents aren't there at dinner, or a lot of them aren't. I think until you get a society that lays out very clearcut norms for kids . . . you're going to have excesses, you're going to have fraternity deaths. . . . The hazing intensity is there because we're dealing with a society that is very self-focused. We're dealing with people that are so concerned with their own needs, what do they care about somebody else's? If you're other-directed, you're concerned about others, and if you're concerned about others, you don't do things to them. You don't hurt them, you don't haze them."

Sigal cites the wisdom of Emile Durkheim, the grandfather of many sociological precepts, to support some of his conclusions about contemporary society. Sigal identifies suicide and hazing as twin prongs on the devil's pitchfork in social eras when the individual feels estranged from society. The Frenchman Durkheim refers to this sense of rootlessness as "anomie" in his book *Suicide*. Durkheim recommends that people understand what is happening in society in order to feel a greater sense of control over their environment.

The fraternal world today — and society as a whole — would benefit from its academic connections in the struggle to blunt the force of that diabolical pitchfork. The Greek system, like any other bureaucracy, has only the law and order that it as a group gives its members. The influence for good or evil is powerful. Moreover, when values break down and individuals in various institutions — college administrators, faculty, fraternity executives, politicians, you-name-it — no longer work together for mutual interdependence, this can be disastrous in a society such as ours, dependent upon what Durkheim calls organic solidarity.

Fraternities, for example, assemble to feel that satisfying wholeness we as human beings get when many are one. The difference today is that the symbols of this collective oneness — the items used in secret rituals — no longer have the same meaning for many of today's Greeks that they had for Sigal, for Don King, for Fred Kershner. Nor has the fraternal world figured out how to make those ceremonies impressive again, perhaps because many in the Greek world debunked them during the 1960s when the flower-child generation perceived such rituals to be unworthy and childish.

Some fraternity leaders today caution that the trend to do away with pledging could have disastrous consequences for the fraternal system, further knocking askew important shared values. On the other hand, hazing — an aberration of those desirable rituals — is what such leaders want to deemphasize and eliminate. Somehow the adult leaders of the fraternity world must unite to help their younger brethren get their acts back together. Through education, young people — in the Greek world and beyond — must relearn what their lives and their rituals are about.

Eileen can count on one hand her invitations to speak to sororities. Nonetheless, many sorority women pack the auditoriums whenever fraternities have her address campus Greeks. She has long known that problems in sororities are mild compared to those in men's fraternities, but innocents the sisters are not.

As social boundaries break down and feminism has gained strength, things have changed in sororities as well, particularly as women have made economic and status gains in the workplace. Sigal notes that when the media started emphasizing "unisex this or unisex that," definitions of *male* and *female* became less distinct. As a result, Sigal is not surprised that hazing has become more uniform between the sexes, particularly as alcohol use becomes more extreme.

Female hazing is following a path similar to what happened in women's athletics when the media began playing up female accomplishments in track and field. Suddenly some women began taking steroids, flirting with dangers traditionally associated with male athletes. In a similar vein, a black sorority at Ball State University found itself in trouble with the school early in 1990 for committing acts of physical hazing, unfortunately a more common sorority problem in general these days.

Eileen Stevens has learned about "goldfish bowling," a practice in which pledges are blindfolded while actives scream at them, forcing them to reveal personal flaws.

She has learned from a heavyset Rutgers University pledge about sisters who forced her to stand on a table while they criticized her weight. The pledge told Eileen that she sobbed in her room for hours and had fleeting thoughts of suicide afterward.

She has been told of blindfolded pledges who have been seated in a circle and forced to reveal intimate details of their first sexual experience, only to find out the grinning sisters had recorded them.

A Gamma Phi Beta from Syracuse University wrote Eileen to say that in her era as a sister, "One girl became quite upset and stayed upset for a week or so" after members shined bright lights in her face and asked personal questions during a hazing session.

An Alpha Sigma Alpha from Adrian College in Michigan wrote about her experience with mental hazing. It caused psychological trauma that required counseling. "Sometimes the mere idea of a confrontation can shake me," she confessed. "I'd love to knock some sense into the girls for their rude, uncalled-for tongue lashing. I wish at times they could experience the hurt they so willingly inflicted. . . . If that is brotherhood or sisterhood—our society is in trouble."

A Sigma Iota Beta member from Bryant College in Providence, Rhode Island, wrote a gutsy letter about her 1970 initiation, hoping that her experience might help Eileen save other young people from victimization. She said, in part:

> On several occasions [the pledges] were instructed to duck-walk long distances. . . . One evening we were told to have knee races in the icy, slushy parking lot of a local bar on our bare knees. Under the covering of slush was a solid bed of ice into which was imbedded rocks, broken glass, etc. (This was February . . . and it was dark so nothing was visible.) After the initial shock of cold, we felt nothing because the ice acted as an anaesthetic. When the "race" was over we stood up & suddenly felt blood running down our legs. All of us—& there were about 30 pledges—suffered serious contusions and abrasions; some of us had blood poisoning; and one of us—me—had such serious permanent damage that I spent the next 2 wks. on crutches.
>
> The sisters were frightened when they saw all those bloody knees—but not because of the damage done but rather because of the repercussions from the College. We were told the sorority would pay for any medical expenses incurred but this entire incident had to be hushed up. . . . Of course, this is in no way comparable to the hazing deaths you are publicizing. But it does point out that sororities are not immune from inhumane hazing rituals and further, that left to their own devices, and given the power to command someone who reveres them, many college students lack common sense & foresight. The potential for the abuses of this power is reflected in these hazing deaths.

The realities of sorority hazing had struck even closer to home for Eileen than she knew. In fact, the very act of attending Chuck's funeral became the turning point for his friend Nanci Lunati in her attitude toward her sorority. Lunati had suspicions about her friend's death, feelings that grew directly out of her own hazing experiences.

Picture the average American father receiving a call from his daughter, the sorority pledge. Darling Clementine exclaims that she has just received her invitation—THE BID!!!—from the sorority of her choice. She would have died had they overlooked her, but they just knew by looking at her that she was one of them. Daddy says, "That's nice, dear," and goes to bed. He is startled at Clementine's euphoria and wishes that she might transfer some of that enthusiasm to her freshman composition class. As his head hits the pillow, a video of his daughter's pledging plays in the VCR of his mind. He sees Clementine selling cookies to raise sorority funds. He sees the wealthy president of the jock fraternity planting a chaste kiss on Clementine's cheek and, eventually, an engagement ring in her diet cola at the senior prom. Maybe he sees Clementine seated in the midst of sixty other darling Clementines. They sing a sorority ballad while twenty platinum-haired alumnae weep with the joy of sisterhood.

But if Nanci Lunati's father harbored such a vision for his daughter, he couldn't have been more wrong.

Picture another scene, Mr. Lunati. Your Nanci is a student at the State University of New York College of Technology at Delhi, a two-year technical college located in the lovely Catskills. Imagine a huge room in a rambling house that belongs to the brother fraternity of Alpha Beta Chi sorority. Picture those brothers seated amongst the females of Alpha Beta Chi. The show is about to begin, and the eyes of the audience are on the combined pledge classes. During the two-week pledging period, the female Alpha Beta Chi pledges, with their male counterparts, must put on skits dreamed up by an audience of their potential sisters and brothers. The skit your daughter has to perform with one of the fellows isn't something you'd like to share with your boss tomorrow, Daddy. The required assignment is to pantomime fifteen different positions of sexual intercourse. Yes, they keep their clothes on, but that doesn't keep your daughter from feeling like a siren of sleaze.

Besides, a few days later she will take off her clothes, most of them anyway. The good sisters of Alpha Beta Chi have given all their pledges cutesy nicknames. Because Nanci is long-haired and athletic and pretty enough to play an extra in a Hollywood beach movie, she's been dubbed "Surfer Girl." Here she is now prancing in front of the college men and her cheering future sisters. The men are whistling, clapping, and ogling every inch of her that a bikini fails to cover.

"Hey, surfer," they cry. "Hey, honey."

She feels cheap and abused, and that's precisely how the members want her to feel. They want to put this cookie from Sayville in her place. While her pledge sisters sing the words to the Beach Boys' rendition of "Surfer Girl," Nanci stands in front of the audience. She tried to tell the sisters where they could shove their "sick little play," but they told her that if she didn't perform, one of her pledge sisters would take her place. So here she stands, center stage, tears dropping onto her bikini top. She tries to sing, but all she can do is gag. Seconds later, she grabs her surfboard and runs away in shame and fury. The members send the pledges to coax her back. As she resumes her place in line, it's the turn of the heaviest young woman in the pledge class to cavort before the audience. And, my, aren't the fellows happy to see her in the flimsiest teddy imaginable. Someone shouts her nickname. "Hey, Pillsbury Doughgirl!"

After this night ends, the sisters award tee-shirts to the pledges with "Surfer Girl" and the rest of their nicknames on them. Your daughter has almost become a sister. She has only Hell Night to go.

Hell Night was the final event for Lunati and her pledge class. The evening began with intense physical and mental hazing. In the midst of the indignities, Lunati's roommate, a tall, blonde knockout, had enough and quit. The other pledges tried to convince her to stay, but she wanted no part of Alpha Beta Chi. Lunati and the others remained, figuring that they had come too far to stop now.

At midnight the members drove the remaining pledges to the base of a tall fire tower. After the pledges piled out of the cars, they formed a line and members tied a long rope around each one's waist. Each was given a six-pack of beer. They were told to climb the tower and chug the beer. They were not to come down until every can was empty. If five-one, ninety-eight pound Nanci could drink only three beers, the pledge the sisters called the Pillsbury Doughgirl had to drink nine.

"If one drop spills, we'll send up another six-pack," a member warned them.

Four cars illuminated the tower with headlights as the girls climbed. If one person fell, the other girls, in theory, would catch her and help her regain her balance. None of them dared think of what might happen if all of them should go sailing into space. The pledge class reached the top of the tower and toasted the accomplishment with their first beers. Sometime during the drinking session, the members drove away, leaving the pledges in darkness. Not even a moon to celebrate with them. Somehow Lunati made it back to her dormitory before morning broke. That evening there was a sorority party in the new members' honor. Her roommate watched Lunati get ready.

"You asshole, I can't believe you didn't do it," Lunati said to her.

"You're the asshole for doing it," she fired back. "I can't believe you let them do it to you."

Many years after pledging, Lunati sits at a kitchen table, her former roommate on her mind. "I admire her for quitting," she says. "I just wish I'd been right behind her."

Lunati listens to a story about an experience Eileen Stevens had many years after becoming head of an anti-hazing group. She received a telephone call from a distraught father. He refused to give his name but said that his daughter had been a sorority pledge at a college in Virginia. Eileen was hesitant to speak, not sure that this wasn't a prank call. The father told her that his daughter had been abused at a joint pledging session of his daughter's sorority and a brother fraternity. After a few minutes, Eileen believed he was sincere.

The father said that his daughter's ordeal began when she picked an assignment out of a hat. Because the father was so evasive, Eileen pictured a gang rape or molestation until finally it dawned on her that the members had required the girl to submit to an enema. Why she complied, the father did not know, but she had. Her pants had been pulled partially down; her buttocks, exposed. The brothers made crude remarks. The girl became hysterical. She had since dropped out of school, believing her reputation permanently scarred.

Lunati listens. Assuming the story's truth, could the one-time Surfer Girl see the person she had been eleven years earlier doing such a humiliating thing?

"If that was Hell Night, yes," she says.

Could she envision the so-called Doughgirl or the other pledge sisters submitting to similar abuse?

"Absolutely."

Women do not often go on the record advocating hazing. In fact, sorority representatives are even more vehement in attacking the practice than are their male counterparts. Nonetheless, a woman will occasionally speak in favor of hazing, and her reasons invariably echo those more commonly uttered by men. "As a member of Kappa Kappa Gamma, one of our nation's oldest and most prestigious college sororities, I am continually dismayed by attempts of the media and other outsiders to disparage the Greek System," Nancy L. Haigwood wrote the *News-Post* of Frederick, Maryland, in 1983. "I am especially incensed at vitriolic attacks on our practices of 'hazing,' which non-Greeks fail to realize serve numerous valuable functions."

According to Haigwood, "hazing strengthens the mettle of pledges" by putting them through trials they'll have to face sooner or later in life. "Secondly," she says, "hazing builds loyalty to the pledge class and to the overall organization." Her third defense is that "hazing is the final stage of the all-important weeding-out process."

Haigwood argues that Greeks should not be abused by the press. She says, "Charges that actives are to blame for accidental injuries which sometimes occur during pledge hazing are totally without foundation. No active ever forces any pledge or initiate to do anything in a sorority or fraternity—an individual is free to depledge at any time.

"Charges that hazing and other related activities are detrimental to the academic performance of pledges obviously come from individuals who don't realize that the primary education in a college or university environment doesn't come from reading a book or sitting in a classroom, but rather from dynamically interacting with one's peers."

Jenny Frank Helderman of Gadsden, Alabama, the vice president of Kappa Kappa Gamma and a member since 1959, says that "Haigwood does not speak for the fraternity and never has," and adds that it is a "most isolated" occurrence to have a sorority woman come out in favor of hazing, which is "strictly prohibited" by the national.

Suzanne Kilgannon, an Alpha Sigma Alpha member and employee, reveals some disturbing experiences she had while visiting chapters across the country in an article in the sorority magazine *The Phoenix.* She saw "pledges do horrible things in order to prove their worthiness to be Alpha Sigma Alphas." She believes that hazing undermines a chapter's goals and causes pledges to feel misled about the sorority's ideals as presented during the rush period.

Klan's Richard Klein suggests that as women have evolved into more aggressive drivers and smoke and drink more often, they might also imitate undesirable male hazing practices. Some cases suggest that Klein's perception may not be too far off the mark:

■ In 1978 the Alpha Kappa Alpha chapter at the University of Texas was found guilty of such hazing offenses as "requiring pledges to ingest unpleasant food, to recite sorority history and other information excessively and under duress, and to do physical exercises for failure to perform expected tasks," said assistant dean of students David McClintock.

■ Alpha Delta Pi sorority at the University of Southern California was found guilty of hazing after an intoxicated pledge had to have her stomach pumped in 1982.

■ A University of Maine sorority, Alpha Chi Omega, was suspended in 1988 after members branded blindfolded pledges in a cemetery. Three pledges received minor burns when a metal brand—bearing the group's Greek initials—heated over a candle flame was pressed against their flesh.

■ During the late eighties senior Sara Hardon, a Delta Nu sorority president at Dickinson College, resigned because "some girls felt that hazing was the backbone of the sorority." Among other things, pledges were forced to sit on a block of ice and tell jokes until they made the sisterhood laugh. The sorority was censured by the college for two years after pleading guilty to hazing charges.

In the eighties some universities took the positive step of banning little sisters' groups, which are created out of inherently sexist attitudes and sometimes lead to sexual abuses. Women are rushed for little sisters' groups much the way male pledges are recruited. A smug tee-shirt sold in a Bloomington, Indiana, mall during the Christmas season in 1989 summed up the problem, perhaps unintentionally. It read, "What does a Little Sister really have to do?"

One of the most controversial cases dealing with little sisters involved an alleged gang rape in 1984. The fraternity was Pi Lambda Phi, which eventually reached a settlement with University of Florida officials. A woman who agreed to have sex with one man to secure a "secret bid" after a little sister rush party then alleged that she was gang raped. The state disagreed, calling it a case of group sex instead of rape. "It's a not-so-uncommon event," a Pi Lam wrote the student paper, discounting it as merely "a train by a group of guys and a willing girl."

Advisor Ben Patterson resigned. "They seemed to think that what happened was just another case of 'boys will be boys,'" he complained. When a group of women marched down Fraternity Row, the fraternity men jeered. One condition of the settlement was that the fraternity end its little sister program.

Sexual problems involving sorority pledges who attend joint sorority-fraternity parties have also occasionally occurred. In 1988, for example, a University of Mississippi Chi Omega sorority pledge said she was raped after a mixer with Sigma Alpha Epsilon. School officials suspended the chapter, charging an "extensive period of disruptive behavior."

In 1985 Phi Sigma Kappa fraternity was disbanded at Eastern Illinois University after a party it cosponsored with the Sigma Kappa sorority. During the party a nude woman was handcuffed to a staircase for five hours.

Another publicized case involved Pi Kappa Alpha fraternity at Ferris State College, which was accused in 1984 of abducting Ann M. Doherty and forcing her to drink a bottle of tequila. The college's Interfraternity Council required the fraternity to apologize and partake in an alcohol-awareness program. It recommended no other punishment.

Even panty raids, a long-practiced college prank, have been discouraged, with good reason, by school administrators. Angry Delta Zeta sorority sisters at the University of Nebraska demanded that Alpha Tau Omega compensate them for eleven hundred dollars after members ransacked the house in search of women's underwear. The women did not appreciate a remark made by an ATO that the raid was "an age-old fraternal custom that got enjoyably out of hand."

National fraternities love to peddle the image of the fraternity gentleman. Few care to admit (except to one another or off the record) that the image of fraternities today is as bad as it was during the fifties when their racist and anti-religious membership requirements were denounced by fair individuals. In addition to the killing, breaking, and demeaning of pledges during initiation rites, fraternities today have a well-deserved infamy for sponsoring racist theme parties, encouraging sexual crimes and anti-feminist attitudes, and breaking alcohol and drug laws. Too often, fraternities are regarded as unpleasant neighbors and, in extreme cases, as a danger to the community.

The staggering weight of fraternal problems has led such former strongholds of Greek life as Amherst and Franklin and Marshall colleges to disband fraternities and sororities—a decision that Alfred's Don King denounces as "a copout." Eliminating all Greek organizations does ignore the basic constitutional right to organize fraternities and sororities—the majority of which present no insurmountable problems and which, arguably, do much good for their members. But it is also unfair and unwise to leave unpunished those Greek organizations that are habitual offenders and the epitome of *Animal House* behavior. The board of directors of the American Council on Education recommended in 1990 that colleges set strict standards of conduct for Greek organizations that include penalties for those that break rules.

Organizations do have merit even if they exist purely for social reasons, so long as those groups do not brazenly violate alcohol and hazing laws, according to Fred Kershner. Many college-age students crave the group reinforcement of a fraternity or sorority, particularly on isolated campuses or large, sprawling campuses. But simply doing legitimate community service makes many Greeks feel they are immune to criticisms from the press and public. One of the most galling occurrences for parents after a child dies during an initiation is the inevitable fraternity defender who will remind us that this same group had a blood drive or charity beer blast—as if somehow that act of charity balanced an act of barbarism.

The Greek system has accused the media of covering only its negative side. Unfortunately, given the significance of the hazing problem, media criticism has actually been light. Although there are exceptions, newspapers generally investigate hazing only after serious injuries or deaths. For many years, newspapers, magazines, and television actually glamorized the hazing aspects of pledging and the military plebe system. Witness the following:

> ■ *Munsey's* magazine in 1901 said: "A man makes his vow to his fraternity in only a less degree of awe than to his wife. To one, as to the other, he pledges a loyalty that lasts through the years, but when the initiation is finished, bedlam breaks loose, and the new member is treated to a veritable sorry go round of mixed emotions. It is not permitted to more than suggest this indescribable hour. It is an unfortunate fact that there has been a serious or even fatal accident to the candidate, usually due to some action of his which his comrades could not have foreseen, but none the less deplorable on that account. It is a mooted question whether this part of the initiation should not be prohibited. Football is also a

mooted question, but the good features of both institutions have kept them alive for years, and probably will keep them alive for years to come."

■ The New York *Times* carried a 1915 editorial which said in part: "Anybody who has been to college knows that not all hazing is of the same moral quality—that some of it is criminal, some cowardly, and some mere play, harmless or even beneficial to all concerned. . . . The hazing instinct or impulse is by no means confined to schoolboys and undergraduates. It is characteristic of the whole of humanity, and in one or another form and degree it manifests itself wherever and whenever experience and wontedness give, as they invariably do, a sense of superiority over the newcomer, the stranger. A 'folkway' as old and as widespread as this should not be hastily condemned as either wicked or useless, and he assumes an almost hopeless task who undertakes its ending."

■ In 1919 the New York *Times* reported an incident in which a Colgate University freshman drowned after trying to escape from an island where sophomores had marooned him. Taking the position that the incident should be called "accidental," an editorial said: "There was hazing, but it was not brutal or cowardly hazing—was not, that is, unless those epithets are applicable whenever college boys by force of numbers compel one of their number to do something against his will, and such an extension of the terms is forbidden by common sense. It will be demanded only by those who have forgotten or never knew the real nature of boys."

■ In 1920 the *Times* said about hazing at Annapolis: "As a general thing, hazing does not take a malignant form; quite the contrary. The victim is not persecuted, but played with, and he enters into the spirit of the occasion if he is a normal boy. It is not unnatural for upper classmen to impose modesty and introspection upon the 'plebes,' who may be the better for it; anyway, hazing blended of a feeling of superiority and a spirit of mischief will always be so hard to eradicate that a wise Superintendent, while he should draw the line at excess, is inclined to let boys be boys." The next year, a young man was injured in a hazing, and testimony emerged that Rear

Admiral Henry B. Wilson, Superintendent of the Naval Academy, had made remarks that he wanted the "freshness . . . taken out of these plebes." Wilson said he must have been misunderstood.

- "Hazing, or running, had its basis in sheer necessity," said a *Saturday Evening Post* writer in 1923. "It was not cruel, save in those very occasional instances where, as in every university, it was degraded from the real purpose behind it. That purpose was the subordination of the individual to the welfare of the mass, which meant, naturally, the welfare of the academy and ultimately the welfare of the Navy."

- "Frosh Just Love to Be Miserable" read a 1949 headline in *Life* that depicted hazing at New York University. "Hazers were careful not to injure anyone seriously," the magazine clucked. Photographs depicted the immersion of freshmen into troughs of icewater and their subsequent paddling by a gauntlet of seniors.

- "Hazing isn't all bad," read a 1981 editorial headline in the *Sun News,* a Myrtle Beach, South Carolina, paper not long after Barry Ballou's death. "Hazing, we would argue, encompasses a wide variety of activities, and some of them are not only not dangerous, but downright fun. The emphasis, then, should accrue to the students who conduct college club initiations—Who said a head-shaving was dangerous?—and to the administration of the state's colleges. . . . The state should stay out of hazing otherwise, remembering that students don't have to undergo hazing because they don't have to join those organizations which include hazing."

- "Except for MIT and a handful of other schools, where college pranks survive as a tradition, pranks aren't what they used to be," lamented Nathan Cobb of the Boston *Globe* in 1983.

Hazing has always been self-perpetuating. Many pledges who vow that they will end the system when they become brothers instead become some of the worst hazers when it comes their turn to break the initiates. "The group itself does not think of these things as impossible demands," the author of *Victims of Groupthink,* Irving Janis, says. "They themselves have gone through the initiation rite. The members merely tend to think of what they are doing as simply parallel to what they endured. It's a matter of misjudgment. None of them wants to commit manslaughter. It's a very sloppily made decision, one made in the stages of conviviality. Everyone perceives what is happening as in the range of what has always been done."

Janis says that the concept of peer pressure cannot be overestimated, citing studies that show people typically take risks in a group setting that they would never take when alone. In the case of Chuck Stenzel and Klan Alpine, victim and aggressors reinforced one another, a clear case of "group polarization." According to Janis, when pledges or brothers see their peers approving of something dangerous, silly, or inappropriate, they are likely to join in even if they would never have believed themselves capable of such acts.

It is shocking but certainly understandable in terms of group psychology that, as Chuck lay dying, Klan members continued to party, visited a sorority house, and went off to shower or sleep. In "When Will People Help in a Crisis?" John M. Darley says that it would be atypical for someone in a large group situation either to halt the aggressive behavior of another participant or to take positive action of any sort. It would seem that the more people who watch a victim in distress, the more chance there is someone will act to avert the tragedy. But the opposite happens. If each member of a fraternity is aware that other people are present, he will be less likely to act even if he thinks there is an emergency.

"These days nobody wants to be accountable," says Roy Stevens, hitting the hazing problem squarely on the nose. Without doubt, if hazing is to end in the Greek system, both alumni and fraternity executives must get involved at the field level and stay involved. One such volunteer is Mark N. Popovich, the Indiana state director of Sigma Chi, a large national fraternity founded in 1855. "Extreme hazing has not been a problem" in Indiana, says Popovich, although "some mental hazing does occur from time to time, I think." To regulate behavior, the national fraternity employs "assistant executive secretaries" who evaluate all 211 Sigma Chi chapters annually, spending two to three days with each. "They try to be around for initiation/indoctrination week and serve as watchdogs in that capacity," says Popovich. They also make sure that the fraternity hazing policy is posted in each chapter house, among other things.

In addition, chapter alumni do spot checks to make sure that a local group doesn't add hazing to the normal Sigma Chi ritual. Many chapters have a so-called "house corporation" made up of alumni who serve as watchdogs over finances, upkeep of the house, and the fraternity's observance of risk management policies regarding alcohol, hazing, and drug abuse.

Unpaid volunteers such as Popovich are always concerned with their own personal liability, and thus they stress to all chapters the need to follow strict guidelines recommended by the fraternity's Risk Management Foundation so that its insurance carrier won't raise rates or, worse, cancel coverage. Popovich visits all nine Indiana Sigma Chi chapters at least once annually. He says that the performance of chapters under his jurisdiction is "a matter of personal pride and a source of competition among him and other praetors [the fraternity term for his position]." Should violations such as hazing be detected under his command, he would feel that he had been derelict.

Unlike several fraternity executives, Popovich has no problem talking freely about his concerns about hazing and expressing why he, at forty-eight, is involved with young men. "I feel that I have made a commitment to work with college-age men by providing guidance and counsel to them whenever they feel they need it," he says. "I think the fraternity experience is a unique experience because it can only happen in a college environment. It gives the undergraduate the opportunity to learn leadership, organizational, social, and academic skills all in one experience. I try to be available to help them understand just how important that experience can be to them and then provide advice and 'wisdom' on an individual basis if they feel they need to talk with someone.

"I try to provide a viewpoint that is outside their own peer group in an objective and nonauthoritative manner. In some sense I serve as a father figure—cheering them on when they accomplish their goals and kicking their butts when they get involved in mindless blunders, as they sometimes do. I try to do all this and remember that it is their experience, and not mine.

"I find it a rewarding experience because I am working with the future members of our society. Their wit, energy, and enthusiasm help to keep me young in spirit. In our fraternity we say that Sigma Chi is a lifelong experience. I am an example of the fact that such is the case, and that is the kind of example that I provide for the young men in our fraternity."

Who can be blamed for the problems of fraternity hazing? As Rich Sigal says, some of the problems are simply emblematic of society as a whole. On the other hand, the Greeks themselves must take full responsibility for hazing excesses attributable to them alone.

The National Interfraternity Conference is a weak, ineffectual operation when it comes to eradicating hazing. Studied in a historical context with regard to hazing, the NIC has been a colossal failure. Because it was never intended to be a legislative body, the institution cannot force its fifty-nine individual member fraternities and their thousands of chapters to obey its leadership. It can't yank charters; it can't metaphorically grab throats and shake people. Hence, a good segment of its undergraduate population has been unresponsive to NIC requests to eliminate hazing for seven decades; worse, far too often the NIC has given assurances that hazing was gone while undergraduates indulged behind closed doors. Inept at washing its dirty linen, the fraternity system nonetheless has resisted suggestions that they send it out to be cleaned.

The NIC is hardly the Vatican when it comes to power. It's nowhere close to possessing the power the National Collegiate Athletic Association

(NCAA) possesses in the area of college sports. "Our group is much like a Chamber of Commerce," says Jonathan Brant, the executive director. "We try to provide the best possible information to our fifty-nine individual membership groups, and then they have their own decision-making process. We're not a rules-and-regulations body."

The NIC's many critics say the organization is not much of anything. In fact, one of Brant's strengths is that he is more vocal on the hazing issue than was his predecessor, Jack Anson. As individuals, both Brant and Anson are unquestionably against hazing. But their personal views have not led to successful implementation of anti-hazing strategies. Anson tried to keep the hazing monster under control by employing only pro-fraternity people to conduct educational workshops. He deplored the efforts of Greeks to work with the media and legislators to combat hazing, saying that such outlets could only bash fraternities, not clean them up. He believed that the media exaggerated the number of hazing incidents yet never authorized an impartial research study to ascertain whether his perception was correct.

If the National Interfraternity Conference is a wheel, picture the fifty-nine member fraternities as spokes, not all of them the same length, thickness, or strength. They are so divided on important issues that it would take a Greek version of *perestroika* to unite them. The national sororities and women's fraternities also have their version of the NIC called the National Panhellenic Conference. Both the NIC and NPC are located in Indianapolis, the Athens of American Greeks. The NPC isn't much different from the NIC, but hazing simply isn't as extensive or as brutal in women's groups as it has been in men's, although any hazing is still a problem, acknowledges Diane C. Gregory, president of the National Panhellenic Association of Central Office Executives.

The NIC's Brant has been in office since 1982, and under his leadership hazing has not significantly diminished—at least there is no documented evidence of such a trend. The NIC still has not authorized significant studies to say with certainty whether hazing-related incidents have increased or decreased. Nor can the organization say whether non-Greek hazing in dormitories, clubs, and bands is more or less of a campus problem than Greek hazing.

The fraternity system would appear to have an ethical responsibility for maintaining a clearinghouse of statistics on hazing deaths and injuries. Certainly, the Greeks have the funds and capabilities to do so. But, for whatever reason, the NIC allows haphazard and inaccurate death totals to appear in the press on a regular basis because it lacks a clear appraisal of the hazing problem.

Some executives say it's on the rise, some say it's on the decline, and some say that public perception of hazing is on the increase. All these claims are suspect, based on hearsay and limited personal observation, evidence that an educational institution that often touts its educational value to members—the fraternity system—has little interest in intellectual pursuit of truth.

The NIC boasts that its membership is at an all-time high (more than 400,000 members in 1990 although an NIC spokesman said "There's no way we know exactly how many we have"). When many men find fraternity life attractive, members can subject them to more hardships than were required, say, during the sixties when most of a generation rejected what the Greeks had to offer. Brant says that only five percent of NIC members haze, the lowest figure cited by any national Greek spokesman. The Sigma Tau Gamma executive director estimates that thirty to forty percent of his active members haze, for example. Considering even Brant's estimate to be accurate, that's still twenty thousand-plus young men hazing each year. At the other end of the statistical spectrum, Greek advisors at two large midwestern colleges estimate that half of all fraternity chapters haze; that would involve more than 200,000 men each year. With from twenty thousand to 200,000 men hazing—in national fraternities alone—the odds are that something, somewhere, is going to go wrong. And those chances are upped considerably when local fraternities, sub-rosa drinking clubs, sororities, and black fraternities (nationals—none of which are members of the NIC) that haze get tossed into the statistical hopper.

Fred Kershner believes that self-criticism properly directed is needed to reform a system gone haywire. He once told Brant that alumni and the nationals had let the Greek system down.

"We have been too easy on the hazers. We have tended to pacify the administration, reduce the public relations that's unfavorable, promise reforms—but we haven't done enough to the hazers. . . . I don't want to get nasty about it, but hazing as it now operates is illegal," Kershner says. "It is criminal. It breaks national fraternity rules and laws. It's so bad an offense I can't understand why we're so nice to the [offending] boys.

"I have a feeling that we run more risk and spend more money [on the hazers] than we do on our scholarship people, our public service people, campus leaders. Those that are good and obey the law ought to fight and fight hard. Their dues are being blown on public relations programs to smooth over the ill effects of those who have broken the law. We give a signal that we're really knocking ourselves out for those hazers that we say we don't like. They draw that lesson very well. We don't treat fire prevention in a chapter house that way, do we? But we're not rough on hazing. If we want the public and . . . administrators to get rough on hazing, it should start with fraternities to show that they are aware of the gravity of the situation."

Relatively few dissertations and scholarly papers have addressed the problem of hazing. In 1983 two Texas Tech researchers published the results of an attitudinal survey of alumni and active members "at a large southwestern state university" in the *Journal of College Personnel*. Contrary to Don King's conclusion that required drinking is not a hazing activity, one hundred percent of all active members (and ninety-nine percent of all alumni) considered such an activity to be hazing. But the survey clearly demonstrated that the definition of hazing varied with active members and alumni. By way of example:

- Ninety-four percent of actives considered calisthenics to be hazing; only seventy-seven percent
  of alumni did.

- Eighty-three percent of actives considered kid-
  naps and road trips to be hazing; seventy-five
  percent of alumni.

- Sixty-seven percent of actives considered pledge
  class lineups to be hazing; forty-nine percent of
  alumni.

- Eighty-one percent of actives considered yelling
  and name-calling to be hazing; seventy-five percent of alumni.

- Seventy-seven percent of active brothers and
  sixty-three percent of alumni thought hazing
  served a valuable purpose. More than half said it
  "builds pledge-class unity."

The researchers concluded that alumni were more accepting of hazing,
offering the explanation that alumni "may have become somewhat desensi-
tized to these practices." Both active and alumni members thought their
peers were more in sympathy with hazing than they were. The authors
found that only ten percent of actives and thirteen percent of alumni
thought hazing was a problem in their own chapters, concluding that the
"'it's somebody else's problem' syndrome appears to be a primary hin-
drance to the reduction or elimination of hazing in college fraternities."

Jonathan Brant is tall, slim, inconspicuously low key—pretty much
what a bureaucrat who has fifty-nine bosses needs to be in order to survive. He has conservative views, wears conservative clothes, and spouts pat
conservative phrases that he uses over and over again in interviews. Those
views are partially molded by Lind and White, a firm that is trying to do
for hazing and fraternities what other PR firms have undertaken for tainted Tylenol, explosive Ford Pintos, and oil-laden Alaskan beaches. The
emphasis on public relations drives Kershner mad. "You're simply paying
to prove you're hypocrites," he tells his fellow Greeks. "We tend to be
blinded by our own self-sympathy or bias."

How do you explain away the scandal in Brant's own fraternity, Beta
Theta Pi, after members scribbled on a passed-out pledge's body with
Magic Markers? How do you tell a father that his Delta Kappa Epsilon
pledge had to eat a turkey head or pig fetuses? How does Louisiana State
University justify its Delta Kappa Epsilon chapter's presence, when the
group is infamous for having a member dance nude at a sorority house, for
decorating a Christmas tree with dead skunks, for making obscene gestures in a university parade, and for dousing their dates in beer on an

NBC television special? How do you explain to black America why some white pledges from Virginia Tech had to travel to Kenyon College in Ohio to kiss black women and bring back photographic evidence of what they had done? How do you overcome the negative publicity after a Sigma Alpha Epsilon pledge was kicked in the eye by members and had dead rodents and human excrement placed in his room? How do you explain to mother after mother after mother that her son has died in pledging-related shenanigans?

Answers: You can't. But you try. And try. And try. You try to point the blame at local and black fraternities, and while those outfits have serious hazing problems, so do NIC members. And the American public—unaware of how the fraternity system works and fails to work—has accepted the NIC's schmoozing year after year since the roaring twenties. Headlines clearly show that the fraternal chamber of commerce has tried, unsuccessfully, to eradicate hazing since the 1920s:

■ In 1929 the NIC conducted a survey that showed ninety percent of the membership was opposed to hazing, although only fifty-six percent wanted steps taken by the organization to prevent it.

■ In 1935 the membership faced the crisis of hazing. A speaker urged the NIC's annual convention to have "convictions" instead of mouthing platitudes. Another speaker assailed the alumnus who comes back year after year to inflame the undergraduates by telling them "what a hell-raiser he was in his day." Fraternities that year were trying to rebound from Depression membership losses; thus, the NIC was trying to restore public confidence in the Greek system. The president of Williams College had cautioned freshmen against joining, saying fraternities might be "an anachronism in the future."

The NIC adopted six ideals and presented them to the membership on an illuminated scroll. Those ideals are not a bad standard against which to measure how well the fraternity system has achieved its aims: (1) to promote fraternity objectives which will be in accord with the aims of colleges in which they are located; (2) to impress upon all fraternity members that their primary loyalty is to the college, and that formation of a chapter involves responsibility of the group for the individual; (3) to promote through fraternities conduct consistent with good morals and taste; (4) to create in each chapter an atmosphere of intellectual achievement; (5) to promote sanitary and wholesome conditions in all fraternity buildings, and (6) to inculcate sound business practices in managing them.

■ The 1938 and 1939 conventions, on the brink of World War Two, concluded that fraternities had beaten hazing. "Hazing has been ruled out of every self-respecting college and university in the country," said a Greek spokesman. The NIC blasted the press for "cheap and sensational journalism" when it published photographs of hazers in the act. As if to show the hypocrisy of the NIC's announcement that all was well, half the undergraduates surveyed at the 1939 convention said they favored hazing. They argued that paddles "used judiciously" were effective enforcers of discipline.

■ In 1948 the press dutifully reported that Greek Week had been recommended as a substitute for Hell Week. Greek Week, said a fraternal spokesman at the NIC convention, "is a substitute for the harmful features characteristic of the pre-initiation period."

■ In 1949 Alpha Tau Omega started Help Week as an alternative to Hell Week. The idea was adopted nationwide to save fraternal images at a time when racist and anti-semitic policies had the frats in trouble.

■ In 1959 a New York *Times* headline read: "Fraternities Bar Harmful Hazing." A resolution banning hazing was adopted that year at the NIC's fiftieth anniversary convention.

■ In 1960 the NIC affirmed its opposition to hazing at its annual dinner.

■ "Hazing has no place in the fraternity experience," said Jonathan Brant in 1989. "We absolutely forbid it."

Brant's remarks were made at a press conference, the standard PR gimmick in the age of television. At the microphone Brant is sleek, groomed, nonthreatening. With fifty-nine fraternities to answer to, he cannot say a great deal without displeasing one organization or another, so he doesn't say a great deal. He sounds best in three-minute television bites, less impressive in in-depth interviews. Hence, he gives many short interviews, avoids long ones, and sugarcoats his criticism of academia so that it comes out praise. Lacking both bark and bite, he moves through the fraternity world, putting paws on fraternal shoulders to let them know he's there but never hard enough to knock anyone down.

And therein lies the problem. When Brant asks fraternity men to stop hazing, he comes across with all the authority of the substitute teachers they terrorized in high school. Fraternities have hazed for more than a century. They've also been accused of sexism, racism, and anti-semitism. The young men who haze — particularly those who haze maliciously — aren't afraid of Brant. They know the NIC is powerless. It can't even get the member fraternities to agree on whether pledging is good or bad.

One fraternity spokesman, Alpha Tau Omega communications manager Steve Glaser, says that the NIC's inability to get things done is no reflection on the organization or Brant. Rather, he says, it reflects "an unwillingness among its members to give up portions of their autonomy. . . . Believe me, if the national organizations could be made to wish for a well-fanged interfraternal body, the NIC would be rapidly fit with strong dentures."

Glaser senses a move toward Greek unity afoot. He calls former NIC president Patrick I. Brown "a strong voice for interfraternal self-regulation" and believes others are coming to agree with Brown. Glaser says that both the Fraternity Executives Association (FEA) and the Fraternity Insurance Purchase Group (FIPG) are other examples of interfraternal cooperation. Fraternity organizations that agree to FIPG principals have agreed not to haze or abuse substances. Glaser says that in 1988 FEA officials seriously considered the concept of having an interfraternal "commissioner" who would have the power to revoke charters in "animal houses" and to expel hazers in any NIC chapter. "Many fraternities' unwillingness to give up autonomy proved a roadblock," he says, "but the serious discussion today may pave the way for acceptance tomorrow."

Some Greeks think pledging invariably includes hazing. Others swear that positive pledge programs can be run without hazing. Lambda Chi Alpha has for years run an associate member program as an alternative to pledging. Tau Kappa Epsilon and Zeta Beta Tau — following the example of Phi Beta Sigma, Charles Wright's fraternity — gave no-pledging a whirl in 1989. The rest of the NIC members are watching, waiting for their rivals to fail or to succeed so that they can steal the idea. Glaser insists that getting rid of pledging is neither a "gimmick" nor "a public relations sham." He says "a fairer characterization might be 'an act of desperation.'"

Brant himself walks a tightwire on the issue. He doesn't dare say whether he thinks pledging is good or bad for fear of alienating NIC members. "We're not coming to a point where we're going to recommend one direction or another," he says. Many individual fraternities do, however, plan to eliminate pledging in the nineties.

Early evidence suggests that fraternities may have gotten rid of pledging, but not hazing. In February 1990 the Bloomington [IN] *Herald-Times* ran a story about Tau Kappa Epsilon and Zeta Beta Tau chapters at Indiana University that were "happy with [their] 'no-pledge' policy." But the article also mentioned that new men still had to clean up after parties although members "often helped." Despite the hoopla, personal servitude in some form is still part of the system.

Adam Lashinsky, a 1989 University of Illinois graduate and former fraternity member, says that he has no doubt that abolishing pledging won't eliminate hazing; it merely forces the activity behind closed doors. Sigma Pi executive Kevin O'Rourke insists that "pledging is not synonymous with hazing" and suggests that fraternities try to convince the American public that hazing "is a societal problem" that other organizations also need to abolish.

Those that advocate the elimination of pledging, such as Ron Taylor of Zeta Beta Tau, argue that fraternity founders were successful without it. According to Fred Kershner, the practice of pledging started when universities had so-called "preps" or pre-freshmen, adolescents who attended college classes prior to the creation of a public high-school system. Fraternities "pledged" these men to be initiated as soon as they became college freshmen. Then pledging became a way to weed out undesirables before initiation. According to Kershner, by 1880 one alumnus of Delta Tau Delta, his fraternity, recommended "pledging men" to place them "on a sort of probation."

Unless the NIC becomes a rules and regulations body, the press — including college journalists — should regard the organization's news releases as propaganda. Nor should the press have applauded, as it did in 1989 and 1990, the end of pledging in some fraternities — not without proof positive that hazing would decline as a result.

College journalists in particular have tended merely to tweak their peers about hazing. Renee Hobbs, advisor to the student newspaper at Massachusetts's Babson College in 1986, says her student editor had to decide whether to use a photograph he obtained accidentally: a group shot of a Babson fraternity smiling while one young man — teeth bared in a grimace — was, apparently, sodomized with a golf club. The photograph was too objectionable to be published, the editor decided, but for complex reasons — including his fear of ruffling student and faculty feathers at this affluent private business college — he chose not to investigate the story at all. No story was printed that might damage "Babson's image," says Hobbs, although the photograph strongly suggested to her and the editor that the Massachusetts hazing law had been violated. Since Hobbs could only advise, not mandate policy, she was dutybound to accept the editor's decision.

But, as a Massachusetts citizen, Hobbs had a moral dilemma: should she report an apparent act of hazing? In the end she did nothing, which bothers her. She has a strong sense that one is obligated to do the ethically right thing at all times. "I chose allegiance to the newspaper and advisees over my responsibility to the larger community," says Hobbs. "I'm aware of how students can make bad decisions, and I end up with the consequences of those decisions."

Hobbs sympathizes with fraternity advisors in Texas, for example, who supposedly are compelled by law to report all hazings. If Greek advisors quietly squash an incident of hazing but fail to report it, they could be found guilty of violating the state's anti-hazing law.

The NIC's fifty-nine members have expanded to five thousand chapters on eight hundred campuses in the United States and Canada. The NIC needs to consider that unplanned growth might be harmful. Like doctors with too many patients, some fraternity nationals simply cannot keep track of all their chapters; others require exhaustion-level commitment from their people in the field. Few colleges, for example, have hired additional advisors and other personnel to deal with the Greek boom. Many administrators, in fact, don't want to hire more advisors lest their actions be attacked by tuition-paying non-Greeks who don't want anything to do with such organizations.

Rather than blame the NIC, Brant blames the schools. He compares the need for Greek advisors to the need for directors and hall advisors for every residence hall on campus. Yet, he charges, most campuses get by with a single advisor for hundreds or thousands of Greek students, and many of them are assigned other duties as well. The Ball State University fraternity advisor, for example, not only oversees fraternities but also works with disabled students. "It often suggests that there's far less attention given by the universities to the fraternities than is given to the university residence halls," says Brant. "The Greek advisor is trying to work with hundreds of people and just can't possibly do it effectively or as effectively as he or she could if there were more of them to work with the students. . . . We think it's important for the university to have a full-time person working on this, and perhaps additional people as well."

Brant perceives another problem from his discussions with veterans in student affairs. Today's university structure has become so stratified that where once advisors dealt directly with the vice president of student affairs or a dean of students, they now deal with a lesser bureaucrat — an associate dean of student activities perhaps, who reports to the higher administration. "It would be our opinion that if in some way we were talking with policy makers as opposed to those who are implementing the policy, we may return to a time when we would have far more cooperation and coordination with what the university is doing," says Brant.

Once upon a time there were highly respected administrators who served as "dean of deans." Thomas Arkle Clark was a nationally known pro-fraternity educator at the University of Illinois. He was not only a disciplinarian but also a much-loved friend of students during his years as dean from 1901 to 1931. In today's educational system, too often the university simply hires an entry-level person to serve important functions once the responsibility of men such as Clark. Often these young people stay at a school only for a year or two as they pursue graduate degrees or save some money to go elsewhere for their terminal degrees.

In the first half of this century Greek advisors were esteemed, wise old bucks who had been on campus for many years. Both faculty and students revered and respected them. Today's typical advisor is only one to three years away from active fraternity life himself. These entry-level jobs typically pay in the teens and rarely attract or hold top people for long.

Obviously, there are exceptions. At some schools the dean of students or a vice president for student affairs gets very involved with fraternities. Other advisors, low pay and all, stay and work through the ranks. Eileen Stevens refers to these topnotch advisors as "true unsung heroes." But low pay, frequent handling of crises, and being the target of media criticism have taken their toll. Brant says many advisors "definitely are in burnout positions," and he sees a need for hazing and alcohol problems to be solved so that advisors can help students achieve "loftier goals." One of Brant's primary goals is to eliminate the public perception that only fraternities haze. Another is to convince the public that the NIC constantly has to restart the educational process for its members, for whom there is a hundred percent turnover every few years.

"I think it is realistic to recognize that we're dealing with, in some ways, a new chapter every year," says Brant. "Certainly, every three or four years we have complete matriculation of a class. We're constantly mulling over the same information, trying to carry the same [anti-hazing] message." He recalls a time when he headed Beta Theta Pi's national organization. A housemother from a local chapter at Miami of Ohio came to see him. "You know, Jonathan, I've been here for sixteen years and nothing's changed," she complained. Suddenly, he said, the implications of what she had said hit her. She began to laugh, realizing that part of being a housemother, a fraternity executive, a dean of students, an advisor, or a faculty member is that everyone in education has to start from square one every autumn. "We have to go over the same topics and often the same experiences for the individual to really move through the process of maturation," he says.

Brant says that schools such as Alfred, when Chuck Stenzel was a pledge, present another problem. A faculty member such as Steven Peterson couldn't possibly give the Klan Alpine members as much time or focus as a full-time advisor does. "When I think of the fraternity advisor, I think of a development officer," says Brant, "someone who's proactively involved in trying to help students make the right decisions and to be responsible in whatever they're doing."

Many parents of prospective Greeks have little idea of the difficulty a faculty advisor has in trying to keep order while maintaining the semblance of a good working relationship with hundreds of students. Nor can the advisor possibly know all these students as individuals. The problems of alcohol abuse and hazing have taken a toll on Greek advisors during the 1980s. More and more have made public complaints, saying that these problems have been unfairly dumped on their already overburdened shoulders. Highly regarded advisors have quit to find less stressful work outside academe. Their complaints are telling:

- "We don't have the time to check every single thing a frat or sorority is doing," admitted Craig Little, a University of Oklahoma fraternity advisor in 1988.

- "Most schools look upon it as an entry-level job," says administrator Ed King of Bradley University. "I'm very well paid, but I also have other responsibilities. The academic unit has not made a commitment."

- "I'm mad! And I'm frustrated! And I'm disillusioned!" said Barb Robel, a Kansas State University advisor for Greek affairs.

Too often graduate students are put in charge of individual chapters. The case of Edwin Taylor makes clear the dangers inherent in using an immature nonprofessional in such a sensitive position. A graduate student advisor, Taylor went berserk in the aftermath of a hazing in October of 1974 at Bluefield State College. He fired a gun that had been used to intimidate pledges during a mental hazing session prior to a Tau Kappa Epsilon initiation, killing a member, Mike Bishop, and wounding Frank Hollis. "This is how we did it in Vietnam," said Taylor, as he shot Bishop in the head from a few feet away. College president B. L. Coffindaffer at first denied that the gun had been used in the initiation. But during the advisor's trial it was revealed that cans were set on pledges' heads. Then the gun was fired while members used sticks to send the cans flying. Taylor pleaded guilty to manslaughter.

Activities similar to hazing are present in other cultures. The Germans had dueling societies, mock-dueling societies, and other associations that had pledging and hazing. Their most controversial aspect, according to historian Robert Waite, was having a *schmisse* — a facial badge of honor carved in their cheeks with a blade. "That scar means you've been accepted," says Waite. "You don't stitch it or you stitch it roughly so it remains a large, open scar — the larger the better."

Raumer's *History of German Universities* contains an exchange between a father and his son: "You think, perhaps, that in the universities they sup pure wisdom by spoonfuls . . . but . . . you will find that you must be made a fool of for the first year," he said. "Consent to be a fool for this one year; let yourself be plagued and abused; and when an old veteran steps up to you and tweaks your nose, let it not appear singular; endure it, harden yourself to it." Hazing in Germany had gotten so bad by 1818 that a voluntary group of students from fourteen universities formed an anti-hazing association.

In 1909 a hazing scandal rocked the Borussia Corps at the University of Bonn. This had been the fraternity of choice for the German kaiser, crown prince, and other aristocrats since the days of Frederick the Great.

In the Netherlands in 1962 there was an uproar because freshmen (*foetuses* in Holland) were given "the Dachau treatment," a reference to the dreaded World War Two concentration camp. According to *Time,* one freshman suffered a brain concussion when an upperclassman tried to knock a ball off his head with a hockey stick. In another custom more than two hundred young men were packed naked or half-naked into a small room. The upperclassmen then performed such barbarities as walking on the foetuses' heads, drenching them with beer, and releasing a laxative-bloated pig into their midst.

France has also had its problems controlling young men. The French term *brimade* includes hazing, fagging, silly and dangerous jokes, and forced drinking. During the 1920s in France, a nationwide campaign raged against brimades. The minister of public instruction forbade them in all French schools, and the minister of war ordered an end to such practices. According to a 1928 notice in the New York *Times,* "brimades . . . have too often gone beyond the limits of fun, and, especially with nervous boys, have often amounted to persecution and cruelty. In the military schools practical jokes have been pushed much further." The ministers of instruction and war emphasized that new boys must be welcomed cordially, fairly and kindly.

Brimades have also been a problem in Canada, perhaps because that country has imported such customs from the British, French, and American Greeks. Hazing activities flourished on the Canadian frontier just as they did on our own. Many incidents reported in Canada occur during orientation week, the traditional system for introducing new students to college life. Some examples:

- The Supreme Court of Alberta awarded fifty-six thousand dollars to a Calgary attorney whose son went insane after being hazed at the University of Alberta.

- In 1984 a male University of Saskatchewan student was found dead at the bottom of a seven-story elevator shaft. His body was covered with whipped cream and fire extinguisher fluid.

- In 1984 a female residence advisor at Wilfrid Laurier University was crushed to death under a chartered bus while trying to control an orientation crowd.

- During the early 1980s a Ryerson Polytechnical Institute student who had been drinking was killed when he dove off a ferry boat containing students headed for an orientation picnic.

■ In 1984 and 1985 School of Forestry students at Lakehead University in Thunder Bay, Ontario, were pressured to partake in a foolish and degrading activity called "The Shit Pits." According to Canadian anti-hazing activist Andy Hueton, this involved repeated immersion of the first-year students by drunken upperclassmen in ditchwater filled with cow manure, fermented wheat, and sawdust. There was also a degrading ceremony for women, called the "Miss D.B.H. Contest," in which their breasts were measured in the same way that foresters measure the "diameter breast height" of a tree, charges Hueton. R. G. Rosehart of Lakehead University subsequently issued an initiation policy.

■ In 1986 an eighteen-year-old University of Toronto freshman endured indignities such as having a pie thrown into her face, being forced to chug beer from an engineering student's hard hat, and having to wriggle on the ground like a bug. Under university supervision she and other students marched in a chain-gang parade.

■ Other 1986 indignities at Canadian institutions of higher learning included having freshmen dive into pools of Jell-O (University of Ottawa, Carleton University), suffer yeast, rotten eggs, and fish heads to be poured atop them while they tried to fight their way past upperclassmen to put a piece of cake on a sundial (Trinity College), and being jammed inside a sweatbox with 160 other freshmen (McMaster's coed residence dorm).

In Reykjavik, Iceland, adolescent males entering secondary schools experience hazing abuses such as having their faces marked with indelible ink, their clothes splattered with animal blood, and their hair covered with cod liver oil and other disgusting substances. Efforts to introduce welcoming barbecues sponsored by older students have been only partially successful.

In relation to the number of crimes committed annually, hazing laws are seldom invoked by district attorneys. In New York state, for example, the first conviction for hazing did not come until 1985, and it involved a high-school fraternity. Steven Naso, eighteen, was convicted for paddling a pledge who had applied for membership in Alpha Sigma Phi, an unsanctioned fraternity at West Hempstead High School in Long Island. The pledge, John Isaacson, required emergency surgery to control internal bleeding.

High schools have hardly been hazing-free. In 1905, for example, thirteen-year-old William Taylor of Lima, Ohio, died of pneumonia after "being 'hazed' by a number of schoolmates who stuffed snow into his clothing," said the New York *Times*. In 1924 two Brooklyn girls, Helen Chapman and Helen Steingester, of Erasmus High School, and a woman from a business college had Greek letters burned onto their foreheads with a solution of nitrate of silver. They also had crosses drawn on their backs. Their skin turned black the next day, accompanied by severe pain, but they recovered. "The sorority has no connection with Erasmus High School," the principal said in the New York *Times*. "It is not an Erasmus Hall affair and there is nothing the school can do."

Eileen Stevens has answered dozens of letters from parents whose high-school-age children have been hazed for admission into fraternities, clubs, and athletic organizations. Typical is a letter from Alan S. Bobowski of East Lansing, Michigan, who wrote in 1988 to complain that his son and other freshmen had been sexually abused by upperclassmen on the Waverly school district's swim team. Bobowski said that the older boys called their actions not "hazing," but an "initiation thing."

Some activities were merely bothersome, such as pouring shampoo and toiletries on the freshmen's clothing. Others were more disturbing. Bobowski charged that at least one boy had been urinated on, one had had toothpaste smeared all over his body, more than one had been held down while seniors sucked on their necks to give them "hickies," and all the freshmen had been stripped and tossed nude into the snow. He also charged that upperclassmen forced the freshmen to do pushups and then whipped them with towels while they did the exercise.

Bobowski says that after he phoned Waverly Superintendent of Schools Jon Reynolds in 1988 the practices were promptly stopped by a new swim coach and athletic director. Reynolds says that some of Bobowski's hazing charges certainly are true, but he is unable to recall some of the incidents. He says that he "put the coach on notice" that such practices had occurred. He believes that the athletes, mainly sophomores, had started the initiations to create "group solidarity" and "a team feeling." He believes that the practices went on "unbeknownst" to school employees until Bobowski made his accusations. Bobowski says he is satisfied with Reynolds's handling of the hazing practices. Bobowski wrote to Eileen because he feared such practices on the high-school level might "lead to serious problems" when the hazers and hazed entered college. He says, "It may be that in high school boys learn that it's OK to humiliate and abuse younger kids."

Mary Lenaghan, the mother of dead pledge Jay Lenaghan, has the passion to end high-school hazing that Eileen Stevens feels for ending college hazing. Because she also works full-time, she concentrates her anti-hazing efforts in western Massachusetts, where she lives.

Lenaghan and Eileen had some contact after Jay Lenaghan's death. Lenaghan formed an organization called CHORUS, an acronym for

Campus Hazing's Offensive Rituals Undermine Schools. She knew about hazing from personal experience, having been in a high-school sorority that required her to dress in a silly costume and sing songs in Harvard Square. CHORUS helped inspire an anti-hazing law in Massachusetts, just as Eileen and CHUCK had done in New York, and Joan Cerra, Ray and Maisie Ballou, and Dorothy Flowers had helped achieve in Wisconsin, South Carolina, and New Jersey, respectively.

In 1988 Lenaghan learned that hazing had been a part of the Watertown High School football program for as long as eight years, including when her son was a student there. Since the high school had an annual two-thousand-dollar scholarship given to a senior player in his name, she was incensed that abuses could go on. A subsequent investigation determined that hazing was rampant, including the shaving of heads, fagging, and perverse sexual harassment, says Lenaghan. Those abuses had included an incident in which a boy was forced to sit in urine while he vomited in disgust, an incident in which a boy was stuffed in a duffel bag and kicked repeatedly, and a so-called "cookie run," in which new players, naked, stuffed cookies in their buttocks and ran across a field. In the last event those who dropped the cookies were required to eat them, according to Lenaghan and a Boston *Globe* investigation. Watertown High School administrators subsequently suspended head football coach John Barbati and dropped five players from the squad, including all three team captains. Up to thirty players had been involved in the incidents.

The case of a former member of the Lowell High School hockey team, Michael DiGiovanni, is typical of the work CHORUS does. DiGiovanni suffered two broken ribs in a brutal 1985 hazing. He and his parents have brought suit against the city in hopes of discouraging hazers and to "inspire" other hazed youths to "speak out." DiGiovanni says he has been severely harassed by former teammates for taking a stand. Significantly, his fight has been made more difficult by an editorial writer for the *Sun,* the Lowell paper, who said "the [Di]Giovannis should drop their case against the city lest it turn against them and they lose entirely the sympathy people now feel for them and their son, Michael."

Eileen Stevens has come to believe that the public has too complacent an attitude about hazing because the perception is that only fraternities haze. For her, the public's misjudging hazing as "only" a Greek problem is like mislabeling AIDS "only" a homosexual disease.

Alfred University's Gary Horowitz agrees that fraternities have unfairly taken the isolated rap for hazing. According to Horowitz, one of the sadder ironies is that other male secret societies and organizations rarely suffer unfavorable press for hazing. "If you look back in history, Americans like rituals," he says. "They come up with all sorts of strange things. Look at the Masons—look how much of that has been perpetuated. Or the Elks now—getting into their lodges there are strange rituals that you go through. And these are grownups who have not [always] been part of a fraternity. Kiwanis doesn't do that stuff, but the Elks do and they're strong. Masons are strong. What I'm trying to suggest is that [hazing] is more pervasive than just at colleges."

Horowitz may be right. The Moose organization quietly outlawed hazing several years ago, but not before two Birmingham, Alabama, men — the president of the local Chauffeur's Union and an iron moulder — were killed in an initiation that made use of an electrical device, according to *A Dictionary of Secret and Other Societies*. Following the deaths, for a time, the organization still had initiation abuses occurring during the second degree, or Legion, ceremony, according to one member. In 1909 an organization called the Fraternal Order of Eagles, founded in Seattle, discontinued the use of electricity in its initiations but continued to permit tests "of a humorous yet instructive character" in its chapters, or aeries. Another organization called the Woodmen of the World, whose members are in effect buyers of the company's insurance, required new members in one North Carolina chapter to be blindfolded and to stick their hands in a smelly, gooey pile passed off as manure, according to Irvin Howard, who was himself initiated that way.

The Shriners have a custom of swinging people in blankets, as well as more elaborate hazing rituals that have gotten them in trouble from time to time. In South Carolina, Greenville's Hejas Temple and the Imperial Council of the Nobles of the Mystic Shrine of North America were sued by George Blanton Easler who was injured by hazers. According to the *State* of Columbia, South Carolina, "The initiation included a hazing event known as the 'mattress-rotating barrel trick,' which required the candidate to slide eight or nine feet down a metal board onto a series of connected mattresses." Candidates were then required to climb over a spinning barrel. As Easler, thirty-seven, maneuvered over the mattresses and barrel, the members smacked him with so-called "fun-paddles." Instead of landing on the soft mattresses, he banged into the barrel. The mishap required him to have neck vertebrae surgically fused; he now moves his neck with pain. The *State* cited medical testimony that predicted the injury will worsen as he ages "because of rapidly developing arthritic changes along the line of fusion."

Easler, the father of four and a carpenter, claimed that the injury caused stress in his marital life, interfered with his work, and prevented him from partaking in recreational activities. A jury found in his favor, awarding him $361,800 and his wife $37,500 for damages to their marital relationship. The case was upheld on appeal by the Supreme Court.

In St. Petersburg, Florida, Vernon Lee Johnson alleged that as a result of a hazing incident at Joshua Masonic Lodge No. 5 he became a quadriplegic. The Johnson incident occurred when the blindfolded initiate was bounced in the air on a piece of canvas, reported the St. Petersburg *Times*. Johnson landed violently on his head, fracturing his neck and leaving him crippled.

The Masons actively engage in initiations. Even the Mason offshoots, such as the Swords of Bunker Hill in Terre Haute, Indiana, have nonsensical hazings. "They ask you before they initiate you if you have a bad heart," says one member. "Well, how do you know if you have a bad heart?" Among other foolishness, the members play mind games, pretending that they are going to shove a sword up someone's buttocks, and they throw initiates' shoes into an electrically charged pile. When the initiates pick up their shoes, they get shocked.

The initiation ritual for the Ancient Arabic Order of Nobles of the Mystic Shrine, an organization that accepted only Knights Templars and 32nd degree Masons, was printed in a 1903 edition of *The Mystic Shrine Illustrated*:

> The "Bumper" is next used . . . a box about six feet high: perpendicular on one side and concave on the other side. A ladder is then placed on the concave side. The candidate ascends the ladder and is seated on the top, his legs hanging over the concave side. Then he is told to take hold of the end of a large rope, about two feet long, held up by a small string or thread. He is told under no circumstances to let go of the rope, which he firmly grasps, when the box falls to pieces, and he is shot down the concave side of the box, thumping his head and buttocks on a partition that is fixed to receive him. He is then conducted to the Grand Potentate, whom he is commanded to approach with humble and great reverence, stooping very low on his knees, his head near the ground, his buttocks elevated where he receives the "Grand Salaam," that is, a blow on his buttocks with two pieces of board between which are placed some torpedoes that explode with a loud report when they come together. This is called the Grand Salaam or stroke of introduction. He is then introduced to the Grand Potentate, near whom is a Galvanic Battery, so arranged (under the carpet) that when the candidate is introduced to the Grand Potentate, he receives a severe electric shock.

Next one of the members made a loud hue and cry, claiming he had been robbed. Previously, some trinket had been secretly placed on the initiate's person. The initiate was searched, stripped of his clothing save his drawers, and then tried in a kangaroo court, where he was made to sit on a large sponge soaked with ice water. After that ordeal, the stripped candidate was blindfolded and taken into a room. Unknown to him, seated in the dark room were members disguised as women. A member then said to him: "This is the place where our brethern stop to sprinkle the Devil's pass with urine. You will contribute a few drops of urine to commemorate the time and place where all who pass here renounce the wiles and evils of the world to worship at the Shrine of Islam. Only a few drops will do." When the candidate's urine was in mid-stream, a member snatched the blindfold. The initiate beheld the members dressed as women, their bodies partially concealed by a screen. The embarrassed candidate usually ran from the room, followed by the laughter and catcalls of those watching.

Jack Ratliff, the chairman of a committee that studied hazing abuses at the University of Texas, once compared hazing to prostitution. "It's a crime with two willing participants who are both interested in keeping it a secret," he said. Ratliff may be right in some cases, but his oversimplification is dangerous. Many hazing victims experience demeaning and life-threatening indignities. True, some pledges are willing to be hazed; some may even demand to be hazed, as the Greeks claim. But far too many human beings have had to suffer too many indignities to humiliate them further by calling them willing participants.

Gary Horowitz says that hazing is hard to eradicate because some version of it comes with the territory for many professionals. "Graduate students sometimes joke that the PhD process is very much like hazing," he says. "The faculty members . . . beat you into the ground with psychological hazing to make you part of the fraternity of the PhD. To some degree all our professors have done this."

He also pointed out that doctors, for years, hazed their interns, requiring unbearably long shifts for days on end until the interns were physically beaten and hardly at their best to treat patients. "They used to work twenty hours a day for no money," says Horowitz. "They had to prove themselves—that they really wanted to be doctors. Isn't that a form of hazing in a way?"

In such instances as PhD and intern harassment—as with pledging—the abuse ends when the outcasts are allowed into the metaphorical treehouse. Horowitz says that he doesn't want the term *hazing* to become meaningless by making it so generic that it loses all definition, but nonetheless he believes it's worth looking at ingrained American behaviors with a critical eye. "Maybe it's not so bizarre what the kids do," he says. "We all have to prove ourselves. This might tell us it's broader than just what the colleges are doing. There's something ingrained in the American society that buys into this. . . . There's something inherent within our psyche that we keep creating new ways for people to prove themselves to become part of the tribe. . . . That's why I'm not sure it will ever end. You hope it will and you work toward it, but maybe it's going to be with us forever—I don't know."

Hazing of medical students and interns is hardly limited to long hours. For many decades in this country, medical practitioners have hazed their underlings. In June 1927 the New York *Times* reported that three Jewish interns at Kings County Hospital in Brooklyn were savagely hazed. The victims were hauled from their beds, bound, gagged, and immersed in a bathtub filled with icy water. Two of the three were coated with shoe blacking or ink. Six doctors arrested in the assaults had charges dropped in exchange for writing letters of apology.

Eileen Stevens once consulted a psychiatrist who likely would have testified against Alfred had her case gone to court. He told her that while he was in medical school older students blindfolded him and placed a bent elbow against his cheek, making him think it was an erect penis; to frighten him further, a medical student started gagging in the background, making him think that a fellow student was being violated. The psychiatrist was hardly an exception according to Henry K. Silver, MD, who conducted a survey at one major medical school and found that "46.4 percent of all respondents stated that they had been abused at some time while enrolled in medical school, with 80.6 percent of seniors being abused by the senior year." Moreover, 16.2 percent said the abuse "would always affect them," according to Silver's article for the *Journal of the American Medical Association.*

Silver prefers "to use the word *abuse* instead of *hazing*" when describing medical school incidents. Nonetheless, some practices he describes certainly would be sufficient to charge fraternity men with hazing, had they done similar things; these include verbal abuse, threats of physical harm, and actual physical harm. One student reported being kicked in the "testicular region by an attending physican and required medical attention for his injury." Ninety-two percent of all medical students agreed with the statement that "Sleep deprivation has little direct value in training me to be a good physician." Many female students reported sexual harassment.

Silver has been a pioneer in the study of medical student abuse. Certainly similar studies could and should be done to isolate and confirm instances of "abuse" or "hazing" involving PhD candidates, law students, and aspiring professionals in other occupations as well.

A handful of people have written Eileen Stevens to say that they have been hazed on the job and to encourage her efforts to enact legislation in all fifty states. A stockbroker trainee from New York wrote that he had suffered a nervous breakdown after a superior harassed him. Eileen began hearing other stories. Managers of W. T. Grant were smacked with custard pies or suffered other demeaning hazing if they failed to meet quotas. A female sheriff's deputy alleged that she had been handcuffed to a jail fence and sprayed with water by veteran deputies in Sacramento, California. A former volunteer fireman in Mauston, Wisconsin, alleged that his leg was shattered in an initiation required for admission to the group. Author Natasha Josefowitz studied hazing on the job for a year, concluding that women and minorities are hazed the hardest. She distinguishes hazing from harassment, saying that the latter is designed to make employees quit, while hazing is used to teach, test, or tease them.

Rochester, New York, newsman Read Kingsbury has written that "Students who learn the traditions of hazing carry its immature and dangerous attitudes into the workplace. There it becomes okay to overwork, isolate and ridicule junior workers . . . to lubricate the corporate gears with alcohol, to play vicious pranks, to require agonizing 'rites of passage' because 'I had to endure this, so you do too.' Good managers and personnel directors spend a lot of energy defeating their consequences. Most of it would be unnecessary if maturity were a more certain benefit of a college education."

Hazing and initiation rites are still a part of many professional sports teams. The Quebec Nordiques of the National Hockey League, for example, shaved nineteen-year-old rookie center Joe Sakic's head in 1988. According to hockey writer Jeff Hale, Sakic objected and promised that he wouldn't continue the hazing rite when he became a veteran. By and large, however, hazing at the professional level has generally been limited as salaries have escalated. No veteran wants to face a coach's wrath by injuring a six-million-dollar rookie quarterback in a hazing incident.

Some incidents from amateur sports have made headlines:

■ In 1971 a student on a University of Oklahoma wrestling scholarship, Kenneth Thompson, had paint dumped on him by upperclassmen in a hazing ritual. He suffered first-degree chemical burns when he tried to remove the paint with gasoline and turpentine. "They strip you down, carry you outside, put bubble gum in your hair and under your arms, spray you with paint all over and finish you off with a coat of varnish," a fellow wrestler charged.

■ In 1974 student Choya Campbell said that he had been paddled and grilled under hot lights while pledging the University of Oklahoma Ruf-Nek Athletic Spirit Club. An administrative review board suspended the Ruf-Neks for such offenses as stuffing prospective members' mouths with chili peppers and chewing tobacco. Other allegations made were that prospects were paddled, forced to do hour-long calisthenics, and doused with mouthfuls of beer.

■ "Our practice is not to tolerate hazing in any form," said University of Michigan athletic director Don Canham after a 1980 incident involving a hockey player. A resident advisor at Mary Markley Hall complained that senior hockey players had stripped a freshman, shaved his body hair, and locked him in a car trunk for nearly an hour. When two reporters from the student paper tried to attend a closed meeting they believed to concern the incident, they were arrested and led away in handcuffs.

■ In 1981 a soccer team hazing rite called "Freshman Kill Day" was exposed at Toms River High

School. The annual ceremony had gone on for at least eight years at the New Jersey school and included a gauntlet in which freshmen were punched and kicked by upperclassmen. Freshmen were also hosed down and thrown in the mud.

■ In Arizona, after an alleged sexually oriented hazing initiation involving seven junior varsity baseball players on a school bus, the Nogales High School school board reprimanded four men who were coaches or trainers in June 1983.

■ The Kent State University hockey team was suspended for one year in 1988 following a hazing incident. Five freshmen were given mohawk haircuts, had pubic hair shaved, and were asked to drink a mixture of rum and beer. One student was hospitalized because of a violent reaction to the alcohol.

Eileen Stevens also gets occasional calls from parents concerned with high-school and college band hazing. Historically, many elite marching bands have relied on peer pressure to whip their members into shape. The University of Gettysburg once even had a secret group of hooded sophomore band members whose function was to haze freshmen. The masked students are pictured in Gettysburg yearbooks from 1912 to 1918. Sophomore band members became hazing enforcers at several colleges, including the Black Avengers, a disciplinary body of Columbia College (NY) sophomores, and the so-called "mystery chairmen" on each dormitory floor at Barnard College.

Eileen believes band hazing may be widespread, but investigative reporters and campus newspapers simply haven't devoted any time to the matter. One of the most publicized incidents involved the Florida A&M University band — known locally as the "Incomparable Marching 100." A nasty hazing involved its twelve-member flag corps, "The Dirty Dozen." In 1981 associate band director Julian White took direct measures to halt hazing after seventeen-year-old Otis Lawrence was beaten, according to the Miami *Herald*. The newspaper reported that shaved heads were common in the band, and that in the past "shakedowns for petty cash" and "compulsory polishings" of members' shoes were common initiation abuses. Lawrence was beaten after band members suspected him of telling "Doc" White about a nonsanctioned band event, which got the leaders in trouble. Lawrence was admitted to Tallahassee Memorial Regional Medical Center with multiple contusions, according to the *Herald,* and left school for a semester. White suspended four members for violation of Florida's hazing law. The University of Akron's band fraternity, Kappa Kappa Psi, was also charged with hazing in 1984.

Other incidents may be relevant as well, but members just don't refer to certain practices as hazing. In a positive article on the University of Southern California's Trojan band camp, the *Chronicle of Higher Education* quoted Arthur C. Bartner, the band's director and drill sergeant of ten years, as saying he urges the upperclassmen to lean on newcomers. "I believe in competition between classes," said Bartner, who admitted that he had to crack down on wild students in 1984. Band members, for example, used to pull each other's pants down in public. "It's the old members against the freshmen. Peer pressure makes this band great."

According to the *Chronicle,* "The band camp is akin to a rite of passage in which freshmen are constantly reminded (in phrases speckled with four-letter words) of the lowly place they occupy in the pecking order of the band." If newspaper accounts of such incidents are correct, fraternity leaders are justified in saying they are singled out more than other campus groups for their actions. If a USC fraternity or sorority lined up its freshmen pledges and cursed them — or told them to take a lap as the saxophone section of the USC band must do if they blow a number — their advisor would swoop down on them like Attila the Hun.

The tenth anniversary of Chuck's death made his mother grieve afresh. The milestone also forced her to reflect. Her efforts to end hazing had not gone unrecognized. She had won many of the most prestigious awards the fraternity and secular worlds had to offer. In 1984 the Association of Fraternity Advisors presented her the Jack Anson Award to honor her having turned a "very negative experience into something positive from which others could benefit." Even Jack Anson, the former NIC head, had become a supporter of her cause. Nineteen eighty-four also brought the Clara Barton Annual Humanitarian Award. Still to come was the Distinguished Service Award from the Fraternity Executives Association, composed of the executive directors of fraternities belonging to the NIC.

Although grateful for the tributes, Eileen still occasionally despairs. "Those things won't bring him back," she wrote in her diary.

In the late eighties hazing incidents continued to make headlines. Skip Cline died at the University of Mississippi in 1987 after Kappa Alpha fraternity brothers encouraged him to drink to the point of intoxication. School officials refused to call the death a hazing. Also in 1987 Pi Lambda Phi pledge William Burns had a close call at the University of Lowell after members forced him to crawl inside a sleeping bag in a hot attic; after the members added a heater to the potential death scene, Burns's temperature shot up to 109 degrees.

In 1988 another hazing incident, this one at Rutgers University, shocked the country. The Rutgers death was preceded by a weekend of drinking binges at Princeton University's eating clubs. Forty-eight students were hospitalized or treated at the infirmary at that New Jersey school. On February 11, 1988, the Rutgers Lambda Chi Alpha chapter served fourteen associate members an estimated three hundred kamikazes (a concoction made of vodka, triple sec, lime juice), encouraging them to drink all in one hour or until they vomited. Lawyers for fifteen Rutgers students indicted on hazing charges stressed that the associates were strongly "encouraged" to drink but could have refused. They were reciting a litany all too familiar to parents of Lost Chapter members.

Two associates were in deep trouble by the time the last kamikaze was swilled. One was taken to a hospital and saved. Not so fortunate was James Callahan, eighteen, who was pronounced dead at 7:46 A.M. on February 12, 1988. His blood alcohol level was .434.

The Rutgers death dejected Eileen. She again wrote in her journal to mourn a soul "filled with promise and life." Just as Gary Horowitz and

Steven Peterson had known many nice people in Klan Alpine, she held several Rutgers Lambda Chis in high regard. A couple of alumni routinely sent her Christmas greetings, even valentines. She had attended their weddings, accepted honorary memberships, rejoiced when they sent birth announcements, and cheered when they mailed business cards as proof of their successes. Worse, she viewed Lambda Chi's George Spasyk as "a special man" and friend. She wrote Spasyk a note, saying that their anti-hazing efforts were needed more than ever. If such a thing could happen to a chapter well-educated to the dangers of hazing and alcohol abuse, what might have happened had she not started her crusade?

The Rutgers incident also forced Eileen to empathize with how Don King, Richard Rose, and Steven Peterson must have felt when their choice came down to talking honestly with a grieving mother who might sue or protecting an institution they loved and were paid to serve. Never before had it been so clear to her that hazing was an issue in which allegiance to institutions often took precedence over the rights of individuals. Who would ever have thought, the day she bent over that cold table in the morgue, that she would become one of the best friends fraternities ever had? Of course, she empathized with the victims of hazings, but she also felt for her friends in national fraternities who were publicly humiliated whenever a single chapter let the organization down.

Eileen's relationship with fraternities was much on her mind after a Texas mother, whose son had been injured in a hazing incident, chastized her. The woman's attorney had contacted Eileen, asking her to testify against a fraternity as a paid expert witness. Eileen demurred because her role demands that she remain a friend to fraternities, colleges, and victims alike. The attorney upped the ante. "I can't do it for any amount of money," she said. She told the attorney that she hoped his client would understand her predicament. She did not. The irate mother telephoned Eileen to express her anger.

Eileen was miserable when she hung up. A few years earlier, during her suit against Klan Alpine, she might have sold her soul — or at least an Alfred administrator's — for just one witness who could win her case for her. Now, here she was, traveling from campus to campus, breaking bread with fraternities. Eileen approached Roy. She told him about the call.

"Be honest with me, Roy," she said. "Am I a hypocrite?"

Roy took his time. He can't make the English language do tricks the way Eileen can, and he sometimes fights to find the right words. He told her how, in the tool-and-die business, he sometimes compromises with his sales staff in ways that make him a villain in his employees' eyes. "The way I see it," he said, "you're either a friend to attorneys or you're a friend to victims, schools, and fraternities. The attorney is dutybound to be friends with one person — the client. Therefore, if you become the attorney's friend, you're the others' enemy."

Eileen accepted his answer, but she was still troubled. She confided in Spasyk. He told her not to worry. He said that if a prosecuting attorney asked her questions requiring her to say truthful but negative things about fraternities, there would also be a chance for the defense attorney to ask what good they do. She could truthfully say that fraternities have the most visible problems with hazing but are also the most active force for its eradication.

Although she doesn't testify against fraternities, Eileen speaks out whenever there is a hazing death. That's hard, particularly when she knows friends in the unfortunate fraternity prefer that she remain silent. But speak out she does. In the end she can only try to be honest and ethical; if her fraternity friends are true friends, she believes they will applaud her stand. Chuck's death is her touchstone, helping her separate duty from her emotional attachment to the Greeks.

The Callahan death paralyzed the entire Lambda Chi organization and made its associate member program look like a sham to the public.

George Spasyk, in remarks made at a National Interfraternity Conference legal seminar, called the Rutgers affair "the most devastating experience in my thirty-eight years on the Fraternity staff." He said that the episode caused him to exhaust "every conceivable emotion . . . shock, sorrow, fear, anger, frustration, humiliation, embarrassment, and, ultimately, a sense of gratitude and optimism."

The call to Spasyk came mid-morning the day of Callahan's death. He was supposed to be lecturing in Baton Rouge on values and ethics, a talk that might have been of some use in New Brunswick, New Jersey, the previous evening. But snow in Indiana kept him at the office, where he watched the story develop. Advisor Roy Lenardson phoned to fill Spasyk in on what had occurred. Then the media began to barrage the headquarters in Indianapolis with phone calls. Other officials handled most of these, Spasyk told the seminar, not surprising given his well-known aversion to talking to the media, one shared by many other national executives.

Spasyk had little information about Callahan's death, and much of it was incorrect. By Friday night the story was receiving major play in the New Jersey area. "RU Frosh Dies after Frat Party," said the headline in the Central New Jersey *Home News*. "None of the Lambda brothers expected that to happen," Rutgers sophomore Gary Gechlik told the paper. "It was an accident . . . the fraternity is not to blame."

The Rutgers administration also became the focus of a media blitz, and Spasyk thinks university president Edward Bloustein handled the matter poorly. "Some of President Bloustein's early comments were clearly hysterical," he told the NIC, "calling on the national fraternity to revoke the charter immediately and permanently and shutting down all fraternity and sorority activity indefinitely."

City officials padlocked the chapter house a few hours after Callahan's death, citing violations of sundry building, health, and safety codes. Spasyk questioned this hurried action, noting that a few weeks earlier the house had passed a city inspection. But his complaint does not take into account the damage members did the night of the out-of-control swill session. A city construction code official said the house was "literally destroyed." He told the *Home News* that "there were doors and windows broken" and "all the fire extinguishers were emptied out. Exit signs were ripped out and the pool table busted. . . . The only thing working was the fire alarm."

Spasyk made light of that report to the NIC. "Our own investigation showed that the house was indeed 'a pit,' but if you've been in any of your chapter houses in recent years, I think you'll agree that very few of them exhibit cathedral-like qualities." He added, "There is no question but that city officials were pressured into closing the house as a public demonstration that swift action was being taken against the fraternity."

Instead of thinking that Bloustein might have been acting in good conscience when he blasted the Rutgers chapter, Spasyk blamed media pressures. He cited a university spokesman who said, "There is no indication at all that this is a hazing incident." That the university would try to take the onus off a fraternity and try to put it on Callahan would not and did not surprise Eileen and other Lost Chapter mothers who followed the case with interest.

Spasyk, unlike Bloustein, refused to speak with the press. "I would make no statement or take no action without legal advice," he told his colleagues at the NIC. "In fact, we had four lawyers on the phone all weekend, one of them in Hawaii on vacation."

When the Lambda Chi board of directors (known in fraternity jargon as the Grand High Zeta) had enough information and legal counsel, they did declare the Rutgers chapter inactive, which stopped its normal activities. In so doing, the board followed its own procedures for due process. "Suspension or revocation of a charter requires, under our laws, preferring charges, conducting a thorough investigation, permitting a defense . . .," Spasyk said, "all of which takes time." However, because the national fraternity handled the chapter with kid gloves on the advice of its attorney, the Rutgers members felt betrayed when the Lambda Chi Alpha national office did shut down their house the following April and reacted with outrage.

The university was apparently unconcerned with due process. "They wanted to hear the words *suspended* or *revoked*," Spasyk said at the convention. He tried to inform the school that inactive status had the same short-term function that pulling the Rutgers chapter's charter would have had. As of February 13, one day after the death, operations were suspended, and the chapter was no longer considered an official unit of the national fraternity. However, Spasyk said he could and should have satisfied the university and press by playing a little word game with both. "I should have announced that 'operations of the chapter have been suspended,' which was technically correct," he said, "and the press would have reported that we had suspended the chapter or suspended the charter, and everyone would have been satisfied."

Spasyk told the NIC, "Soon after the shock and sorrow had subsided, I was consumed with anger. We (the whole fraternity) had been blindsided by one chapter! How could they do this to us? We have policies on hazing, alcohol abuse, drugs, open parties, dry recruitment; we have printed articles and published material on risk avoidance, legal liabilities, date rape, and on and on."

Spasyk concluded that because his national fraternity has 224 chapters and more than twelve thousand undergraduates, "there will always be some who aren't paying attention or who maintain the fantasy that 'it can't happen here.'" But instead of despairing he and his fraternity elected to work all the harder to educate young members "to the dangers and consequences of irresponsible behavior." The fraternity sent a notice on February 29, 1989, approved by four lawyers, that demanded an "absolute end to selling alcohol, serving minors, hosting open parties, purchasing alcohol with chapter funds, sexual harassment, and the use of illegal drugs."

Lambda Chi's action was commendable although unfortunately too late to save James Callahan. At the convention Spasyk also announced plans to film a video presentation of the Rutgers tragedy. He had earlier ordered all Lambda Chi chapters to view a Sigma Phi Epsilon tape on an incident at the University of Texas. "I think it had an impact," he told the NIC assembly, "but it's not the same as seeing your Greek letters on the screen, seeing one of your chapter houses padlocked, seeing some of your members interviewed on national television."

He also noted that reaction from Lambda Chi alumni was mixed. Some members resigned; others sent donations to fight alcohol abuse in Lambda Chi chapters and to prevent a second tragedy. Spasyk said that he was considering many alternatives to combat the bad publicity generated by the Rutgers incident, including retaining a public relations firm. However, he ultimately decided that silence was more prudent than making statements that might be misinterpreted in the few months remaining before his retirement. Thus, the public lost the opportunity to benefit from his perspective.

Spasyk admitted that the Lambda Chi national office never contacted the family of James Callahan. The reasons he gave were undeniably human. He said, "Frankly, I didn't know what to say. I still don't. I felt that whatever I said would be wrong, would sound hollow, or self-serving. That's when I experienced the fear of doing the wrong thing."

Moreover, Spasyk had a temporary bout of cynicism in the aftermath of another tragedy at Rutgers. "Three Rutgers football players got drunk in a residence hall, got in a car, crashed it, and one was killed," he said. "Cynically, I thought—why don't they ban football at Rutgers; why don't they close down the residence hall for five years?"

Ultimately, Spasyk said in his talk, he "got over" his "despair." He said, "I looked around and saw thousands and thousands of fine young Lambda Chis, and I saw many positive things happening as a result of this tragedy."

One not-so-positive result, apparently, was the perception of some Lambda Chis across the country—perhaps reinforced by members of the national staff—that what happened to James Callahan was not a hazing. A member of the Butler University chapter appeared on Dick Wolfsie's *AM*

Indiana show in 1989 and insisted that the Rutgers incident was not haz-ing. His statement was refuted by panelist Richard Harris, the fraternity advisor at Ball State University.

Despite such strong denial evident in Lambda Chi, Spasyk's closing remarks to the NIC bear attention. They give an indication of his and the fraternity's grief and concern regarding hazing. Unfortunately, his expression of those feelings had to be reserved for an occasion when he didn't have four lawyers advising him what to say and not to.

"I want to help others to prevent such a tragedy, as Eileen Stevens has done," said Spasyk. "To paraphrase John Donne: This young man's death diminishes me, diminishes my fraternity. . . . For that we are truly sorry."

Coincidentally, one of the most respected authorities on male behavior, anthropologist Lionel Tiger, teaches at Rutgers. Tiger believes that male hazing rituals stem from basic competitive drives that include sexual com-petition for desirable women and a need to find a comfortable niche in a group. One Howard University member of Omega Psi Phi, for example, told the Washington *Star* that he joined his fraternity "because Omegas always have the most athletes and the prettiest women. . . . When you tell some college girls that you're an Omega, you've got instant respectability."

Tiger occasionally lectures to college groups to discuss a chapter on fraternity behavior in his 1969 book *Men in Groups,* which Greek leaders routinely cite as the best available interpretation of why men haze.

He believes that hazing often reflects "in pathological ways" what might be normal relations between young males and slightly older males in fraternities and other organizations. Hazing allows males to see themselves as powerful. Other variations would be the ancient knight-squire connec-tion or today's relationships between mentors and the young people they take under their wing. "I think the hazing situation is a kind of acting out or working out of that general process," says Tiger, "but with a very practi-cal and often punishing kind of reality. To have a taboo against hazing per se would involve a kind of level of self-consciousness that I don't think young males are likely to have. After all, these are the most volatile and complicated people in a society to discipline."

Nonetheless, Tiger says, those who deal with young males must find institutional solutions to deal with hazing and alcohol-related abuses because the problems are "not going to go away." He thinks it is foolish for fraternal leaders to make an announcement that hazing has stopped, then expect young men to comply, particularly in fraternal groups that lose and replace approximately a quarter of the membership every year. Hazing cannot be dealt with by raising consciousness—that presumes a higher awareness than most teenage males possess—and therefore the Greek elders must try to solve the problems by highly structured means, says Tiger. He points out that recent innovations such as dry rush can help stop hazing deaths. "But there is something intrinsic to the relationship between older and younger males in this kind of semi-secret or secret environment that can get out of hand," warns the anthropologist. He adds that males at this age are far more likely to be susceptible to peer group pressure than to moral qualms, a fact that college and fraternal authorities must keep in mind when they attempt to eradicate hazing.

Tiger says that educational programs such as Eileen Stevens's anti-hazing lectures do serve a useful purpose. "There is this tremendous power that a mother has," says Tiger. "These are young men away from home, very often for the first time, and they are acting with a certain amount of bravado because they don't have a mother any longer. . . . Certainly a careful and responsible statement by the mother of a dead potential fraternity brother has a real impact, as it should. She may be effective whenever she speaks, but where she's not around, there needs to be an institutional structure."

Tiger relates contemporary hazing to the Big Picture: males in our culture experience difficulty in defining their maleness. The old notions of heroism and the male as hunter, he says, "have become faintly silly," and the women's movement has long criticized traditional male "machismo" and behavior patterns. "The confusion that this may engender may lead men to act among themselves more aggressively than they might other-wise," says Tiger, particularly among college males who today find them-selves in coeducational environments with rare exceptions. If men have to compete with women in their classes, as well as allow women more and more to dictate sexual boundaries and the means of contraception, Tiger says that they may "find it more self-expressive to compete with each other in a secret society."

He says that some males would quite naturally find the largely sub-servient women in little sister organizations to be appealing and reassuring to them. The fraternities "are not going to say it's sexual — they're going to say it's social — but it's potentially a reproductive training relationship." Likewise, women who gravitate toward little sister groups find males desirable who most conform to the male "stereotype of the fifties," says Tiger.

Tiger also coauthored a book entitled *The Imperial Animal,* which points out that young males constitute a special block of society. Society must figure out what to do with that block. Biologically, of course, says Tiger, the aggression is directly linked to massive increases of testosterone, a male hormone. "It's as if they've been given a drug, and they have been . . . except they've been given it by evolution," he explains. Some societies might send these young men to war. Some might turn them into novices in a religious enterprise. Contemporary American society, terrified of roving gangs on city streets, has generally approved of fraternities, the FFA, the Boy Scouts, and other such organizations to channel the energies of mem-bers of the community who otherwise might turn to crime or other unsavory ventures.

The Rutgers tragedy, heavily covered by both the New Jersey and the New York media, practically ensured the passage of a tougher statute against hazing. New York's governor, Mario Cuomo, signed a beefed-up version of the state's previous anti-hazing law. Now any hazer who puts an initiate at risk of injury can be found in violation. No longer does injury or death have to occur for an arrest to be made after a hazing incident. The bill, sponsored by Assemblyman Arthur J. Kremer, chairman of the committee on standing committees, was supported by CHUCK, several statewide PTA groups, and the Student Association of the State University of New York. The new violation is punishable by a maximum fine of $250 or as many as fifteen days in jail.

One of the best minds at Alfred, according to Greg Belanger, is no longer in the classroom. Gary Horowitz, now director of alumni-parent programs, is a brilliant man whose memory is the envy of Alfred police chief Tiny Jamison, another of Horowitz's fans. In addition to advising Klan Alpine, Horowitz's job requires contact with successful alumni, among them many Klan members.

Horowitz doesn't have a clearly defined idea of how Alfred can overcome its image as the school where a kid died at a fraternity house. He says there was talk on campus about awarding Eileen Stevens an honorary degree, an idea that was nixed when some faculty scoffed that the well-intentioned gesture of good will might be misperceived as a blatant attempt to buy her off.

Horowitz blanches if his phone rings at eight-thirty A.M. on a Monday morning. He knows "it's the vice president for student affairs [Don King] asking me, 'Do you know what Klan did this weekend?'" he says. Although Klan may get in trouble now and then, Horowitz is impressed with his students. "You have kids who are nineteen to twenty-two, who have a budget close to $200,000 a year, $250,000 a year. They pay taxes, they maintain the structure, they hire a cook to cook the food, they pay their own bills, they discipline themselves. . . . Fraternities to a certain degree serve a very useful function—for some kids. It's not for everybody and I understand that.

"But I think fraternities to some degree have taken a bad rap. Again, they do stupid things and they deserve whatever punishment they get. But there's a very positive side to fraternities, and that's why I want to be advisor to them. I think it does help kids grow. I sometimes wake up on Saturday morning in a cold sweat, thinking, have they done anything stupid this morning?"

With Horowitz on the minds of members, if not on their tails, Klan Alpine won't have another death if he can help it—but he can't offer any guarantees.

As Klan advisor, Horowitz has chastized social chairmen who send newsletters to alumni that mention parties with lots of beer. "I say, 'Alumni don't care about that,'" says Horowitz. "Once you're out of here for three or four years you're no longer concerned about how much beer you drank. Your life becomes very different. Alumni don't want to read about that. They want to know, 'Are you active in [varsity] sports?'; 'What are you doing for the community?'; 'Is the house doing OK?'" he says.

Horowitz admits that being an advisor isn't easy. "There's no support given to advisors," he says. "It's one of the great failings here." He also talks about the built-in frustrations that all advisors—be they in charge of Greeks, the student newspaper, or cheerleaders—have. Namely, all you can do is advise. Advisors who try to determine a kid's life are out of line, he says. The good ones let students have the final say in student matters, and that is how it should be in a learning environment. Unlike a so-called dean of discipline, a term that's fallen into disfavor, an advisor has no power unless he can bend wills through negotiation, the power of suggestion, or—in Horowitz's case—an occasional tongue-lashing.

Horowitz won't go to tapping nights either, but he defends his decision in a way that's hard to criticize. It also raises the question of whether Steven Peterson and Robert Heineman, in all fairness, should be criticized for never attending Klan Tapping Night ceremonies in the late seventies. Does being an advisor entail being a cop or a hall monitor?

"I'm forty-seven years old," Horowitz says. "I will act as advisor to Klan, but I will not go to their parties. I like the kids, I enjoy being with them, and I will work for them, but I am not their social friend. I am not going to be at forty-seven years old this arrested adolescent who's going to go down to every party they have to sit in their TV room and watch sports with them. . . . I'll be damned if I do that. In fact, I think people like that are fairly sad. . . . So there is this dilemma about what responsibilities do I have as an advisor. To what extent am I responsible for what happens there? I don't feel it's fair to assume that I'm going to be there at all times."

What he does do, during pledging, that Steven Peterson did not do in 1978, is regularly summon the Klan president. He repeats and repeats the message: "Hazing's wrong." He tells the president to use common sense, to expect the unexpected and to be aware that a pledge may have hidden health defects. "I keep stressing that," he says. "But will a court hold me responsible for not doing more? I'm not sure that's fair. So in a way I am caught in a dilemma, and I could lose a helluva lot."

Horowitz says that he acts as advisor; he refuses to act as a house father. He's willing to give his time to Klan, his advice, and to be the supporting adult that they can come to in a pinch. "The alternative is for me not to do anything," he says. "Then no adult will go over there. I'm not sure what the courts expect out of advisors."

Horowitz likes to tease the Klan members by saying that they look like "leftover kids," but he insists there is something special about the members. "That is why this whole thing with Stenzel doesn't make sense," he says. "It happened. Clearly the kid is dead. It's just the maligning that they took is truly not deserved for Klan as a group." Historically, he said, they may be Alfred's most successful graduates. Joel Moscowitz, the man who wrote that stirring letter about Klan Alpine fraternity, has served for several years on the school's Board of Trustees. Another is a college president at Rose-Hulman Institute of Technology, a school that invited Eileen to speak.

Horowitz refuses to give the names of specific Klan success stories, but he readily supplies their occupations: "There are several MDs, including psychiatrists, a shitload of lawyers, a partner in Morgan Stanley, executive vice president of Payne Webber, presidents of insurance brokerage houses, people who work on the commodities exchange in New York, a president of a ceramic company, president of a carpet company, president of services for the aging, a professor of law . . . dentists—lots of 'em, schoolteachers in secondary schools, nurses, ceramic engineers, accountants."

During a quarter-century spent working with young people Horowitz has come to certain conclusion: they never think anything bad is going to happen to them; they never think their foolish actions can kill someone else. Unless the students are veterans, it's unlikely they've seen death. When grandparents die while students are in college, quite often they're shaken. The personal experience with death overwhelms them. "This is why with DWI laws college kids will still continue to drink and drive," he says, or fail to take precautions to prevent AIDS. They know kids die, but they convince themselves it can't happen to them. "So when they do these dumb-ass things with drinking, it's never malicious," he says. "It's sheer stupidity. It comes because they don't think anything's going to happen." Despite one crippling Alfred stair-diving injury, he said that "the kids are still doing stair-diving in the same fraternity. They saw it, and some of them see this kid every day. But that happened to him; it's not going to happen to me. How do you get it through their heads?"

Horowitz believes that hazing can be solved or curtailed over time, but only through harsh measures. When the little sisters of Zeta Beta Tau chapter at Alfred were scattered like broken dolls when a car hit them, Horowitz was disturbed. "I mean, you talk about hazing," he says. "In my mind there is no clearer act. They were out on a country road supposedly blindfolded, and they were hit by a car. First of all, why was that car there? No one's ever on that road. There had to be something more to it . . . something absurd. But the kids don't think about it; they just don't think about it. . . . It's stupid. There's no justification for it, except the kids will justify it by saying that it builds a love for fraternity. You go through that shit and you learn to really love it. Basically, it's the goddamn sophomores who went through it the previous year who want to get even, so they make it worse."

He is skeptical that education and litigation can have an effect on hazing. "It doesn't work, I'm telling you," he says. "Litigation is not the key with these kids because it doesn't mean a thing to them." For him, the only thing that can change hazing on campus is a fundamental attitude change in young people. "I don't know if [hazing] will last," he says. "I think kids are changing, and they're not going to buy this crap anymore. How long it takes, I don't know. I don't see any justification for hazing."

Steven Peterson apologizes for the wreckage in his office. The former Klan Alpine advisor occupies a book-strewn room in one of the more modern buildings on campus. Peterson has mixed feelings about CHUCK but stresses that he thinks Eileen's story deserves to be heard and that he sympathizes. "I hate to see that kind of price paid to have an impact," he says, adding that in his opinion Eileen has taken a beating over time in addition to her son's death. "There's no question that this particular hazing ritual was stupid, and as a parent . . . I'd sure as hell seriously consider whether or not I would want to have some kind of punitive suit against whatever actives seemed appropriate."

Chuck's death has had a profound effect upon Peterson. As a result, he has tried to help students make good and positive decisions. "This is my legacy to Chuck," he says. Significantly, he doubts that Klan Alpine undergraduates have learned very much from the agonies of their predecessors. "The fact is that Klan, if anyone would, would have changed," says the former Klan advisor. "But from what I understand . . . they still go through dumb rituals."

Don King agrees that the current Klan members haven't fully grasped the significance of the tragedy that occurred in their house in 1978. "They can't relate to it . . . except that they do have that stigma," he says. "They don't want to hear it because they weren't part of that." King has had a difficult time deciding precisely what the Stenzel incident has meant to Alfred. "A stigma's there," he admits. "It's real." He says the administration even talked about suing Eileen. "But it's very, very difficult," he says. "She has the right to [say] anything she believes is factual. If you sue her and prove different, she can come back and say, well, this is the information I received."

King's decision not to contact Eileen for a clear-the-air talk has hurt Alfred's recruitment on Long Island and probably will continue to hurt the school's image. From Alfred's perspective, however, the number of nasty incidents involving fraternities there has been comparable to other schools its size. King claims that the press has failed to see its good points. The feeling on campus, unquestionably, has been that both Alfred and King have been castigated unfairly over the Stenzel incident.

Even with time, some stigmas never go away. Kent State University is forever linked with National Guard troops mowing down students on a grassy knoll; the University of Texas, with Charles Whitman atop a campus tower unleashing bullets everywhere. At Lehigh University a female student died in a grisly rape. People remember.

Another university might have made an effort to turn a disaster to its advantage in some public way that demonstrated remorse, compassion, and a will not to repeat its past. Alfred has, to a degree, done all three in quiet, private ways but has persisted in regarding Eileen as the enemy instead of as a potential ally.

King maintains that he did what he could, under trying circumstances, to accommodate the Stevenses. He steadfastly asserts that a pledge initiation, even one in which students are placed in a trunk and forced to play drinking games until they vomit, is not hazing. Eileen's crusade "certainly has . . . raised the consciousness level of many, many people," says King. "But obviously I have some real biases as to how she's used this specific incident, in a sense, to try to blackball Alfred University. . . . She really was not able, willing, to look very carefully [as to] what responsibility her son had to what transpired. . . . The institution by no means is condoning what transpired that evening . . . but until you have knowledge of these things there's no way you can act or respond." Once again, he says that his actions toward the Stevenses were based on the imminence of a lawsuit, not on insensitivity. "We were advised by our attorneys to be careful, you know, what we were saying, because we knew at that point, you know, that we were going to be sued."

He also points out the difficulties of his job. He has had to deal with parents whose children have committed suicide on campus—including one who died of a self-inflicted slashed throat; students who have turned into vegetables because they took LSD, and many who have died in accidents. "Was [Chuck's death] the worst moment?" he asks himself. "It was a difficult moment, certainly. The thing that goes through your mind was part of you . . . is mad. . . . You're angry because somebody allowed this to happen. On the other hand, you try to keep things in perspective and try to deal with the situation in as objective a manner as you can. I would only say that I've obviously been touched and hit by lots of . . . tragedies that have affected my life in many ways."

King has concluded that Eileen, "probably generally with good intentions . . . began to, I think, take things out of perspective, to exploit beyond what actually transpired, and where some of the responsibility actually lies."

King finds students unwilling to listen to advice concerning their own safety. Many students from both colleges in Alfred have been killed or seriously injured on a certain road leading into town, a pattern of repeated behavior that proves students don't listen. "It's a bad road and they speed," King says. "As much discussion as you have, students will continue to believe that it's not going to happen to them."

King says that he has tried to improve the fraternity system at Alfred, and certainly he has taken some positive measures. Since 1986 he has gotten assurances from fraternity presidents that they will take an intoxicated or injured student to the health center first without worrying about possible repercussions. It is clear in his mind that he must and will take action whenever he comes across a life-threatening or illegal situation of any type on his campus. He has advised fraternities not to throw open parties. During the 1988-89 school year he authorized the campus Greeks to show a videotape of Eileen's talk.

King has also been instrumental in eliminating pledging for first-semester freshmen and freshmen who fall below a 2.0 GPA (out of 4.0) at Alfred. "I feel very strongly about that," he says. "I think it's an unfortunate thing to allow students to come in the first week . . . and start pledging right away." He believes students need at least one term on campus to find the Greek organization best suited to their individual interests, lifestyles, and personalities. As a matter of practice King also reacquaints fraternity and sorority presidents with the state's anti-hazing law. "You've got to use certain benchmarks every year . . . to bring it to their attention. You've got to walk it through with them," he says.

Alfred University has introduced a hard-hitting statement on hazing, initiation activities, and irresponsible drinking into its official catalog. The administration also requires the policy to be incorporated into the bylaws of every organization operating on campus. But King admits that Alfred is still not immune to tragedy. National fraternities such as Lambda Chi and Zeta Beta Tau continue to wring their hands over the management of alcohol risks at Alfred. "Young people are transient . . .," King says. "They come and go quickly. The tradition stays on. The traditions of fraternities and sororities are very, very heavy. I really do believe lots of campuses — and specifically this campus — have modified, new programs, but I still believe some of their activities have the potential of somebody possibly getting hurt."

King also stresses that Alfred doesn't have the problem with homicides, rapes, and robberies that many other universities have. Statistics back his contention that the law has been enforced, despite Alfred's using student security officers instead of trained campus police.

King refuses to leave Alfred University, despite the Stenzel incident, "because I don't believe one should leave situations because of something they didn't have any control over," he says. "I shouldn't leave Alfred because of that incident. . . . If I left for that reason . . . it's a cop-out. So I stay here because Alfred has been a good place. . . . I also like the students who are here. I've been here now twenty years. I've served four presidents, and I think as far as a student affairs division and myself, I believe we've served students in our community very well. This kind of incident taints things, but there has never been a time when a faculty member or anyone else on this campus put blame on myself for what transpired. . . . I may have been more overly sensitive than people think I should be in respect to this whole thing, because I took it personally, but that's me as a person. I've never felt apologetic or defensive about it because I didn't have any control over what transpired."

Eileen Stevens says that she has tried of late to see the incident from Don King's perspective. She can understand that he feared saying the wrong thing or too much, thus jeopardizing the school and himself in the event of a lawsuit. "Having interacted with so many administrators I've come to see the politics of it all, but that doesn't make [his actions] right," she says. Her silent treatment from the school and district attorney's office provoked her into starting CHUCK. Eileen believes the so-called "veil of confidentiality" that universities use to keep information from the public and press has been abused, used to cover up slapped wrists that should have been kicked tails.

* * *

In 1989 vandals said to be pledges of an Alfred fraternity caused six hundred dollars' worth of damage to the Theta Theta Chi sorority house sign. "The same fraternity has been accused of several other acts of vandalism over the last few years," said the campus paper on November 8, 1989. Also in 1989 members of Alfred's Sigma Alpha Mu fraternity told the *London Telegraph* that hazing was a major part of its pledging program. Pledges "have to trust us that we're not going to kill them," said chapter president Jeff Mora.

In contrast to the reports of Greek scandal, a Klan Alpine advertisement in *Fiat Lux* in the fall of 1989 proved that a man's experiences after college bear little resemblance to the reckless days of fraternity life. The ad congratulated "Brother Jeff Maurer '69 on becoming President of U.S. Trust Company." The fraternity was proud to proclaim "Another Klan Brother climbs to the pinnacle of success!"

The university's public relations problems continue. The campus paper reported that from spring to November 1989 eight members of the university relations staff had either "resigned, retired, been fired, or switched departments." Career choices and burnout due to job frustrations were the reasons cited for the departures. The school advertised in the *Chronicle of Higher Education* for an executive director of public relations whose duties were to include "counseling key administrators on public relations issues."

In August 1989 Alfred once again made the New York *Times,* this time as the Zeta Beta Tau chapter found itself shut down and in serious trouble with its national fraternity. According to the *Times,* ZBT national president Frederick E. Schatz said that the Alfred chapter was "an accident waiting to happen." He charged that the house had demonstrated "blatant disregard" for the image that the national had been trying to cultivate. The *Times* interviewed ZBT executive director James E. Greer, Jr., who said the Alfred chapter's problems included drug abuse, alcohol violations, and financial mismanagement. The *Times* also interviewed Don King who "expressed irritation that he was not notified before the [national's] move" and said he hoped "to reactivate the chapter as soon as possible." Chief Tiny Jamison said that Zeta Beta Tau had not been a major problem in the community although there had been minor fights.

The *Alfred Reporter,* the alumni newsletter, tried to put its brightest light on the scandal. "It has been emphasized that the charter has not been revoked, but withdrawn until a new group of undergraduates can resume active membership," said the newsletter. The actives were, in effect, kicked upstairs after the national fraternity granted them alumni status.

Zeta Beta Tau's action was not as forceful as it might seem. The bounced brothers—unbeknownst to Greer, he claims—were given permission by the Alfred Inter-Greek Council to continue their participation in Greek functions. There was an "understanding," says Alfred's Gary Horowitz, that the national was going to allow Zeta Beta Tau to recolonize in

January. "Let's be realistic," says Horowitz. Fraternities are "big business," to use Horowitz's language. Zeta Beta Tau did not want to sacrifice income from an inoperative Alfred chapter. Horowitz, a pragmatic man, understands that the fraternity world is no more ideal than the rest of society. The national's dealings with a rowdy chapter are, at some level, going to be colored by financial considerations.

Withdrawal of recognition at Alfred hadn't changed much in the twelve years since Chuck Stenzel's death. The major punishment suffered by the Alfred chapter of Zeta Beta Tau was bad press and a missed chance to pledge in the fall semester. Since first-semester freshmen were, under King's new policy, unable to pledge until second semester, the punishment was a tickle, not a slap. Alfred suffered a far greater loss of face from the *Times* article than did the unnamed students of its ZBT chapter.

In February 1990 Zeta Beta Tau's national fraternity, after a suspension of just one semester, allowed the Alfred chapter to recolonize. The chapter included many of the same members who had been kicked upstairs to alumni status. The move was inexplicable in view of a personal letter sent from Robert J. Eschman, ZBT chapter consultant, to a friend in the fraternity world on June 12, 1989. Eschman criticized Alfred's atmosphere regarding fraternities. "Frankly . . . I am very concerned about the risk management environment for the entire Alfred campus," said Eschman. "One would think after the Chuck Stevens [sic] tragedy that the campus would shape up but it appears that this is not the case, at least in the area of alcohol risk management."

In another document handmarked "confidential," Eschman says, "Based on our observations of and visits to our own chapter, we are very concerned about . . . violations at the Alfred University campus. We have directed our chapter to cease all known/rumored behavior that violates . . . Risk Management Policy. We urge all National Staffs with a chapter at Alfred University to keep each other posted on trends, attitudes, and specific violations."

Richard Rose continues to serve as president of Rochester Institute of Technology. He gets his greatest satisfaction as an educator when young people realize their potential "through the vehicle of education."

In the military he participated in ceremonies that would be defined as hazing by the New York law, but he "didn't see that as hazing, really—it was just keeping a tradition alive." Such behavior—he "personally saw people going down a garbage chute"—is harmless in his opinion.

Rose is unwilling to condemn categorically all types of hazing. He distinguishes between "fun things" and "brutality," thus taking the position that Eileen Stevens took for the first two years of her crusade. However, Eileen subsequently came to believe that *no* form of hazing is permissible. Rose is unequivocally opposed to brutal acts of hazing. He abhors groups' threatening lives for amusement and thinks Chuck Stenzel's death has lessons to teach all that it touches.

"All of us obviously can learn from that experience," he says. "We talk to fraternities here periodically—the officers—and remind them of that and the fact that we have a policy opposed to hazing. It's not just hazing where you threaten lives; it's hazing where you intimidate people, where you embarrass them in front of their peers. It's one thing to have fun—even ridiculous fun is okay—it's healthy. But when you do something to impose yourself on another person against their will and create situations that are potentially dangerous and humiliating, then I feel we need to step in and say this is not to be tolerated and you ought to know better."

Rose believes that colleges and universities can influence students positively through quality advising. "I think that when it becomes evident that there is hazing, we shouldn't go to halfway measures. . . . They know it's wrong. We should say that it's absolutely wrong . . . absolutely not to be tolerated, take whatever steps it takes to eliminate it," he says.

He feels Klan Alpine put more emphasis on hard drinking than did other groups on campus during his tenure at Alfred. But he also perceived the Klan members, several of whom he knew personally, to be good people. He says, "The last thing they wanted was to hurt somebody; that wasn't their motivation at all."

Rose recalls experiencing frustration in the aftermath of Chuck's death. Charges of personal insensitivity, made by Eileen Stevens and the press, still disturb him, even though bad publicity per se doesn't. What truly bothers him is that he believes Klan Alpine members "could have saved [Chuck Stenzel] if the group had been a little more mature in their behavior." It also troubles him that "there's a young man who is not living a fulfilled life, and [his] family's been devastated." Rose has seen tapes of Eileen Stevens speaking and feels that "what she's done has been very positive."

George Francis left the district attorney's office in 1982. The Stenzel case was not the only controversy of his tenure as Allegany County DA. The Buffalo *News* reported that an official had criticized Francis's tendency to drop cases in which he obtained indictments. In 1981 charges of arson and conspiracy against an Olean businessman were dropped after the DA neglected to file important motions before deadlines.

In 1982 the bearded, diminutive ex-Marine was elected State Supreme Court Justice. He ran, unopposed, on the Republican ticket. The Erie County Bar Association gave him merely a C (Qualified) rating, said the *News*. An A rating is superior.

Now based in Buffalo, Francis continues to be involved in controversial cases. The *News* speaks of strong supporters who believe Francis to be a bright, dedicated jurist. He also has critics who rightly or wrongly have found him soft on white-collar crimes and sexual offenses. Others defend him, saying he agonizes over every sentence he metes out. Eileen Stevens is not the only person to claim that Francis is insensitive to the rights of victims. In 1983 a Buffalo police officer received only a two- to six-year sentence from Francis, despite having crippled his wife when he pumped six bullets into her belly with a service revolver. In 1985 Francis released Arthur Kohler, who had been convicted of attempting to molest an eight-year-old girl. Eleven days after his probation began, Kohler raped a woman. In 1988 Francis sentenced a repeat sex offender to only six to twelve years in jail after finding him guilty of brutally sodomizing a woman in the washroom of a Buffalo college. All these victims and their families have complained about Francis in print. Suffice to say, he's not a hanging judge. But many people that he's sentenced think he's Solomon reincarnated for giving them another chance to put their lives on track.

Not all hazing incidents make the newspapers. National fraternities routinely investigate many cases that never reach the public, disciplining the offending chapters as they see fit. By 1989 several fraternities had informed their members that they were willing to yank charters if necessary to enforce discipline. But there are disturbing indications that some incidents occur that are not uncovered by the press or by the national fraternities. Louise Owens, an Indiana physician, treated a young man who had been told to drink vodka by a university organization. Owens saved him by placing him on a ventilator and pumping his stomach. His blood alcohol level was in excess of .40. "It would be unusual to live with a blood alcohol of that level," Owens says, and the young man was comatose for several days. "I think they're underreported . . .," says the doctor. "I didn't see any publicity about this boy at all in the Bloomington paper."

The president of the Carnegie Foundation for the Advancement of Teaching, Ernest Boyer, has said that college students don't want the university involved in their lives but do want administrators concerned about their lives. That may be a reasonable request. But students who have chosen to live in a university setting haven't taken a sabbatical from their responsibilities either. Students should be considerate of the rights of administrators and their institutions. The thoughtless actions of Klan Alpine in 1978 forever changed Don King's life.

Students today have every imaginable freedom, says sociologist Richard A. Bogg, and that freedom has been construed "as the right to party." The issue of alcohol consumption by college students isn't too far off the subject of hazing, says Bogg, who has studied the so-called "party animal." According to Bogg, "Booze complicates the hazing issue. . . . Members are likely to dream up dangerous and demeaning things for pledges to do that they might not otherwise concoct when sober. The same goes for pledges. The liquid courage makes them think they not only can do whatever dangerous and dumb stunts the members have ordered, but exceed such demands as well."

Fraternities will go a long way toward solving the hazing problem when they eliminate the stereotype that being Greek means being able to hold your booze. Beer distributors alone spend an estimated fifteen million dollars annually on the college market, according to *USA Today*, and certainly a fair share of that amount is targeted toward fraternities and sororities.

Lon A. Turner, Jr., an educational leadership consultant, visited Alfred's Lambda Chi Alpha chapter from March 12 through 14, 1989, talking with eight associate members and forty-eight initiated members. There were five freshmen, sixteen sophomores, twenty-three juniors, and twelve seniors in the group. Turner's conclusions in a confidential report are harsh. "Due to its remoteness and a hands-off policy by the University, this campus is plagued with large alcohol and hazing problems," he said. "Vice President of Student Affairs, Don King, classifies Lambda Chi Alpha as his least worry and lowest risk. But by our standards, [the chapter] still falls way behind."

The Alfred Lambda Chis told Turner alcohol violations were inevitable because the fraternity couldn't compete with other Greek organizations for members of status if their chapter's alcohol policies were not similar to others'.

During Turner's tour of the chapter house with a Lambda Chi higher-up called the "High Alpha," he discovered that members and non-members alike — including underage drinkers — had "free and unlimited access" to two kegs of beer. Lambda Chi had further violations and "poor risk management," the consultant found. In fall 1988, for example, the chapter threw a twenty-nine-keg party for seven hundred. Rather than refuse to serve minors, the Alfred chapter devised a ploy "with the help of an attorney." All guests had to sign a contract upon entering that said they were not connected to or affiliated with any law enforcement agency.

The consultant also found abuses in Lambda Chi's recruitment efforts. Events included chugging contests and drinking games that matched prospects with members. Turner found the Alfred chapter defensive and somewhat surly about its use of alcohol. The High Alpha told him that they would give up national status and become a local fraternity [like Klan Alpine] "before they would follow the [required] alcohol policies."

On a positive note, the alumni of Lambda Chi Alpha did eventually agree to back the national's strong stand on alcohol, and the chapter ultimately agreed that there was a need to implement changes, not to circumnavigate rules. "Much of the conversation focused on the realization of needed change and how alcohol was attracting low quality members," said the consultant. "Their focus was to work with many of the younger members who unfortunately were there for alcohol only."

The Alfred chapter of Lambda Chi Alpha has also refused to abide by the "associate member" rules and regulations mandated by the national organization, said Turner. George Spasyk once said to a seminar in Indianapolis, "We have associate members rather than pledges — the press never did pick up on that distinction." The Alfred chapter suggests that some Lambda Chis themselves share the press's problem with the distinction. "Many members still use 'pledge' terminology," read the consultant's report. "Associates are required to clean the house on a weekly basis, be at the house for interviews at set times, and wear suits on Wednesday. The associates also must go through three 'grill' or 'hot box' sessions in which they are quizzed about Lambda Chi Alpha." One session is extremely harsh. Associate members are verbally abused for wrong answers.

After discussing Turner's report, the Alfred chapter decided to shape up rather than ship out, according to another confidential document, addressed to Lambda Chi Alpha headquarters in Indianapolis:

> Our recent visit from Lon Turner has made the issue of alcohol a top priority at our chapter. No quick, feasible solution to our alcohol problem exists. As you know, Alfred has a poor, nonetheless true, reputation concerning alcohol. Alfred University is a school of approximately 2500 students. But unlike other college towns, Alfred has very limited recreational facilities and thus offers few diversions. The nearest theater is fifteen miles away while the nearest shopping mall is nearly sixty-five miles away. . . . The one establishment offering any form of nighttime entertainment to students under 21 is a bar which allows those over 18 to enter for a $3 cover charge. With so few activities available, the seven fraternities fill the void by offering free entertainment with access to alcohol for most university students. The fraternities are the center of social activity at Alfred. Since the fraternities on campus enjoy this distinction, prospective members are invariably attracted by social functions which usually focus upon alcohol. In light of this, a drastic change by one fraternity alone would not change Alfred University and could easily eliminate the chapter.
>
> We understand that such activities cannot be totally safeguarded, not even by the alcohol policy our chapter has enforced over the past year. When our chapter becomes the only dry fraternity at Alfred, our existence at Alfred University will be seriously threatened. . . . Of course the failure of our chapter is the last thing we want to see happen. Thus, we are requesting your assistance in our transition to a dry fraternity. We do not have the funds to pay higher liability insurance premiums, nor do we wish to lose our association with Lambda Chi Alpha. Going dry is best for all involved; however, we need time for Alfred University's fraternities to collectively become dry, spurred on by pressure from our chapter and the university administration. This topic will be addressed for the first time by our president at this week's Inter-Greek council meeting,

which will also include Donald King, the Vice President of Student Affairs. . . .

Eileen Stevens doesn't know how many more colleges she can visit, conventions she can attend, seminars she can give; how much more lobbying she can do at her own expense to promote anti-hazing laws. The 1990 CHUCK is cash-poor, and friends have urged her to insist upon honorariums, instead of relying on a handful of sensitive Greek organizations and schools for financial support. Yet she has not done so. Because CHUCK has had national publicity since 1978, many fraternities believe that it must have coffers to match Scrooge McDuck's or their own national's annual budget.

The Stevens family continues to live in the same Marion Street house that they have owned since the mid-sixties. The most visible sign of wealth is Eileen's Cadillac, now several years old. After Zeta Beta Tau — annual national budget: one million dollars — implemented its "no pledge" program, one undergraduate member of the organization called to ask if CHUCK would share any future contributions with ZBT, a "pioneer" in the anti-hazing movement. Stunned by this misperception of CHUCK's supposed wealth, Eileen wrote a nice note to decline and read the letter to Roy. "They've just asked the poorest organization in the world for money," he said.

Financial worries aside, Eileen is content with what she does. She still wants to see anti-hazing laws on the books in the states that don't have them. She hopes a congressional committee will be formed to look into the Coast Guard hazing of Joe Branson and the hazing problems in America's high schools and colleges. Her immediate desire is to find a university interested in taking over CHUCK's files as the basis for a thorough study of the hazing problem and to serve as an accurate clearinghouse for deaths attributable to hazing and other causes. She also actively supports anti-hazing efforts at Gallaudet, an independent liberal arts institution for the deaf in Washington, DC. Gallaudet, she charges, is a bastion of hazing practices.

Eileen has used her interpretation of Mike Moskos's study to supply reporters with a count of hazing deaths since 1980, but some of the deaths reported by the press should be attributed to other causes. Several people have written to CHUCK about deaths or serious injuries at institutions, but the schools are unwilling to provide factual data to reporters, making it difficult to come up with definitive numbers. Without a doubt, the number of hazing deaths reported from 1980 to 1989 in prestigious papers such as the New York *Times* is inaccurate, and almost certainly exaggerated. Other hazing-related incidents may have missed the attention of the press or been listed as suicides or accidents.

Eileen lacks the scholarly credentials to provide an accurate count of hazing deaths. Nor does she have any way of verifying claims about deaths at universities such as Cornell, which have no basis in fact but have been reported in newspapers and studies. The fictitious Cornell incident, widely spread by word of mouth, concerns a young man who supposedly fell to his death in a coffin suspended over a cliff.

Self-studies by the fraternities are needed, but the anti-intellectual climate noted by Fred Kershner has prevented the National Interfraternity Conference from launching an all-out study of the hazing problem by legitimate researchers. The highly touted Center for the Study of the College Fraternity at Indiana University is little more than a pile of books and papers that would fit into a single eight-shelf bookcase. The fraternity world does have educational foundations, but Kershner dismisses them as "tax dodges to a certain extent," failing to turn out significant research that would help the Greeks solve their hazing problems.

The best single study of a fraternity's problems was commissioned by the University of Texas, a school once plagued by hazing deaths and incidents, but which has now considerably reduced its problem thanks to the determination of President William H. Cunningham. Another institution that is a model of Greek reforms is Indiana University, largely because of strict guidelines established by Dean of Students Michael Gordon.

The three Stevens children are adults now. Suzanne still lives at home. She has a photograph of Chuck in his red baseball cap on her wall and uses his old pillow, tattered now and ready to be retired. Steven resides in New York City and refuses to discuss his brother's death with the press. He is fiercely protective of his privacy but supports his mother's work. Scott has married and works nightly with Roy to remodel an older house he bought. He collapsed at the finish line during a marathon in 1988 and had to be revived by an ambulance crew. His parents witnessed his close call and feared that the worst had happened yet again.

After working as a journalist, Greg Belanger began teaching college journalism in New Haven, Connecticut. In the classroom he tries to get students to think for themselves and to argue with him. His model is his old mentor, Stuart Campbell. Today's students occasionally exasperate him and have convinced him that he is addressing a generation more concerned with final grades than with learning concepts or how to think for themselves. "It's like a quotient," he says. "If I do X, I get a B. If I do Y, I get an A." The other survivors from the gang of seven have settled all over the country. In April 1990 Jimmy Arnoux and his wife, Nanci, abandoned Long Island for cleaner waters in Wilmington, North Carolina. Their infant son — middle name, Charles, for Chuck Stenzel — moved with them. There they joined Billy Vollmer, who builds houses. Before Arnoux left, Eileen fixed him a goodbye meal. She wanted it to be extra special, so she cooked him a batch of chili, Chuck's favorite meal. "He ate every last bite," she says.

How long can Eileen Stevens keep up her crusade?

"As long as I'm able," she says. "Or until I burn out. Maybe one day I'll wake up and say I've had enough. Let somebody else take the ball and roll with it. But at this point that time has not come—there's so much to be done. Surely I'm not out to save the world. Roy teases me and calls me 'Carrie Nation.' But after all these many . . . years arousing interest, stimulating people, urging colleges and fraternities and legislators to see my point . . . I'm not about to stop. It's too important and too vital. The fact is that I have seen good things, positive things, come from my work.

"God, I expected to fall on my face. Who would have thought that me, someone who didn't go to college, who never spoke in public in her life, who never left home, who never went anywhere without her husband, who had a very limited existence, would have the chutzpah to do what I do? . . . I've learned that if we believe enough in something and care enough about something, we really can move mountains. I'm hopeful, I'm optimistic. I've seen positive things come out of something so dreadful and tragic. I thank God every day that I have the strength and the ability to do what I'm doing. . . . Even when I run into indifference and apathy, and people placate me and . . . let me down, I still feel I have accomplished something. I feel what I'm doing is right, and what I'm doing is a labor of love.

"I'm not doing it for money, and God knows it's cost me a lot more than I've ever recouped. Those early days when Chuck's tuition refund came and . . . even the insurance money—those things were all put to use to help this little organization get off the ground. It's my baby. I love it with all my heart. When I see the [concern] in the faces of those students, when I see their response, and I read that what I had to say made a difference, that what I say gave them the courage to try to go back and implement change . . . then each and every one of them has a special place in my heart. They have given me the strength to do what I do."

Eileen stood at a podium while giving her anti-hazing lecture at the convention of one of the nation's stronger fraternities. Unknown to her, two executives from the organization stood outside the packed ballroom.

"Is she still telling her tired old story?" grumbled one man.

His companion shot him daggers. "Yeah, she is," he said, "and eight hundred kids are still listening. You can hear a pin drop in there."

Eileen's allies have told her that she has a charismatic talent, but she shrugs away such analysis. She prefers to say that she slips into her listeners' foreheads and leaves them thinking. "I'm not a threat to them," she says. "I'm not an administrator, I'm not a professor. I'm just somebody's mother."

APPENDIX

A Selective Chronology of College Hazing Incidents and Related Miscellanea

Hazing incidents rarely make headlines unless a death occurs. The intent of this appendix is to provide a comprehensive list of hazing and miscellaneous tragedies that have occurred on college campuses. Although most hazing goes undetected and many instances are quietly punished or covered up, this list indicates that hazing is neither isolated nor unplanned.

Included here are episodes of class (upperclassmen versus lowerclassmen), athletic, band, and Greek hazing. When known, rulings on whether an incident was officially termed a hazing are provided. Many deaths that appear to be hazing-related are ruled accidents by local and school authorities, however. Also listed here are miscellaneous Greek deaths from alcohol overdoses and other causes, which reflect the mindset that leads to hazing deaths. Many of these deaths are erroneously included in hazing-death totals by national periodicals.

Every attempt has been made to provide accurate data and documentation. In some cases, where information has been obtained from clippings in CHUCK files and from other sources, documentation is incomplete. Readers who wish to report additional incidents or to correct information can write to the author in care of the publisher. Enclose complete documentation and a stamped, self-addressed envelope for reply.

Future printings of *Broken Pledges* will incorporate new and amended information.

Nineteenth-Century

1838
Franklin Seminary
Simpson County, Kentucky
Class hazing

John Butler Groves died in a hazing incident.
His grieving parents refused to send another
child to college.

1860
Harvard University
Cambridge, Massachusetts
Class hazing

Eight men were expelled for hazing by the
president of the college.

1873
Cornell University
Ithaca, New York
Kappa Alpha Society

A blindfolded pledge and two members
walked the countryside in a nineteenth-
century version of a fraternity kidnapping.
The members said they removed the
blindfold after they realized they were all
lost. Nonetheless, the pledge, Mortimer N.
Leggett, died when he plunged over an open
cliff above Six Mile Creek.

1874
University of Michigan
Ann Arbor, Michigan
Class hazing

After six students were suspended for hazing,
eighty-one students signed a paper protesting
the university's action. All protestors were
suspended as well.

1878
Princeton University
Princeton, New Jersey
Class hazing

After freshmen retaliated for hazing offenses
against them by shaving the heads of two
sophomores, a fight occurred in which one
student was shot in the leg. He was not
seriously wounded.

Trinity College
Hartford, Connecticut
Class hazing

Fifteen freshmen and three juniors were
suspended for hazing after several incidents
resulted in injuries to participants. Several
pistol shots were fired.

1881
University of Illinois
Champaign-Urbana, Illinois
Class hazing

A group of freshmen intent upon uprooting a
tree planted by seniors was blasted with
shotguns by upperclassmen. One freshman
had more than one hundred pieces of
birdshot removed by friends.

1882
Bowdoin College
Brunswick, Maine
Class hazing

A suit for ten thousand dollars was brought
against eight students for hazing.

Bucknell University
Lewisburg, Pennsylvania
Texas Rangers

The Texas Rangers, a social club, terrorized
faculty and students alike. One student
rushed after the group with an ax, vowing to
"clean out the crowd."

University of California
Berkeley, California
Class hazing

The university suspended fourteen students
for hazing.

1886
Illinois College
Jacksonville, Illinois
Class hazing

The college president had to put down a
revolt of student hazers.

1889
University of Wisconsin
Madison, Wisconsin
Class hazing

A student named D. M. Flowers was
convicted of hazing. He was fined ten dollars
and court costs.

1893
Harvard University
Cambridge, Massachusetts
Dickey Club (later Delta Kappa Epsilon)

286

A young man died accidentally after a hazing activity.

Ohio Wesleyan University
Delaware, Ohio
Delta Omicron Alpha, Sigma Zeta Nu

Students were suspended after faces of initiates were temporarily blinded with nitrate of silver.

Princeton University
Princeton, New Jersey
Class hazing

The faculty dismissed four students (allowing two to return) and suspended five others for hazing.

1894
Cornell University
Ithaca, New York
Class hazing

As a prank, one or more students released chlorine gas into a group of undergraduates during a class dinner. The gas killed a female server.

1899
Conference Seminary
Buckhannon, West Virginia
Student prank

College security guards opened fire on a group of seminary men who were burning the school's president in effigy. One bullet seriously wounded Martin Williams, penetrating his brain.

Cornell University
Ithaca, New York
Kappa Alpha (also known as Kappa Alpha Society)

In a pre-automobile version of a fraternity ride, twenty Cornell students dropped eight pledges off a train about one mile from Geneva, New York. One was given orders to pin a piece of paper to a tree about a quarter-mile away. The pledge, Edward Fairchild Berkeley of St. Louis, walked in darkness and plunged accidentally into a canal. His body was recovered two hours later. The New York *Times* said, "It is the general opinion that it could have been avoided."

New York University
New York, New York
Class hazing

During a sophomore ducking of freshmen, a member of the class of 1903 received a scalp wound when he banged his head on a horse trough.

Rutgers University
New Brunswick, New Jersey
Class hazing

Freshmen celebrated charter day, the commemoration of Rutgers' 133rd anniversary, by pulling a prank on the sophomores. The freshmen hoisted their banner in Monument Square, cutting the halyards so that it could not be removed without someone's risking his life.

1900-1909

1901
Lehigh University
Bethlehem, Pennsylvania
Hazing of instructor

One hundred students seized physics instructor Howard Logan Bronson, abused him with switches, and ordered him to plunge fully clothed into the Lehigh River.

Purdue University
Lafayette, Indiana
Class hazing

Two students were beaten with clubs during a class "rush" between members of the freshman and sophomore classes.

United States Military Academy
West Point, New York
Cadet hazing

A House of Representatives committee held an inquiry into the death of Cadet Oscar L. Booz. They found that brutal hazing was common at West Point but could not with certainty attribute the young man's death directly to hazing.

1902
St. John's College
Annapolis, Maryland
Class hazing

The annual hazing of freshmen by sophomores broke into a three-hour melee in which more than one hundred students and one professor participated. "Several heads were broken," said one newspaper account.

St. John's College
Annapolis, Maryland
Class hazing

An attempt by upperclassmen to haze preparatory students led to a fight in which several participants were injured. A college instructor took part in the struggle as leader of the prep students.

1903
University of Maryland
Baltimore, Maryland
Phi Psi Chi

Dental student Martin Loew's death remained a mystery after he died following a fraternity initiation in which pledges were hit with a "slapjack" (blackjack) and tossed in the air, among other indignities. Although Loew's body was bruised, the coroner ruled that he had died from "contagion of the lungs caused by gas or some deadly drug unknown to the jury." The president of the fraternity was exonerated following the investigation.

Massachusetts Institute of Technology
Boston, Massachusetts
Class hazing

A party of upperclassmen tortured and killed a pig, the freshman class mascot.

1904
Cornell University
Ithaca, New York
Class hazing

The sophomores branded forty Cornell freshmen on the face with a solution of silver nitrate and made them wear grotesque costumes in a parade. Three years earlier, the college president had announced that hazing had been ended at Cornell.

St. Stephen's College
Annadale, New York
The Kaps Society

Three boys were beaten in a hazing incident, one nearly to death, according to the father of one of the victims.

Wesleyan College
Middletown, Connecticut
Class hazing

The faculty suspended six sophomores for blinding freshman Howard Richard in one eye during a hazing incident. The Wesleyan College Senate (made up of undergraduates and faculty officers) said it thought the faculty's penalty too harsh for the circumstances.

1905
Columbia College
New York, New York
Class hazing

Kingdon Gould, the grandson of Jay Gould, was severely hazed by a secret group of upperclassmen called the Black Avengers. According to a newspaper account, Gould was blindfolded, set astride a barrel, and told to give an exhibition of "pony polo." A sudden kick sent the barrel from under its rider, and Gould was declared unhorsed. Additional hazings were reported following autumn, and three sophomore leaders were suspended by the faculty for one year.

Columbia College
New York, New York
Class hazing

Freshmen from the class of 1909 defied Columbia's new anti-hazing rule by painting their class year on a fence and shouting "Quack, quack, quack, quack, 1908" in unison at sophomore class members. A brawl began between the classes. The school's president and a dean passed by without interrupting it. Three members of the sophomore class were suspended.

Cornell University
Ithaca, New York
Class hazing

Police arrested five sophomores who had chopped a hole in a boardinghouse roof to reach freshmen who had barricaded themselves in the attic.

Franklin and Marshall
Lancaster, Pennsylvania
Class hazing

Oscar Gingrich, a freshman, fired a revolver into a crowd of sophomores after one, he alleged, had struck him following a kangaroo court trial. One sophomore, Roy Ulsh, was wounded in the shooting.

Kenyon College
Gambier, Ohio
Delta Kappa Epsilon

Freshman Stuart L. Pierson waited for brothers to return to a railroad bridge where they had abandoned him, but somehow he rolled onto the track and was killed by a locomotive. Newspapers claimed the boy had been tied to the track because a detective spotted "marks" on the boy's wrists and ankles. That charge was never proved. Another possibility was that the boy had been deprived of sleep prior to his abandonment. In that case he may have fallen asleep and rolled onto the track, particularly if he had been given alcohol to drink. The death remains a mystery.

University of Michigan
Ann Arbor, Michigan
Class hazing

Fearing his hair would be cut by members of the sophomore class, a freshman student stabbed two sophomores with a knife, seriously wounding H. H. Corson and L. A. Warren.

United States Naval Academy
Annapolis, Maryland
Midshipman hazing

Midshipman Jerdone P. Kimbough was found unconscious in his room after being hazed by upperclassmen.

1907
United States Military Academy
West Point, New York
Cadet hazing

The commandant of West Point, Colonel Robert Lee Howze, threatened to throw out the entire plebe class for hazing but had to back down, admitting he could not stop his charges from ostracizing a first-year man.

United States Naval Academy
Annapolis, Maryland
Midshipman hazing

Hazing (or "running") of fourth-class men, as it had come to be termed, again cropped up at the Academy. Fourth-class men were required to do silly stunts such as the "elephant dance," a routine which required the newcomers to hit each other with slippers and other objects.

1908
Gettysburg College
Gettysburg, Pennsyvania
Class hazing

Three masked sophomores punished three freshmen who refused to wear the mandatory dink (a black cap with a green button). While the freshmen were blindfolded and subdued, their heads were shaved. Then their faces were stained with iodine. They were told they would be pushed into the path of a train.

University of Oregon
Eugene, Oregon
Class hazing

Upperclassmen ducked a freshman in a bath of icy water, and he ran away in terror. He was committed to a mental institution and locked in a padded cell. Professors of the victim, Ralph Bristol, said they had observed nothing abnormal about the young man before the hazing occurred.

1909
University of Illinois
Champaign-Urbana, Illinois
Class hazing

Sophomores H. D. Emmert and Arthur W. Ide were expelled for hazing.

Muhlenberg College
Allentown, Pennsylvania
Class hazing

Faculty suspended the entire sophomore class for hazing six freshmen. The offenders cut half the hair off their victims for their refusal to wear the traditional green buttons.

United States Military Academy
West Point, New York
Cadet hazing

Six or seven cadets were dismissed in the wake of a hazing scandal.

Washington and Jefferson College
Washington, Pennsylvania
Class hazing

After freshman William R. Cowleson chased away sophomore hazers at gunpoint, he was ducked under a water pump. At least three sophomore students paid fines for assault and battery.

1910-1919

1910
Texas A&M University
College Station, Texas
Corps of Cadets hazing

A sleeping cadet suffered serious burns when burning sulphur was placed alongside him. The hazer was dismissed.

United States Military Academy
West Point, New York
Cadet hazing

Several cadets were found guilty of hazing, and public support of hazing ran high enough that the Senate passed a bill to give the superintendent permission to inflict lighter punishment on hazers. All told, seven cadets were dismissed. One offense found hazers guilty of punching a cadet and attacking him with tent poles, putting the youth in the hospital for twenty-one days. Another involved cadets who required plebes to race on their hands and knees like horses. The plebes were then auctioned off as a further means of humiliation.

United States Naval Academy
Annapolis, Maryland
Midshipman hazing

An investigation into hazing at the Naval Academy commenced shortly after the superintendent had issued a warning to stop all hazing.

Wesleyan University
Middletown, Connecticut
Class hazing

Several freshmen desecrated graves during an initiation ceremony in Saybrook, Connecticut. The college president paid for damages to keep students from being prosecuted.

1911
University of Texas
Austin, Texas
Class hazing

A freshman shot and killed a young man who was hazing him.

1912
University of North Carolina
Chapel Hill, North Carolina
Class hazing

Freshman Isaac Rand fell from a barrel onto a broken bottle, slitting his jugular vein. He lived ten minutes. (Novelist Thomas Wolfe later fictionalized this episode.) Three students were found guilty of manslaughter, but their sentences of four months' imprisonment were dropped on the condition that the court costs be paid. They were released into the custody of their parents. The faculty expelled eight students, suspended twelve, and reprimanded two others that it found guilty of hazing.

United States Naval Academy
Annapolis, Maryland
Fourth-class tradition

William L. Bullock fell to his death while attempting to fulfill the tradition of piercing his cap on the spike of the main mast on the *Hartford*. Another tradition was to have new midshipmen shinny twenty feet up a greased obelisk known as the Herndon Monument. Supposedly, the first to touch the top was destined to become an admiral.

United States Naval Academy
Annapolis, Maryland
Midshipman hazing

Two midshipmen stood accused of forcing an Indiana cadet to stand on his head for a prolonged time, a practice that years earlier had caused a man to lapse into a coma. Both were court-martialed.

1913
Purdue University
Lafayette, Indiana
Class hazing

A youth from South Whitley, Indiana, Francis W. Obenchain, died as a result of the annual fight between freshmen and sophomores.

Texas A&M University
College Station, Texas
Corps of Cadets hazing

After vicious hazing incidents that prompted the Texas legislature to pass a law against the practice, the university reinstated 466 students who had been expelled for hazing. To get back into the school, the cadets took an oath to stop hazing. Two of them broke their vow and were expelled. Hazing included the stripping of cadets and beating their bare buttocks with leather straps.

1914
Lafayette College
Easton, Pennsylvania
Class hazing

Administrators suspended fifty-four sophomores and put eighteen others on probation for hazing freshmen. A resolution signed by five hundred students promised to end hazing at Lafayette.

New York University
New York, New York
Class hazing

Upperclass students petitioned the faculty for permission to resume ducking of students in tubs of water. "The freshmen this year have wounded the susceptibilities of the upperclassmen so deeply, it is said, that they feel nothing short of a ducking party will assuage their injured feelings," said a reporter.

St. John's Military College
Annapolis, Maryland
Class hazing

A freshman (apparently at the urging of four confederates) fired a pistol shot through the door of upperclassmen William R. Bowlus after a hazing incident. Bowlus died as a result.

University of Washington
Seattle, Washington
Class hazing

Sophomores continued to conduct mock trials after a faculty order to decease. Several suspensions resulted.

1915
University of Kentucky
Lexington, Kentucky
Class hazing

After winning a tug of war with sophomores, the freshmen victors ran through the streets of Lexington. A streetcar on Broadway and Third hit the cable they were carrying. One student died of a fractured skull.

New Mexico Military Institute
Roswell, New Mexico
Class hazing

Ludwig Von Gerichten, Jr., died from pneumonia as a result of a class prank in which young men were taken miles from town, dunked in a horse tank, and left to walk back in chilly weather, said a family member.

United States Naval Academy
Annapolis, Maryland
Midshipman hazing

President Woodrow Wilson issued orders that punished twenty-five midshipmen for hazing.

Wesleyan College
Middletown, Connecticut
Chi Psi

Stuart Grant Peck died of spinal meningitis. He took ill the morning after his initiation into the fraternity. College authorities insisted the death was not due to the initiation. "Every member of the fraternity voluntarily swore that not a thing had been done toward hazing," said Carr W. Peck, the dead youth's father.

1916
University of South Carolina
Columbia, South Carolina
Class hazing

A freshman was beaten with electric wire until he bled. When he reported the incident to the president's office, the hazers attacked the victim again to gain revenge.

1917
College of the City of New York
New York, New York
Phi Sigma Kappa

William Ashcom Bullock died of spinal meningitis following an initiation in which he was rolled on the ground in a wet blanket. He had been in poor health prior to the initiation.

United States Military Academy
West Point, New York
Cadet hazing

Once again, members of the third class were involved in a hazing scandal.

1919
Colgate University
Hamilton, New York
Class hazing

A Kane, Pennsylvania, freshman who had been left on an island lake by sophomores decided to swim for shore. Frank McCullough "became distressed" and drowned.

United States Naval Academy
Annapolis, Maryland
Midshipman hazing

Midshipmen Henry C. Wetherstone and P. H. Seltzer tried unsuccessfully to kill themselves, and a third youth suffered a nervous collapse. One of the youths admitted that he had been hazed but said overall conditions and his poor schoolwork had been stronger contributing reasons for his actions.

University of Wisconsin
Madison, Wisconsin
Class hazing

Sophomores threw more than one hundred freshmen into a cold lake in defiance of school rules against hazing.

1920-1929

1920
St. John's College
Annapolis, Maryland
Hazing rebellion

One hundred and seventy students went on strike to protest school rules against hazing.

United States Military Academy
Annapolis, Maryland
Midshipman hazing

Charles Edwin Snedaker, third class, of New York City submitted his resignation following an investigation into hazing. As tradition mandated, all members of his class were requested to observe his shame. Instead, nearly everyone defied the admiral by cheering Snedaker's departure. The admiral ordered them confined to their quarters for the remainder of the day.

1921
College of the City of New York
New York, New York
Secret society hazing

A college senior, Louis Warsoff, was "severely beaten" by students tapping him for admission into an unnamed organization. A New York magistrate dismissed the charges against one attacker, poohpoohing the incident. "In my time we hardly considered these things as disorderly conduct," said the magistrate, who laughed when the defendant said he'd taken an oath not to reveal the name of the secret society. "There was no breach of the peace but was only loving evidence of the regard one class had for the other, or one society for an individual," he said.

Columbia College
New York, New York
Phi Kappa Psi

Five freshmen candidates were arrested after brothers abandoned them near Hicksville, Long Island. The five "appropriated" a car to get back to campus. At the request of the presiding magistrate, the car owner later dropped charges.

University of Maine
Orono, Maine
Dormitory hazing

The faculty suspended fifty-six sophomores for making freshmen run a gauntlet in which they were paddled.

Northwestern University
Evanston, Illinois
Class hazing

One of the most mysterious possible hazings occurred the morning of September 21, 1921, when Leighton Mount disappeared after a freshman-sophomore class rush. In April 1923 his bleached skeleton was found beneath a pier at the foot of Lake Street in Chicago. His body was covered with seven or eight rocks, which weighed from fifty to one hundred pounds each. (Despite that evidence, university officials maintained that Mount had committed suicide, although a jury found him a victim of murder.) One theory is that Mount's hazers panicked when he died accidentally during a confrontation, then decided to hide the body to conceal the evidence.

University of South Carolina
Columbia, South Carolina
Fraternity membership

President J. S. Currell announced that he would expel or suspend students found guilty of joining "sub-rosa" fraternities. State law at that time prohibited fraternities.

Texas A&M University
College Station, Texas
Corps of Cadets hazing

Administrators ordered a stop to the whipping of "fish," as freshmen were called at A&M.

University of Wisconsin
Madison, Wisconsin
Class hazing

During a confrontation between the freshmen and sophomore classes, bombs made of such materials as sulphuric acid, sugar, and potassium iodine severely injured eight students. The Student Senate voted to abolish hazing, including the wearing of traditional green caps.

1922
Brown College
Providence, Rhode Island
Class hazing

Upperclassmen decided to substitute mental torture for paddling to imbue freshmen with a "proper sense of . . . unworthiness."

Cooper Union
New York, New York
Class hazing

The eighteen-year-old president of the freshmen night-school class was struck with a blackjack, chloroformed, and dumped in Troy, New York, by members of the sophomore class.

Lafayette College
Easton, Pennsylvania
Class hazing

A seventeen-year-old freshman was found unconscious after having been paddled, kicked, and punched in a rough hazing incident. The boy's father, the Reverend Henry Cunningham, a Presbyterian pastor, forgave the perpetrators.

Mercer University
Macon, Georgia
Class hazing

The university president gave sophomore hazers a choice: expulsion or a drubbing with straps by the senior class. All chose a whipping.

United States Naval Academy
Annapolis, Maryland
Midshipman hazing

Witnesses in a hazing court-martial were doused with water at night in their rooms to intimidate them. One of the witnesses was ostracized by nearly all students because they believed it was his parents who first brought hazing violations into the public eye. One witness — freshman William H. McGregor of Indiana, Pennsylvania — testified while he was on crutches, a victim of hazing injuries. The trial of Midshipman William H. Robinson, first class, demonstrated that hazing was carried out to an extent far beyond the charges originally made. Five seniors were punished for hazing, and another senior had his punishment set aside. Two midshipmen testified that Rear Admiral Henry B. Wilson, Superintendent of the Naval Academy, made remarks to a group of midshipmen that intimated that he wanted the "freshness . . . taken out of the plebes." Wilson said he must have been misunderstood.

1923
University of Alabama
Tuscaloosa, Alabama
Sigma Nu

A local youth died "from psychic effects of excitement" following an initiation at the fraternity's house. A coroner determined that Glenn Kersh, son of a Tuscaloosa city clerk, likely had had a bad heart.

Franklin and Marshall College
Lancaster, Pennsylvania
Class hazing

Ainsworth Brown, a sophomore, died of injuries suffered during the annual class rush. The university ended rushes following the death of the Tenafly, New Jersey, student.

Hobart College
Geneva, New York
Class hazing

Freshman Lloyd Hyde was beaten and thrown down an embankment into Seneca Lake. Two star football players, both seniors, were expelled for "breach of discipline." Three other senior athletes were punished, including the president of the senior class.

1924
Earlham College
Richmond, Indiana
Class hazing

Eight students were suspended for hazing.

Harvard University
Cambridge, Massachusetts
Class hazing

The Harvard Freshman Discussion Club voted in favor of hazing, overruling a minority who feared injuries might result.

1925
Rensselaer Polytechnic Institute
Troy, New York
Class hazing

Administrators suspended four upperclassmen for painting the faces of freshmen and requiring them to perform undignified stunts on the streets of Troy.

United States Naval Academy
Annapolis, Maryland
Class hazing

The Interior Department awarded a pension to William H. McGregor of Johnstown, Pennsylvania. McGregor was seriously injured in a hazing incident. He resigned from the Academy, fearing that his career was over because fellow students regarded him as a "blabber."

1926
College of the City of New York
New York, New York
Fraternity hazing

A patrolman arrested two City College students involved in a fraternity initiation. The two students, clad in scanty track suits amid the throng of suited men on Broadway, were captured by heavyset John Brown of the West 47th Street station. The crowd cheered Brown when he nabbed Moe Bandler, eighteen, and David A. Davidson, also eighteen, on disorderly conduct charges. At least one of the boys was carrying a raised umbrella while running, which slowed his escape.

Columbia College
New York, New York
Class hazing

A sophomore suffered a head injury after being hit with a lead pipe by a freshman.

Connecticut Agricultural College
Storrs, Connecticut
Class hazing

A student alleged that he had been struck with a paddle and injured during a pajama parade.

University of Maryland
Baltimore, Maryland
Fraternity hazing

Dr. Lewis Battle charged that one of his patients was branded with a hot iron or similar instrument of torture at the University of Maryland during a fraternity initiation.

University of North Carolina
Chapel Hill, North Carolina
Class hazing

Two university students were arrested for hazing. They required freshmen to parade with trousers rolled up to their knees.

United States Military Academy
West Point, New York
Cadet hazing

Four seniors were suspended for one year on charges of hazing seven plebes.

1927
Amherst College
Amherst, Massachusetts
Fraternity hazing

Fraternity brothers placed a burlap bag over Howard Hurley's head, and he walked over a cliff. Hurley was disfigured, required plastic surgery, and dropped out of college, according to his best friend, Freddy Morin.

Amherst College
Amherst, Massachusetts
Class hazing

A sophomore was injured while attempting to capture the freshman class chairman, an annual tradition that was ended after the accident.

Virginia Military Institute
Lexington, Virginia
Class hazing

Upperclassmen at VMI were confined to barracks for a month after a hazing incident.

1928
Gonzaga University
Spokane, Washington
Class hazing

Hazing had reached such "refinement," wrote school historian Wilfred P. Schoenberg, S.J., that freshmen and sophomores "shanghaied" each other's leaders and shipped them, shoeless and penniless, to Hope, Idaho, and Pasco, Washington.

University of Texas
Austin, Texas
Delta Kappa Epsilon

Nolte McElroy, nineteen, was stripped, wet down with water, and required to crawl through two mattress springs charged with electrical current, using a rheostat from the lighting wires. The Longhorn football player (who had played in a game earlier on the same day) was electrocuted.

1929
Columbia College
New York, New York
Class hazing

Despite a vote by the sophomore class to abolish hazing, twenty to thirty sophomores painted a freshman with black shoe polish.

Indiana University
Bloomington, Indiana
Delta Chi

The parents of George P. Steinmetz, Jr., blamed their son's death from lung disease on rough initiation. The chapter and the university told the parents that they intended to abolish "rough week." Both later did so.

Indiana University
Bloomington, Indiana
Sphinx

In protest of rough initiation (hazing) and alleged shortcomings of this social club, nine members resigned. The men quit during the initiation ceremony. Those resigning included the club's president, Byron Wallace, and Branch McCracken, a member of the class of 1930. McCracken was destined to become a respected coach at Ball State University and Indiana University.

Louisiana State University
Baton Rouge, Louisiana
Class hazing

Despite opposition from university officials, upperclassmen shaved fifty freshmen bald in a darkened dormitory. Perpetrators disconnected all lights before descending on the men with shears.

1930-1939

1930
College of the City of New York
New York, New York
Class hazing

A free-for-all brawl occurred in a New York hotel during the annual "frosh feed." Sophomores tried to rescue two of their officers whom the freshmen had captured. Combatants suffered black eyes and scratches. The freshman advisor "tried in vain to quell the fight, but the efforts of ten policemen were more successful."

1931
University of Illinois
Champaign-Urbana, Illinois
Fraternity hazing

A campus official complained that a battered student said his black eyes and need for a breathing apparatus were caused by "a little pre-initiation ceremony." Also injured was a pledge with a broken thumb and one whose "right side of the face looked as if it were in the last stages of putrefaction."

1932
United States Military Academy
West Point, New York
Cadet hazing

After forty years without a black cadet's enrolling, West Point had a black cadet who was subjected to a form of hazing known as cutting, which meant social ostracism. Nonetheless, the cadet persevered and won over his detractors, graduating in 1936 near the top of his class.

1939
Eastern Michigan University
Ypsilanti, Michigan
Fraternity hazing

Pledge Robert Hendee was kidnapped in the middle of the night and taken to a remote Michigan island. He returned safely. School officials denounced the practice.

St. Mary Mercy Hospital School of Nursing
Gary, Indiana
Probationer hazing

A young "probie," as the student nurses were called, suffered severe headaches for thirteen and one-half years after being shoved during a hazing.

1940-1949

1940
University of Missouri
Columbia, Missouri
Theta Nu Epsilon

Hubert L. Spake, Jr., a twenty-one-year-old junior from Kansas City, died after participating in a required drinking marathon held by an unrecognized drinking fraternity. The school banned the club from campus after the death. One Missouri student later became a lifelong opponent of hazing. That student is James Kilpatrick, the nationally syndicated columnist and a member of Sigma Alpha Epsilon.

1942
Syracuse University
Syracuse, New York
Gamma Phi Beta

Sorority pledges were made to feel as if they were being interrogated by members. While bright spotlights were shined in the faces of the young women, embarrassing questions were asked.

1945
St. Louis University
St. Louis, Missouri
Phi Beta Pi

Robert Perry, twenty, died. He had been
made to lie naked on a table and receive
shocks on his skin, which was coated with
collodin (a substance used in film
developing) and lampblack. A spark from the
shocks ignited, and Perry went up in flames.

1946
Ohio State University
Columbus, Ohio
Sigma Chi

Two World War II veterans suffered head
injuries during Hell Week after a sixty-foot
plunge into rocks at the bottom of a stone
quarry. At three A.M., the two were looking
for a drive-in theater on a scavenger hunt
when a car's headlights blinded them, and
they mistook the quarry for a field. Brothers
called it an "unavoidable accident," not a
hazing. The university's Council on Student
Affairs ruled that Sigma Chi showed a "lack
of judgment and a poor sense of values," but
ruled that the "fraternity and its officers
cannot be held responsible for the accident."

1949
Piedmont College
Demorest, Georgia
Class hazing

A freshman was dropped off in the woods in
Georgia rattlesnake country wearing only
shoes and shorts. Mortified, he dropped out
of college. The incident convinced the college
president to outlaw hazing.

1950-1959

1950
Wittenberg University
Springfield, Ohio
Alpha Tau Omega

Two pledges were hit by a truck while
sleeping on the road after fraternity
members left them in the country. Dean
Joyce Niswonger died, and Jerome Wendell
suffered a fractured arm. Alcohol was not
involved, but previous sleep deprivation may
have been a contributing factor.

1952
Hofstra University
Hempstead, Long Island
Crown and Lance

Seven students in this fraternity were burned,
one in the eye, after they were smeared with
a strange mixture of substances.

1954
Swarthmore College
Swarthmore, Pennsylvania
Delta Upsilon

Peter Mertz, a member of a family that has
long been a generous benefactor of
Swarthmore, had been required to find his
way back to campus after being dropped off.
He was struck and killed by a car. No alcohol
was involved. A conscience-stricken brother
wrote Eileen Stevens a letter about the
incident, which read, in part: "All of us — no
matter how hard we told ourselves that it was
an automobile/pedestrian accident rather
than a hazing — have been unable to shake
the realization that it would not have
happened without the hazing. We prided
ourselves on avoiding the 'silly' and
dangerous practices of other
fraternities. . . . But the accident happened
to us. . . . Its memory will *never* be far below
the surface for me."

1956
Cornell University
Ithaca, New York
Alpha Zeta

The Interfraternity Council fined the chapter
for hazing.

Massachusetts Institute of Technology
Cambridge, Massachusetts
Delta Kappa Epsilon

Pledge Thomas Clark, eighteen, drowned
beneath a snow-covered reservoir after Deke
brothers dropped him off in a deserted area
and told him to find his way back to campus
during a pre-initiation rite known as the
"one-way ride." Clark's father, who had
joined a fruitless, week-long search for his
son, said his boy was "another victim of a
criminal fraternity prank." According to
Time magazine, the fraternity's national
headquarters told its chapters "to see to it
that there should be no such victim again."

Michigan State University
East Lansing, Michigan
Phi Kappa Tau

296

The Interfraternity Council fined Phi Kappa Tau for abandoning a pledge away from campus.

University of Texas
Austin, Texas
Delta Sigma Phi

After two pledges were hurt, including a former paratrooper who was hospitalized for a week with a neck injury, Delta Sigma Phi received a minimum two-year suspension.

1957
Santa Barbara College
Santa Barbara, California
Fraternity hazing

Max Caulk's fraternity brothers thought he was joking when the twenty-two-year-old neophyte said he couldn't swim. They threw him into a harbor during an initiation ceremony. He drowned. A jury found no member accountable.

1959
Cornell University
Ithaca, New York
Fraternity hazing

Six students were injured in hazing incidents during the fall term.

University of Southern California
Los Angeles, California
Kappa Sigma

Richard Swanson, twenty-one, choked to death. Swanson was preceded by six other pledges who successfully swallowed a thick, oil-soaked piece of raw liver roughly the size of a club sandwich. Swanson had tried to swallow the liver three times before his last attempt. An ambulance was called immediately, but Swanson died because fraternity members refused to divulge that meat was lodged in the victim's throat, according to the ambulance driver.

Valparaiso University
Valparaiso, Indiana
Freshman hazing

Officials ordered all freshmen hazing stopped after nine coeds were injured during initiation proceedings.

1960-1969

1961
Pasadena City College
Pasadena, California
The Regents

A municipal judge fined six members of this social club amounts of one hundred dollars to $150 for tarring eight pledges and chaining them to a Bakersfield fence on a cold, rainy night. They were convicted of hazing. Should they not pay the fines, the magistrate gave them the option of spending thirty days in jail.

1962
University of Southern California
Los Angeles, California
Zeta Beta Tau

Pledge Harold Davidson "began gasping for air" during an initiation exercise in which pledges passed raw eggs to one another by mouth. He suffered from "hyperventilation and mild shock." The university suspended the chapter.

1963
Brown University
Providence, Rhode Island
Delta Kappa Epsilon

A sophomore pledge was hospitalized in "serious" condition following an all-night initiation. University officials disbanded the organization.

1964
Washington State University
Pullman, Washington
Phi Kappa Tau

The Dean of Men suspended the fraternity from all chapter activities for hazing.

1965
Georgetown College
Georgetown, Kentucky
Pi Kappa Alpha

Richard (Dick) Winder drowned while attempting to throw an active brother (who had been "pinned") into Elkhorn Creek. Winder and the active brother were swept over a dam, killing Winder. The active brother survived, making this a rare incident in which the hazer, not the hazed, perished.

1967
Baylor University
Waco, Texas
Baylor Chamber of Commerce

A student was made to swallow a foul-tasting concoction. After participating in strenuous exercises at the club's behest, John Clifton regurgitated the mixture, sucking it into his windpipe. He choked to death. The state examining court ruled the death accidental. No charges were filed.

University of Colorado
Boulder, Colorado
Delta Tau Delta

A freshman track man claimed he suffered permanent injuries after complying with an order from actives to run with a cement block up and down three flights of stairs for forty-five minutes.

1968
Monmouth College
West Long Branch, New Jersey
Phi Delta Sigma

A former pledge alleged that he and his fellow pledges had to carry a telephone pole on their shoulders for seven miles without ever being allowed to put it down. He suffered a pinched nerve in his left shoulder and required electrical shock treatment to regain full use of his arm. He also alleged that he had to drink warm salt water until he threw up.

1970-1979

1970
Eastern Illinois University
Charleston, Illinois
Alpha Gamma Delta

While being dropped off by pledges in the country, member Donna Bedinger, nineteen, was accidentally killed in a fall from a vehicle.

1971
Tulane University
New Orleans, Louisiana
Delta Kappa Epsilon

Seventeen-year-old Wayne Paul Kennedy drowned in Lake Pontchartrain. The New Orleans *Times-Picayune* said that "what apparently was part of a series of playful pranks at a Tulane University fraternity rush party . . . has turned out to be a tragedy."

1972
University of Maryland
College Park, Maryland
Sigma Alpha Mu

Brian Cursack, who had a diseased heart, died after performing strenuous calisthenics, according to a Sigma Alpha Mu fraternity brother, Dr. Mark Taff. Taff later became an expert on the forensic aspects of fraternity hazing.

Pierce College
Los Angeles, California
Chi Chi Chi

In late December three fraternity brothers dumped Fred P. Bronner in the Angeles National Forest. He did not have his glasses with him when he was taken by the members — supposedly to cure his attitude problem — and fell over a five-hundred-foot cliff to his death. The members were fined up to two hundred dollars and spent a sentence of ten days at a U.S. forestry road camp.

1973
Lehigh University
Bethlehem, Pennsylvania
Delta Phi

Pledge Mitchell Fishkin apparently jumped from a speeding car filled with active members. The district attorney ruled that Fishkin died of a fractured skull from "spontaneous horseplay," not hazing.

Louisiana State University
Baton Rouge, Louisiana
Delta Kappa Epsilon

Frank David Carlson, a minor pledging the LSU fraternity, was battered during pledging activities, requiring hospitalization and surgery.

United States Military Academy
West Point, New York
Cadet hazing

A dehydrated cadet resigned after being hazed.

1974
Bluefield State College
Bluefield, West Virginia
Tau Kappa Epsilon

Michael Bishop, twenty, was shot and killed during an off-campus pre-initiation in the woods. Although Bishop was a member, not a pledge of the fraternity, he was present at a pre-initiation ceremony. Blindfolded pledges believed that cans would be shot off their heads. Instead, the cans were knocked off with sticks at the same time that shots were fired into the ground. Edwin Taylor, twenty-eight, was found guilty of voluntary manslaughter. Taylor was the fraternity advisor (graduate status) and fired at random at those present. Another member was shot in the neck.

Grove City College
Grove City, Pennsylvania
Adelphikos

Seventeen pledges of a local fraternity were walking along a road when a car plowed into them, according to Ross A. Foster, the vice president of student affairs. Four students perished in the accident. "We take a hard line on this stuff," said Foster. "If they have any alcohol during pledging, we lift the charter."

Monmouth College
West Long Branch, New Jersey
Zeta Beta Tau

Members ordered five pledges to dig six-foot "graves" on a sandy beach on the Atlantic Ocean. The five then lay down in the graves while members threw handfuls of sand atop them. The grave of William E. Flowers, Jr., collapsed, and he began inhaling sand. He died of asphyxiation. A grand jury called the death "accidental," clearing seven Zeta Beta Tau members who had been arrested on charges of manslaughter.

1975
Cheyney University of Pennsylvania
Cheyney, Pennsylvania
Class hazing

Theodore R. Ben, nineteen, was carrying another student on his back during a traditional hazing initiation when he was pushed against a wall, sustaining a terrific blow to his head. He later died. The incident was part of an initiation conducted by sophomores at the school.

The Citadel
Charleston, South Carolina
Disputed death

The official version was that David Ohlhorst and other cadets were horsing around with a cocked and loaded gun when a .22-caliber bullet killed Ohlhorst instantly. But a coroner disputed that version, calling it a "clear case of manslaughter." The county medical examiner, an instructor for The Citadel's pistol club, ruled that the slaying was accidental. The only witness to the shooting refused to discuss the incident with a *Newsday* reporter investigating the shooting. The student who fired the fatal shot dropped out of school and paid a twenty-five-hundred-dollar settlement to the dead youth's mother.

University of Nevada
Reno, Nevada
Sundowners

John Davies, a Nevada-Reno football player, died during an initiation rite for this sub-rosa drinking club. He was required to drink large quantities of wine, beer, and liquor, including potent Everclear. A grand jury called the fraternity morally responsible but assessed no criminal penalties.

Northern Illinois University
DeKalb, Illinois
Wine Psi Phi

Pledge Richard Gowins died of alcohol poisoning as a result of drinking a half-gallon mixture of gin, tequila, and wine.

Tennessee State University
Nashville, Tennessee
Delta Sigma Theta

Three sorority members were suspended for injuring four pledges with paddles. The state Supreme Court upheld the suspensions in 1978.

Washington State University
Pullman, Washington
Tau Kappa Epsilon

Jon Asher died of bilateral pneumonia during a TKE initiation ceremony. A University Senate investigation committee found no evidence of physical abuse or misconduct despite findings that pledges had been deprived of sleep and forced to do calisthenics.

University of Wisconsin
Stevens Point, Wisconsin
Siasefi

David Hoffman, twenty, died of acute alcohol poisoning after members of this social club took him to a number of bars in a ritual known as the "death march." Members pleaded no contest to a hazing charge.

1976
Iowa State University
Ames, Iowa
Fraternity hazing

Dennis Redenbeck died of alcohol poisoning.

Manhattan College
Riverdale, New York
Sigma Delta Beta

State police pulled over five cars in Carmel, New York, breaking up a bizarre initiation. Three semi-nude pledges — coated with a mixture of beer, honey, molasses, and eggs — were forced to sit in an open convertible in forty-degree weather. Sixteen members were cited for harassment, a misdemeanor.

University of Nevada
Reno, Nevada
Alpha Tau Omega

An ATO suffered brain damage when he fell from the roof of his house during a drinking party.

University of Rhode Island
Kingston, Rhode Island
Fraternity hazing

A woman wrote the student paper to complain that a coatless young man had been dumped near her home at two-thirty A.M. in midwinter. The Interfraternity Council determined the incident was not a hazing because pledges had kidnapped a brother, not vice versa.

St. John's University
Jamaica, New York
Pershing Rifles

Pledge Thomas Fitzgerald, twenty, was fatally stabbed in the chest with a non-regulation hunting knife during Hell Night in mid-November. The National Honorary Society of Pershing Rifles subsequently was banned from campus. However, the school maintained that the accident was merely a "training exercise" that had gone wrong.

University of Texas
Austin, Texas
Texas Cowboys

A Cowboy initiate was brained with wooden boards, causing him to be placed in a hospital's intensive care ward. In the fall, the campus newspaper published pictures of an alleged initiation ceremony in which members brandished cattle prods.

Texas Tech University
Lubbock, Texas
Pi Kappa Alpha

Member Samuel Mark Click was killed by a train in a freak accident during a scavenger hunt in which both actives and pledges had been participating.

Tulane University
New Orleans, Louisiana
Delta Kappa Epsilon

The fraternity was put on campus probation after a pledge was struck by members.

United States Military Academy
West Point, New York
Cadet hazing

Senator Adlai Stevenson III demanded an investigation into the hazing of cadet Stephen R. Verr.

1977
Bradley University
Peoria, Illinois
Alpha Phi Alpha

A pledge claimed he had been beaten with fists and paddles. He was treated for acute kidney failure. Twelve members pled guilty to hazing charges.

University of Missouri
Rolla, Missouri
Kappa Alpha, Daughters of Lee

Randall L. Crustals, twenty-one, died when a cannon exploded. The firing of the cannon was traditionally used in Kappa Alpha's little sister (Daughters of Lee) initiation. Susan E. Diehl suffered cuts and a broken ankle.

North Carolina Central University
Durham, North Carolina
Omega Psi Phi

A pledge dropped dead after calisthenics. The chapter was not officially recognized by the national.

University of Pennsylvania
Philadelphia, Pennsylvania
Omega Psi Phi

Robert J. Bazile died of a heart attack after overexerting himself in pledge-related exercise sessions. The fraternity wasn't recognized by the school as an official Greek group.

University of Rochester
Rochester, New York
Psi Upsilon

A pledge received Last Rites from a priest at a local hospital emergency room after chugging non-stop a quart of whiskey as part of his initiation into the fraternity. He survived.

University of Texas
Austin, Texas
Kappa Sigma

The fraternity was suspended for six months after a pledge became ill from ingesting a concoction made of raw eggs, limburger cheese, cod liver oil, and jalapeno peppers.

University of Texas
Austin, Texas
Phi Delta Theta

Police stopped a rental truck that was weaving down a highway. Inside the truck were twenty-seven pledges covered with corn flakes, molasses, eggs, and Tabasco sauce. Some had been stunned with a cattle prod.

Tulane University
New Orleans, Louisiana
Delta Kappa Epsilon

A pledge was kicked into a wall while doing pushups. He suffered a reoccurrence of an eye injury he had suffered two weeks previously. He also alleged that blindfolded pledges had to crawl along the Mississippi River. Pledges were forced to sit in a boarded-up room for twelve hours while listening to radio static. The pledges were also forced to bathe in a tub of ice. A goat was brought into a room, and pledges were told they would have sex with the mascot. This proved to be only a threat, intended to scare initiates. On one occasion beer was poured down initiates' throats. After the pledge became a brother, members began to harass him after the youth's parents learned what had caused the injury.

1978
Alfred University
Alfred, New York
Klan Alpine

Chuck Stenzel died in a traditional night of drinking for new pledges. The university has refused to term his death a hazing incident. His death led to the formation of CHUCK, the Committee to Halt Useless College Killings.

University of Arizona
Tucson, Arizona
Sigma Phi Epsilon

Pledges kidnapped a brother and dropped him off in the countryside. He was handcuffed, inebriated, and disoriented, according to a news account.

Case Western Reserve University
Cleveland, Ohio
Zeta Psi

Michael Quaintance, twenty, died when he fell from the roof during a fraternity "Welcome Back" party.

Loras College
Dubuque, Iowa
Gamma Psi

Stephen J. McNamara, a member of this sub-rosa fraternity, drank himself to death.

University of Texas
Austin, Texas
Alpha Kappa Alpha

After a pledge was admitted with bruises to the student health center, an investigation determined that the sorority practiced hazing. Pledges had to "ingest unpleasant food, recite sorority history, and perform physical exercises." It was never determined how the pledge received the bruises.

1979
University of Arizona
Tucson, Arizona
Sigma Phi Epsilon

A Sigma Phi Epsilon brother came close to death after four pledges kidnapped him, pressured him to drink a bottle of tequila, then dumped him on the floor of a convenience store. He wore only a grocery sack, shoes, and balloons. His vital signs took hours to stabilize, and Tucson General Hospital emergency room technicians feared they would lose him. This was the second near-fatality involving this fraternity in two years.

Carroll College
Waukesha, Wisconsin
Delta Rho Upsilon

A pledge was hospitalized when he ruptured his bronchial tube after yelling all night as an initiation requirement. Four other pledges from the same fraternity were hospitalized in a four-year period for physical problems incurred during exercise sessions.

University of Florida
Gainesville, Florida
Omega Psi Phi

Eighteen pledges were violently hazed, resulting in a one-year suspension of the fraternity. "You name it, I got it," pledge Michael Lawrence told reporters. "They had a heyday with us." One pledge spent a night in a psychiatric ward. Other pledges charged they were forced to consume large amounts of marijuana and alcohol.

Harvard University
Cambridge, Massachusetts
Pi Eta

Paul Callahan, twenty-two, a one-time Harvard basketball player, was paralyzed after a wrestling match which occurred following initiation ceremonies between new initiates and actives on a beer-coated linoleum floor. In other activities of this eating club, pledges were required to run naked from their clubhouse to a library, check out a book, and then run across Harvard Square to buy a candy bar.

Louisiana State University
Baton Rouge, Louisiana
Theta Xi

Bruce Wiseman, eighteen, was struck by a car in an accident while walking with five other blindfolded pledges across a highway. Wiseman died. The others suffered broken legs.

University of Missouri
Rolla, Missouri
Delta Sigma Phi

A pledge suffered brain damage after being unmercifully beaten by persons unknown. He charged that his fraternity abandoned him along a rural road without his glasses. The president of the fraternity complained when Delta Sigma Phi was put on social probation, saying members had once helped repair a church. He called the punishment too severe just days after the pledge underwent brain surgery for the removal of a blood clot. "I guess it depends on what definition of hazing you use," the president told a local paper.

State University College of New York
Geneseo, New York
Delta Kappa Tau, Prometheus

Initiation parties sent two pledges to the hospital, one with an alcohol overdose and one with a head injury suffered in a fall. The dean of students ruled that neither case was a hazing.

University of North Dakota
Grand Forks, North Dakota
Sigma Nu

Afraid he would be slapped until given a "pink belly" by fellow fraternity members trying to discipline him, a nineteen-year-old member stabbed and killed a fellow Sigma Nu who had forced his way into the member's room. The student was cleared of the charge of involuntary manslaughter.

Northeast Missouri State University
Kirksville, Missouri
Tau Kappa Epsilon

Pledge Stan Baldwin, a junior, collapsed during TKE's Hell Week after he had been deprived of sleep and food. "Had he not been basically a strong kid, he would have died," said Dean of Students Terry Smith. Another pledge was blinded temporarily when he rubbed his eyes with gasoline while trying to remove tar that brothers had used to cover him and two fellow pledges.

University of Oklahoma
Norman, Oklahoma
Sorority and fraternity hazing

A member of an unidentified sorority revealed inane hazing practices, including the forcing of pledges to eat off a plate on the floor without silverware and counting the urinals in a fraternity house. A fraternity brother revealed such practices as beatings, lineups, abandoning naked pledges in isolated areas, and pouring liquor down a man's throat until he vomited.

Rutgers University
New Brunswick, New Jersey
Delta Phi

Richard C. Fuhs, Jr., died in a car crash after being roused out of sleep to drink excessive alcohol at a dawn session at a Piscataway tavern. Fuhs was a passenger in the car. Officials ruled the drinking session "voluntary" and declined, therefore, to charge the fraternity. "I wasn't too keen about him joining," said Richard Fuhs, Sr. "I heard those places had wild parties and things. But he assured us it wasn't that kind of place." The fraternity immediately issued a statement denying responsibility for Fuhs's death.

Southeast Missouri State University
Cape Girardeau, Missouri
Tau Kappa Epsilon

A former little sister of TKE wrote CHUCK to reveal hazing practices in the fraternity, including the plunging of a brother's head into a toilet and paddling.

University of Tennessee
Knoxville, Tennessee
Alpha Psi

Pledges accused brothers of forcing them to clean an apartment at gunpoint, beating them during a ritual known as "slap boxing," and paddling them.

United States Military Academy
West Point, New York
Cadet hazing

Upperclassmen forced a woman to bite the head off a chicken to cure her squeamishness. Hazing was hardly confined to a single incident. A male cadet was disrobed and bound; shaving cream was sprayed over his genitals. Other hazers, including one black upperclassman, dressed in Ku Klux Klan robes to intimidate their victims.

Virginia Polytechnic Institute and State University
Blacksburg, Virginia
Phi Delta Theta

Paul Hayward died of head injuries in a fall at the fraternity house.

Virginia State College
Petersburg, Virginia
Beta Phi Burgundy and Wine Psi Phi

Two pledges — one from a male social club, the other from a female club — drowned in the Appomattox River during an initiation ceremony. Approximately twenty male and female pledges and members were present. Accounts varied, but one witness charged that pledges were required to swim in the river while fully clothed. "It's sort of like . . . baptism," a student explained. The dead youths were Robert Etheridge, twenty-one, and Norsha Lynn Delk, twenty. Etheridge was wearing combat boots when his body was found during dragging operations. The college president dissolved both groups following the incident.

1980-1989

1980
Albion College
Albion, Michigan
Sigma Chi

A fraternity brother was found guilty of a traffic offense after running over a pledge with a Jeep, injuring the initiate, during a "water-balloon war game." As a result, Albion fraternities also were ordered to stop their tradition of hurling pledges into the Kalamazoo River.

Carroll College
Waukesha, Wisconsin
Delta Rho Upsilon

Two pledges were hospitalized for "extreme exhaustion" following hazing activities.

Fisk University
Nashville, Tennessee
Fraternity initiation

Fifteen fraternity members participating in an initiation rite in public were victims of a lone armed robber. They were forced to strip to their shorts and leave the area.

University of Georgia
Athens, Georgia
Chi Phi

Administrators suspended Chi Phi after hearing accusations of hazing and substance abuse.

Harding University
Searcy, Arkansas
Social club

A pledge of a social club was burned with silver nitrate during a pre-initiation ceremony.

Ithaca College
Ithaca, New York
Delta Kappa

Fraternity brothers forced pledge Joseph Parella, eighteen, and others to perform arduous calisthenics in a steam room. The pledges were bundled in heavy clothing while exercising. Parella died of heat exhaustion and hyperthermia. A grand jury report said Parella "was in a real sense murdered by collective stupidity, collective insensitivity, and collective irresponsibility." The fraternity had been reprimanded the previous spring for its rough hazing practices.

University of Lowell
Lowell, Massachusetts
Delta Kappa Phi

Steve Call, nineteen, died of hyperthermia after participating in grueling calisthenics during a pre-initiation rite. He was hospitalized with a fever of 108 degrees.

University of Michigan
Ann Arbor, Michigan
Athletic hazing

"Our practice is not to tolerate hazing in any form," said athletic director Don Canham, following a "traditional initiation ritual" in which a hockey player was stripped, roughly shorn of pubic hair, locked in a car trunk, and dumped on the dormitory steps. The player's dormitory advisor said the player's complexion was blue. The initiate was drunk, covered with eggshells, flour, and cologne. Four other freshmen were also roughly treated.

Millersville State College
Millersville, Pennsylvania
Fraternity hazing

Police charged one of eight pledges dropped by members along a rural road with public drunkenness.

Mississippi State University
Mississippi State, Mississippi
Pi Kappa Alpha

A twenty-year-old member died of head injuries after jumping from a car to avoid being dunked in a mudhole by pledges who were celebrating his birthday.

University of Missouri
Columbia, Missouri
Phi Kappa Psi

Investigators ruled that "horsing around," not hazing, caused the death of a pledge. A fraternity brother said that Lex Dean Batson died during a football practice in which fraternity brothers and pledges "urinate all over Thomas Jefferson's statue." Batson fell off a bluff when he and his companions scampered upon seeing approaching lights. Batson had been drinking but was legally sober. The activity was not sanctioned by the fraternity's written rules.

University of Missouri
Columbia, Missouri
Sigma Alpha Epsilon

Former SAE pledge Michael Morgan said he suffered mental anguish and damage to his right knee during his three-month pledgeship. Two former SAE pledges confirmed his charges.

Northeast Missouri State University
Kirksville, Missouri
Alpha Kappa Lambda

David Andres, nineteen, died of alcohol poisoning after drinking whiskey and beer at a mixer with a sorority. He voluntarily drank the alcohol, said fraternity spokesmen. His blood alcohol level was 0.43 percent (four times the amount required to be legally drunk).

Ohio Northern University
Ada, Ohio
Delta Sigma Pi

A pledge was hospitalized and spent nine days in an intensive-care ward after performing calisthenics that shot his temperature up to 106 degrees.

University of Richmond
Richmond, Virginia
Fraternity hazing

Fraternities at the University of Richmond claimed hazing had "diminished." Nonetheless, Theta Chi admitted "kidnapping" pledges and taking them on "rides." A Sigma Phi Epsilon member admitted he had been paddled as a pledge. A Pi Kappa Alpha member admitted he'd been pelted with eggs and vinegar, as well as shot with a fire extinguisher, during his pledgeship.

San Diego State University
San Diego, California
Sigma Chi

The fraternity was suspended by both the university and its national for activities such as ordering pledges to vandalize rival Greek houses and wrapping a pledge in toilet paper after filling his pants with peanuts and glue.

University of South Carolina
Columbia, South Carolina
Sigma Nu

L. Barry Ballou, a pledge, died in a fraternity initiation after drinking what proved to be a lethal dose of alcohol, then being forced by brothers to do calisthenics.

Stetson University
DeLand, Florida
Pi Kappa Psi

Several members of the Chi chapter were expelled from the fraternity for shocking pledges with an electrical device. Seven years later the entire chapter was suspended for one year in a similar incident, possibly involving the same electrical device.

Vanderbilt University
Nashville, Tennessee
Kappa Alpha, Phi Delta Theta

When Kappa Alpha kidnapped the Phi Delta Theta mascot, a goat, and engineered at least one other prank, the Phi Delts retaliated by kidnapping KA pledges and making them drink beer until they vomited. The story was broadcast by Tom Brokaw, leading to a claim in the campus paper that the story was blown out of proportion.

Virginia State University
Ettrick, Virginia
Kappa Alpha Psi

The Alpha Psi chapter was suspended for infractions of rules, and its advisor was fired. The group was investigated because hazing charges had been brought against the chapter by a concerned student. VSU officials denied that hazing was a factor in their decision to suspend Alpha Psi.

Washington University
St. Louis, Missouri
Fraternity hazing

A campus official acknowledged that a pledge had been hospitalized for an alcohol overdose as part of a fraternity initiation.

1981
University of California
Los Angeles, California
Beta Theta Pi

Administrators suspended the fraternity after a battered prospective member was found in Palos Verdes where members had abandoned him — a ritual known as "bagging" him.

University of Delaware
Newark, Delaware
Sigma Phi Epsilon

The Sig Ep national kicked the Delaware chapter out of its house after pledges Jeff Furek and Chris Colgan were blindfolded and injured by industrial-strength oven cleaner poured over them by brothers. The blindfold, said Furek, saved him from being blinded. They were also paddled and covered with beer and fire extinguisher foam.

Florida A&M University
Tallahassee, Florida
Band hazing

The beating of a FAMU band member, allegedly for reporting a hazing incident, brought to light long-standing hazing practices. Alleged violations included head shavings and unsanctioned midnight practices.

University of Kansas
Lawrence, Kansas
Alpha Tau Omega

University officials suspended ATO for unspecified hazing violations.

University of Minnesota
Minneapolis, Minnesota
Kappa Sigma

Pledge Joe Pasquale charged that he and another pledge of the Beta Mu chapter were sexually abused by brothers. He said that while nude he was bound to the other pledge, who was also nude, and smeared with petroleum jelly and cake frosting. While he was helpless, said Pasquale, fraternity members painted his toenails, wrote on his body with lipstick, and documented the event with photographs. Kappa Sigma's national organization suspended several officers of the chapter. In March 1982 the University of Minnesota judicial board of the Interfraternity Council suspended the chapter for one year.

University of Nebraska
Lincoln, Nebraska
Kappa Sigma

A pledge belonging to the Alpha Psi chapter said he suffered extensive dental damage when he was struck accidentally in the mouth with a chair while eating a pie off the floor in a required pledging exercise.

University of Nevada
Reno, Nevada
Coffin & Keys

The office of the student newspaper was broken into and several items were stolen, including a file on a secret campus organization called Coffin & Keys. The perpetrators spread animal manure all over the office and damaged certificates of merit earned by the paper.

St. John's University
Jamaica, New York
Delta Sigma Phi

University officials suspended the group for two years for a hazing violation. "We [the university] viewed it as a very serious incident," said the dean of the office of student development.

State University College of New York
Cortland, New York
Beta Phi Epsilon

A pledge vomited blood after a Beta hazing ritual. He swallowed a mixture of "strange" substances, which broke blood vessels in his stomach. A second pledge suffered a skin rash from bathing in ice, Tabasco sauce, and vinegar.

State University of New York
Old Westbury, New York
Omega Psi Phi, Phi Beta Sigma

A district attorney found several examples of sadistic and dangerous hazing during an investigation, including branding with hangers while the victim was involuntarily restrained, forced eating of dogfood and laxatives, as well as sleep deprivation. Some pledges were not allowed to bathe for one month. "There is a possible handful of students involved in the hazing," claimed the school's president.

North Carolina Central University
Durham, North Carolina
Alpha Phi Alpha, Omega Psi Phi

The university temporarily suspended pledging after an Alpha pledge was twice hospitalized because of an "extreme illness." An Omega pledge, identified only as "number eight," was hospitalized with a groin injury. Pledging was allowed to resume even before the initiation was concluded, according to the student newspaper.

University of Oregon
Eugene, Oregon
Kappa Sigma

A pledge was hit by a car after being abandoned in a rural area. He suffered brain damage and a fractured skull.

University of Pittsburgh
Pittsburgh, Pennsylvania
Alpha Phi Alpha

Two students were hospitalized in hazing incidents, one after being paddled.

University of Southern California
Los Angeles, California
Delta Tau Delta

Administrators expelled the fraternity for brutal treatment of initiates.

University of Southern California
Los Angeles, California
Sigma Nu

The fraternity was suspended by the university and its national organization after two pledges were stripped and tied to a signpost in Bakersfield, California. "It is a . . . lower-class neighborhood, and it's got a real high crime rate," said Deputy Sheriff Michael Dentley of the Kern County Sheriff's Department. "It is not a safe place to be tied up to a sign, to walk, or to drive through."

Stanford University
Palo Alto, California
Zeta Psi

The fifty-five-member Zetes were suspended for hazing after two bound, stripped pledges were found face down in muck near the university stables. The day was cold, and adhesive tape was used to tie the pledges. Three months before the pledge incident, the fraternity—Stanford's oldest, founded in 1891—knocked a woman unconscious and threw her into a pool for having an unfriendly attitude, according to the victim.

Syracuse University
Syracuse, New York
Fraternity hazing

Delta Tau Delta president John Stevens, in a commentary for the campus newspaper which urged the adoption of positive pledging programs, revealed Hell Week practices he had observed in rival fraternities, including forced pushups and lineups.

University of Virginia
Charlottesville, Virginia
Theta Delta Chi and other fraternities

Kidnapping pledges at the University of Virginia is called "rolling." Eleven of twenty-two fraternities who responded to a student newspaper poll said they rolled pledges; six additional fraternities refused to participate in the survey. Other practices were forced exercise sessions, forced drinking, and miscellaneous pranks. One Theta Delta Chi pledge admitted he had been rolled three times.

University of Wisconsin
Platteville, Wisconsin
Phi Sigma Epsilon

Double irony existed when Billy Benes mysteriously fell from the roof of Phi Sigma Epsilon. For one thing, the affable chapter president was termed "one of the better leaders in the group" by a chancellor. For another, Benes's major was occupational safety.

University of Wisconsin
Superior, Wisconsin
FEX

Rick Cerra, twenty-one, died while undergoing severe mandatory exercise, wearing heavy clothing. Cerra, a former high-school athlete, could possibly have been saved had he been taken to a hospital instead of to an FEX member's apartment, charged his mother. School officials denied that he had been hazed.

1982
Adrian College
Adrian, Michigan
Alpha Sigma Alpha

A former sorority pledge charged that she had suffered psychological trauma after receiving verbal abuse from members.

Alabama A&M University
Normal, Alabama
Omega Psi Phi

The university banned the fraternity for multiple offenses. Reports said the members abducted a student to throw him over the cliff.

University of Arkansas
Pine Bluff, Arkansas
Fraternity hazing

University officials suspended two fraternities for paddling incidents. One pledge was hospitalized with internal bleeding.

Ball State University
Muncie, Indiana
Delta Tau Delta

The fraternity's "Road to Ruin" rush party resulted in the hospitalization of three visiting students with an alcohol overdose.

University of Georgia
Athens, Georgia
Chi Phi

The university suspended Chi Phi for alleged hazing and drug use.

University of Maine
Orono, Maine
Phi Eta Kappa

Two pledges suffered reactions, both requiring hospitalization, after being forced to eat onions.

Rider College
Lawrenceville, New Jersey
Kappa Alpha Psi

Rider students pledging a nearby Trenton State College fraternity were injured in an unspecified hazing incident. A security director said that injuries to one pledge were "substantial."

University of Southern California
Los Angeles, California
Alpha Delta Pi

The sorority was suspended for two months after a pledge suffered an alcohol overdose during a scavenger hunt. Doctors pumped the young woman's stomach.

Syracuse University
Syracuse, New York
Phi Kappa Psi

The fraternity was found guilty of hazing offenses: depriving pledges of sleep and forcing them to wear garbage bags.

University of Texas
Austin, Texas
Sigma Nu

John Calkins died of a lack of oxygen to the brain caused by an alcohol overdose. He had lapsed into a coma for nine days after chugging a bottle of tequila.

Towson State University
Towson, Maryland
Alpha Omega Lambda

Victor (Ricky) Siegel, twenty, had been deprived of sleep for days when he fell asleep at the wheel of a car that flipped over, killing him. Two other initiates were also injured, one seriously. The fraternity had just entered Hell Week that day. Siegel was dressed as a Playboy bunny when he died.

West Virginia University
Morgantown, West Virginia
Sigma Phi Epsilon

The last of thirty pledges undergoing initiation was severely burned over twenty-three percent of his body in a ceremony the youth's father termed "pagan." Brothers poured alcohol on John Payne's chest and lit it. The fire jumped to a bowl (apparently containing more alcohol) that someone was holding, and that person dropped it on the victim. The burns extended from Payne's chin and earlobes to his navel. He wore a rubberized suit for eighteen months to stave off infections.

Western Maryland College
Westminster, Maryland
Delta Pi Alpha

The fraternity was suspended after a seventeen-year-old pledge was paddled and required hospitalization for an overdose of alcohol.

University of Virginia
Charlottesville, Virginia
Phi Kappa Sigma

A Virginia court held the house liable for $125,000 in damages after a pledge, on the premises, received a serious head injury from being struck by a can of beer.

University of Virginia
Charlottesville, Virginia
Sigma Chi

A U-Haul van carrying dozens of members and rushees to a party at Randolph-Macon College veered onto the wrong side of the road and collided with a VW. One student was killed at the scene, another died later in the hospital, and sixty-three were injured in the wreck. The driver and many of the students had been drinking.

1983

University of California
Berkeley, California
Kappa Delta Rho

University officials suspended the forty-five-member fraternity after sixteen pledges, naked and decked out in greasepaint, charged through a dozen sorority houses on an annual raid. The pledges tore one woman's dress, confronted a young woman who had just stepped out of a shower, and attempted to kiss several other women.

California State University
Chico, California
Tau Gamma Theta

Jeffrey Long, twenty-three, a senior pledge was killed by a car during a fraternity game. Newspaper accounts demonstrated that the members stonewalled the investigation. Parents of the dead youth settled in February 1988 for $115,000.

Carnegie-Mellon University
Pittsburgh, Pennslyvania
Zeta Beta Tau

The chapter was suspended after two freshmen became severely ill after a drinking session. One student came near death after drinking two dozen shots of whiskey in twenty-four minutes. Another drank twenty shots in rapidfire succession. In 1984 the chapter was booted off campus for repeated fighting. "Fraternities are here at the pleasure of the university," said the school's dean of students.

East Carolina University
Greenville, North Carolina
Omega Psi Phi

A judge dismissed hazing charges against three fraternity members, claiming the statute was too vague. A pledge had been knocked unconscious during his initiation and was hospitalized.

Indiana University
Bloomington, Indiana
Theta Chi

Two students signed affidavits charging Theta Chi with hazing. Results of a hearing were not disclosed by university officials.

University of Maryland
College Park, Maryland
Alpha Epsilon Phi

Pledges stole property worth in excess of a thousand dollars during a scavenger hunt required for admittance into the fraternity.

University of Maryland
College Park, Maryland
Omega Psi Phi

According to a pledge, an active member struck him for being too clumsy in doing the "step," a sort of choreographed dance, which is an important part of this fraternity's ritual. The pledge suffered a ruptured eardrum. Other pledges charged that they were swatted with table legs.

University of Missouri
Columbia, Missouri
Sigma Pi

Three pledges and two brothers were charged with stealing a hubcap from a police car and other objects during a mandatory scavenger hunt.

Montana State University
Bozeman, Montana
Sigma Alpha Epsilon

A Sigma Alpha Epsilon member froze a kitten in a block of ice and dropped it in a punch bowl as a party decoration.

University of New Mexico
Albuquerque, New Mexico
Sigma Alpha Epsilon

The campus newspaper called for an investigation after several people were hospitalized for eating contaminated duck eggs during a "dinner." The chemical burns occurred during Hell Week.

University of Oklahoma
Norman, Oklahoma
Phi Delta Theta

Pledge Lyle Payne had a section of his liver surgically removed after being pelted with snowballs during a ritual known as the "Phi Delt Border Crossing."

Oregon State University
Corvallis, Oregon
Alpha Gamma Rho

Police freed a pledge who was tied to an anchor in front of Alpha Gamma Rho. He was clad in his undershorts and told police the stunt was all in fun.

Southeast Missouri State University
Cape Girardeau, Missouri
Sigma Tau Gamma

College administrators suspended Sig Tau members for hazing "pranks" that a spokesman called "one of those dehumanizing activities that you would associate with fraternities of twenty years ago."

University of Southern California
Los Angeles, California
Phi Delta Theta

The house was put on a year's probation after two students suffered acute alcohol poisoning.

Stetson University
DeLand, Florida
Lambda Chi Alpha

Unsavory photographs of associate members being hazed were stolen from Lambda Chi Alpha and distributed widely on campus. Campus security was asked to investigate the burglary. Lambda Chi was found guilty of hazing violations and ordered to contribute $750 to CHUCK.

Syracuse University
Syracuse, New York
Delta Kappa Epsilon

Resident advisor Robert Hildreth charged that a pledge was bruised and exhausted following a hazing session. The Syracuse *Herald* cited sources who claimed the pledges, behind locked doors and blacked-out windows, were made to sing and dance for seven hours while clad only in jockstraps. Pledge Ronald Quill claimed he and four initiates were forced to eat pig fetuses and a turkey head. They also had hot wax poured over them and endured other indignities during the thirty-six-hour ordeal, said Quill.

Tennessee State University
Nashville, Tennessee
Omega Psi Phi

Pledge Vann L. Watts and eight other pledges endured a night of terror in which their bodies were badly beaten with switches and they were forced to consume incredible quantities of alcohol. Watts died sometime after three A.M. His blood alcohol level was 0.52 percent. Watts had switch marks on his body. The fraternity was given a five-year suspension after one pledge admitted he'd been hazed. Seven other pledges stuck to their denials, saying no hazing had occurred.

Texas Christian University
Fort Worth, Texas
Sigma Alpha Epsilon

Angered when its national organization suspended the chapter for hazing, SAE trashed a dormitory, causing damage estimated at two thousand dollars. Despite its bad reputation, SAE was allowed to recolonize by the university.

United States Air Force Academy
Colorado Springs, Colorado
Cadet hazing

Thirteen freshmen cadets were hospitalized and 136 more treated after rigorous Hell Week activities. Most were treated for dehydration.

West Georgia College
Carrolltown, Georgia
Omega Psi Phi

An associate professor of sociology charged that pledges of the fraternity were required to be branded as part of their initiation ceremony. Advisors denied the charges, saying branding was voluntary.

1984
University of Akron
Akron, Ohio
Kappa Kappa Psi

The Associated Student Government Supreme Court heard a petition charging this band fraternity with hazing.

American National College
Springfield, Massachusetts
Zeta Chi

Jay Lenaghan, nineteen, died of alcohol poisoning. His blood alcohol level was 0.48 — almost five times the state's recognized level for legal intoxication. Lenaghan was urged to eat spaghetti and drink massive quantities of wine, then vomit in a trash can and repeat the process. Lenaghan passed out and was carried to the bathtub and sprayed with cold water. Later, around midnight, a fraternity member realized that Lenaghan wasn't breathing and called an ambulance. But it was too late. Other ZX pledge activities included paddling, spraying pledges with water in mid-winter, branding the fraternity symbol on their buttocks, and giving electrical shocks. "It was a macho fraternity," said the district attorney. "Their claim to fame on campus was that they had the toughest initiation. . . . It does strain the imagination that someone on campus did not know this was going on." American eventually banned fraternities and sororities.

Arizona State University
Tempe, Arizona
Fraternity hazing

The campus paper, the *Daily Wildcat,* published photographs of pledges trying to climb atop a wall smeared with peanut butter. Campus officials ruled the event was not hazing. Active brothers attacked the student photographer.

Ball State University
Muncie, Indiana
Beta Theta Pi

The university and national organization suspended the social fraternity's charter for undisclosed hazing violations.

Ball State University
Muncie, Indiana
Kappa Alpha Psi

School officials suspended the fraternity chapter for three years after determining that brothers violently hazed pledges and forced them to consume alcohol.

Florida Southern College
Lakeland, Florida
Fraternity hazing

Some campus fraternities haze by throwing pledges into Lake Hollingsworth, said Dean of Students Hugh Moran, Jr.

Hampden-Sydney College
Hampden-Sydney, Virginia
Theta Chi

After alcohol was believed to have contributed to the death of a Theta Chi fraternity member (although he was not legally intoxicated), Hampden-Sydney students signed a pledge not to drive under the influence of intoxicants.

Indiana University
Bloomington, Indiana
Sigma Chi

Ironically, pledge activities saved lives during a four A.M. house fire at IU. The Sigma Chi pledges were headed for "an early breakfast" when they spotted flames coming from the Zeta Beta Tau fraternity house. They roused the occupants, saving thirty lives. One man died in the fire, which was set by an arsonist.

Lamar University
Beaumont, Texas
Little sister hazing

A fraternity advisor investigated two complaints made by little sisters against the fraternities with whom they were associated. A girl reinjured a hernia as she got a brother a beverage within a one-minute time limit. A second woman complained that members ostracized her.

Louisiana State University
Baton Rouge, Louisiana
Delta Kappa Epsilon

The university banned the chapter after pledges damaged a dormitory room, causing more than one thousand dollars in damages.

University of Maryland
College Park, Maryland
Alpha Epsilon Pi

A campus judicial board recommended that the fraternity be suspended for four years if members did not demonstrate an earnest attempt to eliminate hazing. Pledges had stolen property worth more than a thousand dollars during a scavenger hunt.

University of Maryland
College Park, Maryland
Gate and Key

This honorary fraternal society pressured a prospective member to swallow a pitcher of beer in a single gulp, causing him to vomit and tear his esophagus.

San Diego State University
San Diego, California
Fraternity hazing

A university official told the Los Angeles *Times* that four fraternities in the past five years had been disciplined for hazing. "Everybody does it," one fraternity member told the reporter. Said another, "I did it; it's no big deal." Tau Kappa Epsilon was charged with mentally abusing pledges.

University of Southern California
Los Angeles, California
Phi Kappa Tau

The chapter's charter was suspended for two months because of hazing violations.

University of Texas
Austin, Texas
Phi Kappa Psi

Several members of Phi Kappa Psi were handcuffed and bound with tape, according to a police incident report produced by the university student newspaper. The incident happened poolside at a local apartment complex, and the complainant was the manager, who feared the handcuffed men were about to be thrown into the freezing water. Austin police officer Edmund Garza found five men handcuffed, and six active members laughing at them. Because the bound brothers refused to press charges, Garza did not file any. Two years later Phi Kappa Psi pledge Mark Thomas Seeberger was handcuffed and died following an alcohol overdose.

University of Texas
Austin, Texas
Sigma Alpha Epsilon

A pledge was injured while performing calisthenics at two luncheons attended by more than 140 fraternity brothers. The victim suffered "muscle tissue breakdown." The charter was suspended, but the group was allowed to reorganize.

Texas A&M University
College Station, Texas
Corps of Cadets

Freshman Bruce Goodrich, from upstate New York, perished as a result of being forced to perform extensive calisthenics until he dropped. "If something positive doesn't come of this, we're damned fools," said the commandant of the corps. Three students pleaded guilty to hazing charges. Another student was found guilty of destroying evidence in the case.

Tulane University
New Orleans, Louisiana
Delta Kappa Epsilon

Tulane officials kicked the Delta Kappa Epsilon fraternity off campus after a series of serious offenses, including a hazing incident in which pledges had cords attached to their genitals, which, in turn, were tied to bricks. Although the pledges didn't know it, the bricks were attached by a slipknot that kept the victims from being hurt.

1985
Arizona State University
Tempe, Arizona
Sigma Alpha Epsilon

A pledge claimed one of his eyes was permanently damaged as a result of rough hazing practices. He said he was kicked in the eye while doing pushups. He also alleges that members threatened him with bodily harm, placed human feces and dead rodents in his room, and gave him the "silent treatment."

California University of Pennsylvania
California, Pennsylvania
Kappa Alpha Psi

A pledge charged that he had been beaten repeatedly by members, including his roommate.

University of Colorado
Boulder, Colorado
Kappa Alpha Theta

Pledge Sherri Ann Clark accidentally fell to her death after drinking heavily at a party sponsored by two sororities. Her blood alcohol level was 0.298, almost three times the amount needed to be legally intoxicated.

Illinois Institute of Technology
Chicago, Illinois
Alpha Sigma Phi

A student placed in a coffin as part of an initiation ritual suffered second- and third-degree burns when a mixture of alcohol and salt ignited. Pledge Martin Badrov, nineteen, was lying in a darkened room, said reporter Wes Smith. The coffin had a glass window so that the remaining pledges could see Badrov. Fraternity members insisted the ceremony wasn't hazing.

University of Kansas
Lawrence, Kansas
Alpha Phi

Jeanna M. Carkoski was killed in a fall from the third floor of the sorority house.

University of Kansas
Lawrence, Kansas
Sigma Alpha Epsilon

University officials suspended SAE for two years for unspecified hazing violations.

Michigan State University
East Lansing, Michigan
Kappa Alpha Psi

Michigan State suspended the KAP chapter after two students suffered severely burned feet in a hazing incident at Lansing's Potter Park.

University of Mississippi
Oxford, Mississippi
Delta Kappa Epsilon

Administrators at Ole Miss suspended the chapter after a pledge was hospitalized after an initiation rite.

University of Missouri
Columbia, Missouri
Fraternity hazing

Two student reporters interviewed men who had quit pledging to ask them to reveal illegal hazing practices. The former pledges talked about demeaning lineups, sleep deprivation, forced dropping of trousers while a brother shined a light on a pledge's bare buttocks, and verbal abuse. The fraternities involved included Beta Theta Pi, Phi Gamma Delta, Sigma Nu, and Beta Sigma Psi.

University of Missouri
Columbia, Missouri
Lambda Chi Alpha

A fraternity brother driving a rushee from a rush party crashed into a concrete drain, killing his passenger. Liquor was served at the party, according to an Alpha Tau Omega newsletter describing the event.

Oklahoma State University
Stillwater, Oklahoma
Fraternity hazing

Oklahoma State officials toughened campus hazing statutes after pledges, clad only in underwear, were dumped in downtown Stillwater.

Princeton University
Princeton, New Jersey
Eating club hazing

Eighteen initiates were treated for alcohol overdoses at a Princeton health center.

Southern Methodist University
Dallas, Texas
Alpha Tau Omega

ATO's national revoked the SMU chapter's charter for hazing and other infractions. Two members who had given women fraternity pins were tied to a lamppost and basted in raw eggs and cooking oil. Three pledges also suffered alcohol overdoses.

Southern Methodist University
Dallas, Texas
Lambda Chi Alpha

An associate member suffered a broken ankle and torn ligaments while attempting to resist brothers' attempts to dunk his head repeatedly in a toilet, an action frequently called "swirlies" by fraternities.

Stetson University
DeLand, Florida
Sigma Nu

DeLand police received six citizen complaints charging that items recently stolen from them turned up at a Sigma Nu scavenger hunt sale. The school put the fraternity on social probation for one month.

University of Texas
Austin, Texas
Kappa Kappa Psi

Initiates entering this honorary band society received dry ice burns during mental hazing in which members told them they were about to be branded.

Texas A&M University
College Station, Texas
Cadet hazing

A member of the Corps of Cadets was suspended after violating a university rule prohibiting hazing.

Texas Tech University
Lubbock, Texas
Sigma Alpha Epsilon

The son of Congressman Charles Stenholm collapsed while performing calisthenics and was hospitalized. A university administrator said there had been about fifteen hazing incidents the previous school year.

Tulane University
New Orleans, Louisiana
Sigma Nu

A pledge lost his arm after falling in front of his drunken big brother's car and then being dragged through city streets. No charges of hazing were made.

Washington and Lee University
Lexington, Virginia
Fraternity hazing

Interfraternity Council President David Perdue said that "dumping" pledges in the countryside is "a kind of joke and everybody goes along with it" at Washington and Lee. He defended the practice "as long as somebody keeps an eye on what's going on." He said "dangerous hazing" is nonexistent on his campus.

Washington and Lee University
Lexington, Virginia
Fraternity hazing

Scott Stockburger, a columnist for the school paper, the *Ring-tum Phi,* wrote that "hazing is a serious problem at W&L." He quoted dormitory counselor Bob Tomaso, who said, "Every fraternity hazes to a certain extent." He cited unlawful scavenger hunts that required pledges to steal public and private property, including McDonald's flags and highway signs listing the mileage to women's colleges.

1986
Bowling Green State University
Bowling Green, Ohio
Phi Kappa Psi

Scott Davis, a twenty-two-year-old senior from Portage, Indiana, drowned accidentally when he fell into the icy Portage River after leaving a formal fraternity party.

The Citadel
Charleston, South Carolina
Cadet hazing

Black cadet Kevin Nesmith resigned after upperclassmen dressed in hoods and sheets harassed him and left behind a charred cross. "The harassing and terrorizing to force a kid to leave The Citadel happens every year. I know," said Pat Conroy, author of *The Lords of Discipline,* a novel about the hazing of a black plebe at a fictional military school. Conroy is a Citadel alumnus. "The kids who did the hazing made a mistake only in symbolism. If they had done it without sheets, they would have been seen as only doing their duty."

Dartmouth College
Hanover, New Hampshire
Beta Theta Pi

University officials suspended the fraternity for numerous violations, including hazing.

Florida Southern University
Lakeland, Florida
Phi Sigma Kappa

A campus dean observed five pledges jogging around Lake Hollingsworth with ten-pound weights and threw the fraternity off campus. The pledges insisted that they were merely trying to get ready for basketball season. The incident occurred at five A.M. Previously, the pledges had been seen toting a ninety-pound tombstone around the lake.

University of Georgia
Athens, Georgia
Alpha Tau Omega

Georgia's Alpha Beta chapter went on probation for a hazing incident. Less than one week later, the fraternity committed a second hazing violation.

Gustavus Adolphus University
St. Peter, Minnesota
Alpha Phi Rho

A sorority pledge suffered an injured jaw during an "air raid" drill in which pledges had to dive repeatedly to the floor.

Gustavus Adolphus University
St. Peter, Minnesota
Omega Kappa

An OK pledge suffered a broken arm while resisting brothers who wished to force him into a car.

Gustavus Adolphus University
St. Peter, Minnesota
Phi Alpha

Ten Phi Alpha students were burned with silver nitrate (a chemical substance commonly used in silverplating) when brothers tried to impose the fraternity's symbols on their backs. The pledges also had to perform daily calisthenics at six A.M., refrain from speaking to women, and perform menial tasks such as washing members' laundry.

Hope College
Holland, Michigan
Dormitory hazing

A student sued Hope College, claiming it failed to protect him against harassment. A school spokesman expressed displeasure, not denying the harassment, but saying that appropriate disciplinary measures had already been taken.

Indiana University
Bloomington, Indiana
Alpha Sigma Phi

Two pledges suffered from an alcohol overdose and one lay near death with a 0.46 blood alcohol reading after they "voluntarily" imbibed during a scavenger hunt.

Long Island University (C. W. Post Campus)
Brookville, New York
Phi Beta Sigma

Five pledges who had complained about paddle beatings to university officials changed their stories and said they had not been beaten.

Manhattan College
Bronx, New York
Beta Sigma

On one of the coldest nights of the winter, pledge Michael Flynn, nineteen, was abandoned naked on an isolated country road in Putnam County, New York. During the drive by automobile to the drop-off point, fraternity brothers poured beer on his feet, ignoring two pleas from Flynn that his feet were freezing. The wind-chill factor outside the car was thirty-five degrees below zero. Flynn's feet were seriously frostbitten. He was hospitalized for two weeks and suffered permanent health problems. A judge acquitted four defendants, saying he could not determine that the brothers had knowingly subjected Flynn to frostbite.

University of Maryland
College Park, Maryland
Tau Kappa Epsilon

A pledge was hospitalized after members forced him to consume large quantities of alcohol at the campus golf course. TKE expelled the hazers. One pledge's body temperature dropped to ninety-four degrees during the drinking bout.

State University of New York
Old Westbury, New York
Kappa Alpha Psi

Two pledges were rendered unconscious after a "slamming" — a ritual in which they were hung upside down, beaten, and dropped on their heads. Two members were expelled, two suspended, and one reprimanded.

North Carolina A&T State University
Greensboro, North Carolina
Omega Psi Phi

Eight Omega Psi Phi pledges were beaten in a hazing incident, including seven who were hit in the head with a two-by-four. One student was hospitalized with a blood clot to the brain. Fraternity member Steven Jones was sentenced to jail on hazing and miscellaneous charges.

North Texas State University
Denton, Texas
Sigma Phi Epsilon

A pledge collapsed and was rushed to the hospital by ambulance. The fraternity denied that it had been hazing him.

University of Oklahoma
Norman, Oklahoma
Sigma Alpha Epsilon

A pledge was admitted to the university health center after being punched in the stomach by a member after answering a question wrong during a quiz session on fraternity facts. A newspaper report said the pledge suffered a broken rib.

Princeton University
Princeton, New Jersey
Eating club hazing

Twenty-one male and female students were treated for intoxication following a night of initiations. All were assisted into the health center.

St. John's University
Jamaica, New York
Pi Lambda Phi, Lambda Epsilon Chi

Pi Lambda Phi members used tape to tie a pledge to a chair in a hazing incident. The pledge was unhurt. Brothers of Lambda Epsilon Chi were observed in an act of hazing by the school's president as they wrestled pledges to the ground. Both chapters were suspended by the school.

College of St. Thomas
St. Paul, Minnesota
Alpha Kappa Psi

Alpha Kappa Psi conducted strenuous exercise programs for pledges, made them eat dogfood and onions, and get drunk on Wopatooee, a mixed drink composed of vodka, rum, club soda, and fruit.

San Diego State University
San Diego, California
Pi Kappa Alpha

The university expelled the fraternity for multiple violations, including hazing, alcohol violations, and obscene behavior.

University of South Carolina
Columbia, South Carolina
Omega Psi Phi

A student said that he had been slapped and punched as part of the initiation into Omega Psi Phi.

University of Southern California
Los Angeles, California
Delta Pi

A school panel found the sorority guilty of hazing after a student had to have her stomach pumped because of alcohol poisoning.

Stetson University
DeLand, Florida
Delta Sigma Phi

The Alpha Chi chapter went on social probation for hazing activities, including a scavenger hunt and a road trip to the University of Florida in Gainesville, where pledges were forced to find a way back home.

Syracuse University
Syracuse, New York
Zeta Beta Tau

Pledges were sprayed with oven degreaser, beer, and food. Five required hospitalization.

University of Texas
Austin, Texas
Alpha Tau Omega

The university suspended the Gamma Eta chapter for hazing abuses. Pledges were deprived of sleep, confined in isolation, and pelted with raw eggs, resulting in the hospitalization of two young men. Approximately half of the pledges sought medical treatment. Former pledge Lee Roever eventually settled with ATO for a large but undisclosed amount of money. He had sued after injuring his hand in a hazing incident that caused him to incur a fever of 106 degrees. The ATO High Council shut down the Gamma Eta chapter entirely for hazing. "ATO is committed to the elimination of all hazing," said a spokesman.

University of Texas
Austin, Texas
Phi Kappa Psi

After being asked to drink by fraternity brothers, pledge Mark Seeberger consumed sixteen to twenty ounces of rum in two hours or less while on a "ride" for the purpose of dumping him in the countryside. He died of alcohol poisoning. Fellow pledges signed sworn statements that Seeburger had been handcuffed while drinking the alcohol. Fraternity brothers pleaded their Fifth Amendment rights, refusing to cooperate with a grand jury's investigation. The death was not ruled a hazing.

University of Washington
Seattle, Washington
Alpha Delta Phi

Thomas John White, Jr., died after falling three floors out a window. He had been drinking at a party that he organized.

University of Washington
Seattle, Washington
Sigma Alpha Epsilon

A student sued the fraternity after he fell from a fire escape. He suffered a broken thigh.

University of Wyoming
Laramie, Wyoming
Sigma Alpha Epsilon

A member and a non-member suffered first- and second-degree burns after both fell while racing over hot coals at an annual celebration called Bushman's week.

Xavier University
New Orleans, Louisiana
Fraternity hazing

Kirk White charged that he had to drop out of college temporarily after receiving "kidney slaps," punches to the back that caused him to urinate blood.

1987
American University
Washington, DC
Alpha Epsilon Pi

School authorities suspended the fraternity for a hazing violation.

Arizona State University
Tempe, Arizona
Phi Delta Theta

A photographer for the Tempe *Daily News Tribune* was assaulted by Phi Delta brothers after taking a photograph of a pledge bound with tape and hanging from a chaise lounge. The Greek Relations Board put the fraternity on probation but refused to label the incident as hazing. Phi Delta Theta was "not found guilty of hazing because hazing is such a fine line, and everyone has their own definition of hazing," Greek Relations Board president Alex Duhamel told a *State Press* reporter.

Arizona State University
Tempe, Arizona
Phi Gamma Delta

"Hell Week Journals" kept by the fraternity said that pledges had their group pictures taken while they were covered with human waste. Jewish pledges allegedly had to chant "six million," a reference to the number of Jews killed during World War II. Then they had to say, "And I should have been one of them, sir." The fraternity received a two-year suspension.

University of Arkansas
Fayetteville, Arkansas
Pi Kappa Alpha

The parents of Todd Prince, a rushee killed by a car while involved in a hayride sponsored by the fraternity, lost their suit against the fraternity because Arkansas law at the time of the death said that one who furnishes alcohol to a minor or to someone inebriated is not liable.

Evangel College
Springfield, Massachusetts
Athletic hazing

A school disciplinary committee suspended four starters, including the team's quarterback, for shaving the legs of another player.

University of Georgia
Athens, Georgia
Lambda Chi Alpha

Lambda Chi Alpha was suspended for alcohol violations and alleged disorderly conduct. University policy prevented the exact incidents from being published.

Gettysburg College
Gettyburg, Pennsylvania
Tau Kappa Epsilon

University officials found freshmen unconscious in the grass after TKE brothers set up fifteen bars in the house. Angry faculty members began a movement to eliminate fraternities on campus that nearly succeeded.

University of Illinois
Champaign-Urbana, Illinois
Beta Theta Pi

A pledge sued the Sigma Rho chapter for neurological damage and partial disability he said were caused when members made him drink a "near fatal" amount of alcohol during an initiation.

Iowa State University
Ames, Iowa
Pi Kappa Alpha

At an initiation dinner where alcohol was served, big brothers each gave their little brothers a bottle of booze. One pledge drank his gift in an hour, began bleeding from the mouth and nose, and was rescued by emergency paramedics. The youth's blood alcohol content was 0.44.

Kansas State University
Manhattan, Kansas
Phi Delta Theta

Sophomore Jeffrey Nolting, twenty-one, fell from the roof and died of massive head injuries. Students were engaging in an annual ritual that involved flinging stereos, televisions, and other equipment off the roof of the fraternity house.

University of Lowell
Lowell, Massachusetts
Pi Lambda Phi

Pledge William Burns was hospitalized in a temporary coma with a temperature of 109 degrees after being buried to the top of his head in a sleeping bag inside a hot attic. To add to his discomfort, brothers turned a heater on.

Memphis State University
Memphis, Tennessee
Sigma Chi

Fraternity members and campus police
clashed after twenty-five to thirty pledges
streaked the neighborhood near their
fraternity houses. A security guard said the
pledges were nude. The fraternity
maintained the men wore "skin-colored boxer
shorts."

Michigan State University
East Lansing, Michigan
Band hazing

Cynthia Maggard, a member of the school's
marching band, alleged she had been hazed.
The student, of Navajo descent, said that two
band members forcibly shaved the hair off
her neck and shoulders despite her protests.
After informing the MSU band director of
the incident, she quit the band.

University of Mississippi
Oxford, Mississippi
Kappa Alpha

Harry (Skip) Cline, Jr., eighteen, died of
injuries after a fall during a drinking session.
University officials ruled that the death was
"accidental" and not "hazing," even though
fraternity brothers had encouraged drinking
to intoxication. "Pressure to drink an
excessive amount in a short period of time
was implicit in the exercise," said officials.

Monmouth College
West Long Branch, New Jersey
Alpha Sigma Tau

Six women accused the sorority of hazing
violations, including forced drinking,
kidnapping, and mental and physical abuse.

Morehouse College
Atlanta, Georgia
Phi Beta Sigma

In 1989 a blackballed pledge of Phi Beta
Sigma sued members for damages, alleging
that he had suffered a concussion while being
struck in the head "with unknown objects"
while trying "to crawl on hands and knees up
a hill against the force of the fraternity
members."

University of Oklahoma
Norman, Oklahoma
Beta Theta Pi

The school suspended the fraternity's charter
for hazing. Both mental and physical
violations were committed, administrators
charged.

University of Oklahoma
Norman, Oklahoma
Sigma Alpha Epsilon

The chapter was put on probation following
charges of hazing its pledges.

Oklahoma State University
Stillwater, Oklahoma
FarmHouse

A local newspaper reported that FarmHouse
had been placed on probation by OSU
officials after a pledge fainted in a lineup
and was taken to a hospital. "FarmHouse did
build brotherhood and unity, but they did it
through terror and humiliation," charged one
pledge in the OSU student newspaper.

Pennsylvania State University
State College, Pennsylvania
Delta Sigma Pi

Paul J. Walsh was intoxicated when he fell to
his death from the fraternity house's roof.

Radford University
Radford, Virginia
Fraternity hazing

A chapter was put on inactive status after an
intoxicated student was injured while
members had taken him on a ride.

Seton Hall University
South Orange, New Jersey
Omega Psi Phi

An outsider was bitten when he tried
touching the collar of a pledge who was
walking on his leash for Omega Psi Phi.

University of South Carolina
Columbia, South Carolina
Sigma Nu

Already on probation for the death of pledge
Barry Ballou, Sigma Nu pledges were
detained for defacing Interstate 26 with
white paint. One brother was arrested in the
incident (for scratching the fraternity's
initials into the paint of a patrol car whose
officer was investigating the situation) and
another was ticketed.

Stanford University
Palo Alto, California
Zeta Psi

David Dunshee, twenty, died of drowning at
a fraternity rush party held on Lake
Lagunita.

Stephen F. Austin State University
Nacogdoches, Texas
Sorority hazing

School officials investigated a sorority after underage new members allegedly participated in a scavenger hunt that required them to drink.

Stetson University
DeLand, Florida
Pi Kappa Phi

The Chi chapter was banned for one year by its national for hazing activities, including shocking pledges with an electrical device.

Texas A&M University
College Station, Texas
Corps of Cadets hazing

The Dallas *Morning News* reported that three hazing incidents had occurred in 1987.

University of Virginia
Charlottesville, Virginia
Delta Sigma Phi

Pledges were arrested while stealing items for a fraternity-mandated scavenger hunt.

1988
Carnegie Mellon University
Pittsburgh, Pennsylvania
Delta Tau Delta

Stella Goldberg sued Delta Tau Delta and Carnegie Mellon University. She claimed that the two failed to regulate the use of alcohol and marijuana at a party that preceded the stabbing of her daughter, Jeanne.

College of Charleston
Charleston, South Carolina
Pi Kappa Phi

An associate member, the fraternity's alternative to a pledge, had his stomach pumped after drinking two pints of gin at a fraternity party. Glen Dickson, the national Pi Kappa Phi spokesman, blamed the associate member for what occurred. The youth's mother disagreed, arguing that the associate members had been told not to come to the party without alcohol.

University of Florida
Gainesville, Florida
Sigma Alpha Epsilon

A visitor to the house, twenty-one-year-old Jason Todd Miller, died when he fell from a balcony.

Frostburg State University
Frostburg, Maryland
Tau Kappa Epsilon

After pledge Tim Speicher was mentally hazed and required hospitalization, Frostburg State began an investigation of TEKE that led to the group's dissolution. He alleged that he crushed a gerbil to death to fulfill a pledge obligation. Sixteen students continued to operate in defiance of the school order. One was suspended, and others were put on probation.

Hope College
Holland, Michigan
Arcadian fraternity

The fraternity was placed on indefinite suspension after being found guilty of pledging violations. Pledges were required to wear blue jock straps while warm water was squirted on them to "make them feel they were being urinated on," said Brian Breen, editor of the Hope *Anchor,* the newspaper that first printed the allegations.

University of Houston
Houston, Texas
Alpha Phi Alpha

A member, Anthony Lee Cole, was fined five hundred dollars for hazing a blindfolded pledge by striking him in the chest.

Iowa State University
Ames, Iowa
Delta Upsilon

A fraternity pledge was so humiliated by what he underwent in a hazing that he dropped out of school. School officials barred the Ames chapter from university activities the remainder of the school year. They declined to name either the pledge or what had been done to him.

Johns Hopkins University
Baltimore, Maryland
Fraternity hazing

An unnamed fraternity was put on probation for hazing.

Kennesaw State College
Marietta, Georgia
Sigma Pi Alpha

The Student Activities Council (SAC) suspended Sigma Pi Alpha for eight years after finding the organization guilty of physical and mental hazing, as well as abusive and illegal use of alcohol. Charges against the fraternity were brought by its cofounder, Jason Rutter.

Kent State University
Kent, Ohio
Athletic hazing

The Kent State hockey program was suspended for one year following an off-campus hazing incident.

University of Lowell
Lowell, Massachusetts
Fraternity hazing

William Burns nearly died after active members placed a sleeping bag over his head and lined up electrical heaters along his body. A fraternity brother died in a 1980 incident at Lowell. As a result, the school disbanded all Greek-letter organizations in July.

University of Maine
Orono, Maine
Alpha Chi Omega

University officials refused to recognize the sorority after an incident in which sisters used a metal stamp to brand sixteen initiates with the letters of the organization.

Miami University
Oxford, Ohio
Delta Zeta

School officials suspended the sorority after three pledges were forced to drink. One was hospitalized.

Michigan Technological University
Houghton, Michigan
Beta Sigma Theta

The Alpha chapter was suspended for hazing after a pledge was hospitalized for an alcohol overdose.

Monmouth College
West Long Branch, New Jersey
Tau Kappa Epsilon

Brothers ordered pledges to consume portions of goldfish and catfood while screaming that they wanted to join the fraternity. One person was hospitalized when a cyst on his esophagus burst during the hazing.

State University of New York
Albany, New York
Tau Kappa Epsilon

During a pledging exercise, twenty-year-old pledge Bryan Higgins was electrocuted when he entered a lake that had electrical current. In addition to the death, four pledges required hospitalization.

State University College of New York
Oneonta, New York
Phi Kappa Sigma

Pledges allegedly endured hazing during a party thrown by fraternity brothers. Public safety officers had to assist pledges who were too intoxicated to function normally.

Norfolk State University
Norfolk, Virginia
Omega Psi Phi

During one of several so-called "inspiration" sessions, pledge Christopher Peace suffered a broken jaw. He charged that he and other pledges had been slapped, punched, and beaten with paddles.

University of Pennsylvania
Philadelphia, Pennsylvania
Zeta Beta Tau

The all-white fraternity hired two black strippers and, at one point, asked them to dance with a prospective pledge. The women performed suggestive dances while the fraternity shouted racial epithets at them.

University of Rhode Island
South Kingston, Rhode Island
Psi Kappa Phi

For making pledges sit naked on blocks of ice, guzzle beer through funnels, and endure an egg-throwing session, the fraternity was suspended by the university until 1990.

University of Richmond
Richmond, Virginia
Pi Kappa Alpha

Lack of sleep during pledging contributed to the death of Matthew S. McCoy, eighteen, who apparently fell asleep at the wheel on Interstate 64 and died in a crash. He and other pledges had voluntarily stayed up to discuss pledging matters after a party. During the night McCoy and pledge Chip Cummings went to a Charlottesville train station to pick up a fellow pledge, but they never arrived. Cummings was injured in the accident that killed McCoy. Leonard Goldberg, vice president of student affairs, said he would have "nailed" the brothers had they been responsible for the pledges' lack of sleep, but his investigation ruled out that possibility. He said the pledges themselves had enjoyed their overnight outing, which did not involve alcohol or drugs.

Rider College
Lawrenceville, New Jersey
Theta Chi

A group of pledges, rushing to buy booze for a traditional party in which they kidnapped the pledgemaster, crashed into a parked truck. The impact killed one pledge, nineteen-year-old Sean Hickey of Hazlet, New Jersey. Police arrested the driver, John Delesandro III, whose blood alcohol level was more than twice the legal limit. He was driving at a speed of up to seventy miles per hour in a twenty-five-mile-per-hour zone when the fatality occurred. The college denied that it or the fraternity could be held responsible. Delassandro was sentenced to a maximum of 364 days in the county jail.

Rutgers University
New Brunswick, New Jersey
Lambda Chi Alpha

Brothers ordered associate members to "drink 'til you're sick" during a hazing session, killing eighteen-year-old James C. Callahan. Pledges wore bags to catch falling vomit, admitted Callahan's fellow associate member John Deliso. Brothers had set up more than two hundred kamikazes, mixed drinks containing vodka, triple sec, and lime juice. Only one year earlier CHUCK president Eileen Stevens had met with the group at their invitation to discuss hazing hazards. University officials revealed that they had disciplined eight fraternities for hazing violations from 1985 to 1987.

University of Texas
Austin, Texas
Delta Tau Delta

Pledges chased member Scott Phillips, twenty-one, telling him they planned to throw him into a pool. He fell from a 125-foot cliff, breaking his neck. A sheriff's department spokesman said he didn't consider the incident a hazing.

United States Military Academy
West Point, New York
Military hazing

A twenty-four-year-old second-classman (junior) was drummed out of West Point after he twice had failed Military Development, a class in which his leadership had been scrutinized. He claimed that his failure was due to his inability to abide by the plebe system and the inhumanity it suggested to him.

Valparaiso University
Valparaiso, Indiana
Sigma Phi Epsilon

Brother Steven R. Jenny, twenty-three, was stripped and coated with four gallons of a hot mixture that included peanut butter, urine, and feces. This ceremony was performed whenever a member gave a lavaliere to his girlfriend.

1989
Alfred University
Alfred, New York
Sigma Alpha Mu

Members of the fraternity admitted to a reporter that they hazed but said they drew the line at dangerous activities.

Alfred University
Alfred, New York
Zeta Beta Tau

The ZBT national fraternity put the Alfred chapter here into the care of a local alumni group after it found evidence that multiple drug and alcohol violations had been committed.

Arizona State University
Tempe, Arizona
Sigma Alpha Epsilon

A student won a civil suit award of $8,865 for severe headaches he said he incurred as a result of hazing. His report of his hazing included the placing of a dead rat and human waste in his room. He was injured, he said, when he was kicked in the eye.

University of California
Santa Barbara, California
Phi Kappa Psi

According to the *Interfraternity Bulletin,* a brother claimed he had been severely hazed as a pledge and wanted his membership ended for that reason.

The Citadel
Charleston, South Carolina
Questionable death

Dr. John H. Gilligan, Jr., the Alexandria, Virginia, father of a freshman cadet who died when he was in the company of seniors on a school-sponsored diving trip, said that certain aspects of the death have made him question whether hazing might have been involved. The school insisted that it was not, said the physician, but he still has doubts about what occurred in the underground cave where his son passed away. In February 1990 Dr. Gilligan filed a lawsuit, charging the college and the president of scuba diving club with negligence.

Clemson University
Clemson, South Carolina
Alpha Tau Omega

Shannon Ashley Gill, a twenty-year-old coed, fell to her death outside room 307 in the ATO house.

Colgate University
Hamilton, New York
Delta Kappa Epsilon

Archives stolen from the Delta Kappa Epsilon house had passages describing hazing practices, sexual assaults, and illegal drug use.

University of Colorado
Boulder, Colorado
Delta Tau Delta

According to news accounts, a pledge was hospitalized for alcohol poisoning during a required drinking game while his pants were soaked with his own urine. The fraternity refused to leave its house when alumni ordered them to vacate the premises. Those who stayed severely damaged the house by punching holes in the wall, hurling bottles, and other acts of vandalism.

Connecticut State University
New Haven, Connecticut
Phi Alpha Omega

Administrators disbanded the black fraternity for brawling with white students. The incident allegedly occurred while Phi Alpha Omega was hazing its pledges.

Cortland University
Cortland, New York
Pi Lambda Phi

Three fraternity brothers stuffed a handcuffed pledge into a sack and dumped him into the back of a pickup truck while they drove him around town. The three brothers were charged with a second-degree hazing.

Dickinson College
Carlisle, Pennsylvania
Alpha Chi Rho

After consuming eight to ten drinks at an outdoor ceremony in which he was invited to pledge Alpha Chi Rho, freshman Steven Butterworth fell to his death out a bedroom window. The fraternity's alcohol violations may have contributed to the death of the pledge, but the death was ruled accidental.

Fort Valley State College
Fort Valley, Georgia
Kappa Alpha Psi

A twenty-one-year-old pledge was dehydrated and suffered kidney disfunction after members paddled him, drubbed him with canes, and battered him with their fists. "It was like being in hell," the pledge said. Another was hospitalized with a sprained back.

Georgia Southern College
Statesboro, Georgia
Alpha Tau Omega

During a "prank" pulled by members, pledges were frightened by a bull and cows that the initiates had irritated.

Georgia Tech
Atlanta, Georgia
Alpha Tau Omega

Three brothers were bound, blindfolded, and "baptized" during a fraternity intiation reserved for members to celebrate pinnings, lavalierings, and engagements, according to newspaper reports.

University of Illinois
Champaign-Urbana, Illinois
Sigma Alpha Mu

Pledge Jed Seltzer, from Pomona, New York, said that he suffered bruises and a head injury after brothers punched him and slammed his head into a wall during a lineup. They also spat on him, he charged.

Miami University
Oxford, Ohio
Beta Theta Pi

School officials suspended the Oxford chapter for one year after brothers wrote on a pledge's body with indelible markers. The pledge had passed out from drinking too much alcohol.

University of Michigan
Ann Arbor, Michigan
Zeta Beta Tau

Four pledges from Long Island ran naked through the Gamma Phi Beta house on a panty raid. They asked women to autograph their bare buttocks and grabbed underwear from drawers. The four were fined by a judge.

Michigan State University
East Lansing, Michigan
Alpha Tau Omega

The university suspended ATO after an alleged hazing incident in which pledges were required to drink alcohol while trying to guess their big brothers' identity. One pledge said that he suffered facial abrasions and alcohol poisoning.

University of Mississippi
Oxford, Mississippi
Beta Theta Pi

Members of the Beta Beta chapter stripped a pledge and a member, painted racial slurs on their bodies, and dumped them on the campus of predominantly black Rust College.

Morehouse College
Atlanta, Georgia
Alpha Phi Alpha

Joel Harris, eighteen, collapsed and died during a three-hour hazing ritual. The medical examiner said that pledges were struck if they were unable to recite "historical facts."

State University of New York
Stony Brook, New York
Kappa Alpha Psi

A Kappa Alpha Psi pledge filed hazing charges against three fraternity brothers he said beat him and others during pledging. During the beating, the pledge blacked out. University officials suspended the fraternity indefinitely from on-campus activities. The university suspended the hazers for one year. The national fraternity denied responsibility, claiming that this was a renegade group that had not been sanctioned.

University of Oklahoma
Norman, Oklahoma
Kappa Alpha

Citing a regular pattern of hazing against him the previous spring, former pledge Eric Ashlock filed a two-million-dollar lawsuit against the fraternity. Ashlock claimed that he had to undergo an operation for a shoulder that was separated when he was jumped by brothers. The advisor for the OU Interfraternity Council said the incident wasn't hazing, "just horsing around." Later in the year, an entertainment company that ran a haunted house sued Kappa Alpha for damages incurred when the brotherhood of the Beta Eta chapter allegedly were responsible for the partial trashing of the building in which the haunted house was constructed. The brothers were also alleged

to have hit a woman in the head with a mallet, causing her injury, according to a complaint filed in Oklahoma County District Court.

University of Oklahoma
Norman, Oklahoma
Phi Delta Theta

A student suffered a broken neck after diving into a shallow pool, which had been decorated for a fraternity party. The boy and some of the other fraternity members smelled of liquor, said police.

University of Oklahoma
Norman, Oklahoma
Sigma Alpha Epsilon

The chapter was suspended for alleged hazing and physical abuse of pledges.

Pace University
New York, New York
Delta Kappa Epsilon

Pledges who had been dropped off by members were strip-searched and issued disorderly conduct tickets by a police officer.

Pennsylvania State University
State College, Pennsylvania
Delta Theta Sigma

Members hung a fellow Delta Theta Sigma from a tree in freezing six-degree cold. He was clad only in his underwear while brothers pelted him with food and buckets of water and vomit in a traditional ceremony to acknowledge a brother's engagement.

Purdue University
West Lafayette, Indiana
Alpha Phi Alpha

Purdue University officials yanked privileges of the local chapter for a minimum of three years for mentally and physically hazing a pledge the previous fall.

Rider College
Lawrenceville, New Jersey
Zeta Beta Tau, Theta Chi

A police drug bust on Fraternity Row resulted in eleven arrests for possession of three pounds of marijuana, hashish, cocaine, LSD, and psilocybin. Earlier in the decade, the college had closed the Tau Kappa Epsilon house for disruptive behavior and vandalism.

Stetson University
DeLand, Florida
Pi Kappa Alpha

The fraternity was suspended for four years for degrading its pledges, among other charges.

Virginia Polytechnic Institute and State University
Blacksburg, Virginia
Delta Kappa Epsilon

The fraternity was banned for four years after it was determined that pledges were ordered to take pictures of other pledges kissing black women.

1990-

1990
National conference
Jacksonville, Florida
Alpha Tau Omega

A delegate to a national ATO leadership conference tried unsuccessfully to climb a bridge after he had been drinking. He plunged to his death.

East Texas State University
Commerce, Texas
Pi Kappa Alpha

The chapter was suspended in the aftermath of an incident in which four active members were bound in duct tape and abandoned in downtown Commerce.

Florida Southern College
Lakeland, Florida
Phi Sigma Kappa

Although the chapter had been thrown off campus in 1986 for hazing, Phi Sigma Kappa again was caught hazing in a local park. Eight students were suspended for a semester.

Gallaudet University
Washington, DC
Kappa Gamma

An editorial writer for the school paper listed fraternity practices that might be construed as mental hazing.

State University College of New York
Plattsburgh, New York
Sorority hazing

The student newspaper chastised an unspecified sorority pledge class that was photographed in an act of hazing. An editorial said that "More and more, the actions of pledge classes are interfering with the rights of students not affiliated with the Greeks, and subsequently hindering their education."

Northwestern State University
Natchitoches, Louisiana
Kappa Alpha Psi

The university suspended the chapter for two years after a pledge alleged that he had been hazed.

United States Military Academy
West Point, New York
Military hazing

An internal report prepared by academy officials, staff, and cadets said that the Fourth Class System contains undesirable hazing practices. Freshmen are forced to perform menial tasks and subjected to "pinging," an unnatural rapid walking gait.

United States Naval Academy
Annapolis, Maryland
Midshipman hazing

Gwen Marie Dreyer alleged that she was carried into a bathroom and handcuffed to a urinal by upperclassmen. She left the school.

University of Vermont
Burlington, Vermont
Kappa Sigma

Brett Klein died in a fall from the roof of his fraternity house while drunk.

University of Washington
Seattle, Washington
Theta Xi

The campus judicial committee expelled the chapter for abusing animals and breaking hazing rules. During initiation week, police — acting on a complaint — found pledges dressed in their underwear with white grease on their hands and peanut butter on their bodies. The pledges were in the company of two "overheated and agitated" sheep. The university said that it couldn't discipline the students because the incident happened off-campus.

Washington State University
Pullman, Washington
Kappa Sigma

Fourteen pledges pleaded guilty to stealing items valued at seventeen hundred dollars. They received light sentences.

West Texas State University
Canyon, Texas
Phi Delta Theta

A student fraternity board suspended the Phi
Delts for two years after pledge Jason
O'Neill charged that his kidney was bruised
when he was kicked during a pledge lineup.

GLOSSARY

Active member — one who has been initiated

Alumnus — graduated member

Associate member — a program used as an alternative to pledging, in which those selected have many of the rights and responsibilities of full members

Black organizations (national) -- eight fraternities and sororities which agreed in 1990 to end pledging. Fraternities formerly referred to pledges as line brothers.

Chapter — fraternities and sororities have individual chapters which are designated in sequence by a letter of the Greek alphabet. Thus, the first chapter founded would be the Alpha chapter; the second the Beta; and so on.

Chips (or legacies) — sons and daughters of alumni

Fraternity — a Greek-letter society of either men or women

Initiation — the ceremony in which a pledge or associate member becomes a member of a fraternity or sorority

Local — a Greek organization unaffiliated with a national organization

National — fraternity that is a member of the National Interfraternity Conference or sorority that is a member of the National Panhellenic Conference

Pledges — uninitiated males or females who are participating in a series of rites designed to make them aware of the traditions of their particular group

Rush period — series of parties or get-togethers (often called smokers by black fraternities) in which members and potential members check each other out and court one another

Rushees — potential members who have expressed an interest in joining one Greek group or another

Sorority — common name for female fraternities

Sub-rosa club or fraternity — organizations not sanctioned by a school. Often these are strictly drinking clubs.

Tapping Night — a celebration on the night on which rushees have been "tapped" for membership

WORKS CITED

Editor's Note: When known, page numbers are included below. Because many clippings given to the author by various sources lack page numbers, citing specific pages is not possible in all cases.

ONE

Fiat Lux 19 Nov. 1979: 1+.

Horowitz, Gary S. ed. *A Sesquicentennial History of Alfred University.* Alfred: Alfred UP, 1985.

Jenkins, Peter. *A Walk Across America.* New York: Fawcett, 1980.

Rochester [NY] *Democrat and Chronicle* 6 Mar. 1978.

TWO

Boston *Globe* 24 Feb. 1984.

Chicago *Tribune* 9 Mar. 1985.

Pascal, John. "Mrs. Stevens' Crusade." *LI [Long Island],* 3 Dec. 1978: 30+.

Stolz, James. "Fratricide." Buffalo *Courier Express* 9 May 1982: 10-14.

THREE

Sunday Spectator 26 Feb. 1978: 1+.

FOUR

Belanger, Greg. "Chuck and His Brothers." *The Washington Monthly* Nov. 1988: 42-43.

FIVE

Nuwer, Hank. "Dead Souls of Hell Week." *Human Behavior* Oct. 1978: 53+.

SIX

Fiat Lux 19 Feb. 1979: 7.

MacArthur, Douglas. *Reminiscences.* New York: McGraw-Hill, 1964.

United States Cong. House. *Testimony Taken by the Select Committee of the House of Representatives.* 56th Cong., 2nd sess. Washington: GPO, 1901.

SEVEN

Alfred *Sun* 2 Mar. 1978: 1+.

Taunton [MA] *Daily Gazette* 29 Sept. 1979: 2.

EIGHT

Slavitt, David R. *Cold Comfort.* New York: Methuen, 1980.

NINE

Atlanta *Constitution* 14 Mar. 1988: 8A.

Bishop, Morris. *A History of Cornell.* Ithaca: Cornell UP, 1962.

Iona College *Ionian* 14 Mar. 1979.

Miami *Herald* 21 Feb. 1979.

Miami *News* 23 Feb. 1979.

New York *Times* 28 Feb. 1909.

——. 11 Apr. 1909.

Nuwer. *Human Behavior.*

Putney, Michael. "The Brutal Brotherhood." *Tropic* 22 Apr. 1979: 10+.

Syracuse *Daily Orange* 10 Dec. 1980.

U of Florida *Alligator* 4 Dec. 1979.

TEN

Birmingham, Stephen. "Are Fraternities Necessary?" *Holiday* Oct. 1958: 50+.

Burstein, Patricia. "Her Son's Pointless Death Spurs an Angry Mother's War Against Fraternity Hazing." *People* 12 Feb. 1979: 31-35.

"Campus Clash." *Literary Digest* 123: 29-30.

Dallas *Morning News* 2 Feb. 1947.

Kershner, Frederick Doyle. "Hazing: A Throwback to the Middle Ages." Delta Tau Delta *Rainbow Magazine* Summer 1977: 39+.

——. *Report on Hazing, Pledging and Fraternity Education in the American Social Fraternity System.* Indianapolis: National Interfraternity Conference, 1989.

Leemon, Thomas A. *The Rites of Passage in a Student Culture.* New York: Teachers College, 1972.

Nuwer. *Human Behavior.*

Olmert, Michael. "Points of Origin." *Smithsonian* Sept. 1983: 150-54.

Reed, Thomas Walter. *"Uncle Tom" Reed's Memoir of the University of Georgia.* Athens: U of Georgia Libraries, 1974.

"School Fagging." *The Spectator* 10 Oct. 1891: 492-93.

"Eton Bids Farewell to Fagging. *Time* 26 May 1980: 96.

Walker, Milton Glenn. *Organizational Type, Rites of Corporation, and Group Solidarity: A Study of Fraternity Hell Week.* Diss. U of Washington, 1967.

ELEVEN

Fiat Lux 19 Feb. 1979: 7.

Buffalo *Courier Express* 8 Oct. 1979.

TWELVE

Alfred *Sun* 2 Mar. 1978: 1+.

Fiat Lux 10 Dec. 1979: 1+.

——. 6 Feb. 1981.

——. 20 Sept. 1985.

Buffalo *Courier Express* 12 Apr. 1980.

"Hazing Had Parallel Among Primitive People." *Science Newsletter* 8 Oct. 1960.

Hornbuckle, Bruce D. *Death by Hazing.* Sigma Alpha Epsilon, 1981.

Kershner. *Rainbow.*

Olmert. *Smithsonian.*

Sigal, Richard. "A Fraternity Death." Unpublished essay, June 1981.

Smith, R.J. "In Buffalo: Bad Taste but No
  Hazing." Buffalo *Courier Express Sunday*
  9 May 1982: 13-14.
Sunday Tribune 24 Oct. 1982.
"University Reform." *Atlantic Monthly* Sept. 1866:
  296+.

THIRTEEN

Fiat Lux 12 Oct. 1982: 1+.
Phipps, Lloyd J. "F.F.A. Hazing." *The
  Agricultural Education Magazine* May 1952:
  252-53.
"University Reform." *Atlantic Monthly.*

FOURTEEN

Richardson, Keith. "Polliwogs and Shellbacks:
  An Analysis of the Equator Crossing
  Ritual." *Western Folklore* Apr. 1977: 154-59.

FIFTEEN

Ceasar, Kimberley. "Branded for Life." Ball State
  University *expo* Winter 1987: 7.

SIXTEEN

Ann Arbor *News* 14 Oct. 1980.
Baier, John L., and Patrick S. Williams.
  "Fraternity Hazing Revisited: Current
  Alumni and Active Member Attitudes
  Toward Hazing." *Journal of College Student
  Personnel* July 1983: 300-05.
Campus Voice Nov. 1984: 25.
Canadian University Press wire report, undated
  (circa 1984).
Fraternity Newsletter Nov. 1984.
———. Dec. 1986.
Journal of the American Medical Association 26
  Jan. 1990: 527.
Kershner. *Rainbow.*
Literary Digest 25 Nov. 1933: 116.
National On-campus Report 25 Mar. 1985.
News release. Dickinson College News Service.
New York *Daily News* 5 Oct. 1983.
New York *Times* 21 Nov. 1909: 1.
———. 30 Sept. 1928.
Nuwer. *Human Behavior.*
Preuss, Arthur. *A Dictionary of Secret and Other
  Societies.* St. Louis: B. Herder, 1924.
Rochester *Democrat and Chronicle* 15 Nov. 1989.
Roanoke *Times* 15 Apr. 1979.
Silver, Henry K. "Medical Student Abuse."
  Journal of the American Medical Association
  26 Jan. 1990: 527-37.
Sporting News 16 Mar. 1987.
Texas Christian University *Daily Skiff* 31 Mar.
  1989.
"The Netherlands, Night of the Pig." *Time* 9 Nov.
  1962: 35.
Toronto *Sunday Star* 7 Sept. 1986.
Tulsa *World* 3 Mar. 1988.
United Press International wire report 3 Dec.
  1981.
———. 14 Sept. 1984.

University of Texas *Daily Texan* 17 Mar. 1978.
"University Reform." *Atlantic Monthly.*
Wall Street Journal 4 Feb. 1977.

SEVENTEEN

Buffalo *News* 31 Jan. 1988: A1, A12.
Moskos, Mike. "Deaths Due to Hazing."
  Unpublished list of hazing deaths updated
  periodically, 1990.
New York *Daily News* 6 Oct. 1983: 44.
Tiger, Lionel. *Men in Groups.* New York:
  Random House, 1969.

APPENDIX

Amarillo *Globe-News* 2 May 1990.
Anderson [IN] *Herald-Bulletin* 19 Oct. 1988.
———. 24 Jan. 1989: 1.
Ann Arbor [MI] *News* 14 Oct. 1980: 1-2.
Arizona *Republic* 24 Feb. 1987.
Asbury Park *Press* 21 Feb. 1988.
———. 26 Apr. 1988.
———. 9 June 1988: A12.
Associated Press 7 Nov. 1975.
———. 25 Jan. 1978.
———. 19 Mar. 1980.
———. 11 May 1986.
Atlanta *Journal-Constitution* 21 Nov. 1976: 2A.
———. 27 May 1979.
Atlanta *Constitution* 17 Oct. 1989.
———. 27 Oct. 1989.
———. 22 Nov. 1989: 1+.
Atlanta *Journal* 4 June 1982.
Arkansas *Gazette* 26 July 1983.
ATO News Feb. 1986.
Austin *American Statesman* 10 Mar. 1982.
———. 20 Sept. 1986.
Ball State U *Daily News* 19 Mar. 1982.
———. 25 Mar. 1984: 1.
Baltimore *Evening Sun* 5 July 1988: A1.
Baton Rouge *State Times* 7 Aug. 1986.
Bentley College *Inferno* 18 Nov. 1982: 9.
Beaumont *Enterprise* 13 Jan. 1985: 5-6A.
Bishop, Morris. *A History of Cornell.* Ithaca:
  Cornell UP, 1962.
Bluefield [WV] *Daily Telegraph* 23 Nov. 1974: 1.
Boston *Globe* 19 Oct. 1984: 71.
———. 31 Oct. 1987: 7.
Boston *Herald American* 10 May 1980: B1.
Buffalo *Courier Express* 8 Oct. 1979: 3-4.
*Bulletin of Interfraternity Research and Advisory
  Council* 1 May 1985.
Burlington County [NJ] *Times* 11 Sept. 1980: 15.
Campus Commentary October 1978.
Campus Echo 6 Mar. 1981.
Cerra, Joan. Personal interview. 1 Aug. 1988.
Chester (PA) *Times* 8 Mar. 1954.
Chicago *Tribune* 19 Oct. 1977.
Chico *News & Review* 1 Mar. 1984.
Chronicle of Higher Education 10 Nov. 1982.
———. 25 May 1983.

———. 11 Apr. 1984.

———. 26 June 1985.

———. 19 Feb. 1986.

———. 12 Mar. 1986: 35-36.

———. 22 April 1987.

———. 16 Sept. 1987: A2.

———. 2 Mar. 1988: 2-3A.

———. 19 Oct. 1988: A2.

———. 5 Nov. 1988.

———. 11 Jan. 1989.

———. 14 Sept. 1988.

Cincinnati *Enquirer* 30 Mar. 1989: C1.

Clarksburg [WV] *Exponent* 14 Jan. 1982.

Cleveland *Plain Dealer* 22 Sept. 1988: 1+.

College of St. Thomas *Aquin* 2 May 1986: 1-2.

College Student and the Courts. June 1988.

College Papers May/June 1980.

"Collegiate Hedlines [sic]." Magna Publications 30 Mar. 1981: 1.

Colorado *Daily* 23 Aug. 1967.

Columbia [SC] *State* 23 Apr. 1986: 2E.

———. 20 Nov. 1986: 1B+.

———. 2 Dec. 1986: 1

———. 11 Feb. 1988: 8C.

———. 5 Apr. 1989: A3.

———. 26 Apr. 1989.

———. 20 Sept. 1989.

———. 4 Oct. 1989: A2.

———. 15 Nov. 1989.

———. 6 Dec. 1989: A3.

———. 13 Dec. 1989: A2-3.

———. 10 Jan. 1990: A2.

———. 7 Feb. 1990.

Columbus *Dispatch* 8 Feb. 1946: 1.

Cornell *Alumni News* Oct. 1982: 32-33.

Curti, Merle and Vernon Carstensen. *The University of Wisconsin, A History (1848-1925).* Madison: U of Wisconsin P, 1949.

Daily Oklahoman 1 Feb. 1989.

Daily Oklahoman and Times 22 Apr. 1989.

———. 1 Nov. 1989.

Dallas *Morning News* 7 Sept. 1984: 16A.

———. 24 Apr. 1985: 22A.

———. 26 Apr. 1985: 25A.

———. 26 Oct. 1987.

Delta Tau Delta Mar. 1989: 5.

Des Moines *Register* 1 Nov. 1988.

Dethloff, Henry C. *A Centennial History of Texas A&M University, 1876-1976,* Vol. I. College Station: Texas A&M UP, 1975.

Detroit *News* 29 Sept. 1980.

Eastern Illinois University *Eastern News* 3 Apr. 1970: 1+.

Emory University *Wheel* 30 Oct. 1987.

Eugene [OR] *Register-Guard* 18 Mar. 1986.

Farrand, Elizabeth M. *History of the University of Michigan.* Ann Arbor: Register, 1885.

Florida Southern *Southern* 12 Oct. 1984.

Fraternity Newsletter May 1980.

———. May 1985: 1.

Gallaudet University *Buff and Blue* 13 Apr. 1990.

Gates, Charles M. *The First Century at the University of Washington, 1861-1961.* Seattle: U of Washington P, 1961.

Glatfelter, Charles H. *A Salutory Influence: Gettysburg College, 1832-1985,* Vol. 2. Gettysburg: Gettysburg College, 1987.

Greek Letter 13 Sept. 1976: 1.

Greensboro [NC] *News and Record* 23 Apr. 1986: C1+.

Gustavus Adolphus *Gustavian Weekly* 24 Apr. 1986: 1.

Holland [MI] *Sentinel* 22 Apr. 1986.

Hopewell [VA] *News* 7 Mar. 1979: A13.

Hubbart, Henry Clyde. *Ohio Wesleyan: First Hundred Years.* Delaware: Ohio Wesleyan UP, 1943.

Indiana *Daily Student* 15 June 1929: 1.

———. *Daily Student* 14 Sept. 1983: 2.

Indianapolis *News* 11 June 1929: 1.

Indianapolis *Star* 8 Dec. 1984.

———. 19 Oct. 1986.

Interfraternity Bulletin 1 March 1987: 3.

Ithaca [NY] *Journal* 14 June 1980: 1.

Joplin *Globe* 9 Feb. 1979.

Kennesaw State College *Sentinel* 8 Mar. 1989: 1.

———. 22 February 1989: 1.

Lancaster [PA] *New Era* 2 Apr. 1980.

Literary Digest 123: 29-30.

Loras College *Lorian* 13 Oct. 1978.

Los Angeles *Herald-Examiner* 6 July 1982: C1+.

Los Angeles *Times* 26 Jan. 1961.

———. 31 Jan. 1962: IV10.

———. 15 Nov. 1981: 1+.

———. 1 Oct. 1984.

———. 19 Oct. 1984: II3.

Louisiana State *Daily Reville* 23 Mar. 1984: 1.

Memphis State *Daily Helsman* 9 Oct. 1987: 1.

Memorandum, Office of the Dean of Students, Washington State, 21 Feb. 1964.

Memorandum, Associate Vice Chancellor for Student Affairs, 16 Jan. 1980.

Miami *Herald* 21 Feb. 1979: 1+.

———. 5 Sept. 1981: 1-2C.

Michigan State University *State News* 24 Apr. 1989.

Mills, Robert L. Letter to Georgetown College Board of Trustees 19 Feb. 1965.

Milwaukee *Journal* 21 Feb. 1980: II1.

———. 20 Feb. 1980.

———. 6 Sept. 1981.

Minneapolis *Star and Tribune* 24 Apr. 1986.

Muncie *Star* 10 June 1988.

Nashville *Banner* 23 Mar. 1984.

Nation 24 Oct. 1959: 243.

National On-Campus Report January 1984.

New Era 16 Jan. 1979.

New Orleans *Times-Picayune* 29 Aug. 1971.

———. 3 February 1973.

———. 24 Mar. 1984: I17.

———. 11 Aug. 1986.

Newsday 3 Apr. 1978.

———. 15 Nov. 1979: 21.

———. 15 Apr. 1986: 7.
———. 11 July 1986.
———. 20 Jan. 1989: 6.
———. 25 May 1989: 21.
———. 28 May 1989: 26.
———. 20 May 1990.
New York *Daily News* 8 June 1988.
New York *Post* 1 Sept. 1981: 3.
———. 14 Apr. 1983.
New York *Times* 4 Nov. 1893: 18.
———. 14 Nov. 1893: 4.
———. 29 Oct. 1899: 1.
———. 30 Oct. 1899: 1.
———. 2 Nov. 1899.
———. 6 Nov. 1899.
———. 11 Nov. 1899.
———. 17 Oct. 1901: 1.
———. 2 Nov. 1901.
———. 10 Jan. 1904: 13.
———. 8 Mar. 1904: 1.
———. 9 May 1904: 1.
———. 11 Mar. 1905: 1.
———. 13 Mar. 1905: 1.
———. 19 Apr. 1905: 1.
———. 28 Sept. 1905: 4.
———. 7 Oct. 1905: 7.
———. 28 Feb. 1909: 1.
———. 11 Apr. 1909: 9.
———. 15 Dec. 1902: 3.
———. 9 Mar. 1905: 1.
———. 7 Nov. 1905.
———. 14 Dec. 1905: 1.
———. 20 Aug. 1907: 1.
———. 8 Sept. 1907: II6.
———. 2 Oct. 1909: 5.
———. 13 Oct. 1909: 7.
———. 19 Dec. 1909: 10.
———. 16 Feb. 1910: 4.
———. 10 Mar. 1910: 3.
———. 4 June 1910: 3.
———. 7 June 1910: 4.
———. 14 Oct. 1910.
———. 22 July 1912: 1.
———. 20 Oct. 1912: 1.
———. 19 Apr. 1914: III3.
———. 29 May, 1914: 1
———. 20 Oct. 1914: 13.
———. 19 Sept. 1915: II11.
———. 2 Oct. 1915: 3.
———. 4 Dec. 1915: 15.
———. 5 Dec. 1915: II19.
———. 11 May 1917: 13.
———. 28 Sept. 1917.
———. 25 Sept. 1919: 7.
———. 9 Oct. 1919: 8.
———. 10 Oct. 1919: 18.
———. 8 Apr. 1920: 17.
———. 23 Nov. 1920: 13.
———. 7 Mar. 1921: 15.
———. 8 May 1921: II6.
———. 9 June 1921: 17.
———. 6 Oct. 1921: 19.

———. 7 Oct. 1921: 7.
———. 21 Oct. 1921: 3.
———. 21 Feb. 1992: 1.
———. 30 Mar. 1922: 1.
———. 23 Sept. 1922: 1.
———. 6 Oct. 1922: 25.
———. 21 Oct. 1922: 12.
———. 22 Oct. 1922: 9.
———. 9 Nov. 1922: 15.
———. 10 Nov. 1922: 12.
———. 11 Nov. 1922: 8.
———. 12 Dec. 1922: 1.
———. 29 Jan. 1923: 1.
———. 2 May 1923: 1.
———. 9 June 1923: 13.
———. 14 June 1923: 21.
———. 2 Oct. 1923: 6.
———. 31 Oct. 1924: 21.
———. 23 Nov. 1924: IV6.
———. 6 Jan. 1925: 13.
———. 4 Apr. 1925: 6.
———. 10 Mar. 1926: 4.
———. 31 May 1926: 9.
———. 19 Sept. 1926: III1.
———. 22 Sept. 1926: 27.
———. 24 Sept. 1926: 19.
———. 12 Oct. 1927: 19.
———. 21 Oct. 1927: 9.
———. 20 Oct. 1928: 10.
———. 1 Oct. 1929: 7.
———. 28 Nov. 1929: 36.
———. 10 Dec. 1930: 34.
———. 11 Mar. 1940: 7.
———. 13 Mar. 1940: 10.
———. 20 Feb. 1945: 17.
———. 17 Dec. 1952: 42.
———. 16 Feb. 1956: 5.
———. 18 Feb. 1956: 1.
———. 23 Feb. 1956: 33.
———. 1 Dec. 1956: 44.
———. 22 Oct. 1957: 24.
———. 18 Sept. 1959: 10.
———. 9 Dec. 1963: 42.
———. 28 Sept. 1973: 68.
———. 24 Aug. 1975: 29.
———. 16 Nov. 1974: 35.
———. 20 Jan. 1975: 60.
———. 19 Sept. 1975: 34.
———. 28 Apr. 1976: 53.
———. 29 May 1983.
———. 8 Oct. 1987: A20.
———. 5 Mar. 1988.
———. 11 Apr. 1988: I16
———. 5 Nov. 1988.
———. 2 July 1989: 27.
———. 3 July 1988.
———. 27 Aug. 1989.
———. 20 May 1990.
North Texas State University *Daily* 23 Oct. 1986: 1.
Oklahoma Daily 31 Oct. 1979.
Oklahoman and Times 31 Jan. 1987.

Oliphant, J. Orin. *The Rise of Bucknell University.* New York: Appleton, 1965.

Oneonta *Daily Star* 14 Oct. 1988.

Orlando *Sentinel* 20 Apr. 1986: I11.

———. 17 Apr. 1987.

———. 4 Feb. 1990.

Packet 11 Feb. 1986.

Philadelphia *Inquirer* 6 March 1954.

———. 17 September 1973: B1.

Piedmont College *Bulletin* Spring 1979: 1.

Pi Kappa Alpha *Forum* Oct. 1987.

Pilot and Ledger-Star 17 Apr. 1988.

Pittsburgh *Post-Gazette* 27 July 1985.

Pittsburgh *Press* 12 Feb. 1989.

Rammelkamp, Charles Henry. *Illinois College: A Centennial History, 1829-1929.* New Haven: Yale UP, 1928.

Record of Sigma Alpha Epsilon Fall 1987: 25.

[UGA] *Red and Black* 30 Oct. 1987.

Reno *Evening Gazette* 29 Oct. 1989.

Richmond [VA] *News Leader* 26 Mar. 1979.

Richmond [VA] *Times-Dispatch* 8 Feb. 1981: D8.

Rider College *Rider News* 12 Nov. 1982: 1.

Roanoke [VA] *Times* 15 Apr. 1979: F1.

Rochester *Democrat and Chronicle* 8 Apr. 1989.

Rockland County [NY] *Journal-News* 15 Aug. 1986: A1.

Rolla [MO] *Daily News* 21 Sept. 1977.

Sacramento *Bee* 11 Nov. 1981: B8.

St. John's University *Torch* 8 Oct. 1986: 1.

St. Louis *Post-Dispatch* 20 Dec. 1979.

———. 14 May 1987.

St. Louis *Post* 26 Oct. 1980.

———. 29 Oct. 1980.

———. 6 Jan. 1984.

———. 1 Apr. 1983: I11.

———. 16 May 1983: I11.

San Diego State *Daily Aztec* 19 Oct. 1984.

San Jose *Mercury News* 21 Feb. 1988.

San Francisco *Chronicle* 30 Jan. 1986.

San Francisco *Examiner* 20 Dec. 1981: A1+.

———. 20 Sept. 1983.

———. 11 June 1987.

Schoenberg, Wilfred P. *Gonzaga University: Seventy-Five Years (1887-1962).* Spokane: Gonzaga, 1963.

Seattle *Post-Intelligencer* 15 May 1986.

———. 6 Aug. 1986.

Shrewsbury [NJ] *Daily Register* 26 April 1979: 10.

Smythe, George Franklin. *Kenyon College, Its First Century.* New Haven: Yale UP, 1924.

Solberg, Winton U. *The University of Illinois, 1867-1894.* Champaign-Urbana: U of Illinois P, 1968.

Springfield [MO] *News-Leader* 1 Oct. 1987: 1A+.

Starkville [MS] *Daily News* 31 May 1980.

———. 13 November 1980.

Stetson University *Reporter* 11 Oct. 1985.

———. 12 Sept. 1986.

Swarthmore College *Phoenix* 9 May 1954.

Syracuse *Daily Orange* 20 Mar. 1981.

———. 13 Apr. 1983: 1.

Syracuse *Herald* 13 March 1983.

Syracuse *Post-Standard* 13 Apr. 1983: 1.

———. 5 Mar. 1986: A-1.

Talbert, Charles G. *University of Kentucky.* Lexington: U of Kentucky P, 1965.

Taunton [MA] *Daily Gazette* 29 Sept. 1979: 2.

Texas A&M. Annual Report, 1920-21: 22-24.

Thornburg, Opal. *Earlham: The Story of the College (1847-1962).* Richmond: Earlham College P, 1963.

Time 5 Mar. 1945: 68.

———. 27 Feb. 1956.

———. 19 Mar. 1956: 86.

———. 22 Nov. 1976: 61.

———. 19 Nov. 1979.

Trinity Tablet 26 Oct. 1978.

Tulsa *World* 3 Mar. 1988.

United Press International 6 Jan. 1980.

———. 30 Aug. 1984.

United States. Cong. House. Investigation of Hazing at the United States Military Academy. *Hearings.* 56th Cong., 2nd sess. Washington: GPO, 1901.

University Mirror Mar. 1882.

U of Akron *Buchtelite* 4 Dec. 1984.

U of Albany *Student Press* 22 Apr. 1988: 1.

U of Delaware *Review* 28 Apr. 1981: 1+.

U of Illinois *Daily Illini* 10 Nov. 1979: 3.

———. 13 Jan. 1982.

U of Kansas *Daily Kansan* 30 Jan. 1981.

———. 21 Aug. 1985: 1.

U of Maryland *Diamondback* 4 Dec. 1984.

———. 10 Apr. 1985.

U of Missouri *Maneater* 23 Jan. 1981.

———. 1 Mar. 1983: 1.

———. 8 Mar. 1985.

U of Nevada-Reno *Sagebrush* 17 Oct. 1975: 1.

U of New Mexico *Daily Lobo* 22 November 1983.

U of North Dakota *Dakota Student* 11 Oct. 1979.

U of Pittsburgh *Pitt News* 27 Mar. 1981.

U of Rhode Island *Good 5¢ Cigar* 25 February 1976.

———. 3 March 1976.

University of Richmond *Collegian* 20 Nov. 1980.

———. 8 Dec. 1988: 1+.

U of South Carolina *Gamecock* 14 Nov. 1916.

U of Southern California *Daily Trojan* 14 Oct. 1981: 1+.

U of Tennessee *Daily Beacon* 9 Mar. 1982.

U of Texas *Daily Texan* 2 Oct. 1928.

———. 10 Jan. 1977.

———. 14 Feb. 1977.

———. 17 Mar. 1978.

———. 25 Oct. 1984.

———. 6 Sept. 1985: 28.

———. 9 Dec. 1985.

———. 21 Oct. 1986.

———. 3 Oct. 1986.

U of Wyoming *Branding Iron* 6 May 1986: 1.

USA Today 5 Aug. 1988.

———. 11 May 1990: 10A.

Vanderbilt *Hustler* 23 Mar. 1980.

Waco *Tribune-News* 11 Oct. 1967.

Washington and Lee U *Ring-tum Phi* 17 Jan.
    1985: 1.

Washington *Post* 3 Apr. 1982: B1.

———. 3 Feb. 1985: B7.

———. 8 Nov. 1987: B1.

———. 7 Aug. 1988.

Washington *Star* 26 Apr. 1977.

Washington State U *Daily Evergreen* 21 March
    1975.

Wertenbaker, Thomas Jefferson. *Princeton:
    1746-1896.* Princeton: Princeton UP, 1946.

Wilson, Louis R. *The University of North
    Carolina, 1900-1930.* Chapel Hill: U of North
    Carolina P, 1957.

Wisconsin *State Journal* 27 Nov. 1889.

Wittenberg *Torch* 4 May 1950.

———. 18 May 1950.

INDEX

Abbey, Edward *x*

Adrian College 228, 307

Agee, James 217

Agricultural Education Magazine 194

Alabama 49, 231, 253, 293, 307

Alaska 132, 241

Albany, New York 101, 109, 132, 142, 319

alcohol 8-10, 14, 16, 21, 26-27, 31, 47-50, 55-56, 67, 72-73, 75, 79, 97-99, 105, 124, 128, 134-135, 144, 147-148, 150-152, 175, 177, 179, 181, 185-186, 212, 214, 225, 233-234, 237, 247, 256, 258, 261-262, 265-266, 273-275, 277-279, 289, 296, 299-300, 302, 304-305, 307-312, 314-316, 318-322

Alfred (Saxon King) 81, 301, 320

Alfred, New York 4-6, 29, 70, 76

Alfred *Reporter* 274

Alfred *Sun* 73

Alfred University 3-5, 11, 19, 22, 30, 32, 36-38, 47-48, 52, 58, 68, 71, 73, 76, 79, 81-82, 89, 100, 103-105, 108, 111, 125-126, 130-132, 146, 148-149, 153, 171, 173-174, 223, 252, 272-273, 275, 279, 301, 320

Allegany County (New York) 29, 52, 80, 87, 104, 141, 223, 224, 276

Alpha Beta Chi 229, 230

Alpha Chi Omega 319

Alpha Chi Rho 125, 321

Alpha Delta Phi 176, 315

Alpha Kappa Alpha 232, 301

Alpha Phi Alpha 217, 300, 306, 318, 322

Alpha Sigma Alpha 228, 232, 307

Alpha Sigma Phi (college) 23-25, 311, 314

Alpha Sigma Phi (high school) 250

Alpha Tau Omega 139, 243-244, 296, 300, 305, 312-313, 315, 321, 323

Arizona 111, 179, 258, 301, 310-311, 316, 320

Alumni Hall 32, 51

AM Indiana 265-266

American Council on Education 176, 234

American International College 26

American Journal of Forensic Medicine and Pathology 27

American Journal of Sociology 115

Amherst College 294

Ancient Arabic Order of Nobles of the Mystic Shrine 254

Animal House 49, 91, 234

Annapolis (See United States Naval Academy) 118, 235, 287, 289, 290-293, 323

Anson, Jack L. 127

anti-hazing legislation 8, 77, 92, 102-104, 126-127, 131-132, 141-142, 153, 211, 213, 230, 239, 246-247, 250-252, 256, 268, 273

Archer, Judith 7-8

Archer, Will 16, 82, 175

Arnoux, Jimmy 9, 33, 35, 40, 59, 66-67, 69, 88, 124, 133, 281

Aronson, Elliott 115

Athens 137, 239, 303, 307, 313, 316

Atherton, Carl 195

Babson College 245

Bachman, Joe 10, 31, 71

Badrov, Martin 312

Ball State University 116, 227, 246, 266, 295, 307, 310

Ballou, Barry 179-181, 188, 220, 236, 304, 317

Ballou, Maisie 99, 180, 182, 252

Ballou, Ray 179

Ballou v. Sigma Nu 188

Barbati, John 252

Barnard College 258

Bartner, Arthur C. 259

Batson, Lex 138

Bayport High Schoo! 101

Bazille, Robert 57

Belanger, Greg 29-30, 33, 39-40, 45, 59, 67, 69-71, 75, 93, 123, 134-135, 224, 268, 281

Bell, David 195

Bell, Marvin 4

Belmont, Randy 5-6, 15-16, 21

Berkeley, Edward Fairchild 120

Bernstein, Melvin 65

Berytus 137

Beta Theta Pi 131, 198, 247, 305, 310, 312-313, 316-317, 321-322

Biaggi, Mario 148

Biner, Paul 116

Birmingham, Alabama 253

Birmingham, Stephen 119

Bishop, Mike 248

Bishop, Robert 195

Black Avengers 258, 288

black fraternities 209-212, 216-217, 219, 240, 242

black sororities 210

Bloomington, Indiana 233, 244, 277, 294-295, 308, 310, 314

Bloomington [IN] *Herald-Times* 244

Bloustein, Edward 263

Bluefield State College 248, 298

B'nai B'rith Hillel Council 65

Bobowski, Alan S. 251

Boethius 5

Bogg, Richard A. 277

Booz, Oscar 62

Borussia Corps 248

Boston *Globe* 16, 26, 236, 252

Bowling Green, Ohio 208, 313

Boyer, Ernest 277

Boys Town 7

Bradley University 17, 300

Branson, Joe 201, 280

Brant, Jonathan 239, 241, 243

Briggs, W. J., Jr. 24

brimade(s) 249

Bristol, Pennsylvania 62, 289

Broken Arrow, Oklahoma 197

State University College of New York at Brockport 5, 36, 302, 305, 319, 323
State University College of New York at Buffalo *x*
Suicide 118, 226
SUNY (State University of New York) Agricultural and Technical College at Delhi 102, 229
Stagg, William (Bill) 194
Steadman, Mark *x*, 120
Steingester, Helen 251
Steinheim Museum 32
Steinmetz, George 95
Steinmetz, George Mrs. 95-96
Stengel, Paul F. 130
Stenzel, Charles W. (grandfather of Chuck) 98
Stenzel, Charles (father of Chuck) 223
Stenzel, Charles M. (Chuck) III 19-23, 25-26, 29-45, 47-50, 53-57, 59-62, 65-71, 73, 75-80, 82-83, 87, 93, 98-99
Stenzel, Doreen 33
Stevens, Blaine 26
Stevens, Eileen 4-6, 9-11, 13-14, 16, 19-23, 25-27, 29-39, 41-45, 48, 61-62, 65-83, 87-96, 98-99, 100-105, 107-117, 120, 123, 135, 137-142, 144-145, 148-154, 171-176, 178-181, 188, 196, 202, 206, 210, 213, 217, 220, 223-224, 227-228, 230-231, 247, 251-252, 256, 258, 261-264, 266-269, 271-273, 275-276, 280-281, 296, 320
Stevens, Roy 11, 16, 19, 20, 26, 37, 76, 77, 154, 237
Stevens, Scott 78, 90
Stevens, Steven 107
Stevens, Suzanne (Sue) 31, 109, 148
Sturgeon Bay, Wisconsin 203
sub-rosa fraternity 141
Suffolk County News 100
suit (see litigation) 16, 53, 67, 81, 89-90, 98, 104, 123, 172, 175-178, 180, 207-209, 216, 224, 239, 252, 262, 271-272, 279, 286, 294, 307, 316, 320
Sullivan, Rick 148
Sullivan, Scott 7, 13, 20, 56, 60, 62, 66, 70-71, 79, 99, 124, 174, 178

Sun (Alfred) 38, 52-53, 62, 65, 67, 77, 97, 140, 174, 217, 236, 252, 299
Sundowner Club 97
Swords of Bunker Hill 253
Syracuse University 52, 100, 228, 295, 306-307, 309, 315
Tallahassee, Florida 305
Taff, Mark L. viii, 27, 213, 298
Tapping Night (Alfred University) 6-7, 11, 14-15, 25, 41, 48-49, 53, 60, 70, 124, 126, 171, 176, 269
Tau Kappa Epsilon 244, 298, 299, 302, 311, 314, 316, 318, 319
Taylor, Edwin 248, 299
Taylor, Ron 245
Taylor, William 251
Tennessee 127, 139, 303
Tennessee State University 212, 299, 309
Terre Haute, Indiana 253
Texas 112, 132, 138, 153, 196, 246, 262, 286, 290, 292, 294, 297-298, 300-301, 307, 309-315, 317-318, 320, 323
Texas A&M 121, 289, 282, 311-312, 318
Texas Tech 240, 300, 312
Theta Chi 180, 304, 308, 310, 319, 322
Theta Theta Chi 125, 274
Theta Xi 108, 302, 323
Thompson, Kenneth 257
Thoreau, Henry David 31, 92
Thunder Bay, Ontario 250
Tiger, Lionel 266
Today 124, 131, 146, 246-247, 281
Tomorrow 135
Toms River High School 257
Town Squire 42
Tri Chi 57
Trinity College 250, 286
Truman, Harry 147
Trunzo, Caesar 103, 132
Turner, Lon A., Jr. 278
Twiname, Eric 150
Union Triad 119
United States Military Academy 64, 287, 289, 291-292, 294-295, 298, 300, 303, 320, 323
United States Naval Academy 289-291, 293, 323
University of Alabama 93, 293
University of Alberta 249
University of Bonn 248

University of Charleston (see Morris Harvey College)
University of Cincinnati 153
University of Colorado 120, 298, 311, 321
University of Florida 212, 233, 301, 318
University of Georgia 119, 303, 313,316
University of Gettysburg 258
University of Illinois 194, 245, 246, 286, 289, 295, 316, 321
University of Lowell 26, 261, 303, 316, 319
University of Maine 171, 232, 292, 307, 319
University of Maryland 213, 288, 294, 298, 308, 310, 314
University of Michigan 12, 176, 257, 286, 289, 304, 321
University of Mississippi 233, 261, 312, 317, 322
University of Missouri 113, 138, 295, 300, 302, 304, 308, 312
University of Nebraska 233, 305
University of Nevada-Reno 299, 300, 305
University of Oklahoma 248, 257, 302, 309, 314, 317, 322
University of Ottawa 250
University of Pennsylvania 57, 299, 300, 311, 319
University of Saskatchewan 249
University of South Carolina 179, 180-182, 291-292, 297, 304, 306-307, 309, 311, 315, 317
University of Southern California 71, 232, 259, 297, 306-307, 309, 311, 315
University of Texas 177, 232, 255, 265, 271, 281, 290, 294, 297, 300-301, 307, 311-312, 315, 320
University of Toronto 250
University of Virginia 95, 306, 308, 318
University of Wisconsin-Superior 98, 286, 291-292, 299, 306-307
USA Today 278
U.S. News & World Report 4
Utah 179
Valley Stream North High School 143
Van Cura, Joseph 13, 18
Vermont 147, 323